Newton Rigg College

085765

CM09000799
71'
£3 95
303
·34
/Mun

D1337340

LEARNING AND INFORMATION
SERVICES
UNIVERSITY OF CUMBRIA

Leadership Symposia Series
James G. Hunt, *General Editor*

Previously Published Titles in the Series

Current Developments in the Study of Leadership.
Edited by Edwin A. Fleishman and James G. Hunt. 1973. ISBN: 0-8093-0635-2. *Out of print.*

Contingency Approaches to Leadership.
Edited by James G. Hunt and Lars L. Larson. 1974. ISBN: 0-8093-0689-1. *Out of print.*

Leadership Frontiers.
Edited by James G. Hunt and Lars L. Larson. 1975. ISBN: 0-8093-9998-9.

Leadership: The Cutting Edge.
Edited by James G. Hunt and Lars L. Larson. 1977. ISBN: 0-8093-0840-1. *Out of print.*

Crosscurrents in Leadership.
Edited by James G. Hunt and Lars L. Larson. 1979. ISBN: 0-8093-0932-7.

Leadership
Beyond Establishment
Views

Edited by
JAMES G. HUNT,
UMA SEKARAN, and
CHESTER A. SCHRIESHEIM

SOUTHERN ILLINOIS UNIVERSITY PRESS
Carbondale and Edwardsville

For lovers of ice creams, both exotic and not
(See chapter 16)

Library of Congress Cataloging in Publication Data

Main entry under title:

Leadership, beyond establishment views.

(Leadership symposia series; v. 6)
Bibliography: p.
Includes index.
1. Leadership—Congresses.   I. Hunt, James G., 1932–   .   II. Sekaran,
Uma.   III. Schriesheim, Chester.   IV. Series.
HM141.L393   303.3'4   81-8739
ISBN 0-8093-1026-0   AACR2

Copyright © 1982 by the Board of Trustees,
Southern Illinois University
All rights reserved
Printed in the United States of America
Designed by Gary Gore

Contents

Tables

Figures

Preface

This book is volume 6 of the Leadership Symposia Series originating in 1971. This series covers the content of biennial symposia held at the Carbondale campus of Southern Illinois University. This volume joins the earlier ones in charting the state of the field. The previous volumes are: *Current Developments in the Study of Leadership* (1973); *Contingency Approaches to Leadership* (1974); *Leadership Frontiers* (1975); *Leadership: The Cutting Edge* (1977); and *Crosscurrents in Leadership* (1979).

This series was established to provide in-depth consideration of current and future leadership directions and to provide an interdisciplinary perspective for the scholarly study of leadership. Taken as a whole the volumes in the series have been designed to build on one another, show the evolution of the field over time, and be at the forefront of new developments.

The format of the volumes has encouraged the achievement of these objectives in a number of ways. First, a mix of work from well-known scholars, widely recognized for many years, and younger scholars whose work has only recently received attention, has been utilized. Second, expert discussant/critiquers have prepared commentaries for the presentations. Third, interchange has been encouraged at the symposia and issues emerging from this interchange have been woven into the introductory part and chapter materials where appropriate. Fourth, an outstanding scholar has provided a broad-ranging overview to put the book contents into perspective. Typically, that perspective has ranged far afield from the contents of the chapters themselves. Finally, in more recent volumes, the editors have provided a considerable amount of additional commentary to help balance the content of the volumes in terms of current thrusts.

To encourage further scholarship in the leadership area and to recognize the contributions of outstanding individuals the Ralph M. Stogdill Distinguished Scholarship Award was established in 1976. That award is given to a leadership scholar "in recognition of his/her outstanding contribution to the advancement of leadership research and for devotion to the development of a new generation of leadership scholars." Thus, the award is intended not only for the scholarly contribution of the chosen individual but, equally important, for the contribution to the development of others in the field. The first award was presented to Stogdill himself and the second to Fred E. Fiedler. The award at this symposium was presented to Rensis Likert, for many years at the University of Michigan and now leading Rensis Likert Associates.

This symposia series has been sponsored by the Southern Illinois University at Carbondale Department of Administrative Sciences and College of Business and Administration. For the current endeavor we are indebted to John R. Schermerhorn, chairperson, and John Darling, dean, for their encouragement and support.

Planning and arrangements for the symposium involved a number of people. First, there was a symposium executive committee from the Department of Administrative Sciences to assist with planning, paper evaluation, and decision-making. In addition to the three editors, the committee consisted of A. N. Azim, Lars L. Larson, Thomas N. Martin, Richard N. Osborn, John R. Schermerhorn, and William M. Vicars.

Second, to host the symposium and implement travel and lodging arrangements, the M.B.A. Association provided valuable help. We would especially like to recognize Julie Garrett, Lawrence Lim, John Maloney, Nancy Muklewicz, and Catherine Pierson.

Third, Judith Miller, a doctoral student graduate assistant, and the departmental administrative assistant, Sharon Pinkerton, and secretaries Bobbi Garrett and Vicki Avery assisted by a number of student workers handled a host of symposium-related duties too numerous to mention.

Finally, the leadership symposium advisory board assisted in advice and helped with paper reviewing. Members of the board are:

CHRIS ARGYRIS
Harvard University

BERNARD BASS
State University of New York at Binghamton

DAVID BOWERS
University of Michigan

ELMER BURACK
University of Illinois-Chicago Circle

JOHN CAMPBELL
University of Minnesota

MARTIN CHEMERS
University of Utah

JOHN CHILD
University of Aston in Birmingham, England

LARRY CUMMINGS
University of Wisconsin-Madison

MARTIN EVANS
University of Toronto

GEORGE FARRIS
York University

FRED FIEDLER
University of Washington

EDWIN FLEISHMAN
Advanced Research Resources Organization

WILLIAM FOX
University of Florida

GEORGE GRAEN
Uniersity of Cincinnati

CHARLES GREENE
Indiana University

EDWIN HOLLANDER
State University of New York at Buffalo

ROBERT HOUSE
University of Toronto

T. OWEN JACOBS
Army Research Institute

STEVEN KERR
University of Southern California

ABRAHAM KORMAN
City University of New York

CHARLES LEVINE
University of Maryland

RENSIS LIKERT
Rensis Likert Associates

JAMES PRICE
University of Iowa

MARSHALL SASHKIN
University of Maryland

CHESTER SCHRIESHEIM
University of Southern California

HENRY SIMS, JR.
The Pennsylvania State University

JOHN SLOCUM, JR.
Southern Methodist University

JOHN STINSON
Ohio University

PETER WEISSENBERG
State University of New York at Binghamton

The paper review process was also aided by a number of *ad hoc* reviewers. These were:

PATRICK CONNOR
Oregon State University

PAUL DUFFY
Market Dynamics

DIAN-MARIE HOSKING
University of Aston in Birmingham, England

JOHN SHERIDAN
The Pennsylvania State University

The advisory board and reviewers have been most helpful in providing a crucially important outside perspective to supplement the inside one of the executive committee.

This symposium could not have been held without the assistance of all those mentioned above. Neither could it have taken place without financial support. The bulk of such support came from the United States Army Research Institute for the Behavioral and Social Sciences. This was supplemented by external support from the Office of Naval Research and the Smithsonian Institution. Internal support came from the department and college.

In closing this preface two additional points are appropriate. First, there is a change in editorship reflected in this volume. Commencing with volume 2, the books were edited by James G. (Jerry) Hunt and Lars L. Larson. Lars has now moved into other areas and Jerry Hunt has been joined by Uma Sekaran of Southern Illinois University at Carbondale and, for the first time, by a third editor, Chester Schriesheim of the University of Southern California. All of us thank Lars for his contributions and Jerry welcomes Uma and Chet aboard in their editorial roles.

Second, once again editors' spouses (Donna and Janet) assisted with proofreading and various other manuscript preparation details as well as putting up with their husbands when various things threatened to put the book behind schedule. To them and to all who helped, we express our heartiest thank you.

Carbondale, Illinois, and   J. G. HUNT
Los Angeles, California   U. SEKARAN
March 1981   C. A. SCHRIESHEIM

Notes on Contributors

Michael A. Abelson is Assistant Professor of Management, Texas A&M University, College Station.

Joseph A. Alutto is Professor of Organization and Human Resources and Dean of the School of Management, State University of New York at Buffalo.

Robert F. Bales is Professor of Social Relations in the Department of Psychology and Social Relations at Harvard University.

Bernard M. Bass is Professor of Organizational Behavior, State University of New York at Binghamton.

Robert S. Bussom is Associate Professor of Administrative Sciences and Associate Dean, College of Business and Administration, Southern Illinois University at Carbondale.

Fred Dansereau, Jr., is Associate Professor of Organization and Human Resources, State University of New York at Buffalo.

MacDonald Dumas is Lecturer in Organizational Behavior, University of West Indies at Trinidad.

Roseanne J. Foti is a graduate student in the Industrial/Organizational Psychology Program, University of Akron.

Dian-Marie Hosking is Lecturer, Oranizational Sociology and Psychology Group, University of Aston in Birmingham, England.

James G. (Jerry) Hunt is Professor of Administrative Sciences, Southern Illinois University at Carbondale.

Daniel J. Isenberg is currently completing a PhD in Social Psychology at Harvard University under the supervision of Robert Bales.

Jeffrey L. Kerr is currently a doctoral student at The Pennsylvania State University, where he earned his MBA degree.

Lars L. Larson is Associate Professor of Administrative Sciences, Southern Illinois University at Carbondale.

Michael M. Lombardo is Research Scientist and Project Manager at the Center for Creative Leadership, a nonprofit educational institution in Greensboro, North Carolina.

Robert G. Lord is Associate Professor of Psychology, University of Akron.

Steven E. Markham is Assistant Professor of Organizations, Virginia Polytechnic Institute and State University.

Morgan W. McCall, Jr., is Behavioral Scientist and Project Manager at the Center for Creative Leadership.

Henry Mintzberg is Professor of Management Policy at McGill University.

Ian Morley is Senior Lecturer and Chairperson of the Department of Psychology, University of Warwick, England.

Richard N. Osborn is Senior Research Scientist at the Battelle Human Affairs Research Centers, Seattle, Washington.

James S. Phillips is Assistant Professor of Organizational Behavior and Management, University of Houston.

Uma Sekaran is Assistant Professor of Administrative Sciences, Southern Illinois University at Carbondale.

Chester A. Schriesheim is Assistant Professor of Organizational Behavior, University of Southern California.

John E. Sheridan is Associate Professor of Organizational Behavior at The Pennsylvania State University.

Rosemary Stewart is Fellow in Organizational Behavior at the Oxford Centre for Management Studies in England.

Henry Tosi is Professor and Chairperson, Department of Management, University of Florida.

William M. Vicars is Associate Professor of Administrative Sciences, Southern Illinois University at Carbondale.

Bernard Wilpert is Professor of Psychology at the Technical University of Berlin, Germany, and visiting Professor of Sociology, Institut d'Etudes Politiques de Paris.

Leadership

Beyond Establishment Views

1

Beyond Establishment Views of Leadership:
An Introduction

JAMES G. HUNT, UMA SEKARAN, and CHESTER A.
SCHRIESHEIM

Many scholars see the leadership establishment as concentrating on narrow, highly deterministic, and rigidly delineated models. Some would defend these as representing the results of application of the scientific method to leadership research. Others argue that they narrow the focus too much, screen out most of the potentially interesting and important things that occur in leadership in the real world, and are primarily responsible for current dismay with the leadership literature. The spirit of this second group is captured well in a quote from James Lester's preface to McCall and Lombardo's recent volume, *Leadership: Where Else Can We Go?*

> A major theme, dominant in setting the tone [of the conference upon which the book is based] was the assertion that we need to *rediscover the phenomena* of leadership; the pursuit of rigor and precision has led to an overemphasis on techniques at the expense of knowing what is going on in a direct human way. As a result, we have masses of "findings" that no one seems able to pull together—they simply float around in the literature, providing nothing from which one can push off to anywhere. (McCall & Lombardo, 1978, p. xii)

The present book strikes a middle ground between those in the establishment who would defend to the death rigor and emphasis on scientific canons in studying leadership and those who advocate the complete scrapping of this emphasis and its findings (in effect, throwing the baby out with the bath water). Thus, although the thrust of this volume goes clearly beyond establishment views, nevertheless rigor and scientific values have not been abandoned entirely, and the contents are intended to appeal to both sides. Of course, they may end up satisfying neither, but that is a risk we as editors felt compelled to take.

While the current theme is consistent with a Leadership Symposium objective of pointing out future research directions, a reader might ask to what extent it meets the objective of charting the state of the field. Quite accurately, we believe. While a number of the presentations and commentaries were invited and were deliberately chosen to move beyond establishment views, these were supplemented with three competitive presentations which we see as innovative but representative of a good bit of current work. Perhaps even more importantly, the two epilogs—one reporting on current thrusts in the U.S. literature and the second presenting European contributions, help round out developments in the field. As a whole, then, we have a volume which moves us beyond establishment views but maintains an anchor with current mainstream developments.

To help focus on the different issues concerned with moving beyond establishment views, the book is divided into four parts. The first consists of four chapters examining the interface between leadership and managerial behavior, and the ways in which the literatures from these two areas reinforce each other. The second part again consists of four chapters, and centers around a triad of new models with a foot in both establishment and nonestablishment camps. The third part considers micro and macro extensions of establishment views and consists of three chapters. The final part contains an applications-oriented overview, two epilogs (one covering U.S. work and the other covering European work), and a concluding chapter concerned with the research-practice controversy, and with summary and conclusions. Together, the four chapters in this part are designed to extend the content of the book in providing a broad perspective on the state of leadership research in 1980.

We discuss in this introduction the content of these parts in somewhat more detail, and this discussion is supplemented with more specific comments in the introductions preceding each part. There we point out a number of specific issues relevant to each chapter and how these fit into other areas. These comments are a combination of our own insights and those expressed by the symposium participants and audience. In addition to these, each of the first three parts contains a concluding commentary chapter with discussants' reactions to the preceeding chapters.

Let's now look at the contents of each of these parts in more detail.

*Part 1. Leadership and Managerial Behavior as Loosely Coupled Systems
for Moving Beyond Establishment Views*

As the title to this part implies these are indeed "loosely coupled systems." They should not be but they are! As Stewart suggests in her chapter, "The Relevance of Some Studies of Managerial Work and Behavior for Leadership Research," the reason for the loose coupling is probably because those researching leadership are different from those researching managerial behavior. That, in turn, is influenced by how one defines leadership. Is it a subset of managerial behavior or, using a role definition, is everything a manager does "leadership" since a manager is often in a leadership role? This is, of course, a perennial question which has come up again and again in previous Symposium volumes and elsewhere.

Our stance is to treat leadership as a subset of managerial behavior but to consider the study of leadership as incomplete without also considering managerial behavior. Thus we see the contribution of Stewart's and other chapters in this part as helping to show how the two largely separate bodies of literature can cross-fertilize each other.

The second chapter, "Unstructured, Nonparticipant Observations and the Study of Leaders' Interpersonal Contacts," by Bussom, Larson, and Vicars, focuses on what police chiefs did during a two-week period of observation. The richness of these data help us to break out of the rigid, overly deterministic mold which some have argued characterizes the leadership establishment. The chapter also points out in some detail how one goes about gathering meaningful observational data with practicing managers.

Lombardo and McCall, "Leaders on Line: Observations from a Simulation of Managerial Work," round out the leadership-managerial behavior material by discussing the behaviors of managers in a complex simulation. They do not attempt to separate leadership and managerial behavior. To them, all of the behaviors are important to getting the work of a manager accomplished.

Wilpert's commentary chapter provides additional perspective on the leadership and managerial behavior relationship by addressing a number of issues in the three presentations. He considers the chapters both individually and as a group and integrates them with his perception of establishment views. That point of view is particularly interesting because he is a German and his views reflect a rich European orientation.

Part 2. Semiestablishment Views and a Triad of New Models

The first three chapters in this part differ from those in the other parts in that they were selected from among numerous competitive paper submissions. Thus, they are quite diverse, especially in comparison with those in Part 1 (which were invited to fill their particular niches). This diversity provided a particular challenge to the commentators, who were asked both to contrast and integrate them. Because of the challenge, two commentators were used—Bernard Bass from the United States and Ian Morley from England.

These chapters reflect the pluralism which we see as becoming more prevalent in the current leadership literature. The first of these ("Multiplexed Supervision and Leadership: An Application of Within and Between Analysis"), by Dansereau, Alutto, Markham, and Dumas, focuses on the unit of analysis issue. It examines the applicability of models emphasizing different units of analysis to the same data set and concludes that each model may be appropriate for different variables within a given set. The second chapter, "A Theory of Leadership Categorization," by Lord, Foti, and Phillips, concentrates on applying object categorization and person perception models to leadership research. The authors develop a model which helps explain the processes by which people categorize different kinds of leaders and by which they differentiate leaders from nonleaders. The third chapter ("Leadership Activation Theory: An Opponent Process Model of Subordinate Responses to Leadership Behavior"), by Sheridan, Kerr, and Abelson applies an opponent process model to the responses of subordinates to leader behavior. The approach is especially interesting because it suggests that the intensity of a leader's behavior may sometimes have more impact than its frequency. The next chapter in the part contains the Bass and Morley commentaries, contrasting and integrating the chapters, and showing where they fit among semiestablishment views. This is followed by brief replies to the commentaries by Dansereau et al. and Foti, Lord, and Phillips, which end the chapter and Part 2.

Part 3. Micro and Macro Extensions to Establishment Views

The chapters in this part, though invited, are again quite diverse. The diversity was designed to illustrate extensions of establishment work at both micro and macro ends of the leadership continuum. The first of these chapters ("SYMLOG and Leadership Theory"), by Bales and Isenberg, focuses on Bales's new System for the Multiple Level Observation of

Groups (SYMLOG) as it applies to leadership theory. The second of these chapters ("Toward a Macro-Oriented Model of Leadership: An Odyssey"), by Hunt and Osborn, looks at a macro-oriented leadership model that has taken more than a decade to develop. The authors not only describe the model but trace the circuitous path involved in its development. The commentary chapter by Henry Tosi uses these two models as a point of departure in describing additional extensions beyond the establishment.

Part 4. Overview, Epilogs, and Conclusion

The first chapter in this part is by Henry Mintzberg. In "If You're Not Serving Bill and Barbara, Then You're Not Serving Leadership," the author takes the field and this volume's content to task for neglecting the practitioner. Although the theme is not new, Mintzberg's treatment is rather interesting and ingenious, and it was written to be as provocative as possible. The next chapter is an epilog by the editors. It covers U.S. developments not treated in the book or treated differently or in less depth. It is followed by an epilog by Hosking and Hunt, which summarizes work from a recent informal leadership/managerial behavior conference held in England. This serves as a dramatic counterpoint to the U.S. work, since the European and American perspectives are quite different.[1]

The part concludes with a chapter by the editors, "Conclusion: The Leadership-Management Controversy Revisited." This chapter is concerned with the research-practice dichotomy which is highlighted by Mintzberg's comments and those of other prominent scholars in the field. In this chapter, the editors deal with a number of key issues which have permeated this dichotomy, including basic questions regarding values, preferred research strategies, and the role of "fun" in scientific inquiry.

In closing this introduction, it is instructive to relate the content to that of earlier Symposium volumes, especially the most recent one, *Crosscurrents in Leadership*. In that volume we suggested that the field appeared to be in what Levinson (1978) has labeled a transitional period, where "the major tasks are to reappraise the existing structure, explore new possibilities . . . and work toward choices that provide a basis for a new structure" (p. 317).

1. Strictly speaking we have taken poetic license here in calling this "U.S. work." It also contains a couple of Canadian contributions and one from South Africa. Nevertheless, the overwhelming preponderance of studies included in this category are from the United States. We thought about using the term "North American" instead of "U.S." when comparing this work with that in Europe but decided that might insult Canadians whose work might be substantially different from that summarized here. We finally decided to retain the "U.S." label.

We see the work in the present volume as falling in this transitional category and as helping to provide a basis for a new structure.

Precisely what the new structure for studying leadership will look like is currently unknown, and we are likely to be in a transitional state for some time to come. The contents of this volume and the other volumes in the series suggest, however, that the structure will be highly pluralistic. We believe, consistent with Karmel (1978), that there will probably be different models for different purposes, in contrast to one or a few grand models. Such a structure would allow for the acceptance of many views and would help reconcile the sharp splits now so prevalent in the literature. One of the most dramatic of these has been the researcher/practitioner split. In a utopian, pluralistic world, researchers and practitioners recognize and use different models for their own purposes, without feeling compelled to be defensive. However, such a world does not yet exist, and this issue is considered further in chapter 16 of this volume. Thus, let's move on to Part 1.

Part 1

Leadership and Managerial Behavior as Loosely Coupled Systems for Moving Beyond Establishment Views

Introduction

JAMES G. HUNT, UMA SEKARAN, AND
CHESTER A. SCHRIESHEIM

Each of the four chapters in this part (including the commentary) subscribes, both substantively and methodologically, to nonestablishment approaches to leadership research. The contributions were specially invited so that a forum could be offered for beginning the much-needed integration of research in the managerial and leadership behavior areas. The three content chapters deviate from traditional questionnaire surveys. Observation, simulation, and multimethods of data-collection procedures are treated. The presentations also highlight the importance of investigating issues not traditionally covered in leadership research and provide suggestions which may help bridge the gap between the two areas.

Chapter 2, "The Relevance of Some Studies of Managerial Work and Behavior to Leadership Research," by Rosemary Stewart, is a first step in the synthesis of managerial jobs and behavior, and leadership. Based on 16 years of research, using interviews, diary records, questionnaires, and observations, Stewart extends her model built around the concepts of "demands," "choices," and "constraints" to contingency theories of leadership. As an offshoot of this synthesis, she concludes with several propositions that can be examined in leadership research. These extensions from managerial work and behavior research to leadership offer the potential for breaking new ground and enriching both areas.

During the discussion following her presentation Stewart treated a number of interesting points which will be useful to keep in mind while reading her chapter. First, she noted that it was her observation that most managers are very demand and constraint oriented. They see many of each, but are not generally aware of the choices (opportunities) open to them. Most managers, according to Stewart, are unaware of what they are doing and do not spend time thinking about it. Thus, to a large extent they fail to recognize options which might be available. One obvious implication of this is in terms of teaching managers an appreciation for different available courses of action or making them more proactive, at least in terms of their own role definitions.

In terms of developing this proactive stance, Stewart focused on the "personal domain"—the opportunities for choice outside a manager's immediate unit. There is often considerable latitude in this area, but managers do not perceive it. Training can aid in focusing attention on this way of opening options beyond those otherwise available.

If one accepts these contentions, a question arises as to why managers perceive the world as they do. Stewart suggested that early job experiences may have a substantial impact. Thus, research directed at how people develop views of their jobs, what causes them to focus their attention in certain ways, and how their general approach to management develops over time would be quite important.

Finally, her demands-constraints model appears useful in the performance appraisal area. Stewart suggested that the model can be used to make managers aware of technological and other constraints faced by subordinates being appraised and thus lead to more realistic evaluations. Such an approach might also be useful in rewriting job descriptions and in rewriting jobs.

While Stewart's chapter is primarily conceptual in nature, chapter 3, "Unstructured, Nonparticipant Observation and the Study of Leader's Interpersonal Contacts," by Bussom, Larson and Vicars, has a substantial nonestablishment methodological emphasis but it also treats some conceptual concerns as well. It is an observational study using a design that is different from most other studies of managerial behavior. Their observational recording is a running—almost minute by minute—narration of the activities of the ten police chiefs whom they observed for about 1200 hours during different periods of the year. These activities were subsequently categorized with a heavy emphasis on coder and observer reliabilities. Based on their preliminary data analysis, the authors propose a leader "contact profiles model." This model includes: pattern (how, where, and with whom contacts occur); content (topic and contact meaning); and the interaction between pattern and contact. The authors argue that further development and refinement of the model would offer valuable insights into the determinants of leader behavior.

This presentation is based on very preliminary data analysis. It was our feeling that it was important to provide a preview of the potential of the methodology and conceptualization. Hence, we opted to invite the contribution now even though a wait would have provided more detailed data analyses. Thus, we have here an exciting contribution in its earliest stage of development.

Of special interest as one reads the chapter are the following. First, though the authors show substantial variations in activities across chiefs, to what extent is there a core of activities common to all? Second, the authors briefly treat "proactive" and "reactive" chiefs. Again, there appears to be a tie-in with Stewart's work with respect to her notion of opportunities recognition. Third, the question of stability of contact patterns is treated by the authors. To what extent are these patterns transitory versus long-term and enduring?

We should also point out a relationship between this work and other current work which may at first appear unrelated. The Bussom et al. data focus on what a manager does in very great detail. The data concern behavior in far more depth than even newly developed questionnaires such as the one by Yukl and Nemeroff (1979). An important stream of research from England by Randell and his colleagues (e.g., Randell, in press) and reported in more detail in the European epilog chapter is interesting to compare with that of Bussom et al. The methodologies and approaches are quite different. Both, however, provide a more in-depth look at what managers and leaders do than establishment approaches.

Chapter 4, "Leader's on Line: Observations from a Simulation of Managerial Work," by Lombardo and McCall, is the last chapter prior to the commentary. It points out some directions for rethinking our research inquiries, methodologies, and conceptualizations. For instance, the authors propose that leadership research would be probably better off treating problems rather than individuals or groups as the unit of analysis. Based on their observations of behavior in a simulation, the authors suggest, among other things, that the impact of the environment on leader behavior is far more complex than has typically been assumed. Also, the term "effectiveness" is a function of who defines it. In other words, the meaning of effectiveness lies in the eyes of the beholder. Thus, Lombardo and McCall's research is not only innovative in the methodology adopted—that of simulating a glass-manufacturing company with a systematic attempt to capture the environmental and organizational complexities true to life—but, the authors also provide a rich description of managerial behavior which moves far beyond establishment views. Like Stewart's work, this chapter culminates with a series of explorable propositions.

Readers will no doubt have questions about the adequacy of the simulation for its intended purpose. Concerns such as: more detail on the nature of the simulation and its design; the adequacy of its six-hour length; the extent to which observations of what occurs in the simulation are a function of the simulation's structure; and the effect of experimenter intervention on the simulation come to mind. These kinds of issues are dealt with in a *Management Science* article by the authors (see McCall & Lombardo, in press). We recommend that article as a companion to the present chapter.

Some possible conceptual concerns focus on: when and where leadership is important (and how important in terms of variance accounted for); what is the trade-off between using a group unit of analysis as in this simulation versus an individual one; what difference might background (e.g. student versus manager) make in approaching the exercise; and the extent to which the simulation will allow methodologies beyond the questionnaires so heavily relied upon by the research establishment.

Wilpert, in his commentary, "Various Paths Beyond Establishment Views" (chap. 5) concentrates on some additional points unique to each chapter. He also focuses on concerns cutting across the contributions. Finally, he looks at the chapters from a uniquely European vantage point and relates them to some of that literature.

2

The Relevance of Some Studies of Managerial Work and Behavior to Leadership Research

ROSEMARY STEWART

The purpose of this chapter is to select and discuss those concepts and findings that are potentially relevant to leadership research from five of my studies of managerial work and behavior. These span the period from 1964 to 1980 and are outlined in Table 1. The argument of this chapter is that leadership studies can benefit from other perspectives than those establishment views that have commonly been employed. It is an appropriate time to put forward this suggestion because of the anxiety recently expressed about the state of leadership research and the need for new directions (e.g., Bennis, 1976; Dubin, 1979; Hunt & Larson, 1979; McCall & Lombardo, 1978a).

"Manager" and "managerial jobs" will be used in this chapter for posts in charge of subordinates above the level of first-line supervisor. When "leader" and "leadership" are used they will refer to the exercise of interpersonal influence in the Katz and Kahn (1966) sense as "influential increment over and above mechanical compliance with routine directives of the organization." The phrase "leadership research" or "leadership studies" will be used broadly to include all those who describe themselves as working in that area.

Separation of Leadership Studies and Research into Managerial Work and Behavior

Historically, leadership research and research into managerial behavior have been pursued independently, so that there has been little or no

TABLE 1

Studies in Managerial Work and Behavior Planned and Supervised by Rosemary Stewart

Title of Project	Date and Duration	Staffing	Nature and Size of Sample	Methods Used
1) Similarities and Differences in How Managers Spend Their Time (Stewart, 1967).	1964–66; 2 years.		160 middle and senior managers mainly in production, marketing and accounting in different manufacturing companies.	Diary for four weeks covering when, how, where, with whom.
2) A Behavioral Classification of Managerial Jobs (Stewart, 1976).	1973–75; 2½ years.	1 research worker full-time 2 years—Judy Slinn. 1 full-time 1 year—Richard Turton.	260 managers in jobs selected for diversity of level and function in different companies. 16 managers chosen to represent different contact types.	Lengthy questionnaire interviews. Interviews, diaries, observations.
3) A Classification of Choices in Managerial Jobs	1977–80; 2½ years.	1 research worker full-time 2 years—Phil Long	96 managers and 96 bosses, cross-sectioned by level and function in one company; varied functions in others. 6 pairs of managers in six different jobs.	Lengthy open-ended interview with managers and with the bosses. One week's observation of each manager comparing behavior of each pair.
4) The Job and Role of the District Administrator in the National Health Service (Stewart, Smith, Blake, & Wingate, 1980).	1978–79; 10 months.	3 part-time research associates—Peter Smith, Jenny Black and Pauline Wingate.	41 district administrators from a stratified sample of districts.	3–7 hour interview. Observation of 11 district administrators lasting 3 days to a week each. Group discussions.
5) Managers' Perceptions of the Choices in their Jobs.	1978–79 15 months.	1 part-time research associate—Judi Marshall.	86 middle managers in production/technical and sales/marketing in three manufacturing companies.	Tape recorded open-ended interviews. Personal background. Job involvement and accommodation questionnaire, Myers-Briggs Test.

Funding. 1) Nuffield Foundation.   2), 3), 5) Social Science Research Council.   4) King Edward's Hospital Fund for London.

cross-fertilization of ideas. This separation has a number of possible explanations. The two fields have tended to attract researchers from different backgrounds and with different interests. Those in leadership studies have been primarily social psychologists, mainly using the predominant tools of their occupation—structured questionnaires and laboratory studies, although there is now more interest in other methods. They have attached, and attach, prime importance to measurement. "Without it [measurement], we have nothing" (Korman, 1974). There is a concern with outcomes, with trying to identify what forms of leader behavior are associated with different types of outcome. The much smaller number of people who have done research into managerial behavior have come from varied academic backgrounds, and more of them from outside the United States. Their main interest has been to identify the nature of managerial work by studying what managers do.

One approach to studying managerial work did stem from leadership studies. It sought to identify the dimensions of managerial jobs by using structured questionnaires and factor analytic methods (Hemphill, 1960; Tornow & Pinto, 1976). It is the other approach that has been pursued independently. This studied what managers do using recorded or observed behavior and semistructured interviews (e.g., Burns, 1954, 1957; Carlson, 1951; Mintzberg, 1973; Sayles, 1964; Stewart, 1967, 1976; Stewart, Smith, Blake, & Wingate, 1980). These studies have developed from a numeric description of the more easily classifiable activities to a more anthroological approach that attempts to identify and describe other aspects of behavior. The earlier work produced some general characteristics of behavior, which were summarized by Mintzberg (1973). Later work has developed different constructs for describing the nature of managerial work and behavior. The development of simulation studies is a further and newer development by scholars who span leadership studies and managerial work and behavior (Lombardo & McCall, this volume).

A Model of Managerial Jobs and Behavior

A model was conceived for analyzing managerial jobs and behavior during the course of the second study listed in Table 1 (Stewart, 1976). This was developed in the third study, and applied to the analysis of a particular job in the fourth. This model will be briefly explained, then illustrated from the fourth study, and its relevance to leadership studies discussed. The aim of the model is to describe differences between jobs and differences between the behavior of individuals in similar jobs. (The word "similar" is used rather than "identical" because even managerial jobs with the same responsibilities and resources are likely to have some differences in their situation.)

The model has three broad categories, each of which has a number of subdivisions. The latter were identified in the second and third studies in Table 1. Some broad comparative measurements were made in the second study, some of which are discussed later. The more recently identified subdivisions have not been used as a basis for measurement, but this could be done. The model and the subdivisions which are likely to be of interest to those in leadership studies are outlined in Table 2. The model describes managerial jobs as consisting of an inner core of *demands*, an outer boundary of *constraints* and an in-between area of *choices*. The idea of constraints and demands is used by Graen (1976) in discussing the determinants of roles, though neither is defined. The definitions of our terms are as follows.

Demands: what anyone in the job must do, that is cannot avoid doing without invoking sanctions that would imperil continuing in the job.

Constraints: the factors internal and external to the organization that limit what the jobholder can do.

Choices: the opportunities that exist for jobholders in similar jobs to do different work and to do it in different ways from other jobholders.

Demands: a behavioral description of the minimum core of the job. They can be identified by observing the behavior of a number of jobholders in similar jobs. They could also be discovered, though less reliably, by questionnaires. "Less reliably" because individuals can give inaccurate descriptions of what they do and have different perceptions of the nature of their jobs (Marshall & Stewart, in press). We found that some managers exaggerate the number of demands and the time that they absorb.

The idea of "demands" has similarities to that of "required" behavior in the Multiple Influence Model in that both are concerned with what the jobholder, or leader, has to do, "some minimum set of behaviors dictated by their position in the organizational hierarchy" (Hunt & Osborn, this volume). The difference is that for Hunt and Osborn these are apparently formal requirements. "Leaders at the same hierarchical levels and heading units with similar goals, environment, and organizational variables are likely to share similar requirements." This would not be wholly true of demands. They are not required behavior in the sense of what the jobholder ought to do, but of what he or she cannot get away with not doing. Much of what could be described as the requirements of the job will be interpreted differently by different jobholders, and thus, in practice offer various choices.

In some jobs there are very few demands. The manager will then have a wide array of possible choices which are limited by constraints. The work

TABLE 2
Subdivisions of the Demands, Constraints, and Choices Model

Demands
Determined by:
  Output specifications
  Need for personal involvement in the unit's work
  Bureaucratic procedures that cannot be delegated
  Relationships: contacts, expectations, need to influence
Constraints
  Resource limitations
  Legal, trade union, and systems constraints
  Technological limitations
  Attitudes to the manager's actions and proposed actions
  Extent to which area of the manager's unit is defined } See the text discussion
  Extent of output acceptance.   } of Domain.
Choices
  General
    Focus of attention between different job responsibilities
    Time spent on supervision compared with other work and contacts
    Aspects of supervision emphasized
  Common, but not available in all managerial jobs
    Amount and nature of delegation
    Whom the manager seeks to influence, including attention given to boundary
    management
  Available in some managerial jobs
    Domain
    Work sharing
    Role played in groups of which a member, especially top management teams

---

Note. Only subdivisions affecting the content of work are included here. A classification of methods of work has been developed, but it is excluded since it is of less interest for leadership studies.

that managers must do themselves, *the demands*, is determined by the following four factors.

1. The extent to which there are output specifications for the work for which they are responsible. This must be considered together with the second factor.

2. The extent to which they must be personally involved in this work.

3. Bureaucratic procedures that cannot be delegated.

4. Relationships, that is whom they must work with, and what they must seek to do with each person, or category of people. This includes the expectations that others have of what will be done, and what consequences will follow if these are not met, as well as the meetings that they must attend.

The existence and nature of output specifications (the first factor) affect demands and are, as we shall see later under Domain, a major determinant of the opportunities for choice. However, the nature of output specifications is only the most general guide to the demands upon the manager, which depend very much upon the second factor, the extent to which personal involvement in the unit's work is necessary. In some jobs, we found, the manager must get involved, it is a demand; in others it is a choice. We shall discuss later, under difficulty of supervision, some of the factors that make it a demand.

A minor, but in some organizations quite time consuming, demand (or third factor) is the bureaucratic procedures that managers must fulfill themselves. These include budgets, authorizing expense claims for subordinates, and doing formal appraisals.

Demands will also depend upon the manager's relationships (the fourth factor). We shall later discuss in detail the manager's contacts and variations in the need to influence. Managers must work with people who have expectations about what they will do and how they will do it (Graen, 1976; Katz & Kahn, 1966; Machin, 1979). The extent to which these expectations are demands that the manager must meet varies between different kinds of jobs (Stewart, 1976). Both colleagues and subordinates, as well as bosses, may have such power, and thus be in a position to ensure that some of their expectations are demands upon the manager.

Constraints: the first four types of constraint listed in Table 2 are easily recognized, but are, we found, complex and difficult to assess. They are:

1. The factors that limit the amount and kind of resources. One example of the complexity is the number of factors relevant to constraints on staffing, including whether there is a fixed establishment, and, if so, whether this is modified in practice by the use of contract labor.

2. Legal, trade union and systems constraints: for example, the manager's choice in behavior to staff may be constrained by legislation on working conditions, by agreements with trade unions, by company personnel policies, and by the computerized staff records.

3. Technological limitations which include those imposed by the kind of equipment installed and by the hazards of certain processes.

4. The manager may be constrained in the making of changes by people's attitudes towards them.

There are two other constraints that we found were important in determining the amount of choice that a job offers.

5. The extent to which the area of the manager's unit is defined. (Unit is the general word for the manager's responsibilities whether it is a department, plant, division, or company.) Some jobs are responsible for a defined area of operation that the manager cannot change, and others have more open-ended responsibilities, which we discuss below under Domain.

6. The extent of output acceptance. That is, present or potential customers' willingness to accept what the manager wants to provide, whether it is a new product, training program, or a different method of costing.

Choices: the definition given above is a description of the possibilities for choice inherent in the position, not of what choices a particular individual may make. The concept differs from that of discretionary leadership in the Multiple Influence Model (Hunt & Osborn, this volume) in that choice is seen as an inherent part of all managerial jobs, whereas Hunt and Osborn treat discretionary leadership as something that a leader may not exercise. They put forward propositions about the effects of the exercise of discretionary leadership on unit outcomes. We can make no propositions about the simple exercise of choice, because all managers will necessarily exercise choice in their leadership activities as in other aspects of their behavior. It is the kind of choices exercised and its relevance to the situation that matters for effectiveness.

The choices are limited by both the demands and the constraints, though these are dynamic, changing over time from changes in the situation and sometimes also, depending upon the nature of the job, from the actions of the jobholder, who may be able to change some of the demands, or, more frequently, some of the constraints. The model of demands, constraints, and choices envisions a number of possibilities that can vary in their kind, number, and dimensions. They are, therefore, potentially measurable. The model posits that the opportunities that a job offers, the area of potential choice, cannot be fully used by one individual because of time pressures, the incompatibility of certain choices, and individual differences in abilities.

Table 2 distinguishes between those opportunities for choice that we found in all managerial jobs and those that are limited to particular jobs. In any managerial job, however formalized, individuals will tend to spend their time in different ways, because some aspects of the job will strike them as more important or will interest them more. This will also apply to the time that they spend in supervision and to the aspects of supervision that they emphasize. Our observation of six pairs of middle managers, each pair in a similar job, showed considerable differences in emphasis between different parts of the job. Nearly all managerial jobs also offer a choice in the amount and nature of delegation, but there are a few that do not do so either because of geographical separation or a very marked difference in the tasks to be performed at the two levels. Most managers also have a choice in whom they seek to influence, which we shall discuss later because of its interest to leadership studies.

An important choice in many jobs is the attention given to boundary management, that is, trying to influence the people, both within the organization and outside, who can affect the works of the manager's unit. Some managers, we found, focus their attention primarily downward to their subordinates, while others give more attention to boundary management. We select from the opportunities for choice that apply in a more limited range of jobs those that are most relevant to leadership studies. The major choice is that of domain, which is discussed in the next section. Some jobs offer the choice of sharing different roles and concentrating upon different tasks with one or more other individuals (Hodgson, Levinson, & Zaleznik, 1965; Senger, 1971). Managers may also have a choice both in the role(s) that they play in the different groups to which they must belong, and in which other groups they get involved. Such group membership can provide a variety of different opportunities for influence.

The Nature and Flexibility of the Manager's Domain

Kotter and Lawrence (1974) in their study of mayors used the concept of domain, which they defined as "that subpart of the total city in which the mayor consciously tries to have an impact." The related definition that is used here is "the area in which the manager gets involved and seeks to have an influence." The word "consciously" is omitted because of the difficulty of determining whether an action is conscious or not (Marshall & Stewart, in press).

Jobs differ in the size of their prescribed domain. This is indicated in job descriptions by listing the scope of responsibilities. We found that jobs differ, too, in whether, and if so the extent to which, the domain is flexible. We also found that individuals in similar jobs differ in the relative emphasis they give to different parts of the domain and, more interestingly, where the domain is flexible, in which domains they get involved and exercise influence. These findings suggest two possible questions for those in leadership studies: "What are the areas in which an individual can exercise leadership in a particular job?" and "In which areas is a particular individual exercising leadership?"

A distinction is made in the choice of domain between the possible flexibility in the unit for which the manager is responsible and the opportunities that may exist for exercising influence in domains outside it. The major factor in determining whether the domain of the manager's unit is fixed is how detailed and encompassing are the specifications for its output. The manager of a melting shop in the steel industry, for example, or of any other prescribed work-flow process, has no flexibility in the unit's domain by contrast with a management accountant who can seek to provide new information and get involved in decisions in other areas of the business.

The general manager of a subsidiary company whose products and market area are defined by the parent company has little flexibility of unit domain compared with the general manager of a subsidiary where the parent company expects a prescribed minimum financial return but imposes no geographical constraints and only broad product definitions. The latter has far more opportunities than the former for choice in the directions in which he or she seeks to lead the subsidiary. A manager's opportunities to change or enlarge the unit's domain can also be constrained by prevailing attitudes toward possible new outputs and by the attitudes of subordinates to any changes in the kind of work that is done. Then there may also be resource constraints including the number and qualifications of subordinates. Many managerial jobs offer at least some opportunities for managers to extend their domain outside their own unit. Many of these opportunities are determined by the kinds of contacts that the job demands or which the manager can choose to have.

The wide flexibility of domain that exists in some posts, and the different opportunities that they can provide for leadership, can be illustrated by the fourth research study in Table 1. This was a study of the post of district administrator in the National Health Service in England (Stewart et al., 1980). It is an example of opportunities for choices of domain outside the manager's own unit. The study is of interest because it provided an unusual opportunity to compare the reported and actual behavior of a large number of senior managers in similar posts, and because of its parallels in other, especially senior, jobs. The district administrator is responsible for the administrative services in a health district. A district includes the hospitals and community health services within a geographical area which can have a population ranging from about 100,000 to over 500,000. The district administrator is a member of the consensus district management team which is responsible for the district's health services, within the resource and other constraints imposed by higher levels in the National Health Service. The team does not have a chief executive or other formal leader, and can choose whether to appoint a chairman, and if it decides to do so, who it will be and for how long he or she will serve.

Forty-one administrators were interviewed for from three to seven hours about their activities during the previous month and more generally about their views of their role, and eleven were observed for from three to five days including a meeting of the district management team. Information about meetings attended and their contacts in the previous month, and about the characteristics of their district, was collected by questionnaire.

The district administrators varied considerably in the size and nature of the domain in which they were active. The smallest domain was that of responsibility for the administrative services, which included acting as secretary to the district management team. Such administrators spent much of their time with their subordinates helping them sort out operational demands, and also responding to personal requests for information and help from doctors and other members of staff. Their role in the management team was predominantly secretarial and as spokesman for the administrative function. Their leadership activities were confined to their subordinates. The largest domain was that of the administrators who felt themselves to be responsible for anything that happened in the district, and therefore sought to monitor the service that was being provided in it, and to influence those who they thought were not performing well. They attempted to lead as if they were the general manager, though the methods that they could use with doctors and nurses necessarily had to rely on persuasion and political sensitivity. Most of the administrators occupied domains that were between these two extremes.

There was considerable variation in which domains were the major focus of an administrator's effort and which were not included in attempts at influence. One major difference was between the majority of administrators who sought to lead their subordinates, and those who delegated this task to one, occasionally a couple of, senior subordinates. Contact with these one or two was mainly for the exchange of information, rather than as their leader. Those who abdicated the leadership role in relation to their subordinates saw their major responsibility as lying elsewhere. Most frequently this was in seeking to guide the district management team, to set objectives, to try and ensure that the problems that mattered in the district were discussed and that agreement was reached on what should be done about them, and then in trying to ensure that such agreements were implemented. The ways in which the administrators sought to lead the management team varied. Some saw themselves as having a primarily educational role, teaching other team members how to think, rather than what to think. Some used their superior access to information to support their attempts at influence. Others led by virtue of their superior preparation for meetings, greater interest in, and dedication to, the work of the district, and a few by the force of their personalities.

Some of the administrators expanded into the domain of a colleague, most commonly the chief nursing officer. Some also paired with another member of the team, most frequently the financial head, and sometimes the representative of the hospital consultants. The pair would then share tasks between themselves and jointly seek to influence the team's discussions.

There were yet other domains in which some administrators got involved. A few acted as the figurehead, known as the spokesman for the health services, and the person to go to with a problem—one was even called "Mr. Health" in the local newspapers. Some were active in seeking to influence decisions about the resources allocated to the district. They made a point of getting to know the chairman and other key members of the Authority who allocated resources between districts. They established friendly relations with the Community Health Council, which is the local consumers' voice, and sought to enlist their support for the district management team's plans. They kept their local Member of Parliament informed about the issues on which they looked for support. In short, they took a very proactive view of their role in making friends and influencing people on behalf of their district—a role that some other administrators would not have seen as theirs. Some, who might have considered it, thought that to do so was to go against the interests of the health service as a whole, in which such sectional lobbying was a mistake. Yet another domain in which some administrators were active was the professional one. They became well known as leaders in their profession, and would be called on to speak and to serve on working parties.

So far we have described the different domains as if the district administrator had a free choice between them. The model of demands, constraints, and choices can help as a reminder that that would be an oversimplification. The administrator may be constrained in the choice of delegation by changes in senior subordinates, or by their caliber. In some district management teams there can be one or more strong personalities competing for leadership. The difficulties that a district faces may also add to the demands and reduce the choices.

The job of the district administrator also illustrates the choices that some jobs offer for work sharing. This took various forms. There was the work sharing that was also domain expansion where the district administrator took on some of the work of the district nursing officer and the district medical officer, and got involved in their problems. There was work sharing within the management team, for example, one or more of its members, which might or might not include the district administrator, could go to a meeting on behalf of the team. There was also work sharing between the district administrator and his or her immediate subordinates. Some administrators worked as a team member with their immediate subordinates, jointly tackling problems as they arose. Work sharing was then a more accurate description of their common activities than delegation.

The district management team also provided opportunities for a choice of roles. Different district administrators played different roles in the teams to which they belonged. These included both the formal one of being chairman and the informal ones such as seeking to get the team to work on particular problems or to cooperate together.

Membership of the district management teams offered the district administrator a variety of choices within the demands and constraints imposed by other team members. These choices included whether to play the formal role of chairman and informal roles such as seeking to get the team to cooperate together. There was also a variety of administrative choices that could affect how the team operated, for example, the selection of items for the agenda, both the subjects and their timing of discussion, encouraging or discouraging other members to put forward agenda items, preparation of papers, and attempting to get prior agreement on contentious topics.

The post that we have described is an unusual one in its membership of a consensus management team, which has no designated leader. It is unusual, too, in the wide variety of choice of domains that it offers. However, the choice of domains has parallels in some of the industrial management jobs that we studied, particularly some of the more senior ones. We also found many examples of domain choices in middle management jobs in a large petrochemicals company (Stewart, book in preparation). The potential variety of domains that some jobs offer poses some interesting issues for leadership studies. These include the determination of the domains in which leadership is being exercised, the factors that make individuals choose to be active in some domains rather than others, and the effects that such choices have on the nature of the outcomes, and on which outcomes should be measured.

Many of the choices of domain that have been described can be considered in terms of the kinds of contacts that the manager is free to make. We found that an analysis of contacts was a convenient way to identify some of the choices, so we shall now consider that separately.

Contact Types

The customary ways of distinguishing between managerial work are by level in the hierarchy and by function. However, even jobs at the same level, in the same function, and in the same company can differ considerably as our second and third research projects showed. One way of identifying some of these differences is by the kind of contacts that must, or can, be made. Stewart (1976) classified managerial jobs into twelve types according to the amount of time spent in various categories of contacts. The first dimension used to distinguish between contacts was whether they were wholly *Internal* to the organization; largely *External*, or in between, requiring some external contacts, *Internal/External*. These were subdivided into four categories. The most common in Stewart's sample across a wide variety of jobs and companies, was called *Hub*, where managers spend time with a wide variety of contacts: peers, bosses, subordinates and other juniors, but where most time is spent with subordinates. Another common contact type was called *Peer Dependent*, where as much or more time is spent with colleagues at or near their own level as with their subordinates. *Man Management* is for those heading a pretty self-contained unit where there are few or no contacts with peers. The last, and least socially demanding, category is *Solo*, for those who have much less contact with others. There are marked differences in the amount and nature of leadership skills required in these different categories. The Hub External require the widest variety of leadership skills to deal with the wide range of contacts that need to be influenced. Man Management Internal is the most specific, as managers only have to know how to lead their own subordinates and, perhaps, also how to influence their boss. Solo jobs may have a wider variety of contacts, but much of the time will be spent on work alone.

These contact types provide a simple, and easily measured, guide to a manager's contacts. Later research showed that for many jobs the contact types were a reflection of choice rather than a demand of the job (Stewart, 1979). Some plant managers, for example, were found who had a Peer Dependent contact pattern, by contrast with the more usual Hub pattern that one might expect. The former delegated much more and concentrated their activities on relations with other departments. A variety of other unexpected contact types were found, thus showing that the contact type can be a useful guide to how the manager interprets the job, including whom he or she is seeking to lead.

How the Need to Influence Varies in Different Jobs

Managerial jobs differ, we found, not merely in whom managers must seek to influence, or whom they can try to influence, but they also differ in the difficulty of doing so. Comparisons of the difficulty of relationships are relevant to leadership studies as they can show where leadership is most needed and where it is likely to require most skill. Stewart (1976) compared the difficulty, irrespective of the particular personalities, of relationships with subordinates, boss, peers, and external contacts in sixteen different jobs. The information was obtained by interviews with the manager and separately with his boss, by a three weeks' diary, and by one day's observation each of the three weeks. Two examples are given. The first, the difficulty of the subordinate relationship, is a guide to the need for personal involvement in the unit's work. The second, boss-dependence, to the need to influence one's boss.

The difficulty of the subordinate relationship was rated under a number of headings. A broad distinction was made between whether subordinates *could* do their jobs without supervision and whether they *would*. The factors rated under "could" were: whether tasks had to be allocated; whether the nature of the work done by subordinates had to be monitored to ensure that they were doing the right kind of work; and whether the quality and quantity of the work had to be monitored. In some managerial jobs the holder can expect to have experienced subordinates working for him or her who will need little monitoring. In others, there may be a succession of short-term inexperienced subordinates who will need considerable supervision. In yet others the subordinates may be less technically qualified. The factors rated under whether subordinates "would" do the work without supervision included three factors assessing the likely degree of compliance: unionization, history of industrial action, and the basis of authority. Additionally the extent to which it is easy to monitor subordinates' work was also rated. Two other factors were included in the overall rating of the difficulty of the subordinate relationship: the number of immediate subordinates and whether their work interlocked and their work interests could conflict. The rating for the sixteen jobs ranged from 2 to 16 out of a possible total of 23 which divided into three distinct groups, high, medium, and low.

This discussion of variations in the difficulty of relations with subordinates has concentrated on differences between jobs. Such difficulties can help to show the extent to which there is a need for leadership. Kerr and Jermier (1978) have an interesting discussion of organizational differences, which can also affect the need for leadership. They suggest that "effective leadership might therefore be described as the ability to supply subordinates with needed guidance and good feelings which are not being supplied by other sources."

Jobs differed, we found, in the extent to which they were boss-dependent. In the more formalized organizations the nature of the job is unlikely to be changed by the boss: branch bank managers is one example, where, at least in the United Kingdom, the bank manager's responsibilities are prescribed and are not dependent upon the impression made upon the boss. In less formalized organizations, particularly in some of the smaller entrepreneurial companies, the scope that the subordinate has will depend very much upon the confidence that the boss has in his or her work. In boss-dependent jobs many incumbents will feel a need to try and influence their boss. Indeed when lecturing at management courses I have often been asked for advice on how to manage one's boss. The management of one's boss is not normally included as a part of leadership studies yet it falls within the definition quoted earlier by Katz and Kahn (1966). If this is accepted as the concept of boss-dependence, with the four categories used in Stewart (1976) to measure it, it is a useful guide to one of the leadership requirements of some jobs.

The analysis of contact type and of the difficulty of different kinds of relationships can provide valuable information about the kind of leadership required in different jobs. Such information can be of help in selection; for example, Peer Dependent jobs with a high rating for the difficulty of the relationship with peers require more political leadership skills than do Man Management jobs. An analysis of contacts can also be a guide to training needs highlighting the skills training that may be needed if a manager is moved between markedly dissimilar contact types. Career planning should ensure than an individual has the experience of jobs that require leadership of peers as well as of subordinates.

Leader Behavior Dimensions

One of the areas in which the divorce between leadership research and the research into managerial work and behavior is most noticeable to someone who comes from the latter tradition is that of the dimensions used for leadership behavior in the broader leadership studies. This can be illustrated by one recent example, the most carefully developed leader behavior scales of Yukl and Nemeroff (1979). The items that they include, and those that they suggest adding to bring in other important aspects of managerial behavior, derive from the classical tradition of management studies, as well as from leadership research, rather than from studies of what managers actually do. The underlying assumption is of a rational actor, with time to think and plan, operating in a stable and definable setting where one can plan and schedule "the work" in advance—a relevant behavior scale for some kinds of jobs, but giving the wrong emphasis for others, if it is unsupported by items that take account of the marked fragmentation that characterizes most managerial behavior and the fluidity of some environments.

A different problem about such scales, shown by some of our studies (Marshall & Stewart, in press; Stewart, 1967), is that words like "planning" can mean very different things to different individuals. The assumption in the use of such leader behavior scales seems to be that similar ratings by subordinates mean the same thing. It is surprising when so much care is given to some aspects of measurement, that the meaning of what is being measured for different respondents is not investigated. The possibility of different ratings by different parties has been discussed by others (e.g.,

Hosking, 1978; Mitchell, 1970) which shows an awareness of the problem of different perspectives, but this is between individuals in different positions, not between individuals in the same category of subordinates.

Leader behavior scales that focus, as most of them do, on superior-subordinate relations, assume that the manager will be spending most of his or her time in supervising their subordinates, rather than exercising their leadership skills in other types of relations. If any conclusions are to be drawn about leadership effectiveness from such studies it is essential that great care be exercised in the selection of effectiveness criteria. In the beauty-salon managers studied by Yukl and Nemeroff this would probably not be difficult. They are jobs that necessarily belong in the Man Management contact type, but in jobs in Hub or Peer Dependent contact types, the selection of criteria becomes more difficult. In as complex a job as that of the district administrator, with such a wide choice of domain, a high scale for leader behavior with subordinates might be accompanied by a neglect of other, and perhaps more important, domains.

Job, Behavior and Perceptions

It may have been noticed that the words "work" or "job" and "behavior" have been used throughout rather than just "managerial behavior." This is to signify that one may need to distinguish between job and behavior, rather than assume that a description of one is a description of the other. Behavior can be described as it can be observed, though there can be great difficulties in categorizing what aspects of a manager's behavior one wants to observe. How does one describe a job? Those in leadership studies who have been interested in doing so have asked individuals to rate the extent to which a number of statements apply to their own job, or to another that they are being asked about (e.g., Hemphill, 1960; and Tornow & Pinto, 1976). There are problems with this approach: individuals may perceive the characteristics of the job differently so that one is getting information about perceptions rather than an objective description of the job; and the statements are often couched in rather abstract language which may not describe actual behavior. The model of demands, constraints, and choices, and the illustrations of some of the choices taken by different district administrators, show some of the limitations to trying to describe a job by asking a particular individual, or even several individuals, to rate different characteristics.

It is easy to raise objections to the rating approach, harder to suggest another that will really describe the nature of a job. It is suggested that there are different kinds of answers to the question "what is a job?" which are relevant for different purposes. One is that a job is a designated post in an organization which has certain prescribed responsibilities, and may carry with it certain pay and conditions. Such a pragmatic definition is sufficient for some purposes, such as advertising for a new incumbent. To understand more about the nature of the job, and the different ways in which it can be tackled, one needs a less formal definition. There are various possibilities, the one that is suggested here is "the summation of all the possible behaviors by different jobholders." Such a definition would have the advantage of highlighting the flexibility of the job. It would show that for many managerial jobs it would not be necessary to "Engineer the Job to Fit The Manager" (Fiedler, 1965) because of the wide choice that exists for different behaviors. However, it has the disadvantage of being difficult to describe accurately and economically. It also tells one nothing about the purpose of the job or about its minimum core of demands.

Two additions could remedy these latter two defects. One is to extend the description to include demands, constraints, and choices. Choices would give the summation of possible behaviors, demands would give the minimum core, and constraints would show the boundaries to the choices. This was the method used for the district administrator study. The other addition would be a statement of desired outcomes. This would help to emphasize that although the job could be done in a wide variety of different ways, they should all contribute to these outcomes; which are likely to contribute most will vary with the situation, including its particular problems, the skills of the individual, and the abilities and preferred roles of other members of the role set, especially subordinates and colleagues.

We have suggested a way of trying to reconcile the differences between job and behavior by recognizing that a description of a particular individual manager's behavior will only tell one about some aspects of the job. The relation between perceptions, job, and behavior is even more difficult to discover than that between job and behavior alone, and is more central to leadership studies because so much of the work uses the perceptions that are held of the leader. A plea was made earlier for those in leadership studies to interest themselves in what the statements used for rating actually mean to their respondents and how these meanings differ for different individuals.

The fifth study listed in Table 1 was an exploratory attempt to discover how managers perceived the opportunities for choice in their jobs (Marshall & Stewart, in press). It was a companion study to the third which analyzed the choices in jobs. The fifth study suggests that managers have very different perceptions of the nature of their jobs. Some describe them analytically in terms of their component parts; some focus on a particular aspect which they see as the key to success in the job, and some see the job in very personal terms, and cannot describe it as existing apart from themselves. Few apparently are aware of making choices in how they do their jobs, unless stimulated to do so by some unusual change. However, a minority do see the job in strategic terms. This study underlines the need to consider differences in perception, and the relation of these differences to effectiveness in different kinds of jobs.

Conclusions and Propositions for Leadership Studies

The previous discussions will be summarized by a series of conclusions from the studies listed in Table 1 and by suggestions for their implications for leadership studies and for leadership research in the form of propositions.

The terms that will be used were defined earlier except for "effective." The use of "effective leader" in some of the propositions will refer to one who contributes more than an ineffective leader to maximizing the organization's goals but those who wish to test a proposition will no doubt develop their own criteria for effectiveness.

1. Conclusion: Managerial jobs offer the jobholder choice in the emphasis that can be given to different parts of the job.

2. Conclusion: Managerial jobs differ in the amount and kind of opportunities for choice that they offer. In some there is a choice of domains. *Implications*: Leaders may vary in which areas of their responsibilities they exercise leadership, and in the relative amount of leadership that they exercise in these areas. Some jobs offer the leader considerable choice as to the areas in which they lead their subordinates. *Proposition*: One factor determining leadership effectiveness is the relevance to the needs of the situation of the areas of the job in which managers choose, consciously or not, to exercise leadership. (Included in "needs of the situation" are the nature and severity of the problems facing the manager's unit, the relative importance of different outcomes, and the particular abilities and interests of subordinates. The phrase "consciously or not" is used because leaders may behave differently, that is make choices, without necessarily being aware of doing so.)

3. Conclusion: All managerial jobs, other than those in the Man Management Internal contact type, may offer the jobholder some choice in the relative emphasis given to working with subordinates compared with other categories of contacts.

4. Conclusion: Some posts, usually the more senior ones, offer the choice of delegating subordinate leadership so that the jobholder can concentrate upon other forms of leadership. *Implication*: Some jobs offer the manager a choice as to who he or she seeks to lead. *Proposition*: Assessment of leadership effectiveness should take account of the choices being made in who is being led and of the relative importance of other leadership opportunities for the goals of the organization.

5. Conclusion: Jobs can be rated by a number of criteria as to the difficulty of each of the different categories of relationships.

6. Conclusion: Jobs differ in the overall difficulty of their relationships and in the relative difficulty of different relationships. *Implications*: The overall difficulty of the leadership task and the way in which it is distributed between different categories of contacts can be rated. In some relationships including those with subordinates there may be little need for leadership. *Proposition*: Effective leaders will concentrate their leadership activities where there are difficult relationship tasks.

7. Conclusion: Managers in some jobs, especially those that are members of a top management team, may have a choice of sharing activities and roles with one or more other members of the team.

8. Conclusion: Managers in some jobs will have a choice of sharing activities and roles with another individual, who may be a boss, subordinate, or peer.

9. Conclusion: Managers in some jobs, especially members of a management team, may have a choice of expanding into a colleague's domain. *Implications*: The opportunities in some jobs for sharing leadership tasks upward, downward, and sideways, and between one or more individuals, and the consequent difficulty of drawing boundaries between jobs, needs more recognition in leadership studies, and its implications need more examination. *Propositions*: In some jobs some aspects of effective leadership may need to be assessed for pairs or groups, rather than individually.

These are conclusions about the implications for leadership studies of the nature of choices in managerial jobs, and of the distinctive choices in some jobs. Finally, there is one relevant conclusion on managerial perceptions from the fifth study in Table 1.

10. Conclusion: Managers differ in whether and, if so in the extent to which, they perceive opportunities for choice in their jobs. They also differ in the nature of the opportunities that they see. *Implication*: One of the leader's personal characteristics that should be explored in leadership studies is the nature of leaders' perceptions of their situation including whether they see themselves as having any opportunities for choice. *Proposition*: More effective leaders will see their jobs in strategic terms. They will recognize opportunities for choice and consider which ones they ought to take. This may be true for some kinds of jobs, and personalities, and not for others.

Table 2 listed different categories of demands, constraints, and choices. There are many opportunities for research in developing measures of these categories, and in seeking to use them in contingency theories of leadership.

It is hoped that some at least of the suggestions that have been made will be found useful by those who are interested in leadership studies, and that this chapter has contributed to lessening the separation between research into managerial work and behavior on the one hand and leadership studies on the other.

3

Unstructured, Nonparticipant Observation and the Study of Leaders' Interpersonal Contacts

ROBERT S. BUSSOM, LARS L. LARSON, and WILLIAM M. VICARS

In the most recent leadership symposia volume, Hunt and Larson (1979) noted that the study of leadership may be in a transitional stage where one of the basic issues concerns the purpose of leadership research. They suggested that the leadership field is populated with investigators who are hypothesis testers rather than descriptive researchers, and thus they concluded that one of the most difficult questions to resolve is how to study leadership.

In his overview of the fourth leadership symposium, J. P. Campbell (1977a) made a recommendation for the way to study leadership. "It would be advantageous for the field if a much greater emphasis were given simply to defining, describing, and measuring leadership phenomena. . . . We need many more descriptive studies that attempt to develop reasonable taxonomies of what leaders and followers actually do when they interact" (p. 234). J. P. Campbell (1977a) has since been joined by others (e.g., Luthans, 1979; Sayles, 1979) in his call for more descriptive research and more chronicling of what managers actually do.

Because we agreed that there is an essential need for programs of systematic descriptive research to discover the properties of managerial work, we began with a basic observational study of top level managers.

Prepared under Grant Number 78NI-AX-0095 from the National Institute of Law Enforcement and Criminal Justice, Law Enforcement Assistance Administration, United States Department of Justice. Points of view or opinion stated in this chapter are those of the authors and do not necessarily represent the official position or policies of the United States Department of Justice.

Newton Rigg
Campus Library

The purpose of this chapter is to focus on those parts of our study that may have particular relevance for the field of leadership. Specifically, the purposes are to: 1) present a framework for the systematic description of leaders' interpersonal contacts, 2) describe, using this framework, the observed interpersonal contacts of top level public administrators; and 3) comment on the relevance of this framework for the study of leadership.

Observational Studies of Managerial Work

In developing our research approach, we relied heavily on previous managerial work studies undertaken over the years. These studies generally address the question: What do managers do? There have been numerous attempts to answer this question in a variety of different types of organizations, at different levels of management, and with different research methods. From our point of view, the most relevant works are observational studies of managers on the job. McCall, Morrison, and Hannan (1978) reported 13 managerial studies that relied on observation at least in part, beginning with the founding work of Carlson (1951), through Mintzberg (1973), and ending with Stewart (1976). We found additional studies by Patterson (1975), Feilders (1978), Pitner (1978), Kurke and Aldrich (1979), and Snyder and Glueck (1980).

McCall et al. (1978) summarized the results from their review of the managerial work literature into the following ten statements. 1) Managers work long hours. 2) Managers are busy. 3) A manager's work is fragmented; episodes are brief. 4) The manager's job is varied. 5) Managers are "homebodies." 6) The manager's work is primarily oral. 7) Managers use a lot of contacts. 8) Managers are not reflective planners. 9) Information is the basic ingredient of the manager's work. 10) Managers do not know how they spend their time.

Although some of these statements have recently been questioned (A. Gingras, personal communication, May 1, 1979; Snyder & Glueck, 1980), they at least reflect the magnitude of our knowledge about managerial work. In almost thirty years, progress has not been rapid—to say the least. Why have we advanced so slowly? Why haven't numerous managerial behavior taxonomies been proposed and tested? Why are researchers in the field still just counting frequencies and reporting "time spent" percentages on basic activities? Why aren't cross classifications, time-series, pattern and profile mappings, and other dynamic analyses being done? In short, what's the holdup? It is interesting to note that Campbell, Dunnette, Lawler, and Weick (1970) asked similar questions a decade ago.

First, with the possible exception of Stewart's (1976) and Hemphill's

(1960) work, there has been little attention to research design and method in the managerial work field. Methodological rigor that has been demanded for some time in other types of organizational and managerial studies (e.g., in leadership) is obviously lacking in most managerial work studies. Second, most observational managerial work studies with which we are familiar utilized *structured* observation, at least to some degree. Either a predetermined categorization scheme was used by the observer to classify events or activities on the spot, or the scheme evolved as observation occurred. While structured observation is relatively easy to carry out, it allows recording of very little information about the phenomenon being studied, and much is lost. Third, unstructured observation research in the natural setting is very expensive, time consuming, frustrating, and exceedingly difficult, requiring a team of scientists to do well. Also, this methodology is more qualitative and "dirtier" than the neat and clean designs with which most of us are more comfortable. If significant advances in our understanding about management and leadership processes are to be made, a series of comprehensive studies of managerial work *in situ* must be undertaken. The section that follows describes one such effort.

Method

Research Design

Our project utilized unstructured nonparticipant direct observation of police chief executives on the job by trained observers over a long enough period of time to reduce observer effects and to gain a representative description of each individual's activities and behaviors. As each police executive was observed, a narrative description of events was produced. This narrative is a detailed record of the activities that occurred throughout every minute of the workday. These included interactions with staff, city administrators, and others who had occasion to interface with the police executive as he performed his job. The nature of incoming mail and outgoing correspondence was also monitored where possible. The resultant data set is a time-series narrative description of how the police executive behaved on the job and what took place within his immediate environment. As an illustration of the type of data that we collected, a page from a hypothetical observation of a police executive is shown in Exhibit 1.

Exhibit 1. Hypothetical Sample of Narrative Data

10:42 A.M.   The meeting ends. The chief goes to his office with the major of administrative services. The major asks the chief the details of the freeze on hiring. The chief will give the major a list of the positions that cannot be filled.

10:44 A.M. The major leaves the chief's office and a Citizens' Action Committee person comes into the chief's office. The person tells the chief about a traffic problem. The chief tells the person that the police have been investigating the problem and are working on a solution.

11:03 A.M. The chief attempts to place a phone call to the traffic bureau. The traffic bureau commander is not in.

11:04 A.M. The chief is off the phone. He takes the person across the hall to the traffic bureau. The chief asks the lieutenant in the traffice bureau if there is anything new on the traffic problem. All three talk at length about the problems with the traffic flow.

11:20 A.M. The chief leaves. A lieutenant comes up to the chief in the lobby area and asks a question about how to proceed on an investigation. The chief gives the lieutenant brief instructions.

11:21 A.M. The chief takes personal time.

11:23 A.M. The chief returns to his office and places a phone call to the director of personnel for the city. The personnel director and the chief will go to lunch.

11:24 A.M. The chief is off the phone.

The format of the record in Exhibit 1 is similar to one first proposed by Ashby (1956) and later implemented by Howland, Pierce, and Gardner (1970) and by Bussom (1973), who used a long protocol, showing in sequence the time events occurred and the nature of those events. In his much-referenced managerial work study, Mintzberg (1973) utilized a slightly different format for his "chronology record," which represented a subject's behavior over time in terms of predesignated activity categories. Since our data collection process sought to minimize abstraction and attempted to record as much about the actual situation as possible, no classification or coding was performed during observation. We, therefore, have labeled our data collection format "narrative record" to emphasize that *all* work-related events and activities were recorded completely in an unstructured written form, to the best of the observer's ability, *as they happened.*

Ten police chief executives of major cities in the continental United States participated in the study.[1] Each was observed throughout every

1. The granting agency required that we limit eligibility to cities that ranged in 1970 population from 100,000 to 1,000,000. We chose to study ten of them because this number both satisfied the requirements of our research design and allowed us to stay within budget.

workday for a four-week period divided into two continuous two-week periods: summer/fall 1979 and winter/spring 1980. Narrative records were collected continuously over the two-week period to reduce observer-observed acclimation (warm-up) effects that could occur if, for example, observation days were randomly selected. The police executives were observed from the time they arrived at work until they left work. Business lunches were observed; social lunches were not. Evening business meetings were also observed. Observers were infrequently excluded from meetings where their presence, in the police executive's opinion, would interfere with the interpersonal interaction process. On occasions when the observer was excluded, the duration of, the participants in, and the reported purpose for the meetings were recorded. The usual topics of confidential meetings included employee personal problems, employee disciplinary cases, department politics, and the police executive's personal business.

We used a form of quota sampling to select participants for this study. Three major characteristics were considered in selecting the sample of 10 site cities from the 143 eligible: geographical location (continental United States), department size (number of sworn police officers), and form of city government (mayor/council or city manager). All potential site cities were stratified on each of these three variables, and then cities were selected to represent proportionately these characteristics in the sample. This procedure reduced the number of eligible site cities down to approximately 50. The resultant sample design is shown in Table 3.

Subjects

To recruit 10 voluntary subjects for the study, 25 of the approximately 50 eligible police executives were contacted. Nine rejected the proposal through correspondence. Each of the remaining 16 police executives was visited by two of the investigators, who described the research project in detail and attempted to gain the subject's approval to be part of the study. All potential subjects were cautioned that the study was not evaluative and that it was not intended to provide specific information that would improve effectiveness or efficiency. However, we did promise to provide feedback to them about their activities.

Six of these 16 rejected our plan for a variety of reasons—for example, unstable political climates in which the police executive was unsure about his tenure, a concern that four weeks of observation would involve too much of his time, and a general negative reaction to research done by academicians because the department had been "burned" by previous research projects. In addition, a few chiefs, especially in some of the larger

TABLE 3
Sample Design

Location	Mayor/Council	City Manager
Northeast (Connecticut, Delaware, District of Columbia, Maine, Maryland, Massachusetts, New Hampshire, New Jersey, New York, Pennsylvania, Rhode Island, Vermont, Virginia)	Medium Size	Medium Size
Southeast (Alabama, Florida, Georgia, Kentucky, Louisiana, Mississippi, North Carolina, Tennessee, West Virginia)	Large Size	Small Size
Midwest (Illinois, Indiana, Iowa, Kansas, Michigan, Minnesota, Ohio, Nebraska, Wisconsin)	Small Size	Medium Size
Northwest (Colorado, Idaho, Montana, North Dakota, Oregon, South Dakota, Nevada, Utah, Washington, Wyoming)	Small Size	Medium Size
Southwest (Arkansas, Arizona, California, Missouri, New Mexico, Oklahoma, Texas)	Large Size	Small Size

Small Size = 100–400 sworn officers
Medium Size = 401–800 sworn officers
Large Size = 801–2,500 sworn officers

departments contacted, declined to participate because direct benefits to the department or to the chief could not be guaranteed.

Of the ten chiefs that elected to participate in the study, three accepted the proposal on the basis of our visit alone and seven accepted only after they were also contacted by professional acquaintances that knew about the study and vouched for it.[2] Their mean age was 49.6 years, with a mean time spent in law enforcement of 24.4 years. They had a mean job tenure of 5.1 years, and seven of them had advanced to their position from within their own department. Their departments ranged in size from the smallest organization with 197 sworn police officers to the largest with 2,232 sworn officers.

2. Naturally, we think that those who agreed to participate are open and progressive; consequently, they may not be completely representative of the population of police chiefs. Nevertheless, from a management point of view, we feel that it is an appropriate sample.

Observers

Five individuals acted as observers for the project: the three authors of this chapter, a staff researcher employed full time on the project, and an advanced graduate assistant. Observers were assigned to different police executives in such a manner as to allow analysis of the data for observer-observed patterns of interaction. The longhand narrative descriptions prepared during the actual observation process were immediately edited for errors and deletions by the observer, then submitted to a project secretary for typing, and finally they were proofread by the observer to ensure as much accuracy as possible.

Observational studies where subjects are aware of the observer's presence must be vitally concerned with the effect the observer has on the observed. We have documented elsewhere some of the major problems associated with observational studies (Bussom, Larson, Vicars, & Ness, 1980). In this study care was taken to address these problems by proper selection, training, and supervision of observers. In addition, advanced preparation of the participating police chiefs was undertaken to attempt further to reduce the chance of significant observer influence. This process allowed the subject to become more familiar with the observers and the observers to become more familiar with the subjects, others in the organization, and the physical facilities prior to commencement of observation. Although observer effects probably cannot be removed entirely, our subjects reported that they became accustomed to the observer within the first couple of days of observation and later were not even aware of the observer's presence most of the time.

Reliability, an important consideration in any study, is especially difficult to measure in observational studies. With the exception of one other observational investigation of managerial work (Scott & Eklund, 1978), our study is the only one we know of that actually made specific provisions for the measurement of interobserver reliability. This was accomplished by having three one-half day periods of simultaneous dual observations, each at a different site with different observers. A preliminary analysis of interobserver reliability at one of the first sites showed a 91 percent agreement between the two observers' records. Those differences that did occur were minor in nature.

The Nature of Leaders' Interpersonal Contacts

A large part of the leadership literature has focused on interpersonal contacts between leaders and followers or leaders and peers. Sayles (1979), for example, indicated that interpersonal contacts in and of themselves are critical for the leader/manager. He suggested that people in organizations demand interpersonal contacts and that "Information gets relayed best, attitudes assessed, and problems negotiated in face-to-face confrontations" (p. 18). A consistent finding of managerial work studies (Feilders, 1978; Kurke & Aldrich, 1979; Mintzberg, 1973; Pitner, 1978) is that managers spend the majority of their time in interpersonal contact with others. For example, the police executives in our study spent almost 60 percent of their time in interpersonal contacts. It is important to investigate in more detail the nature of these interpersonal contacts.

A review of the literature indicated that the nature of interpersonal contacts has been viewed in two rather distinct ways: previous studies have usually focused on either the pattern of interpersonal contacts or the content of the contacts. The pioneering work by Richardson and White (1964) illustrates the emphasis on contact patterns: they focused on frequency of contacts and did not address content at all; in fact, they argued that it is the contact itself that is important, not its content. This is in sharp contrast to the major leadership models, which are typically constructed in terms of content, such as structuring, consideration-giving, directive, supportive, participative, or achievement behavior on the part of the leader. To resolve differences in these two approaches, the nature of interpersonal contacts should be approached holistically through an inclusive conceptual framework that will interrelate all relevant contact characteristics.

A Framework for the Study of Interpersonal Contacts

A leader can be characterized by an interpersonal contact style, based on the nature of the leader's contacts. The characteristics of the leader's contact style can be conceptualized as dimensions in an n-dimensional space. In the observational field study approach, the dimensions are derived from observable characteristics (e.g., location, initiator, or purpose of the contact). Each contact characteristic, regardless of type or kind, can be represented by a score or a value on a dimension. The point in the n-dimensional space, or more accurately the coordinates of the point, comprises a contact profile, representing the leader's interpersonal contact style.

Of course, the use of an n-dimensional space approach is not new to the leadership field (Salancik, Calder, Rowland, Leblebici, & Conway, 1975) or to systems work, upon which our project was partially based (e.g., Howland, 1963). But, as far as we know, this conceptualization has not been utilized to describe leaders' interpersonal contact behavior. With this framework, it is our intent to show that descriptive observational studies can

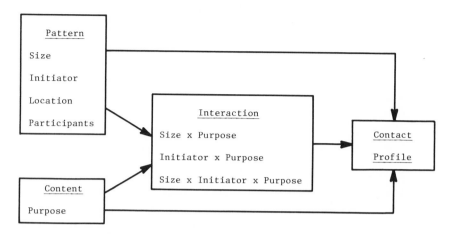

Fig. 1. A descriptive framework of a leader's interpersonal contacts

provide information about *both* the contact pattern of the leader *and* the content of these contacts.

Our conceptualization of the interpersonal contact style profile is represented in Figure 1. Three major elements define a leader's contact profile: 1) pattern, which includes those characteristics that describe how, where, and with whom contact occurs; 2) content, which incorporates into the model the topic and meaning of the contact; and 3) interaction, which represents the relationships between pattern characteristics and content characteristics. Preliminary work with our data suggests that the interaction of the main effects (pattern and content) can be a very important element in a leader's contact profile.

The specific characteristics listed below each major element in Figure 1 illustrate observationally measurable interpersonal contact dimensions. The lists are not exhaustive and could just as well include perceptual constructs. For example, in much of the previous leadership work, these dimensions have been constructs measured by assessment of perceptions and attitudes (e.g., initiating structure, satisfaction). However, in this chapter we will demonstrate the value of the contact profile concept by focusing on observation-based dimensions. What follows is an example of how contact profiles could begin to be generated for the police chiefs who participated in our study. The example is based upon the first two weeks of observation.

Pattern Variables

Tables were constructed to present the percentages of frequency and time of interpersonal contacts for such pattern characteristics as size (the number of people involved), who participated in the contact, who initiated the contact, and where the contact occurred. For illustrative purposes, the data on size are presented in Table 4.

As the results in Table 4 indicate,[3] the majority of a police chief's contacts were one-to-one as opposed to group contacts. All of our chiefs fit this pattern, and there was a difference of only 17 percent between the chief (1) with the highest percentage of one-to-one contacts and the chief (9) with the lowest percentage of one-to-one contacts. However, the total time in contact between one-to-one and group showed much greater variance among the police chiefs. For example, chief 10 spent approximately 68 percent of his contact time in one-to-one situations, while chief 3 spent only 31 percent of his contact time in one-to-one situations.

The results (not shown) on the pattern of the chiefs' contacts with regard to who else was involved showed that subordinates accounted for the largest percentage of contacts in terms of both frequency and time; however, individual chiefs had different patterns, with one spending a large percentage of time with subordinates, while another spent more with outsiders.

The pattern of who initiated interpersonal contacts (not shown), where the frequency of initiation is the most relevant statistic, indicates that the other party tended to initiate the majority of the interpersonal contacts. Again, however, there was a difference in this pattern across the chiefs, with the range of other-initiated contacts being from 36 percent to 62 percent.

The pattern characteristic of location of interpersonal contacts (not shown) revealed, as might be expected, that the large majority of contacts took place in the chief's office, with a range of from 61 percent to 91 percent. Time spent in contacts away from the police chief's headquarters showed a situation where, for some chiefs, all contact time occurred within the unit, while other chiefs spent as much as one-third or more of their contact time away from their headquarters.

Content Variables

A second set of variables that can be used to describe a leader's contact profile concerns the content (e.g., purpose) of the interpersonal contact. While our initial categorization of content uses the Mintzberg (1973) purpose categories, other content typologies could also be used as content variables. There are such large individual differences across the police chiefs,

---

3. Interpretations of results are based strictly on visual inspection and not on statistical tests. Due to small Ns in some cells, care must be taken in interpreting the percentages.

TABLE 4

Percent of Frequency and Time of Paired (One-to-One) and Group Contact Between Police Executives and Others

Police Chief Executive	Frequency of paired contacts as a % of total contacts	Time spent in paired contacts as a % of total contact time	Frequency of group contacts as a % of total contacts	Time spent in group contacts as a % of total contact time	Total number of observed contacts	Total minutes of observed contact time
1	89.02	54.67	10.98	45.33	255	1,990
2	77.34	61.06	22.66	38.94	203	868
3	75.80	30.67	24.20	69.33	157	2,292
4	76.65	31.36	23.35	68.64	424	3,358
5	89.74	67.78	10.26	32.22	341	2,005
6	73.31	34.62	26.69	65.38	236	2,340
7	83.44	60.22	16.56	39.78	163	2,207
8	79.92	55.63	20.08	44.37	259	1,751
9	73.29	45.18	26.71	54.82	438	2,658
10	86.13	67.96	13.87	32.04	310	1,423

in terms of both the percentage of frequency and time for the 12 contact categories, that it is difficult to generalize about the results.

By way of illustration, some of the dissimilarities among the police executives are evident in Table 5, where the percent of frequency of and the percent of time spent in contacts, by purpose of contact, are shown separately for each subject. A noticeable number of the percentages in Table 5 differ substantially from chief to chief. The percent ranges across subjects, presented at the bottom of the table, indicate the magnitude of the diversity among the chiefs. Large differences are particularly apparent for the six purposes that account for most of the contacts—that is, action requests, manager requests, receiving information, giving information, review (and discussion), and other or unknown. Three of the percent of frequency ranges for the six major purposes exceed a width of 20 percent. This result, plus the three ranges of percent of time that are greater than 30 percent, clearly illustrate the variability in the way the police chief executives behaved in the interpersonal contact portion of their jobs. However, there are a few things the chiefs have in common worth noting. 1) The categories of nonmanagerial work, ceremony, scheduling, and stature request represent a small portion of contacts in terms of frequency and time; 2) the strategy and negotiation categories are also relatively low in terms of the frequency percentages; and 3) receiving information, review, and discussion, and manager requests represent the majority of the contact purposes.

Interaction Variables

An illustrative two-way cross classification of pattern and content variables which depicts the interaction of these variables for each chief is presented in Table 6 for contact size by contact purpose.[4] The values show that contacts between the chief and one other person are much more common and take up much more time than those between the chief and two or more others for all the purposes except strategy and negotiation, where the reverse holds. Of course, there are notable exceptions, such as chief 2's complete lack of paired contacts in secondary work. Another exception is chief 3's very small time proportion in receiving information one-to-one and his low reliance on group contacts in strategy and negotiation.

The two-way interaction between contact purpose and form of initia-

4. In order to simplify this complex interaction table, some purposes with low frequencies and natural relations to each other were combined and the other unknown category was deleted. Thus, secondary work is comprised of nonmanagerial work, ceremony, scheduling, and stature request; in addition, strategy and negotiation—both decision making activities—are combined. Percentages are somewhat misleading for the secondary work and the strategy and negotiation purposes, since they occur relatively infrequently.

TABLE 5

Percent of Frequency and Time of Police Executives' Contacts According to the Purpose of the Contact

Police Chief Executive	Non m'grl. work	Ceremony	Scheduling	Stature request (of subject)	Action request (of subject)	Manager request (by subject)	Receiving info.	Giving info.	Review (& discussion)	Strategy	Negotiation	Other or unknown	Total frequency and time of contacts
1	1.2*	0.8	1.6	2.0	14.9	20.0	30.6	10.6	12.9	3.1	0.0	2.4	255**
	9.1	0.6	1.0	0.6	4.4	6.8	37.3	5.5	14.5	14.8	0.0	5.4	1,990
2	0.0	2.0	0.0	0.0	8.9	18.7	18.7	4.9	37.0	1.0	0.0	8.9	203
	0.0	2.3	0.0	0.0	7.5	12.9	13.1	3.1	48.4	8.0	0.0	4.3	868
3	0.0	0.0	6.5	0.0	5.7	12.7	24.2	10.2	26.8	3.2	0.0	10.8	157
	0.0	0.0	2.8	0.0	0.8	3.8	38.4	5.6	26.3	3.5	0.0	18.7	2,292
4	1.2	0.7	3.8	0.2	7.5	11.8	17.0	19.1	26.7	3.3	.5	7.8	424
	7.6	2.1	1.0	0.1	3.2	3.3	6.2	8.6	26.0	3.0	6.9	31.8	3,358
5	0.0	0.9	1.8	0.0	15.2	16.1	22.3	19.0	17.9	3.2	1.2	2.1	341
	0.0	0.4	0.6	0.0	9.0	11.0	11.1	17.2	26.8	10.9	10.3	1.8	2,005
6	0.0	0.9	2.1	1.3	8.9	15.3	20.3	14.8	27.5	5.1	2.1	1.7	236
	0.0	0.9	0.6	0.4	2.4	8.1	8.4	6.6	45.0	15.8	7.6	4.2	2,340
7	1.2	4.3	3.1	1.2	13.5	17.8	14.1	8.0	28.2	3.7	.6	4.3	163
	12.5	2.1	1.4	2.5	5.6	7.9	15.0	2.8	23.1	19.6	0.4	7.2	2,207
8	0.4	1.2	5.4	0.0	9.7	10.4	22.4	10.8	27.0	1.2	.7	10.8	259
	4.2	0.6	1.7	0.0	6.3	6.5	13.2	10.8	28.6	11.7	1.5	15.1	1,751
9	0.7	0.9	2.8	0.9	7.3	19.7	9.1	20.1	12.3	4.1	1.1	21.0	438
	4.1	0.5	0.8	0.3	3.5	7.3	3.2	13.8	22.3	12.1	4.5	27.5	2,658
10	0.3	1.0	1.6	1.3	8.7	13.9	14.5	11.0	21.6	0.3	0.3	25.5	310
	0.1	1.1	1.0	4.2	5.8	6.6	8.6	16.9	21.9	0.3	0.4	33.2	1,423
Percent of frequency range	0.0–1.2	0.0–4.3	0.0–6.5	0.0–2.0	5.7–15.2	10.4–20.0	9.1–30.6	8.0–19.1	12.3–37.0	0.3–5.1	0.0–2.1	1.7–25.5	
Percent of time range	0.0–12.5	0.0–2.1	0.0–2.8	0.0–4.2	0.8–9.0	3.3–12.9	3.2–38.4	2.8–17.2	14.5–48.4	0.3–19.6	0.0–10.3	1.8–33.2	

* The upper value in each cell represents the percent of frequency in each purpose category. The lower value represents the percent of time in each category.

**The upper value is total frequency. The lower value is total time in minutes.

tion was also analyzed for each chief (not shown). Except for review and discussion and to a lesser extent strategy and negotiation and secondary work, initiation by clock/mutual is quite rare. Manager requests and giving information were, as would be expected, largely initiated by the leader, while action requests and receiving information were mostly initiated by others. Review and discussion, secondary work, and strategy and negotiation are more evenly split between self and other initiated contacts. Despite these general trends, there are some striking individual differences among the chiefs.

Finally, the three-way interaction among contact purpose, size, and form of initiation was analyzed for each chief (not shown). The action request, manager request, and receiving information purposes followed an expected pattern. For example, the vast majority of action requests were initiated by others, whether in one-to-one or in group contacts, for all chiefs. Giving information, however, shows some unexpected apparent relations: four of the chiefs spent more time in and had more paired contacts initiated by "other" than by "self." In addition, while three chiefs used "self" as the predominant form of initiation in both paired and group-giving information contacts, six chiefs used reversed predominant forms of initiation for paired versus group contact, and one chief even gave no information in groups. The review and discussion purpose category had the most complexity, with all three forms of initiation and both sizes of the contact generally accounting for a sizable proportion of both frequency and time. This may be due to the fact that review and discussion, like strategy and negotiation, is a complex contact activity. Review and discussion, unlike strategy and negotiation, however, was fairly frequent and absorbed a sizable proportion of contact time.

Contact Profiles: A Contrast

To this point we have introduced the interpersonal contact style profile concept and compared our ten chiefs over a set of observation-based interpersonal contact style characteristics. The elements in this set were selected because they were readily apparent—for example, location—or because they had been used in previous work—for example, purpose of contact categories from Mintzberg (1973). With this preliminary set we found a great amount of dissimilarity and complexity in how leaders carried out their interpersonal contacts.

As stated earlier, our purpose was to demonstrate how interpersonal contact style profiles could be developed. By way of illustration, Table 7 presents a summary contact profile for two chiefs with contrasting contact styles who lead similar-sized departments. For purposes of discussion, the

TABLE 6

Percent of Frequency and Time of Size of Contact by Purpose of Contact

Police Chief Executive	Secondary work	Action request (of chief)	Manager request (by chief)	Receiving information	Giving information	Review & discussion	Strategy & Negotiation
1	86	95	96	90	89	91	12
	69	98	96	50	73	69	2
2	0	67	92	90	100	68	50
	0	55	88	84	100	58	12
3	100	89	90	55	88	86	80
	100	95	91	6	27	59	67
4	84	97	94	92	88	59	25
	14	99	94	93	80	29	4
5	78	94	93	91	94	93	47
	67	85	68	92	78	92	12
6	70	81	92	79	89	62	24
	42	88	82	49	85	24	5
7	50	100	97	83	92	85	43
	28	100	99	56	98	88	17
8	72	96	96	84	89	73	20
	25	75	96	82	62	59	13
9	74	84	81	80	81	61	0
	20	82	71	59	71	26	0
10	59	78	91	96	68	91	50
	27	84	89	92	34	89	60

Note. The cell entries are for paired (one-to-one) contacts; corresponding percents for group contacts can be calculated by subtracting the appropriate cell value from 100. The upper value in each cell is the percent of contact frequency; the bottom value is the percent of contact time.

TABLE 7
Contact Profile Examples

Dimension	Chief 2	Chief 3
Pattern:		
Percent paired contacts	considerable	lowest
Percent time with subordinates	considerable	lowest
Percent time with others	little	highest
Percent time with supervisors	little	average
Initiation	others	balanced
Percent contacts away from police building	none	highest
Percent time spent in office	average	lowest
Content:		
Ceremony	some	none
Scheduling	some	none
Action requests	some	little
Manager requests	high	low
Receive information	average	considerable
Review	highest	average
Interaction:		
Purpose by size		
Action requests	more balanced	paired
Receiving information	paired	group
Percent time giving information	paired	group
Purpose by initiation		
Action requests	other	highest self
Percent time giving information	balanced	low
Review and discussion	other	highest self
Purpose by initiation by size		
Giving information in paired contacts	balanced between self and other initiated	more self-initiated
Review and discussion in paired contacts	more other initiated	more self-initiated
Review and discussion in group contacts	more other initiated	more self-initiated

measures of the characteristics are reported on only nominal or ordinal scales—for example, paired-group, lowest-highest, and little-average-considerable.

The partial profiles in Table 7 suggest that chief 2 is a one-to-one internal reactor type. He spent much of his time in one-to-one contacts with subordinates. Also, he operated primarily in the reactive mode, letting others initiate the majority of his contacts. In contrast, chief 3 appears to be a group-oriented external proactor type. Of the ten chiefs, he spent the least amount of time with subordinates and the most with outsiders, and he also had the lowest percent of paired contacts. Although he displayed a balance of contact initiation between self and other, he showed considerable self-initiation in specific purpose of contact categories, for example, action requests, review and discussion, and giving information in paired contacts.

Interestingly, the characteristics that emerge from the partial profiles are consistent with our clinical appraisal of the two chiefs. Chief 2 rose through the ranks of his police organization and was promoted from within. Generally, his organization operated in the traditional paramilitary form. On the other hand, chief 3 was brought in from the outside and operated in a nontraditional manner. He was interested in innovative approaches to policing and organization and tried new programs. He was as much community-oriented as police-oriented.

Implications for the Study of Leadership

The third major purpose of this chapter is to comment on the relevance of the interpersonal contact profile framework for the study of leadership. What follows are some of our preliminary ideas, based on the initial analysis of the first-phase data collected in the study of police chiefs.

Contact Profile Refinement

While we are excited about the potential of the contact style profile concept to further our understanding of leadership, we also recognize that some aspects of the profile need additional development. The pattern variables list can, of course, be expanded, but we feel that it is relatively complete compared to the content variable section. Even the existing purpose categorization could be refined. For example, while it is useful to know that the chief met for the purpose of receiving information, it would be helpful to be able to classify further the nature of the information. Did the information pertain to a current or potential problem? Was the information a rumor, or was the subordinate passing on information about the Monday night football game? Was the information directly related to the chief's job, or was it only indirectly related to his work? Other possible content categorization schemes could be added to the content variable set, including management functions such as finance, personnel, and public relations (Stewart, 1967); management duties such as supervision, internal control, and technical work (Hemphill, 1960); and types of problems or issues (L. Pondy & A. Huff, personal communication, Sept. 17, 1980).

Impact of a Leader's Contact Profile on Others

Our initial analysis of the pattern and content variables and the inter-action between these two sets of variables shows a relatively high variability among the police chiefs in the study. A natural question is, do these dif-ferences affect the behavior of people in the police chief's sphere of opera-tion, and if so, does this result in differences in efficiency, effectiveness, mo-rale, and so forth, of the Police Department? For example, some contact profiles show chiefs who spend a large proportion of their time away from their office with people who are not part of their units, while the contact profiles of other chiefs reveal that they spend the majority of their time in their own office with their subordinates. Does this external/internal alloca-tion of contact time have an effect on the perceptions of the chiefs' subordi-nates, their effectiveness, or their efficiency?

Impact of Contextual and Leadership Style Variables on the Contact Profile

We have already raised the question of what effect the leader's contact style profile has on others. An equally important question is what factors influence the contact profile? At least two classes of variables have potential to influence a leader's contact profile. The first class of variables is the macro factors such as organizational size and structure, type of supra-organizational structure, and other environmental variables.

The second class of variables is the overall leadership style of the man-ager. The police chiefs in our study had observably different styles of work-ing and communicating, and because of this we are inclined to support the establishment view that leadership style is still a viable concept.

Stability of the contact style profile over time is a related concern. Is the contact profile relatively constant over time or is it highly variable? If either contextual variables or leadership style have a large impact on the contact profile, then the stability of the contact profile may depend on the stability of these other factors.

Conclusions

Certainly one of the challenges that the study of leadership faces is pursuit of the dynamics of interpersonal contacts and the eventual deter-mination of the reasons for and contingencies of the observed differences in leaders' behaviors. We feel that the interpersonal contact style profile conceptualization can be helpful in meeting this challenge. First, the con-tact profile conceptualization forces definition of the elements in the inter-personal contact process and requires operational measures of each. Work with this model will lead to a classification of what is involved in the interpersonal contact process. Second, the contact profile approach emphasizes differences among individuals and thus relies heavily on individual rather than averaged or composite data. For example, much of the information in our data about interaction among characteristics would be lost in the averaging process. This perspective reinforces a similar conclusion by others that work with grouped data may be misleading and unproductive. Third, the profile concept focuses on contact dimensions in combination, considering all elements together, and recognizing interrelationships among them. Pattern, content, and interaction characteristics must all be considered to describe clearly a leader's interpersonal contact style. It demands a holistic approach and emphasizes synthesis as opposed to analysis.

In line with the holistic approach espoused above, our long-term research plan revolves around basic ecological issues and will be mainly concerned with how the various macro and micro variables in leaders' interpersonal environments affect their contact style profiles. Of immediate concern is analysis of the effects of macro variables, such as organization size, form of city government, and geographical location, on the contact profile. Because we gathered data over a relatively long period of time, we also hope to be able to get an indication of the stability of leaders' contact profiles and to find out what factors can change them. While we acknowledge that there are formidable obstacles to be overcome before we can go beyond establishment views of leadership, we are confident that the observational method has given us a strong data base from which to proceed.

4

Leaders on Line: Observations from a Simulation of Managerial Work

MICHAEL M. LOMBARDO and MORGAN W. McCALL, JR.

This chapter is based on a day in the life of a glass manufacturing company and the 20 leaders who run it. Actually, it is the same day repeated 36 times with 36 different sets of managers. Looking Glass is a simulation of managerial work in a complex organization, originally designed as a research tool to generate hypotheses about leadership in organizational settings. The invitation to write this chapter asked the authors to enact this original purpose—to be imaginative rather than traditional or rigorous; to generate some ideas about leadership gleaned from watching leaders on-line.

Accepting that challenge, we have tried to organize some of our impressions and general observations about behavior in Looking Glass. The chapter begins with a brief introduction to Looking Glass, develops a series of propositions with some relevance for leadership research, and concludes with some suggestions for future leadership research.

Origins

Thumbing through the accumulated leadership research may be likened to perusing a songbook where lyrics of various songs appear, but the scores have been omitted. One lyric concerns leader-subordinate relations, another leadership style, another political processes. In themselves, the lyrics may be illuminating or not—but they lack a context, the larger whole from which they flow and which gives them meaning. In themselves, they are pieces that do not sum to a whole because the environmental and organizational context of leadership is not there to give them definition.

It was with this inherent belief—that management or leadership only makes sense when viewed in its entirety—that a complex simulation was designed for use in leadership research. Its goals were both clear and fuzzy: to mirror as realistically as possible the demands of a typical managerial job in a complex organization, to have actual managers run the simulated company as they chose, and to bring multiple methods to bear on learning something new about leadership. By watching a day in the life of managers dealing with the complexity and chaos of organizations, we hoped to develop some more pertinent questions to guide future research on what leadership is, and how and when it matters.

Project Goals

Our area of study lay somewhere in the gap between the sociology of organizations and the psychology and social psychology of individuals and groups. It is that murky area where environmental and organizational forces translate into impact on the behavior of individual leaders, where nonline relationships with people both within and without the organization come to the fore, the land of problems, solutions, and red herrings floating around looking for connections.

We were interested in leadership in complex organizational settings, of which the well-researched leader-group relationship is only a part. The problem was that no one knew too much about it. There is a small pocket of research describing how managers spend their time. A review of these studies (McCall, Morrison, & Hannan, 1978) confirmed the importance of nonhierarchical relationships and framed the hectic, fragmented world of daily managerial life. Other research has questioned how much leadership matters to organizational outcomes (Cohen & March, 1974; Lieberson & O'Connor, 1972; Pfeffer, 1978). The environmental and structural forces we were interested in were obviously affecting what leaders were up to. The most compelling descriptions, however, came from researchers who observed managers *in situ* (e.g., Mintzberg, 1973; Sayles, 1964) and wrote of the demands and contradictions of managerial life in all their complexity.

What we set out to do, then, was to find a way to look more closely at the day-to-day demands of managerial work, at how individuals who found themselves in formal leadership positions coped with the seemingly overwhelming demands thrown at them. As Karl Weick put it: "What worries me is that some of the least important realities about leaders are being accorded some of the largest amounts of attention. I think we need to spend more time watching leaders 'on line,' whether that line is simulated or real. We have to put ourselves in a better position to watch leaders make do, let it pass, improvise, make inferences, scramble, and all the other things leaders do during their *days between* more visible moments of glory" (1978, p. 60).

Our goal, simply put, was to create a tool for systematically observing the on-line behavior of leader/managers. With this tool, we hoped to generate questions about leadership in organizations that could be tested in the field.

Choosing Simulation

The choice of simulation as a tool for accomplishing that goal was not entirely obvious. Why not just observe leaders in complex organizations, capitalizing on the reality of the field and the richness of anthropological techniques? Why not read corporate histories and biographies of leaders to distill new points of view? Why not review the management literature and draw from it new ideas for leadership?

There were many reasons, some logical and some not. On the rational side, we knew that both field observation and historical or biographical accounts suffered from a common flaw: the situations faced by leaders were different in each case. One could never be sure what was idiosyncratic or part of a more general trend. There seemed to be great advantage if one could watch many leaders handle *the same* situations, as long as those situations were strongly anchored in reality. Simulation would allow some control, both in a measurement and an experimental sense—reality could be changed systematically to gauge its effects on leaders (see McCall & Lombardo, in press, for a detailed analysis of using LGI for systematic research).

Building a simulation, it turned out, required the use of the other methodologies. It required a literature review that included the management research (especially diary and observational studies of managers at work), historical accounts of organizational life, and biographies of corporate figures. Trade journals, business publications, and corporate documents also added depth and breadth. It also required interviews and observation, corralling high-level leaders in their organizational lairs for in-depth discussions of their daily work and following the action all the way to the plant floor.

The design effort was obsessively descriptive, identifying in detail what these managers did, the problems they faced, what they read, what they talked about. What the environment actually contained and how it got to a manager's desk was a central question. So was information on how organizations were structured, which pieces mattered and which did not, how they became a part of a manager's daily life. In short, to build a simulation required hammer-and-nail understanding of the mundane, day-to-day, hour-to-hour world of managerial work. We were designers of a set for a play; the managers themselves would write the script and become the actors.

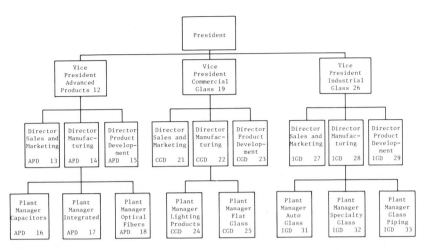

Fig. 2. Looking Glass, Inc. (Reproduced by permission from McCall and Lombardo, 1979)

Evolution

As we got into the project, our decisions took us further from the core of traditional leadership research. Emphasis on leader-organization relationships was at the expense of leader-subordinate interaction; some LGI managers have subordinates located geographically distant from them and accessible only by phone or mail. Considerable effort went into developing specific details of the environmental and organizational context of leadership, sacrificing detail on work group elements.

On the measurement side, criteria were needed that would be compatible with the organizational thrust of the simulation. This meant developing different performance measures for individuals, groups, and the organization as a whole. It meant including the heavy dose of business and problem-specific outcomes, and it meant using a variety of measurement tools, including direct observation, questionnaires, and unobtrusive measures.

Looking Glass: What Happens?

Looking Glass is a six-hour simulation of a moderate-sized manufacturing corporation. In each standardized run 20 participants were assigned to 20 top management roles ranging from President to Plant Manager and spanning three divisions (see Figure 2). Their task: to run the company for a day in any way they want.

The simulation begins the evening before the run with a series of events designed to familiarize participants with the company. During this session, participants and staff are introduced, a slide show explaining the company is shown, participants are assigned roles and spend some time at their desks, and job descriptions and annual reports are distributed. This is followed by some time for socializing.

The following morning Looking Glass opens for business. Each participant spends the first 45 minutes at his or her desk reviewing an in-basket containing today's mail. The in-baskets contain an average of 32 items ranging from the trivial (e.g., wine sales prices) to the significant (e.g., cost figures on plant expansion). After the first 45 minutes, the telephone system is turned on, and the managers are free to call meetings, send memos, place phone calls, and so forth. Using memo or phone, participants can contact anyone inside or outside the company. Trained staff act as "ghosts" and give standardized responses to the most commonly asked questions.

The development of Looking Glass insured that a wide range of management problems and issues exist in the company. These total about 160, and participants are free to deal with them (or ignore them) as they see fit. These problems and issues cover many areas, including finance, personnel, legal, production, sales, R&D, safety, and so forth. Examples of the issues include an opportunity to acquire a new plant, deciding what to do with a plant that has lost money the last few years, pollution and discrimination problems, supply shortages, production capacity limits, a lawsuit with a major customer, and competition with foreign manufacturers.

There are three divisions in Looking Glass, each facing a different external environment. The Advanced Products Division (APD) manufactures products for the electronics and communications industries and exists in an unstable, highly volatile business environment. The Commercial Glass Division (CGD) makes light-bulb casings and flat glass, and faces a reasonably stable, predictable environment characterized by high-volume, low-margin products, and well-established customer relations. The Industrial Glass Division (IGD) faces an environment containing both unstable and stable components because it makes products varying from auto glass (relatively stable) to space-craft windows (highly unstable).

The Data Base

The propositions that follow were drawn from a host of traditional and nontraditional sources. On one hand, Looking Glass was run 10 times as a standardized stimulus with systematic measurements. These included structured observation, questionnaires, and careful records of mail and phone transactions. The resulting data were used to develop simulation norms (McCall, Lombardo, & Rice, 1979) and to examine the content and construct validity of Looking Glass (McCall & Lombardo, 1979).

On the other hand, Looking Glass has been run a total of 36 times, including a host of developmental and training runs over and above the standardized data collection. All of these produced additional data from informal observation, fielding questions asked of "ghost" roles, participating in debriefing and feedback sessions, and discussion with individual manager-participants.

What follows is based on an amalgam of these experiences and is our attempt to make some sense of what we have watched over 600 managers do in the simulation. The propositions are organized around four themes: measurement, environmental impacts on leadership, coupling of oganizational elements, and organizational effectiveness. These traces, like shadows, only indicate what might be asked and what answers might be found in another reality.

What We've Learned Enough about to Ask Some Different Questions of

1. Measurement

Having built a tool to elicit managerial behavior in all its complexity was a far cry from capturing that complexity with a sound measurement system. The measures we adapted or developed ranged widely in method (observation, questionnaire, physical records) and in focus (activities, power, climate, behavior on specific problems). (See McCall et al., 1979, for a complete description.) Our first snag came at the simplest level: We tried to determine the reliability of various ratings by Looking Glass managers. On questionnaires, managers clearly built a new plant; in discussion, the same managers did not recall such a decision. A VP and others would claim a marketing policy change was made, yet the marketing director would state a contradictory policy or claim no knowledge at all. The traditional "true score plus error" approach seemed starkly inadequate when there was not a true score. Managers saw things quite differently because they *were* quite different. What we were trained to call error was a reality well worth explaining.

The question of what happened often was answered as some say this, some say that, and some do not know. We found that even our unit of analysis (basically, each division) did not make sense because neither an individual nor a group ordinarily made decisions. What we found and finally were able to measure was through what positions a problem flowed, who was in a position to implement a solution, and who had to agree with it determined who did what. Whether all managers agreed was far less important than *which* managers agreed.

Over the morning runs, the data finally showed that neither hierarchy nor functional responsibility were more than partial determinants of what happened. Managers were much more interested in where problems were located and who could solve them than in chain of command or other formalities. Except where a rare VP might run a division as a dictatorship, each problem took on a life of its own, with the same positions attacking it time after time. This suggested to us a different unit of analysis than is often considered in organizational research.

1.1. Managerial activity focuses on problems. The problem with its multiple components, multiple solutions, and multiple subsets of actors may be the proper unit of analysis by which to investigate phenomena of interest.

Grouped data are the foundation of models that use averaged perceptual scores for such things as leader behavior, satisfaction, or performance. The problems of aggregation in leadership research have received increasing attention (e.g., Graen & Cashman, 1975; Schriesheim & Kerr, 1974), and our experience with Looking Glass reinforces that concern. What is often seen as measurement error—the failure of different people to agree on what happened—is in fact predictable and an important source of data.

1.2. A perceptual index might be used in tandem with 1.1. This index would measure problem definition and outcome confusion among those who should have known what happened.

Our experience also suggests that using the group as a unit of analysis in leadership research misses the central core of what is happening. Different aggregates of individuals coalesce around different problems as they float through the organization. In that sense we concur with Robert Dubin's suggestion in the 1979 symposium volume: "The skills of leading organizations have to be related to the system problems with which leaders deal. . . . Very few studies of leaders of organizations seem to deal with these central problems as their analytical focus" (1979, p. 230). We would go on to suggest that the problems, as seen by managers, are concrete, tangible things, not abstractions like "coordination," "planning," or "motivating." Managers are purposive; we may understand leaders better if we look harder at *what* they are working on.

2. Environmental Impacts

One of the most prevalent notions in the literature is that effective organizations must fit with the environment(s) they face (e.g., Lawrence & Lorsch, 1967). In general, these models postulate that structural properties of the organization (such as degree of centralization or specialization) must fit with environmental characteristics (such as degree of uncertainty) for an organization to be effective. Looking Glass was designed to reflect three different environments, and our observations of managers in its different divisions suggest some refinement and extensions of the "fit" approach. Central to our extensions are the assumption of the models that environmental differences are linear (e.g., a continuum from certainty to uncertainty) and the currently hazy understanding of how environmental and structural factors impact on leader behavior.

2.1. The effect of environment is nonlinear.

Being caught in the middle is chaotic. The intermediate division (a stable technology and both stable and unstable markets) does not behave as if it lies between the more certain and uncertain divisions on most of the traditional dimensions. It is distinguished by weak integration of functions, and frequent bottlenecks as the linking pin role (the VP) fails to understand that problems are diffused and that different problem definitions are common. The manufacturing roles split off from the rest of the group, and the division retreats into paperwork and one-man rule as a path out of the chaos. Although our results could be simulation artifact, they could also be managerial reactions to a confusing, bimodal environment.

Stability is freedom. The stable division showed the most strategic variability across runs. It either a) behaved bureaucratically, b) met a lot to define problems but did nothing about them, or c) decided the division was slowly dying and launched an offensive. Each strategy was about equally likely. Within this unpredictability there was an easy flow of information and a lack of time urgency that managers insisted characterized stable operations. Certainly, one of our analyses ran totally counter to contingency predictions—managers in the effective stable divisions spent less time with bosses than did the ineffective groups (McCall & Lombardo, 1979). This suggested to us that stability means choice, time to decide, and clear parameters, making time with the boss less necessary.

Uncertainty is predictable. The volatile division was almost unflinchingly consistent. Managers behaved in a fast-paced, fragmented way, holding large numbers of brief meetings involving whoever seemed relevant to a particular problem. Although managers found it nearly impossible to set priorities, this did not deter them from taking action on the most difficult and externally located problems. In sum, managers coped in similar ways with similar problems, as if there were a fire in the theater and it was time for everyone to grab a bucket of water.

2.2. The effect of environment is linear. Many contingency predictions come out as expected. Even in our inadequate sample, Looking Glass produced effects we would expect to take long periods of time to become observable. Managers in effective divisions facing uncertain external environments in contrast with those in effective divisions facing certain external environments a) spent more time with colleagues, b) spent less time with subordinates, c) spent less time on paperwork and more time in meetings, and d) wrote fewer memos and placed more phone calls (McCall & Lombardo, 1979).

2.3. Environments have main effects. Strategic contingencies notions of power state that power flows to those units and positions that are best able to cope with the critical uncertainties facing the organization. As the volatile division could make the most money and is the most visible, we predicted that it would be most powerful regardless of its actual performance. (Conversely, the stable division would be least powerful.) This was true in 34 of 36 runs.

2.4. Environments have no effects. As some research indicates, environment can have little effect (Meyer, 1978). We found, for example, that ineffective divisions leave paper trails of approximately equal weight, and that certain positions are powerful for the same reasons regardless of environmental differences.

2.5. Environment and leadership. The most effective leaders we have observed seem to act in a counter-intuitive fashion, going against the grain of the environment. If the managers in the volatile division predictably fire fight, *effective* VPs of that division are predictably absent, exercising leadership by remote control in a series of brief problem definition sessions. These VPs stay at the strategic level, calling up some new crews and cutting off the water on others. In the most predictable of the divisions, the effective VPs introduce a note of strategic unpredictability.

In the intermediate division, diffused and contradictory, effective VPs seem to provide identity through integrating the functions and fusing the division either literally or symbolically. In the stable division, effective VPs react to overchoice by lessening it—by forcing a strategic choice of what the division should be.

Although the above are only trends, they suggest to us a recognition of the contradictions of life, the tension of opposites that holds us together.

Unpredictability of environment $\longrightarrow$	Predictability of action $\longrightarrow$	Introducing unpredictability by disrupting patterns in behavior that get "out of synch" with the changing environment
Split environments $\longrightarrow$	Diffused effort $\longrightarrow$	Integrating physically where possible and symbolically where not

Stability of	$\longrightarrow$	Freedom of	$\longrightarrow$	Introducing stability by
environment		choice		making the lessening of
				choice an urgent matter

2.6. Behaviors, not structure, fit with the environment. Regardless of their background, once in a volatile or stable division, managers adopt the behavior patterns consonant with that world. Structure, unless forced into consciousness by the President or VP, is basically ignored in favor of problem solving by individuals or *ad hoc* groups. When structure is not ignored, when the chain of command is visibly enforced, the effectiveness of the volatile division usually crumbles under a hierarchical arrangement that makes little sense for its problems. Conversely, the stable division can operate with or without a formal structure, depending on which way it chooses to go—business as usual (the pyramid) or toward a new image (problem-solving groups). This suggests that environment affects *behavior*, but environment only dictates structure when someone decides it does.

In summary, environment is far more complex than it seems: it is both linear and nonlinear, it has direct effects and no effects. To understand how environmental context relates to leader behavior we will have to unpack the apparent contradictions by isolating which elements matter under what circumstances and by looking closely at how environmental factors come to a manager's (or organization's) attention. Some steps in this direction have been taken by Duncan (1972), Meyer (1978), Hunt, Osborn, and Schuler (1978), and Hunt and Osborn in this volume.

Structural factors also need some reconsideration. In Looking Glass, organizational structure acts like a latent variable. It becomes "real" when it eases the flow of routine problems or when a manager needs it for any of a number of reasons. Otherwise, managers seem to ignore the chain of command, doing whatever seems appropriate to solve specific problems. One structural variable that is an exception to this is position; regardless of the effectivess of job incumbents, certain positions are consistently seen as more powerful than others.

Finally, leaders seem to play important roles in mediating both environment and structure. They often make environment matter by interpreting it or calling attention to it. Equally often they neither interpret nor call attention, behaving as if the environment does not exist. How leaders decide to ignore or focus on environment is a critical research question.

3. *Coupling*

The notion of loosely versus tightly coupled systems has received considerable research attention of late.

"Coupling" is still a somewhat amorphous construct (Weick, 1980), but it essentially involves the degree to which elements of a system are related to one another. That is, the degree to which a change in one element will cause a change in another. A "tightly coupled" system would contain many elements that are directly related to one another; in a "loosely coupled" system, elements have little direct effect on one another or relate at one point in time but not another.

Coupling is relevant to Looking Glass on at least two levels: the relationships of divisions to their environments (discussed in the previous section) and how divisions relate to one another. For many reasons tight coupling was expected among the divisions, not the least of which were the common organization chart, policies, and financial system. It was something of a surprise, then, that there has been considerable variance in how much and in what ways the divisions have coupled. Our observations suggest the following:

3.1. Coupling in organizations is a product of behavior. In spite of the logical structure of the simulation, where many problems and functions are tightly coupled, actual coupling is a function of the problems managers choose to tackle and the degree to which managers know what was done. Even when managers from two divisions decided to couple their activities, the rest of the division members usually behaved as if nothing happened and the divisions were as autonomous as before.

3.2. Managers avoid tight coupling on themselves. With one exception, the major problems that are consistently ignored or deferred deal with interconnectedness of the divisions. In general, interdependence that reduces managerial latitude and/or promotes conflict within or between divisions is avoided.

3.3. Managers seek tight coupling as redress. When the acts of another group make life more difficult for a division, that division seeks tight coupling as a means of controlling or neutralizing the interference. When a division is short-changed or transfer pricing or is losing staff to another division, it will seek a corporate policy as redress.

3.4. Managers seek tight coupling to secure what someone else has that they want. Managers of the respective divisions leave one another alone, unless the other has something they want. When a division is short of a raw material (through no fault of the other divisions), it may seek an informal agreement or even a corporate policy to secure a scarce resource.

3.5. Divisions ignore each other as much as possible. Our measures confirm what others have said—organizations are loosely coupled systems and try hard to remain that way. Only when a threshold is reached (need for a scarce resource, redress a grievance) are any attempts to tight coupling made.

So far, our observations suggest that the managerial world (at least in LGI) is a bunch of .3 correlations—most of the elements are loosely related and large changes in any one element have surprisingly small effects on the others. The survival value of this is evident since looseness preserves managerial discretion. As Weick (1980, p. 17) described it, "Loosely coupled systems are sustained by the exchange of inattention." We would add that the appearance of tight coupling, usually through the use or generation of formal policy or structure, identifies a pressure point in the organization. Managers seem to prefer to keep things loose unless they are threatened, usually by some other manager's latitude. They often create tighter coupling by informal agreement or tacit cooperation (note Weick's emphasis on coupling as a process rather than a structure), but usually only on specific issues and when cooperation is mutually beneficial. In the face of potential conflict, they tend to decouple (e.g., avoid joint problems altogether) or to call on structural mechanisms such as policy or chain of command.

Our observations also support Weick's notion of the importance of thresholds. Many views of leadership postulate linear relationships, but it is more common in LGI to see relationships among variables tighten when one element "goes critical." This often happens when the president gets concerned about an issue. Suddenly, the divisions start working together and both roses and thorns appear.

4. Organizational Effectiveness

John Campbell (1977a) has emphasized that organizational effectiveness is a value judgment. He is right. The question is, whose judgments define effectiveness? In Looking Glass, we relied on expert judgments, participant judgments, designer judgments, and even constructed a model of financial effectiveness. All are imperfect; all say little and miss much; and except for the financial model (where value judgments have been converted to an algorithm), all are colored by value judgments, and as such, do not necessarily agree with one another.

In the following sections, we offer some notions about effectiveness in organizations.

4.1. Peer ratings may indicate anything but effectiveness.

4.1.1. Sometimes they indicate distance. The top and bottom positions rate one another quite low while agreeing on the effectiveness of the mid-level positions. In general, the variance is greater and the mean rating lower the further apart the ratee and the rater.

4.1.2. Sometimes they are attributions. The plant manager whose operation is often sold has a near perfect record in manufacturing the product. The financial problems with the product line—the reason the plant is often sold—are in no way under his or her control. Regardless, this position is rated as ineffective by the VP.

4.1.3. Sometimes they indicate structural location. The structural sources of power (working on important problems, a central location, access to critical information) explain both who is powerful and who is effective in Looking Glass. To be the manufacturing director in any of Looking Glass's divisions is, as a rule, to be the most effective division member.

4.1.4. Sometimes they show that a few impressions can be devastating. One plant manager, who inherits high energy costs and a lackluster manufacturing operation, is seen as ineffective and powerless regardless of performance. Since the plant manager cannot be at fault, the powerful attributions that result from such tidbits suggest that being seen as effective/ineffective may be a superficial reality.

4.2. Self-ratings reflect power and position. The powerful often act humble; the powerless do not. The powerful positions consistently rate themselves as less effective than do their peers; the powerless consistently rate themselves as more effective than do their peers.

It may be that people in high influence positions, where many important problems flow, rate themselves lower because they know how much they did not get to. Their peers at lower levels are affected by what was done, and, in a loosely coupled world, not so much by what was not done. At lower levels, managers may rate themselves on how much they did accomplish, most of which is largely invisible to their upper level peers. The higher levels may rate them lower because a) what they did is unknown and b) they did not help much with the problem at the top. These kinds of findings, if confirmed, may aid in the development of multiple rater appraisal systems or dependent variables in leadership research.

4.3. Perceived quality is a function of who is involved in the decision. If a given manager was involved in a decision, the decision was seen as effective by that manager. If not, it was not. Where many of their subordinates were involved in decision-making, the VPs in particular seemed to think decision quality suffered while the lower levels thought it was enhanced. This suggests both how involvement increases commitment at lower levels, and why upper-level managers are reluctant to involve their subordinates in decision-making. Because lower-level managers believe their involvement improved the quality of the decision, they tend to be committed to it. Because higher-level managers believe the involvement of subordinates reduced decision quality, they tend to avoid involvement. To many upper-level managers, participation may be seen as a threat to business success.

4.4. Effectiveness is a function of who defines it. Some leaders' perceptions are others' reality, and as long as effectiveness is based on internal value judgments, whatever they say X is, it is.

In fact, until the external world intervenes in the form of declining profits or bad press, effectiveness may be a matter of perceptual consensus, particularly in hard to quantify areas like staff functions, abstractions like climate, and the inevitably confounded areas of individual and group effectiveness.

The president says the VP of the volatile division is the most effective; divisional data state otherwise; a VP says a given plant manager is the least effective; the data support the opposite contention. In these cases, and many others, leader perceptions define the truth in process. Only in retrospect do their perceptions look erroneous.

4.5. Performance is generally okay but not great. Although the groups and divisions varied, most performed as expected—making a few good decisions, very few bad ones, and leaving the financial picture as it was. This suggests to us that measurement of effectiveness might take several tacks.

4.5.1. Differentiate in the middle range. Many leadership measures do a good job of identifying extremes and predicting the effects of such behavior. Unfortunately, our observations suggest that a) extremes are obvious even without measures and b) most of the action is not at the extremes. Among the better measures we have found for differentiating among managers are (a) who actively seeks to define the major problems facing a work unit and (b) who is seen as responsible for doing anything with these problems.

4.5.2. Extreme cases may be one-tailed. Our observations indicate that at lower levels, it is easy to spot the effective, but almost impossible to spot the ineffective. The effective force their way into major divisional problems and are spotted by peer and observer alike. The majority simply take care of their specific operation and no one can tell whether they are merely efficiently unimaginative or unimaginatively inept. At upper levels, where most of the major problems flow through the positions, spotting an effective VP is extremely difficult because of the 30 problems that could be tackled, who can say which 6 should be? Conversely, a VP who reacts, bumbles or simply does not see any of the problems, is reliably panned.

4.5.3. Effectiveness cuts both ways. Making objectively good choices is an obvious component of effectiveness, but no more so than avoiding bad choices. We found, for example, that the best path to financial effectiveness in our norm group was to make good choices in the stable division and avoid poor choices in the volatile division. This risk avoidance (also supported by field research) may not be salutary, but it is a common route to financial effectiveness.

4.6. Problem definition is a critical skill. In Looking Glass, managers gravitate to the concrete and the tactical and steer away from the fuzzy (problems involving coupling, politics, and long-term effects). The problems rated as most important by managers are those on which the least action is taken. Bad news is sat on until managers can figure out a possible solution. In the interim it is often forgotten.

A perspective for looking at leadership effectiveness might be to see who can: 1) define problems while juggling 20 other things, 2) define the problems that others ignore, particularly the fuzzy, perplexing ones, 3) turn bad news into an opportunity for problem solving, 4) understand the elements of a problem before deciding how to reach a decision on it, and 5) create patterns in streams of decisions (the definition of strategy, according to Mintzberg, 1978). If we had to point to what differentiates effective from ineffective Looking Glass divisions, ability to accomplish the above would be the leading contenders.

4.7. Much of effectiveness has little to do with "the bottom line." Most of the measures we constructed for Looking Glass simply pick up what managers do—deciding on personnel and public policy issues, which raw materials to use and the like—issues that are treated as intrinsically rather than financially important. The vast majority of actions taken do eventually affect "the bottom line" but the relationship is so tenuous and the path so muddled that trying to establish a causal link seems wasted effort.

A complex set of seemingly unrelated decisions by marketing, product development, and manufacturing may interact with the environment to increase profitability without anyone ever knowing who pulled the trigger. A better perspective is, what is the most effective response to a specific problem? What are the relevant elements and how should they be arranged to produce the desired outcome?

4.8. Effectiveness for what? If effectiveness is a value judgment, then we should specify whose values about what. Effectiveness might be construed as changing the environment, reducing costs, improving the quality of life, reaching a high quality decision, being seen as effective, improving return on investment, lowering the crime rate, or any number of things. Effectiveness is certainly no one thing, not even within a work unit or a single problem. Many acts may be construed as effective and they all may be if they attack different facets of a problem. One act may increase profits, another may improve working relationships, and each may negate the effects of the other. Since effectiveness is a value judgment, we believe it must be given meaning within a specific context.

In summary, trying to untangle the reality of effectiveness, even in a simulated environment, brings to the surface all the complexity recorded by research on organizational effectiveness (e.g., Campbell, 1977b; Steers,

1977). Its significance for leadership research is direct: there are no simple dependent variables. As Vaill (1978) pointed out, we have to ask "leadership for what?" Examining "leadership effectiveness" is solving for two equally complex unknowns. We believe leadership research will advance dramatically if a strategically selected set of dependent variables replaces our overdependence on group satisfaction and productivity measures.

Finding a strategic array of variables is, of course, a major task in itself. A first step is acknowledging that for many managerial behaviors, the value judgments made by significant positions in the organization *are* the reality. We spend a lot of time trying to triangulate, trying to find reliability among raters. Perhaps a more useful strategy would be to put that effort into identifying who counts.

Another step is to find better ways to discriminate in the middle range. One promising lead is to look at problems rather than individuals or groups. By watching a problem flow through a system, one can observe how groups and individuals get connected, miss out, make a contribution, or fall apart. This approach might help reduce the illusory effects of context (see 4.2, 4.5.2), and, by looking at selected clusters of problems, we may gain more power than is possible with a "bottom line" index.

Using different levels of analysis as dependent measures in leadership research may raise some tough questions. Using budget allocations as a dependent measure, for example, Pfeffer and Salancik (1978) concluded that individual mayors (as opposed to other sources) accounted for less than 10 percent of the variance. Cohen and March (1974), studying university presidents and using organizational criteria, concluded that performance was largely an act of God. In another unusual study, being Napolean accounted for only 15 percent of the variance in French military success (Simonton, 1979).

We believe leadership can make a difference, but in many circumstances it matters less than expected. In others, it is critical. In short, if we can only account for a bit of the variance, which bit and at what time are important matters.

Conclusions

This overview of findings from Looking Glass was intended to suggest some directions for leadership research that are worth exploring. On our "To Do" list are the following:

1. Stop thinking group. We heartily endorse Dubin's statement, "The study of leadership has been so overwhelmingly concerned with a leader in personal relationship with *some* followers that we simply have ignored a broad range of very important leadership phenomena" (1979, pp. 226–

27). There are other ways to look at what is going on, only one of which is using problems or problem clusters as a basic unit of analysis.

2. Look closely at the dependent variables. The dependent variable in a leadership study is critical. It defines what leadership can be. If a group outcome is the criterion, then we are learning only about leader effects on groups. We are not able to say anything about leader effects on organizations, financial outcomes, specific problems, outsiders, and so forth. Now that we know a good deal about leader-follower relations, we need to find out how that fits in with the larger scheme of organizational functioning. At the very least we need clarity in our choice of dependent variables. The researcher's bias shows clearly in the choice because the criterion says why the researcher thinks leadership is important. It is the researcher's answer to "leadership for what?"

3. Take a fuller look at setting. We built Looking Glass to provide a realistic, replicable, and interpretable setting for studying leader behavior. The relationships between environment, structural factors, and leadership are fascinating but complex. It will not be easy to figure out when what is important. We believe that looking at thresholds, coupling, structure as a latent variable, temporary connections, direct effects, and leader mediation are all promising approaches.

4. Choose samples strategically. In much of the leadership research, the sample has consisted of formal leaders—managers, foremen, crew chiefs, administrators. Implicit in this is that all formal leaders are created equal, or more properly stated, that all leadership positions at roughly the same level are equal. Variance is assumed to reflect something about the individual incumbents rather than their positions. We have to question that. Each of the 20 Looking Glass positions has unique characteristics, regardless of titular, functional, or hierarchical similarities. Aspects of what people will do are predictable from the roles they hold.

Some leadership research might carefully select the leadership roles to be included. For example, the researcher might sample only those positions through which critical problems flow (see Salancik & Pfeffer, 1977). Leadership should matter a great deal in such positions, increasing the chance of finding significant relationships. Or, as Moses (1979) has suggested, one might select samples of individuals previously identified as possessing leadership skills and study what they do in particular positions.

5. Take another look at perception. The attribution approach to leadership (Calder, 1977; Pfeffer, 1978) is a valuable way to understand some of the inconsistencies in leadership research. The important thing is that perceptual disagreement is not all error—it is real, and has meaning. When people disagree, their dissension may flag a fuzzy problem worth looking at. When everyone agrees, something striking must have happened. In ad-

dition, some leaders' perceptions *are* reality, regardless of the objective case. We need to understand better the multiple, evanescent, erroneous, and concrete realities that make up a leader's world.

6. Belay model building. If the manager's world is really a nest of .3 correlations, containing thresholds and constantly changing relations among elements, model building will be a tough proposition. For instance, contingency theories will not do very well because different elements will be relevant at different times and, even if the contingency can be identified, no single behavioral response will necessarily be the best.

Instead of models, which by their nature tightly couple elements, we might look for triggers. What kinds of things happen that bring leadership to the surface? What kinds of acts make elements relate when they did not before? We need more rich description of what leaders in organizations are up to, especially of the problems, the context, the guts of everyday managerial life. Such is the stuff of which new models can be made.

A final observation: Managers participate in Looking Glass in exchange for a developmental experience. In the debriefing they discuss what they were trying to do and what they did. They tell us what they worked on, why, and how. They tell us how they saw the world that day, which is ordinarily as flows of problems, many of which are never solved but only held off a little longer. They do not speak of themselves as leaders; they speak of taking leadership in the soda ash shortage, or in the foreign market question—leadership as an act that changes the relationship between elements at a certain time and place. We believe that they know far better than we what leadership is about, but we do not know how to ask them and they do not know how to tell us. We are both managers, and we cannot tell you either.

5

Commentary on Part 1

Various Paths Beyond Establishment Views

BERNARD WILPERT

The three chapters discussed here reflect indeed three formidable pieces of research. Though different in methodological approach and length of time covered by the research, they are similar in their central focus: to observe *what* managers/leaders do during their time managing/leading. In other words, all three presentations deal exclusively or predominantly with *on-line* observations (Weick, 1978) of managers/leaders in their work over varying time horizons.

Rosemary Stewart's chapter amounts to an attempt to draw the summa—in terms of concepts, models, and findings—of over 15 years of seminal work on managerial behavior of various hierarchical levels, employing the whole gamut of field study techniques from the use of diaries, standardized tests, and questionnaires, to structured/unstructured interviews, group-discussions, and on-line observations.

The other two contributions are more of the nature of progress reports on ongoing, carefully designed, promising research. Bussom, Larson, and Vicars give an inkling of the scientific potential in their impressive data set derived from one of the largest and most thorough field observation studies of top managers hitherto conducted. Finally, Lombardo and McCall present an intermediary evaluation of an ingeniously elaborated simulation study of managerial behavior in a structured organizational setting, which provides at the same time also an impressive data set for a variety of analytic interests.

What should be noted right at the outset—since it has consequences for my own presentation—is the terminological uncertainty in all three contributions with respect to the use of the terms "leader" and "manager." Although some difference of kind is even implied in the titles of two of the presentations (Stewart; Lombardo & McCall), not one of the three contributions elaborates the distinctions, in fact, all use these two terms synonymously. So I will follow suit and assume for purposes of discussion that managers always perform some leadership function due to their organizational position.

My observations are offered in three sections, below. The first section will deal with each of the chapters separately and will raise some issues that I feel are among the most important ones to be considered in the further development of the respective authors' thinking. The second will deal with some encompassing themes arising out of the findings and theorization of the three chapters which I find important to be stressed. And the final section will reflect what appears to be some fundamental issues or problems in the light of this volume's general theme—leadership: beyond establishment views.

Comments on Individual Contributions

Rosemary Stewart's theoretical model differentiates between demands, constraints, and choices. Demands denote the inner core of a manager's job (common to all similar jobs); constraints are outer boundaries for the behavioral variance (choices) in similar jobs. While recognizing that such a nomenclature appeals to the practicing manager because he/she can immediately identify certain aspects of his or her work with such terms, I fear that the conceptual differentiation between demands and constraints may be misleading because of the general and social-scientific use of these terms. Constraints become intrinsic demands for a job and, conversely, demands function as constraints. A conceptualization of core or central versus peripheral and optional job characteristics might help to alleviate this terminological difficulty. Besides, it would give fuller meaning to what the author means by "choice," namely, the exercise of certain variable parts of management behavior. And, if one wants to transcend a strict behaviorism altogether "choice" might be considered as something like "resulting behavior," that is, a consequence of the force field (Lewin, 1951) of "situational barriers" (personal, technological, social constraints) and vectors (goals, valences, expectations). Central and peripheral job characteristics could thus easily be described as a function of varying intensities of field forces.

Bussom, Larson, and Vicars attempt to capture as accurately as possible the "streams of behavior" displayed by police chief executives in large American cities in order to analyze the emergent interpersonal contact patterns. Without questioning the validity and potential significance of their findings (see more on that below) I want to caution about the validity of their claim "that no classification or coding was performed during observation" and that their "narrative record" covered "*all* work related events and activities . . . as they happened" (authors' emphasis).

In principle I would argue that any data collection process implies segmentalization and reduction of reality (Popper, 1961), hence codification and the ordering of phenomena into categories of classification. The practical implementation of this premise is amply exemplified by the authors' care and emphasis in the training and supervision of observers in order to guarantee proper categorization. Furthermore, the selectivity and the quality of categorization of the narrative records can be demonstrated by their "Hypothetical Sample of Narrative Data" (Exhibit 1): it notes nothing of atmospheric characteristics which obviously must have accompanied any one of the described events. Nothing is recorded about change in friendliness, display of differential anxieties, servility, frustration from one event to the other—to give just a few examples. Or must we conclude that this cannot be observed, and hence is not part of events? It seems to me that would be carrying black box behaviorism a trifle too far. Without minimizing the importance of the findings we must recognize the intrinsic methodological limitations of any data collection.

Lombardo and McCall have taken great care in constructing their Looking Glass Corporation in order "to mirror as realistically as possible the demands of a typical managerial job in a complex organization." Within the limits of a one-day simulation they seem to have been quite successful in doing so. I suppose they are as aware of the limits of such a simulation as anyone could be. But since they do not discuss these limits I would like to mention three that tend to constrain the generalizability of their findings: namely, previous socialization, time pressures, and lack of real sanctions. Socialization into an organization's way of operating is one of the fundamental learning processes of any new organization member. The development of and familiarization with such organizational mores which are bound to have impact on the kind of leadership behavior that prevails in the organization is—in LGI—compressed into an evening and a morning session. Hence, one would have to be aware that behavioral artifacts might result that are unlikely in organically grown organizations. Similarly, LGI managers are faced with tremendous decision problems and many might experience the pressure to resolve these within one day while normally processes may extend over weeks and months of study, reflection, and deliberate delays. Finally, I would surmise that in spite of the very intense group pressures which develop in any good role playing situation the nature of negative sanctions in LGI are less existential than for a faulty or unsuccessful managerial action in real life. All three factors might contribute to the emergence of behavior patterns less likely to occur in worldly ventures.

Encompassing Themes

Behavioral Variance

One of the lessons of the three contributions is: The variance of leadership behavior is much greater than naïvely assumed. Flexibility of job domains (Stewart), varying interaction patterns (Bussom et al.), and variety in problem definitions (Lombardo & McCall) are the illustrative terms of the three studies used for this finding. Whence the variety and why? I believe one of the most important lessons of LGI is the insight that managers primarily address problems, even the contention that managers' behavior hinges on how they define problems. I would hypothesize that a great deal of variance in domain choice and interaction frequencies can be explained by such cognitive processes. And if that were so, then we must include the phenomenal world of managers, their *whole life space* in Lewinian terms, into our conceptualizations. Exclusive third party observations as enlightening as they may be, simply cannot do the trick (similarly argue Stewart; Lombardo & McCall).

Importance of Structure

This demand for more holistic considerations repeats itself on the structural level: Stewart's very useful taxonomy of contact types and Lombardo and McCall's insistence on the behavioral consequences of a manager's position within a social system. Both address one of the most important and yet most complicated issues in the study of leadership: How can we do justice to positional differences in comparing leaders of various systems? Bussom et al. by the strategic choice of their sample go a long way to alleviate the problem. In this case we have functionally equivalent positions—police chiefs—that can be assumed to have comparable roles in a functional sense. However, who dares say that the social systems within which these 10 officers are imbedded are identical? This clearly has implications also for the data analysis strategies: we must always judiciously ponder the criteria for choosing an individual *within a system* or, alternatively, a group of individuals *irrespective of their given systems* as units of analysis.

Environment

The difficulties with desirable holistic approaches multiply when we introduce environment into our models (Lombardo & McCall). Traditionally we tend to conceptualize environments in terms of perceived environments (Lawrence & Lorsch, 1967). But there is growing evidence—mainly from European research—that irrespective of their phenomenal representation societal and cultural idiosyncrasies impact on organizational structure and managerial behavior (Lammers & Hickson, 1979; Maurice, Sorge, & Wagner, 1980). This poses tremendous conceptual and measurement problems hitherto largely neglected in leadership research and would drastically expand the scope even of the macro-oriented approach advocated by Hunt and Osborn (this volume).

Importance of Skills

One encompassing theme is also more prominent by its relative neglect in the three studies than by its incisive conceptualization: managerial competence. This is somewhat puzzling because even on a priori grounds one ought to assume that organizational experience, technical and interpersonal competence of managers, of their supervisors, peers, and subordinates must have something to do with how managerial problems are defined and solved, when and where advice is sought, what interaction patterns emerge. On empirical grounds it has been shown that quasi-objective (e.g., level of education) as well as perceived competence in superior-subordinate dyads are among the strongest predictive variables for the emergent decision making patterns (Heller & Wilpert, 1981). It seems that vast areas of fertile ground are here still awaiting to be tilled.

Conclusion: Problems and Prospects

In their emphasis on longitudinal approaches of the study of leadership all three contributions discussed here make decisive steps in a direction to overcome established lines and schools of managerial behavior/leadership research. In doing so the authors implement what many a theoretician and critic have asked us to do but which for lack of concepts, funds, and access we have often neglected. The obvious differences in their methodological approaches and ensuing results once more illustrate the futility of a call for methodological monism in leadership research. In this context it seems particularly inappropriate to deride research efforts that attempt to obtain approximate descriptions of the phenomenal "inner world" of leaders. Problem definition, choice of domain, competence judgements, interpretation of environmental features, perceived threshold stimuli that trigger managerial actions, and the problem of organizational effectiveness and goal setting all pose research issues that can only be attacked by recourse to the perceived world of managers themselves, that is, we must ask them questions about it.

I firmly believe that we need both: strictly behavioristic analyses and approaches (Bussom et al.) and approaches that try to tap the phenomenal realities. The plea for a new look at perceptions (Stewart; Lombardo & McCall) is very timely. A second issue—from the three contributions emerges an apparent need to include organizational situs or structural position into our theorizing and empirical ventures. This raises for me another important problem often left aside in leadership research—the problem of power and conflict (Mulder, 1977). The vulgarized Weberian notion of power as getting one's way even against opposition is so much an evident accompaniment of our everyday naïve leadership experience that it must be included more thoroughly also in our scholarly gropings for an adequate understanding of leadership.

This brings me to a last point—a point where I feel that I can draw on a genuinely European experience and share it with American collegues interested in similar issues. This experience is likely to give a completely different and new meaning to the notion of transcending establishment views which in the context of this symposium is understood as going beyond established lines of scientific discourse.

In established research traditions leadership and management usually connote differences in hierarchy, to be situated on a relatively higher position of the scalar, hierarchical axis of the social system, equipped with easier access to organizational resources, more influence and decision making power. Recent rather heated debates in literally every European country show that strong forces are at work to redress that imbalance in favor of hitherto somewhat less privileged organizational strata further away from the apex of organizations. These demands go under the labels of more "employee participation," "co-determination," "co-surveillance," "self-management," and "industrial democracy." They rely on societal changes and generally on the introduction of new legislation or collective bargaining contracts to increase the say of employees at lower levels (or their representatives as it were) in organizational decision making. As such they are gigantic real life experiments in the wholesale promotion of externally induced organizational change because they stipulate new organizational structures and processes. Hence they will affect also any traditional notion of leadership and management. And, if one wants to take account of these new conditions posed to the excercize of leadership, posed, let us say, to this new developing form of required organizational governance in leadership research, one will be forced to take an evermore systematic account of environmental factors such as legal or other normative prescriptions, of unions' and government agencies' influence, and general sociopolitical ambience.

It is not surprising, then, that the first systematic organization studies of these phenomena took their origin in Europe (e.g., IDE, 1980a, b; King & Van de Vall, 1978; Wall & Lischeron, 1977). Given the situation in the United States it may be still somewhat precocious to direct the attention of North American scholars to these emergent issues for management and leadership research in Europe. However, one ought to be perfectly aware that neglecting them is tantamount to remaining in a traditional establishment view of leadership research in a very specific sense, even though one may advance in many others, as this sixth biennial leadership symposium demonstrates.

Part 2

Semiestablishment Views and a Triad of New Models

Introduction

JAMES G. HUNT, UMA SEKARAN, and CHESTER A. SCHRIESHEIM

The four chapters comprising this part represent "semiestablishment" views in that their roots can be traced back to contemporary mainstream research. The first three were competitively selected from a large number of manuscripts considered by the symposium's reviewers. The fourth consists of expert commentaries on the three presentations, and a reply by two sets of authors to the commentaries. While the first three chapters present illustrative or supportive data, we view their primary focus and contribution as conceptual. Taken collectively, the four chapters represent innovative theoretical treatments which, although linked to establishment perspectives, break new ground in the leadership domain.

Chapter 6, "Multiplexed Supervision and Leadership: An Application of Within and Between Analysis," by Dansereau, Alutto, Markham, and Dumas, is a natural evolution of the work of Dansereau and Dumas (1977) reported in an earlier symposium volume. The unit of analysis question which forms its heart is, in our opinion, a key concern in the entire behavioral science area and is receiving increasing attention (e.g., Lincoln & Zeitz, 1979; Schneider, 1978).

The Chapter begins by proposing a concrete conceptualization of the Average Leadership Style (ALS) and Vertical Dyad Linkage (VDL) models currently employed in leadership research. A general approach is then developed (called within and between analysis, or WABA) which has four conditions and provides a basis for testing whether any set of variables is more congruent with predictions derived from the ALS model, the VDL model, or neither. Data are used to illustrate this approach, its results, and how such results might be interpreted. Finally, the way this approach can align

theory, data, and inference is discussed, along with some important methodological implications and implications for leadership theory, research,
and practice.

In reading the Dansereau et al. chapter, several theoretical issues pertinent to the authors' approach come to mind. Although the authors treat
some of these, at least in part, perhaps they should be highlighted nonetheless (issues concerning their illustrative data are not considered in order to
focus on more substantive concerns). First, the proposed conceptualization
of the ALS and VDL models involves, as the authors put it, pushing both
to their logical extremes. One might question whether ALS or VDL researchers would agree with the natures of the proposed formulations, and
readers might want to give this issue some consideration. For example, the
VDL formulation which is proposed could be thought of as actually making the VDL model a group-based approach, since it assumes that a group-
based referent (the within group mean score for each variable) is somehow
part of subordinate perceptions of or reactions to leadership and other
variables.

This leads directly to a second point: the theoretical model which is
proposed by Dansereau et al. is heavily based upon statistical considerations. One might wonder about its underlying implications concerning associated psychological processes, since these processes are both important
and not explored in the chapter. Third, the conceptual meaning of ag-
gregating individual scores into group scores and the meaning of treating a
group's score as an individual's score (for testing ALS versus VDL models
within some data sets) need to be considered. Such treatments are implied
by the WABA model and have clear statistical interpretations. The theoretical meanings of such variables, however, are less clear. For example,
how would one reconcile this approach with one which argues that group
phenomena are not simply aggregated individual phenomena (cf. Brown &
Turner, in press)?

This also seems important when it is remembered that many ALS variables are group-based (e.g., unit output), while many VDL variables are
based upon individuals (e.g., job satisfaction). Thus, the meaning of testing
conceptually difficult-to-interpret variables within the WABA framework
needs to be kept in mind.

A fourth issue which readers should be alert to concerns assumptions
about groups which are made in the WABA approach. For example, meaningful groups should exist and be examined, in order to test the ALS versus
VDL models. However, determining the boundaries of any particular
group may not be an easy endeavor (group size seems particularly important here, since it might affect the formation of referent subgroups, as well

as raise problems of sampling to get stable and representative group mean scores).

Finally, readers may want to pay attention to some of the conditions which support neither the ALS or VDL models (the authors' "special null" case). While some possible explanations for this situation are discussed, others will undoubtedly come to mind and might constitute useful extensions to the authors' presentation. In sum, the chapter by Dansereau et al. is a provocative one, both with respect to what is and what is not covered within it, and it should serve to stimulate the reader's interest and, we hope, debate in the field over its merits.

Chapter 7, "A Theory of Leadership Categorization," by Lord, Foti, and Phillips, proposes a model of the cognitive structure which underlies implicit leadership theories and leadership perceptions in general. Recent literature on cognitive categorization and person perception is first reviewed, and this is followed by extending this literature by developing a model of leadership cognitions. Finally, some supportive research results are briefly considered, and implications for research and practice are discussed.

In examining the Lord et al. chapter, readers might want to remember the constraints imposed upon the authors by the limited theory and research in the cognitive categorization literature, and by the virtual nonexistance of relevant literature in the leadership field. The conceptualization proposed is therefore general and lacking in detail. The specifics of exactly how categories are developed, modified, and brought to bear remain unclear. Similarly, setting factors affecting these processes are not fully explicated, nor are possible linkages to other literatures, such as those on attribution processes or stereotyping. Still, this chapter outlines what may serve as a useful starting point in applying categorization theory to leadership phenomena, and future work may, we hope, be expected further to develop, refine, and test it.

Chapter 8, "Leadership Activation Theory: An Opponent Process Model of Subordinate Responses to Leadership Behavior," by Sheridan, Kerr, and Abelson, presents an activation model of leadership which is based on arousal and opponent process theories of motivation. The model is shown to suggest that intense leadership incidents may have a stronger influence on subordinate outcomes (e.g., job performance) than the frequency of typical leadership behavior. A test of the model is reported, using a sample of supervisory and managerial employees in an assembly plant. The results suggest some support for the model, and future directions for the model are discussed.

Given the current concern in the field with the measurement of leader behavior, Sheridan et al.'s specially constructed behaviorally anchored rating scales of leadership intensity are of some interest. A couple of recent evaluations of the strengths and weaknesses of such scales (Jacobs, Kafry, & Zedeck, 1980; Morrison & Randell, in press) help put the Sheridan et al. scales in better perspective.

In further examining the Sheridan et al. chapter, it becomes obvious that the data and empirical test are the weakest part of this contribution. In fact, many questions could be raised about methodological issues which seem highly problematic. Questions can also be raised about the theory-data linkage, and whether the empirical test is at all isomorphic with opponent process and activation theories. However, while these concerns are important, they may be viewed as having less relevance for the field as a whole as compared with issues surrounding the application of the theories themselves.

We see the major contribution of this chapter in theoretical rather than empirical terms—a potentially useful extension of major social psychological theory into the leadership area. In exploring the Sheridan et al. chapter, then, besides considering methodological shortcomings and issues, readers may want to think about larger questions about the underlying theory base. For example, what are the theoretical implications for leadership research and practice? What sort of assumptions are needed to extend and test the theory? Is the theory testable and, if so, how might one proceed better to test it? These issues are of considerable importance, and Sheridan et al. have sought to grapple with some of them, at least in part. Perhaps this chapter will stimulate additional theoretical development and testing; at least, that was our purpose in including it in the current volume.

Chapter 9 is the final chapter in this part, and it contains separate commentaries on the first three chapters by Bernard Bass and Ian Morley. These comments are followed by a brief clarification and rejoinder by Dansereau, Alutto, Markham, and Dumas and by Lord, Foti, and Phillips.

Both the Bass and Morley commentaries echo some of the points raised above about the three preceding chapters, although each goes into these points at greater length. Bass discusses the Dansereau et al. chapter from a largely methodological perspective, although theoretical concerns are also given considerable attention. The strengths and weaknesses of the WABA approach, possible alternate statistical designs and underlying assumptions, and problems of sample size, statistical power, and the like are discussed. Possible moderators affecting differential leader behavior toward group members are also considered.

Bass discusses the Lord et al. chapter in terms of the dichotomous nature of the authors' framework, the usefulness of some of their concepts to leadership research (which he questions), and possible attribution theory extensions and adjuncts to their model. The Sheridan et al. chapter is treated with respect to issues of statistical power, measurement quality, the possibility of nonlinear relationships inherent in both the theory and the authors' data, and some possible analytical methods which might be fruitfully applied within the Sheridan et al. framework.

During his comments on the Sheridan et al. chapter, and in the conclusion to his remarks, Bass discusses "transformational leadership"—a concept roughly akin in many respects to charasmatic leadership (House, 1977). He compares it with traditional (transactional) leadership conceptualizations, and highlights its potential importance for theory, research, and practice. He also raises some interesting questions for future research, and the results of a pilot study are briefly presented. Although not new to the leadership domain (cf. House, 1977), the study of transformational leadership seems to be a potentially exciting area, one which may warrant considerable future research. Thus, Bass not only provides expert commentary on the chapters of this part, but also a useful contribution in his own right.

The commentary by Morley is sharply different from that of Bass, in that a strong social-psychological perspective is taken, and the three chapters are examined with respect to two different strategies for coping with the different leadership processes which evolve in different contexts. The first strategy, which Morley sees inherent in the Dansereau et al. chapter, involves dividing theories into mutually exclusive types and testing to see which fits and when. From this perspective, Dansereau et al. are criticized for what is viewed as an extreme position in forcing distinctions between the ALS and VDL models. Some interesting contrasts are also suggested between European and United States leadership research which may prove fruitful for future research.

The second strategy, which Morley sees as characterizing the chapters by Lord et al. and Sheridan et al., involves the identification of basic processes underlying observed behavior. He ties both chapters into cognitive social psychology, and suggests some general and specific directions for each. The Lord et al. chapter is discussed with respect to broader category theory, and he suggests that it does not really need to use category theory and that some relevant research on stereotypes might serve as a more appropriate framework.

The Sheridan et al. chapter is finally discussed, linking it to broader opponent process theory. Morley argues that Sheridan et al. do not actually employ or test an opponent process model, but instead examine the distinction between extreme and commonplace leader behavior. Morley concludes by pointing out that all three chapters deal with the importance of distinctive leadership events, and he suggests that much more research along this vein is needed.

Throughout his discussion, Morley goes to considerable length to link all three chapters back to mainstream research in social psychology, as well as to suggest possible extensions and new conceptualizations pertinent to each chapter. Thus, Morley's comments may be viewed as often insightful, and as providing linkages which the authors and others may wish to pursue.

Replies to the Bass and Morley commentaries, by Dansereau et al. and Foti et al., conclude the final chapter in this part. Dansereau et al. clarify the purpose of their WABA model, as well as consider differences in statistical assumptions and the usefulness of different data-analytic methods for testing ALS versus VDL model formulations. Lord et al. argue that the issues raised by Bass are based on misinterpretations of their chapter. They provide some clarifications in their rejoinder. They also take issue with Morley's contention that research on stereotypes would be a more appropriate framework than the category theory which they use in their chapter.

Taken as a whole, we see the chapters in Part 2 as providing innovative theoretical conceptualizations which might prove valuable to advance contemporary mainstream or "establishment" leadership research, as well as serve as a springboard for "nonestablishment" work. There are some real gems in these chapters, and readers are encouraged to use their imaginations while examining each.

6

Multiplexed Supervision and Leadership: An Application of Within and Between Analysis

FRED DANSEREAU, JR., JOSEPH A. ALUTTO,
STEVEN E. MARKHAM, and MacDONALD DUMAS

Traditional approaches to leadership focus upon 1) differences *between* superiors, 2) differences *between* entire work groups, and 3) the relationship between these supervisory differences and work group differences (e.g., Bowers & Seashore, 1966; Fiedler, 1967; Likert, 1961; Stoghill & Coons, 1957). This traditional paradigm has been labeled the Average Leadership Style (ALS) approach (Dansereau, Cashman, & Graen, 1973). To deny the inherent validity of the ALS model is to ignore the existence of differences between superiors and between entire work groups, and this is rarely a conscious intent. Critical reviews of ALS assumptions do, however, serve to focus on the possibility of a second equally likely alternative model which is quite different from the ALS paradigm.

This alternative model or paradigm (Vecchio, 1979), labeled the Vertical Dyad Linkage Model (Dansereau, Graen, & Haga, 1975), focuses upon 1) differences *within* superiors, 2) differences between individuals *within* work groups, and 3) the relationship between these internal supervisory differences and internal work group differences. Whether by intent or happenstance, critics of the VDL model often find themselves in a position of denying that superiors differentiate between subordinates and that subordinates may differ, and also feel compelled to reject the possibility that such differences may be correlated within work groups.

Although it is possible to argue (perhaps endlessly) about the utility of these two models (Cummings, 1975; Schriesheim, 1979), the purpose of this chapter is to derive empirical predictions from each of the models such that these two paradigms can be simultaneously tested in one set of data.

The Multiplex Approach

In attempting to allow for both paradigms two key questions arise. First, are the VDL and ALS models different from each other? In order to address this question it is helpful to push each model to its extreme and essentially derive ideal VDL and ALS conditions. It is from these theoretical conditions that the differences between these models become apparent. A second key question which must be addressed is, given that the ALS and VDL models can be distinguished from each other, is it possible that both models may be predictive simultaneously? In other words, because of the obvious merits of both the VDL and ALS models it should be possible to allow for the operation of both models simultaneously. Therefore, in the multiplex approach the focus is upon first deriving the *differences* between the models and then second assuring that the theoretical derivation allows for both models to be predictive *simultaneously*.

Identifying ALS Predictions

In the ideal case for the ALS model, superiors differ from each other. For example, one superior supervises more loosely and a second superior supervises less loosely. The schematic diagram in Table 8 attempts to illustrate this condition by the degree to which the circles which represent superiors are filled in. For example, in Table 8 under the ALS model the superior of unit 1 supervises less loosely (the circle representing the supervisor is only partially filled in) while the superior in unit 2 supervises more loosely (completely filled in circle). Moreover, in the ideal case entire work groups are expected to differ from each other. This is shown in Table 8 under the ALS model by the degree to which the circles which represent subordinates are filled in. For example, in terms of Table 8, under the ALS model all subordinates in unit 1 may face tasks which are less unstructured while all the subordinates in unit 2 may face tasks which are more unstructured.

The assumption that superiors differ between each other *and* that work groups vary from each other is critical to the linkage between superiors and subordinates specified by the ALS model. Since subordinates in a work group are viewed as similar there are J work groups (not N subordinates) and these J work groups correspond directly to J superiors. This allows for a one to one correspondence between superior and subordinate analytical units, thereby facilitating examination of the correlation between differing supervisors and work groups. For example, whether superiors who show looser supervision tend to be those who supervise work groups whose tasks are more or less structured is an empirical question.

TABLE 8
Empirical Predictions of the ALS and VDL Models

	Average Leadership Style		Vertical Dyad Linkage	
	Unit 1	Unit 2	Unit 1	Unit 2
Schematic Illustration				
Superiors				
Linkages				
Subordinates				
Theoretical Predictions				
Between Work Group or Supervisor Variation	Valid		Error	
Within Work Group or Superior Variation	Error		Valid	
Empirical Predictions				
Between Work Group or Superior Correlations	Systematic		Near Zero	
Within Work Group or Superior Correlations	Near Zero		Systematic	

Therefore, the first theoretical assumption of the ALS model is that variation between supervisors and between entire work groups is valid variance. However, as pointed out by Dansereau et al. (1973), the assertion that variance between superiors or work groups is valid means that the model also assumes that any variation within superiors and within work groups is error. Since this second assumption involves the specification of error, this assumption of the ALS model has been ignored. In early versions of the traditional approach, only the averages of the scores in each work group were employed (Dansereau et al., 1973). The averages of such scores represent between work group variance and are highly compatible with the focus of the ALS model. However, the problem with the use of *only* between work group scores (and raw scores for that matter) is that the ALS model *also assumes* that variation within cells is error. Consequently, to test fully the ALS model *both* between and within work groups variation should be assessed and compared to the assumptions of the model.

Table 8 includes a summary of the assumptions contained in the ALS model. Specifically, it is possible to view the ALS model as predicting the discovery of valid variance between work groups and superiors and error variance within work groups and superiors. One way to view these predictions is in terms of correlations. If cells are set equal to work groups, then, as shown in Table 8, the ALS model must predict systematic (valid) between work groups correlations and *near* zero (error) within work groups correlations.

Illustrative ALS Hypothesis

An illustrative Average Leadership Style hypothesis is that the degree of looseness of supervision exhibited by different superiors varies with different work group task or role characteristics. Specifically, as hypothesized by Bell (1965), work groups facing less structured tasks are hypothesized to report loose supervision and work groups facing more structured tasks are hypothesized to report closer supervision. Therefore, there should be a positive relationship between the degree to which the tasks which work groups face are unstructured and the perceptions of supervisory looseness. It is important to notice that this hypothesis is formulated in terms of different superiors and work groups. That is, first, superiors are hypothesized to differ *between* each other in terms of the degree of looseness of supervision. Second, entire work groups are hypothesized to differ between each other in terms of task characteristics. Third, these differences between superiors and work groups are hypothesized to be correlated. This ALS hypothesis predicts that the correlations between measures of task structure and looseness of supervision will be systematic between work groups and near zero within work groups.

Identifying VDL Predictions

In contrast to the above formulation, the VDL model predicts that superiors differ within themselves and discriminate between subordinates. This is illustrated in Table 8 in the schematic diagram for superiors where one half of each "supervisory" circle is completely filled in and the other half of the circle is only partially filled. For example, each superior may offer one subordinate a substantial amount of interpersonal support and attention (in Table 8, the side of each superior which is completely filled) while at the same time he or she offers a second subordinate less support (in Table 8, the side of each superior which is partially filled in). The same logic applies to the subordinates in each work group, where some subordinates may be more supportive of a superior while others may be less supportive of the same superior.

The specification that superiors differ within themselves (i.e., differentiate between subordinates) and that subordinates differ from each other in the same work group is crucial to the linkage between superiors and subordinates specified by the VDL model. Subordinates differ from each other and superiors also reflect differences between subordinates. Therefore, the superiors and subordinates align in a one-to-one fashion within each work group.

The theoretical and empirical assumptions of the VDL model can be illustrated by the work of Graen and Schiemann (1978). In their study, support for the VDL model was inferred in part from near zero correlations based upon between work groups scores. It should be apparent that the VDL model, as the antithesis of the ALS model, assumes that the variation between superiors and work groups is error (see Dansereau & Dumas, 1977). In addition, as demonstrated by Markham, Dansereau, and Alutto (1979) the VDL model assumes that the variation within work groups is valid variation. In other words, any VDL model assumes that valid variation occurs within work groups and within superiors, and it also takes the position that variation between work groups should be treated as error. Given this set of theoretical assumptions, as shown in Table 8, in any data set the VDL model can be viewed as predicting systematic within cell correlations and near zero between cell correlations.

Illustrative VDL Hypothesis

An illustrative VDL hypothesis may be presented from Dansereau et al. (1975). According to this hypothesis, if a superior views the performance of his or her subordinate as a contribution to the superior, the superior will tend to provide greater rewards or attention (Graen, Dansereau, Minami & Cashman, 1973). As a VDL hypothesis this means that, first, superiors are predicted to discriminate between subordinates in terms of both the level of attention given and in terms of performance evaluation. Second, within work groups subordinates are predicted to be differentiated in terms of the attention they receive from their superior and their performance contribution to their superior. Third, these differentiated reports are predicted to be correlated. In other words, this hypothesis predicts that the between cell correlations of the superior's attention to subordinates with superior's evaluations of subordinates' performance will be near zero and that within cell correlations of the same measures will be systematic.

Multiplex Predictions

The ALS model views the superior as a whole person, as is traditional in individual difference psychology, and views subordinates as constituting a homogenized work group. In a practical sense, the ALS model predicts that superiors treat subordinates equally and that subordinates are similar. By contrast, the VDL model views each superior as differentiating among the subordinates reporting to him or her, and that subordinates are stratified inside work groups. In a practical sense, the VDL model predicts that superiors treat subordinates unequally and that subordinates are interdependent but different from each other. However, on a single dimension, at one point in time, a superior cannot treat subordinates equally *and* unequally. A superior either treats subordinates equally *or* unequally. Moreover, subordinates are either similar or different on a single dimension at one point in time. In other words, theoretically the ALS and VDL models are mutually exclusive, and distinguishable from each other.

However, if more than one behavioral dimension is considered it is possible for a superior to treat subordinates equally (ALS) on one dimension and unequally (VDL) on a second dimension. In other words, the ALS and VDL models may operate simultaneously. However, we would then expect the variables which are compatible with each model to be quite different.

According to this formulation, the ALS and VDL models are theoretically *distinct* (mutually exclusive), but can operate *simultaneously*. Therefore, the multiplex model predicts that some variables will tend to be compatible with the VDL model and will show systematic within cell correlations and near zero between cell correlations. In addition, other variables are predicted to be more compatible with the ALS model and will show systematic between cell correlations and near zero within cell correlations. This multiplex approach requires only that the possibility of either an ALS or VDL model is allowed. It is then an empirical question whether a specific set of variables appears more compatible with an ALS or VDL inference.

Illustrative Multiplexed Hypothesis

The ALS and VDL hypotheses, as formulated here, allow for a multiplexed situation to be discovered. First, superiors who supervise work groups with less structured tasks may offer looser supervision, while different superiors, who supervise work groups with more structured tasks, may supervise more closely. Second, superiors may also evaluate subordinate performance and offer attention differentially to their subordinates. Consequently, the actual relationship between superiors and subordinates may include both differentiated (or unique) and undifferentiated (common) characteristics depending upon which variables are considered.

Although a distinction between task and relationship dimensions has been made in the literature (Stogdill, 1974), we prefer Jacobs's (1971) distinction between supervision and leadership to distinguish between the illustrative ALS and VDL hypotheses. In other words, superiors may *supervise* loosely or closely based upon the characteristics of work group's tasks and, at the same time, *lead* by developing differential relationships with subordinates. Therefore, a superior is multiplexed in the sense that behavior toward subordinates may involve not only multiple dimensions, but when these dimensions operate differently, ALS and VDL effects may occur simultaneously. From a methodological perspective, an assessment of this multiplexing phenomenon also requires that correlations between the measures specified by the VDL hypothesis be independent or correlated near zero with the measures specified by the ALS hpothesis.

Implications of the Multiplex Approach

The theoretical possibility of multiplexed situations in organizational and leadership settings requires a rethinking of research methods which are designed to understand superior-subordinate relationships. Specifically, if the ALS and VDL models are viewed as equally likely explanations for any variable then it is apparent that raw score correlations between variables can not be employed. This is the case because raw score correlations allow for the testing of only one correlation, and the ALS and VDL models make predictions about two correlations. Specifically, the ALS model predicts systematic between cell correlations *and* near zero within cell correlations. The VDL model predicts near zero between cell correlations *and* systematic within cell correlations. Therefore, an empirical test of these two models (in a sample where there are work groups), should involve 1) partitioning each variable into a between cell (work group) score and within cell (work group) score, and 2) an examination of relationships among these scores. An illustration of this procedure may be helpful at this point.

Within and Between Cell Correlations

The calculation of between and within cell scores and correlations (Dansereau & Dumas, 1977; Dumas, 1977; Markham, 1978; Markham, Dansereau, & Alutto, 1979; McNemar, 1955) can be illustrated by considering the case of a work group composed of Person A who has a score of one and Person B who has a score of three on a variable X. Each individual subject in this work group then has an average cell score ($\bar{x}$) of 2 on this variable. When other units are included in the sample the grand mean (m) of all scores is subtracted from these scores ($\bar{x} - m$) to obtain between cell scores for each individual. The calculation of within cell scores for the same unit involves the subtraction of the raw score (X) minus the cell mean ($\bar{X}$). In the example, Person A has a raw score of 1 and a unit mean score of 2, therefore, the within cell score is -1. Person B has a raw score of 3; the unit mean score is 2, and the within cell score is $+1$. Within and between cell correlations are calculated by inputting the within and between cell scores for each variable into a standard correlation program.

Once these correlations are calculated, it is possible to test whether (1) an obtained between cell correlation is systematic and whether an obtained within cell correlation is near zero, as predicted by the ALS model, or (2) whether an obtained between cell correlation is near zero and an obtained within cell correlation is systematic, as predicted by the VDL model. Consequently, it becomes an empirical question of whether any given data set is more compatible with either the ALS or VDL model.

Drawing Inferences from Within and Between Cell Correlations

Traditional statistics provide one method to test whether a correlation is near zero or systematic. A general equation for this test (see Hays, 1963) is:

$$Z = \frac{Z'_o - Z'_e}{\sqrt{1/(df-1)}} \tag{1}$$

where Z'_o is an obtained correlation transformed to a Fisher Z score and Z'_e is an error or null correlation (also transformed). To test whether a correlation is zero, Z'_e is assumed to be equal to zero, and the standard test of correlation significance results. From McNemar (1955), between cell correlations are known to have $J-2$ degrees of freedom (where J equals the number of work groups of superiors), and within cell correlations are known to have $N-J-1$ degrees of freedom (where N equals the total number of subordinates in this case). Therefore, it is possible to test the significance of between and within cell correlations. This test comprises the first step of the inference process.

If this first step indicates that, for example, a between cell correlation is systematic while a within cell correlation is near zero, then Z'_e (in Equation 1) can be set equal to the within cell correlation and the degrees of freedom are $J-2$ in Equation 1. By contrast, if the first step of the inference process indicates that a within cell correlation is systematic, while a between cell correlation is near zero, then Z'_e can be set equal to the between cell correlation and the degrees of freedom are $N-J-1$. This procedure essentially involves using a near zero (between or within) correlation as a better estimate of error than a correlational value of exactly zero.

When there is no reason to assume that either the within or between cell correlation is error (zero), an alternative test can be employed. Given the independence of the two correlations, the formula for testing the difference between the within (Z'_w) and between (Z'_b) correlations is:

$$Z = \frac{Z'_b - Z'_w}{\sqrt{\dfrac{1}{N-J-2} + \dfrac{1}{J-3}}} \qquad (2)$$

An Examination of the Implications

It may be helpful to point out that from a set of theoretically derived ideal conditions, a set of predictions and a method for testing these predictions has been derived. In theoretical derivations of this type there is always the critical question of whether such predictions and methods are so unrealistic that they could never be useful in a research sense. In order to examine this question, data collected by interviews with managers in the production department of a basic metals extraction firm were employed. In order to use within and between analysis, it is necessary to define "real" work groups and the individual inside the work groups with precision. Therefore, in this study each individual was identified as a member of a particular supervisory work group in three different ways. First, a list of individuals derived from organization records was used. Second, each superior was asked to draw a picture of his unit and indicate reporting relationships. Finally, the name of each individual's superior was listed on each questionnaire and each respondent indicated whether the individual listed was indeed his superior. In this way it was discovered that there were 107 (N) individuals embedded in 30 (J) work groups (for additional details on the setting and scale reliabilities, etc., see Dumas, 1977, and Markham, 1978). All variables are partitioned into between and within cell deviation scores. From Equation 1, at the .05 level of statistical significance for any between cell correlation the degrees of freedom are 28 and a correlation above .36 is required; for any within cell correlations the degrees of freedom are 77, and a correlation above .22 is required.

Illustrative ALS Results

The respondents formed the entire managerial hierarchy in the production department of the organization. As such, upper level managers tended to be ivolved in administrative activities and lower level employees were less involved in decision making. Three measures were employed to assess each subordinate's task structure. First, using the job activity structure questionnaire (Dansereau et al., 1975), each subordinate indicated the amount of time and energy spent on four administrative activities. Second, using a portion of the Alutto and Acito (1974) decision making scale, each subordinate indicated whether he preferred to be involved in six administrative activities. Finally, from organizational records, each individual's job salary grade in points (Hay System of Classification) was employed as an indicator of the skill level required for each individual's job (the skill index correlated .75 with organizational level). This skill index, assessed independently of self reports, was employed to ascertain an estimate of differential skills both within and between subordinate work groups. Looseness of supervision was operationalized using Bell's (1965) approach. Each subordinate responded to six items, dealing with the extent to which his superior checked on his work, required him to follow standard procedures, and the like.

In terms of the illustrative ALS hypothesis, the key set of correlations involve the correlations between the skill index and the subordinate's self-reports. The between and within cell correlations for these measures are shown in the upper portion of Table 9. As shown in the table, all of the between cell correlations are statistically significant. Only two of the within cell correlations are statistically significant. Moreover, these two matrices can be summarized by transforming all the correlations to Z' scores and taking the average of these Z' scores and converting the average back to an "average" correlation. The average of the between cell correlation is .510 and the average of the within cell correlation is .152. Using traditional statistics, the between cell correlations appear systematic ($p < .05$) while the within cell correlations appear nonsystematic (nonsignificant). Therefore, there is reason to assume that the average within cell correlation may represent error ($Z'_r = .152$ in Equation 1) and to test by Equation 1 whether the average between cell correlation (with 28 degrees of freedom) differs significantly from the within cell error condition. A Z score of 2.13 results from this test, which is statistically significant ($p < .05$). A Z score of 1.83 results if Equation 2 is employed, and that is marginally significant ($p < .07$). In any case, it does appear that the between cell correlations tend to be systematic while the within cell correlations tend to be near zero or less systematic, and that the two correlations differ from each other. These results are as predicted by the ALS model (see Table 8).

Essentially, the correlations between looseness of supervision and subordinates task or role structure are more compatible with an ALS interpretation than a VDL interpretation. In other words, the results are more compatible with the inference that some work groups faced less structured tasks and reported their superiors supervised them less closely, while other work groups faced more structured tasks and reported their superiors su-

TABLE 9
Illustrative Results

Illustrative ALS Results

Subordinate Role Characteristics		Between Cell Correlations			Within Cell Correlations		
		(1)	(2)	(3)	(1)	(2)	(3)
Skill Index	(1)						
Time Spent on Administrative Decisions	(2)	.58**			.30*		
Preferences for Decision Making	(3)	.53**	.53***		.22	.24*	
Looseness of Supervision	(4)	.50**	.41*	.50**	.16	−.01	.01
			r̄ = .510*			r̄ = .152	

Illustrative VDL Results

Leadership Attention		Between Cell Correlations			Within Cell Correlations		
		(5)	(6)	(7)	(5)	(6)	(7)
Supervisor Reports	(5)						
Subordinate Reports	(6)	.03			.44**		
Supervisor Satisfaction with Subordinates							
Supervisor Reports	(7)	.44*	−.09		.63**	.39**	
Subordinate Reports	(8)	−.04	.22	−.35	.53**	.49**	.52**
			r̄ = .036			r̄ = .500*	

Illustrative Special Null Results

		Between Cell Correlations			Within Cell Correlations		
Age	(9)						
Tenure	(10)	.82**			.87**		
Experience	(11)	.93**	.86**		.87**	.59**	
			r̄ = .87**			r̄ = .91**	

*p < .05
**p < .01

pervised them more closely. It is quite possible that the propensity of superiors to supervise closely is a characteristic of work group task and/or a superior's own personality. In either case, within the work group it seems plausible that equity considerations may discourage superiors from singling out one subordinate for close supervision and another for looser supervision, or from differentiating as would be predicted by the VDL model. Rather, task factors may justify the degree of closeness or looseness of supervision. Finally, this set of results is compatible with Bell's (1965) notion that the nature of the task faced by a work group is related to the degree to which superiors supervise closely or loosely.

Illustrative VDL Results

In terms of the VDL hypothesis, each subordinate described his superior on the leadership attention scale (Dansereau et al., 1975). The leadership attention scale consists of reports on 11 measures of the extent to which a superior, for example, allows a particular subordinate to influence decisions affecting the subordinate. In addition, on a five point scale each subordinate indicated how satisfied he felt his superior was with his job performance.

Superiors indicated how satisfied they were with each subordinate on a five point scale. This is the same measure as that used by subordinates. In addition, they responded to the same set of 11 leadership attention measures completed by their subordinates, indicating the extent to which he believed each subordinate felt he was providing attention. The key correlations in this analysis are those between superior and subordinate reports.

The between and within cell correlations of these measures are shown in the middle portion of Table 9. As shown in the table, the average of the between cell correlations is .036 and the average of the within cell correlations is .50. This is counterintuitive in a statistical sense in that the between cell correlations have fewer degrees of freedom and should tend to be greater than the within cell correlations. Using traditional statistics, the between cell correlations appear nonsystematic while the within cell correlations appear systematic. Therefore, there is reason to assume that the between cell correlations may represent error (Z'_r = .036 in Equation 1) and to test whether the average within cell correlation differs significantly from the between cell correlation by employing Equation 1. A Z score of 4.50 results for this test, which is statistically significant ($p < .01$). A Z score of 2.31 results if Equation 2 is employed, which also reaches an acceptable level of statistical significance ($p < .05$). It appears that the within cell correlations tended to be systematic while the between cell correlations tended to be near zero or less systematic, and that the two correlations differed from each other. These results are as predicted by the VDL model (see Table 8).

The obtained correlations between superior and subordinate reports of leadership attention and the superior's satisfaction with subordinates are more compatible with a Vertical Dyad Linkage interpretation than an ALS interpretation. In other words, the results are more in alignment with the hypothesis that superiors differentiate between subordinates such that those who receive more leadership attention are those who the superior evaluates more favorably. This interpretation is quite similar to Graen and Cashman's 1976 notion of in and out groups. Subordinates within work groups who receive more leadership attention and who satisfy their superior more could be viewed as "in," while those who received less leadership attention and who satisfied their superior less could be viewed as "out."

The results in terms of the VDL model are also compatible with a reinforcement view of leadership (Sims & Szilagyi, 1975). From this perspective, superiors may reward some subordinates more than others within the same work group. In a sense a superior may differentially administer reinforcers within work groups (VDL model). This is quite different than an ALS hypothesis where some superiors generally offer more reinforcements than others. Moreover, given the similarity between reinforcement theory and exchange theory (Secord & Backman, 1974), the results are also compatible with the notion that in exchange for more leadership attention subordinates offer more support to the superior and vice versa.

Illustrative Multiplex Results

In the case of the multiplex hypothesis, no measures are required. However, in order to interpret the ALS and VDL hypothesis and effects as operating simultaneously, the measures for the ALS hypothesis should be independent of the measures of the VDL hypothesis. The average of the between cell correlations between the ALS and VDL measures was $-.019$, and the average of the within cell correlations between the ALS and VDL measure was .060, and none of the correlations reached an acceptable level of statistical significance (due to space limitations these correlations are not shown).

Given these near zero correlations between the ALS and VDL measures, it appears that both the ALS and VDL models were supported in the data. However, different variables appear to be involved in each model. This may not be too surprising since the "traditional" two dimensions of leadership (task and relationship; structure and consideration) may well operate differently. Specifically, the "task" orientation of superiors may be a style of supervision influenced by the nature of work group tasks (ALS model). By contrast, "relationship" orientation may involve the idiosyncratic ties between leaders and subordinates within work groups (VDL model). The fact that a number of researchers have found independent "task" and relationships dimensions suggests that this is a possibility. These results suggest that the predictions and methods derived in the multiplex formulation may not be so unrealistic as to be untestable, or as necessarily biased against either the ALS or VDL models.

The WABA Model

Derivation of the Model

Thus far we have outlined an approach which moves from theory to methods to data. It is now necessary to close the inferential loop by focusing upon how to move from data back to theory. A critical question which arises in evaluating any theoretical formulation (and which is seldom asked) is the extent to which a formulation determines the data such that inferences from data can only be supportive of a particular theory. Specifically, in this case, it is necessary to ask whether this theoretical formulation allows for effects in the data which would not be interpreted as indicating either a supervisory (VDL) or work group (ALS) effect. In other words, does the formulation allow for negative feedback about itself. This matter should be viewed as not only a statistical issue, but also as a substantive and theoretical question. Note that from a statistical perspective we have allowed for the possibility that both within and between cell correlations could be null in a statistical sense (the traditional null condition). Note also that a set of completely null results is not interpretable in a theoretical sense. Thus, the null condition provides negative feedback about both supervisory and work group effects and the empirical results from a study. In addition, as shown below, the correct formulation also permits systematic (non-null) effects which would not be interpreted as supportive of a supervisory or work group effect.

A level of analysis perspective (Hunt, Osborn, & Larson, 1973) seems particularly helpful in understanding why it may be quite important to allow for systematic effects which have little to do with superiors or work groups. In fact, from this perspective, a within and between analysis (WABA) model which aligns the ALS and VDL models with data becomes visible. In order to illustrate these two points (the need to allow for systematic effects not due to superiors or work groups and WABA), consider the situation where there are N subordinates embedded in J work groups.

First, as in the case of the ALS model, these subordinates can be viewed as J homogenized work groups. Second, as in the case of the VDL model, these subordinates can be viewed as persons within work groups who are dependent upon each other. In this case, there are $n-1$ independent scores in each work group or $N-J$ individuals for all work groups. However, it is also possible that there are really N independent persons ($df = N-1$) whose reports have nothing to do with work group membership. In this latter case, there is no reason to expect that either within or between cell correlations would be nonsystematic or error. On the contrary, it is to be expected that both the between and within cell correlations would be systematic in this case.

For example, it might be expected that individual difference variables such as age, tenure, and experience might vary validly both between and within work groups, since these variables concern individual difference independent of work group membership. Since the 107 individuals in this study indicated their age, tenure, and experience in terms of years, the correlations between these variables are shown in the lower portion of Table 9. As shown in the table, the average of the between cell correlations is .87 ($p < .01$) and the average of the within cell correlations is .91 ($p < .01$). Therefore, both the between and within cell correlations are systematic, and applying equations 1 or 2 reveal no significant difference between them.

The Double Fallacy

For the purpose of illustration, assume that we preferred to interpret the correlation of these demographic variables employing what we might call the "Double Fallacy." The first component of the double fallacy assumes that the ALS model predicts only systematic between cell correlations and predicts nothing about within cell correlations. In this case, 75 percent ($[.87]^2$) of the common variance between the demographic variables would be attributed to the ALS model. The second component of the fallacy involves assuming the VDL model makes predictions only about the within cell correlations and predicts nothing about the between cell correlations. In this case, 82 percent ($[.91]^2$) of the common variance between the demographic variables would be attributed to the VDL model. As a result of the double fallacy, one would have to assert that the ALS model accounts for 75 percent of the common variance between the variables and that the VDL model accounts for 82 percent. This results in the erroneous assertion that 157 percent of the variance between the variables is accounted for by both the ALS and VDL models! While it is empirically the case that both between and within cell correlations are systematic, such a set of results cannot be interpreted as offering support for either the ALS or VDL model. We label this the "special null condition."

Specifically, if the ALS model predicts near zero within cell correlations and, therefore, when zero is squared and added to the squared between cell correlations, the maximum amount of common variance which can be explained is 100 percent. Likewise, if the VDL model predicts near zero between cell correlations and, therefore, when zero is squared and added to the squared within cell correlations, the maximum amount of common variance which can be employed is 100 percent. By contrast, in the special null condition, the partitioning of scores into within and between cell scores is in error because the same effect is represented in two different ways. Therefore, the special null condition is a rejection of the validity of the way in which the cells are constructed (based upon work groups).

This special null condition is theoretically important because it allows for the possibility that levels of analysis other than work groups may best explain a set of findings. Moreover, there are theoretical positions which specify that "real" work groups may have no effect upon reports of leadership (Rush, Thomas, & Lord, 1977). From an empirical perspective, the proponents of "implicit theories" of leadership (Eden & Leviatan, 1975) have shown that systematic correlations can be obtained when there are no "real" superiors or "real" work groups. The special null condition allows for this possibility while at the same time, the procedure presented in this chapter also allows for effects based upon "real" superiors and work groups. Therefore, the special null condition can be viewed as one condition which is just as likely to occur as the ALS, VDL, and traditional null conditions. Like the traditional null condition, it also provides important feedback about the ALS and VDL models' applicability to a given data set.

The General WABA Model

It follows from this that the model which we have employed here actually involves the specification of the following four conditions: 1) ALS, 2) VDL, 3) special null, and 4) traditional null conditions. The rows presented in Table 10 summarize these four theoretical conditions. Essentially, logic dictates that if within cell scores and between cell scores may each be systematic or near zero that four conditions must be permitted. In other words, four conditions are theoretically plausible.

In attempting to understand the general nature of these four conditions, it may be helpful to recall that in the ALS model, inferences are to whole superiors and whole work groups. As a result, the first condition shown in Table 10 (systematic between cell effects and near zero within cell

TABLE 10
The General WABA Model

Theoretical Conditions	Empirical Conditions[a] Between	Within	ALS Variables	VLD Variables	Special Null Variables	Multiple Tests
Average Leadership Model (wholes)	S	0	More likely[b]	Reject	Reject	Reject
Vertical Dyadic Linkage (parts)	0	S	Reject	More likely	Reject	Reject
Special Null	S	S	Reject	Reject	More likely	Reject
Traditional Null	0	0	Reject	Reject	Reject	More likely
Illustrative Results from Table 9			Upper Portion	Middle Portion	Lower Portion	—[c]

[a] S indicates a systematic effect; 0 indicates a near zero effect.

[b] "More likely" is meant here in terms of not rejecting the particular theoretical condition (under classical statistical testing, hypotheses can never be "accepted").

[c] Not shown in Table 9, due to space constraints.

effects) in a more general sense can be interpreted as pertaining to whole or intact entities. In terms of the second condition, it is helpful to recall that in the VDL model inferences are always to superiors who differentiated between individual's inside work groups. In a more general sense, this second condition can be interpreted as pertaining to parts within a particular entity. Finally, in a more general sense, the special null condition can be viewed as indicating the rejection of the hypothesis that the wholes or parts underlie the results. In this special null case, some lower level unit of analysis may best explain a set of findings. Essentially, this special null condition allows for the possibility of other levels of analysis both theoretically and empirically. Therefore, the formulation allows for systematic effects which are not interpreted as compatible with an ALS or VDL inference and can only be assumed to be supportive of neither model.

Note that WABA is applicable when both the ALS and VDL models are of interest, and also when only one model (ALS or VDL) is of interest. Essentially, the four conditions shown in Table 10 can be viewed as equally and mutually exclusive explanations before beginning an empirical study. As a result, in studies where the focus is upon only one model (as in the illustrative results), inference toward the model of interest (e.g., VDL) can be based upon rejection of the other three conditions, since they are equally likely in a multiple hypothesis testing sense (Dunnette, 1966; House & MacKenzie, 1976; Platt, 1964) and can be tested simultaneously.

Illustration of the WABA Model

Although we have considered how to move from theory to method to data and then back to theory, it is quite appropriate to ask whether WABA as a multiple hypothesis testing technique model really allows for data to correct spurious hypotheses that researchers might prefer before data are collected or analyzed. The illustrative results help to demonstrate this characteristic of WABA. Table 10 provides a summary of the structure of the within and between data analysis which was presented in Table 9. The last four columns in Table 10 contain the four sets of relationships of interest. The cells in the table each represent one hypothesis which specifies both the variables and unit of analysis involved in each condition. In Table 10, there are 16 cells and therefore, 16 equally likely hypotheses. In the table, 4 of the 16 hypotheses which were inferred to be more likely are indicated by the term "more likely," based upon the correlational values of Table 9 (see footnotes b and c to Table 10).

In fact, when the study of the 107 managers began, we were committed to the VDL model. We initially conceptualized all the measures as part of the VDL model, and the skill index was viewed as a confounding effect. In fact, all of the results could have fallen in the row labeled VDL (or in any combination of the rows). As the empirical analysis progressed, it became clear that the VDL model was not a more likely explanation of all the results, nor were the ALS, special null, or traditional null models. The VDL model seemed a more likely explanation for only some of the variables. Therefore, one key point is that some hypotheses appeared to constitute less likely explanations for certain relationships than did others. It is the systematic "disproof" of alternative explanations which strengthens an inference to one theory (Platt, 1964). In other words, support for the VDL model comes from the ability to reject the ALS, null, and special null conditions for a set of data. Despite the fact that this procedure pits one theory against another, the results tended to "support" both the ALS and VDL models of leadership, but for different dimensions.

However, raw score correlations do not allow for a choice between the ALS and VDL model based upon data. For example, based upon only raw score correlations, we could have asserted that all correlations between the ALS measures represented differences within work groups, and were compatible with our initial VDL preferences. Employing only raw scores there would have been no way to discover that the within work groups correlations on the ALS measures were near zero (Table 9). If in this study we had relied upon only raw score correlations, a choice between the VDL or ALS models would have been based upon the paradigm to which we were committed, rather than that which best suited our data. This is particularly interesting in light of Schriesheim's (1979) statement that 75 percent of all studies in leadership employ raw score correlations. Of course, it would also have been possible to compare raw score correlations with between cell scores as has been done in some studies. However, these two correlations are not independent and, therefore, their difference cannot be empirically tested; within and between cell correlations are independent, and their difference can be empirically tested. Note that WABA allows for a more direct link between theory and data, particularly when compared to raw score correlations. Therefore, WABA appears to have the correcting capabilities often described in general discussions of multiple hypothesis testing (Dunnette, 1966; House & MacKenzie, 1976).

Applications of the WABA Model

It is important to note that although the development of WABA has focused upon the linkage between data and theory, the real impact for leadership lies in the conceptual and applications area. In terms of theory building, WABA forces a number of critical actions.

Single and Multiple Theories

First, the approach results in increased salience for level of analysis and entity issues. That is, anyone interested in leadership research should begin by positing the entity (e.g., individual or group) assumed to be of theoretical importance and then specifying whether the process involved manifests itself across or within the chosen entity. This emphasis will assist in avoiding confusion that tends to typify leadership research in which entities are ignored or improperly specified (see, for example, Dansereau & Dumas, 1977). Only in this manner can the field systematically develop the conceptual foundations upon which critical research can be conducted.

Moreover, a focus on entities does not appear to constrain theoretical formulations. In addition to the pure ALS and VDL conditions, it is also possible to view superiors as treating subordinates equally (ALS superiors) and subordinates reacting differentially (VDL subordinates). This traditional mixed model has been suggested by Graen and Cashman (1975) and Dansereau and Dumas (1977) as underlying House's Path Goal model. However, logic dictates that an alternative mixed model is equally likely, and that superiors differentiate between subordinates (VDL superiors) but subordinates respond in a similar fashion (ALS subordinates). This latter model, although equally likely as far as we can determine, has received little theoretical or empirical consideration. Therefore, the focus on entities appears not only to systematize contemporary theories, but also allows the development of new theoretical formulations. Moreover, the focus upon entities does not appear to preclude focusing upon non-VDL processes which occur within individuals rather than between individuals (e.g., the Vroom & Yetton [1973] model of decision making within individuals). Rather, WABA is one way for specifying an entity of interest for empirical examination, whether pure ALS, VDL, or mixed models are involved.

Second, the focus of WABA on multiple entities forces consideration of multiple leadership theories, even if one is interested in only one leadership theory. One particularly interesting consequence of this approach is that if a set of effects over a series of studies can be shown to involve ALS effects (rather than VDL effects), this could be quite useful for someone interested in VDL theories. For example, different types of superiors (ALS) may be more or less likely to discriminate (VDL) between subordinates. In this case, the VDL and ALS models can be viewed as interacting in a statistical sense. Moreover, from a WABA perspective, each study (regardless of whether the ALS or VDL model appears more likely) contributes to an overall picture of the type of variables which may fall into the domain of each model. Even, in the case where only one model is of interest, if WABA is employed a VDL inference could only be based upon rejecting an ALS inference for that study, thereby increasing the unique contribution of one study to knowledge and facilitating the interpretation of a series of studies.

Based on this perspective, WABA provides an opportunity to apply a set of statistical procedures designed to accomplish the aims of a social scientist. Traditional techniques, with reliance on raw score and sampling statistics, do not allow for a social scientist to focus on the critical issue of aligning analytical techniques with key theoretical assumptions. The ability of WABA to dictate appropriate statistical linkages between theory and data should result in a more systematic development of leadership theory.

Contingency Theories and Theoretical Constructs

Third, given the fact that WABA involves the specification of theoretically based conditions, it should force attention toward identifying the contingencies under which these conditions may arise. The need to focus upon the contingencies under which various effects are obtained has been established in leadership research, at least partially because of Fiedler's (1967) efforts. The identification of the contingencies which moderate the emergence of ALS and VDL effects will require a substantial effort. Specifically, even in examining contingencies it may be useful to specify the entity to which a particular contingency variable refers (e.g., whole individuals, processes inside individuals, individuals in groups, whole groups, etc.) and to then employ WABA to examine these contingencies while also testing for effects within contingencies.

Fourth, it should be apparent that WABA encourages the development of measures designed to operate at given levels of analysis. Thus, if one develops a theory of leadership suggesting that control over behavior is based upon a group level construct, then the collection and analysis of data is designed to test whether the measure refers to this unit of analysis rather than simply assuming it. Moreover, WABA can lead to the development of rather intricate laboratory studies and simulations, since as a field method it provides information about which sources of variation in specific variables appear to be error and, therefore, suggests sources of variation to be controlled in a laboratory study.

Theory and Data

Finally, in a conceptual sense, WABA provides a self-correcting process for theory development. As a research strategy it is designed to guard against unconscious errors in conceptualizations and data generations. Thus, using WABA, even if one assumes leadership processes involve groups or individuals in groups, the technique forces examination of alternative explanations. Similarly, if one believes measures have been developed which represent only group or individual level phenomena, the technique forces a review of this assumption. In essense, WABA can serve as a means of offsetting the conscious and unconscious biases introduced into theory construction from researcher value systems.

Implications for Applications

One of the problems inherent in the field of leadership research has been the dominance of two diametrically opposed theoretical schools that have had little credibility with those who exercise leadership. It is apparent to most individuals, whether first line superiors, CEOs, elected officials, or military personnel, that the ALS approach is inadequate. All leaders cannot nor should treat all subordinates the same way, even though ALS based questionnaires force such a judgement. The variance that emerges may be either accidental or by design, but real leaders seem to argue that absolute consistency across individuals within groups on all issues, a key assumption of ALS followers, is unrealistic. Similarly, leadership practitioners do not find the VDL model of multiple unique individual relationships to be a generally acceptable description of real life. Such an approach used in all situations can create the perception of inequity among groups members and can be terribly costly of a superior's time and energy. Instead, leaders note that there must be some core of consistency if a superior is to be successful.

Interestingly, up to now, there have been few, if any, methods of examining and developing a hybrid or multiplexed leadership paradigm that may capture the descriptions of leaders when they are not constrained by questionnaires and methodologies designed to force dyadic (within group) or average (across group) responses and inferences. In this chapter we have shown that it may now be possible to identify the context and content of leadership necessary to develop theories that may better capture, and perhaps even clarify, the processes which may underlie the more complex situations frequently described by leaders. Using our simple distinction between leadership and supervision, for example, it may now become possible to identify either two different (though related) sets of behavior or different components of "single" behaviors. We should be able to determine the conditions under which certain differentiated behaviors toward subordinates will occur and yield greatest benefit to a group, leader, or subordinate, just as it should now be possible to identify the types of behaviors and conditions where consistency across group members occurs and is most effective. With WABA these "tests" can be the result of inductive or deductive reasoning processes, but the outcomes would provide a more complete meaning to the concepts of leadership and its effectiveness.

Related to this issue is the question of how can leaders be developed if multiplexed modes of interaction are most effective. It might well be that the interaction approach described previously would be helpful in this area. For example, individuals (ALS) most capable of effective supervision (e.g., of structuring tasks in a similar fashion across members) may find it very difficult to engage simultaneously in effective differential (VDL) leadership behaviors (e.g., individualized negotiations over nontask issues). It may also become evident that in certain situations multiplexed behavior is not effective.

Regardless of these issues, the question remains of how to select and train appropriate leaders. Should we select and/or train based on personality-oriented dimensions (ALS) or based upon the ability to develop specific subordinates into a group, or should we attempt to select and train multiphasic leaders? Even more interesting, is it possible that we can identify "total leadership needs" from a work unit and once having done so, come to the realization that under certain conditions more than one person may fulfill these needs. This model allows for the traditional situation in which a superior teams with an informal leader to provide a set of leadership needs (e.g., differentiated socioemotional and common task) to a group.

If all of this appears to be a resurfacing of old issues, that is probably because it is partially true. What is different is that 1) we now have a means (WABA) of systematically addressing these issues, 2) we now have some scholarly evidence that multiplexed leadership behavior exists, and 3) previous techniques and theories, while insightfully stimulating research, have not provided clear answers to some very basic questions. Nevertheless, in terms of leadership research, it is now possible to address issues of both practical and conceptual significance and to do so with a clear understanding of the limitations of knowledge about content and contingencies.

7

A Theory of Leadership Categorization

ROBERT G. LORD, ROSEANNE J. FOTI, and JAMES S. PHILLIPS

The topic of implicit leadership theories has generated a substantial number of studies in recent years. Most of this research has focused on the effects produced by implicit theories such as their relation to the factor structure of leadership measures (Eden & Leviatan, 1975; Rush, Thomas, & Lord, 1977) or their potential to alter mean responses on behavioral rating scales as a function of contextual information (Lord, Binning, Rush, & Thomas, 1978; Mitchell, Larson, & Green, 1977; Rush, Phillips, & Lord, 1980; Rush et al., 1977). Since relatively little attention has been given to the cognitive structures which may underlie such effects, the present chapter proposes a model of the cognitive structure which we feel to be underlying implicit leadership theories (and leadership perceptions in general). This model generalizes recent work on the cognitive structures inherent to object categorization (Rosch, 1978; Rosch & Mervis, 1975) and person perception (Cantor & Mischel, 1979) to the leadership area. The central premise upon which our model is based is that perceiving someone as a leader involves a relatively simple categorization (leader/nonleader or leader/follower) of the stimulus person into already existing categories. It is the structure of these existing categories and their role in processing information relative to the stimulus person (or to leadership in general) which we will attempt to articulate.

This chapter is divided into three sections. First, we will briefly review recent cognitive literature on categorization, focusing on the principles developed and the trends that have received empirical support. Second, we will use these principles to develop a structural model of leadership cognitions and will present some preliminary data illustrating the potential of this approach. Finally, we will discuss the broader implications of this model for several areas of concern to leadership researchers and managers.

Before describing Rosch's theory of categorization, it is necessary to address one preliminary issue, namely, whether it makes sense to conceptualize leadership perception in terms of a categorization process based on research using common objects. Several areas of research are pertinent to this issue. First, the importance to the leadership area of relatively simple, categorical distinctions is illustrated by early leadership research, much of which focused on discovering traits or behaviors that could be used to distinguish leaders from followers (Carter, Haythorn, Shriver, & Lanzetta, 1951; Kirscht, Lodahl, & Haire, 1959; Mann, 1959). Second, social psychologists concerned with categorization have convincingly argued that the underlying processes are quite general. Taylor, Fiske, Etcoff, and Ruderman (1978) maintain that the cognitive processes (but not content) responsible for sexual and racial stereotypes are similar to processes underlying other categories of objects. They note that stereotypes are merely attributes tagged to category labels that help us organize information about people. Cantor and Mischel (1979) have recently reported an extensive analysis of the internal structure of person categories that revealed striking similarity to the internal structure of the object categories investigated by Rosch and her associates (Rosch, 1975; 1978; Rosch & Mervis, 1975; Rosch, Mervis, Gray, Johnson, & Boyes-Braem, 1976). Finally, research by Fiske and Cox (1979) provides a rationale for explaining why categorization along a leader/nonleader dimension is important to perceivers. They argue that categories pertaining to social relationships are logical cues for accessing person related information since they establish the function of the stimulus person for the perceiver. The importance of functional differentiation associated with leader/follower distinctions has been widely recognized (Bales & Slater, 1955; Bennis & Shepard, 1956; Cartwright & Zander, 1968; Knickerbocker, 1948; Lord, 1977). Thus, Fiske and Cox's premise implies that categorization into leader/nonleader types would provide cues to the perceiver that would help access information about the functions that a stimulus person is likely to fulfill. This interpretation is also consistent with recent work by Miller (1978) that stresses the importance of functional information in object categorization.

In short, this research suggests that people, like objects, are categorized into meaningful, preexisting categories. It also provides a rationale for understanding why categorization along a leader/follower dimension is particularly useful to perceivers, i.e., it helps to assimilate functional information with attributes of the stimulus person.

Categorization Theory

According to recent work in the area of categorization by Rosch and her associates, the world consists of an infinite number of different and discriminable stimuli. One of the most basic tasks of all organisms is to segment the environment into classifications by which non-identical stimuli can be treated as equivalent. A category, defined as a number of objects which are considered equivalent (Rosch et al., 1976), is such a classification. Categorization reduces the complexity of the external world, permits symbolic representation of the world in terms of the labels given to categories, and provides a system of shared names (category labels) by which people can communicate information about categorized entities (Cantor & Mischel, 1979).

Rosch (1978) maintains that categories are organized so as to preserve as much information with as little effort as possible, a principle she labels *cognitive economy*. She also maintains that certain attributes of real-world objects are expected to occur together. For example, creatures with feathers are seen as being more likely to have wings than are creatures with fur. She labels this principle *perceived world structure*.

Rosch uses two additional principles to describe the internal structure of categories. According to Rosch (1978), a category system is structured along both vertical and horizontal dimensions. The *vertical dimension* is structured hierarchically and concerns the degree of inclusiveness, defined as the number of different *kinds* of objects that can be classified into the same category. The broadest and most inclusive level in the system is the superordinate level of categorization; below it is the basic level of categorization, and below it the subordinate level which is least inclusive. For example, if furniture is classified as a superordinate category, table would be a basic level category, and kitchen table would be a subordinate category.

The *horizontal dimension* differentiates categories at the same vertical level of inclusiveness. Thus, it is the dimension along which different superordinate, different basic, or different subordinate categories vary. For example, it is the dimension along which the superordinate categories of vehicle and furniture vary, the basic categories of chair and table vary, or the subordinate categories of kitchen table and living room table vary.

Members of the same superordinate (or basic) level category do not all possess a single set of identical attributes, but vary according to a family resemblance structure. *Family resemblance* describes a pattern of overlapping similarities between category members along the same horizontal dimension in which each horizontal category member has several attributes in common with one or more members, but few attributes are common to *all* category members.

Rosch (1978), further notes two implications that are related to the internal structure of categories. First, not all of the hierarchical levels are equally useful; only the basic level of categorization accurately mirrors the structure of attributes. That is, basic level categories are formed around natural discontinuities in physical and functional characteristics. The second implication is that category distinctiveness is increased by defining categories in terms of their most prototypical attributes. Rosch (1975) uses the term *prototype* to describe an abstract representation of the clearest examples of category membership. Prototypicality has been found to be related to the degree of family resemblance structure among categories (Rosch & Mervis, 1975), that is, the attributes judged to be highly prototypical of a category's members tended to be the same attributes found to be similar across the horizontal dimensions of that category.

The term *cue validity* identifies a final concept developed by Rosch. Cue validity is a probabilistic concept focusing on the ability of an attribute (cue) to discriminate among categories. The validity of a cue as a predictor of a given category increases with the frequency that the cue is associated with this category and decreases with the frequency that the cue is associated with other categories (Reed, 1972). The cue validity of an entire category may be defined as the average of the cue validities for all attributes of that category. A category with high cue validity, therefore, is more differentiated and distinctive from other categories than is a category with low cue validity.

The results of several experiments (Rosch 1975; Rosch & Mervis, 1975) have shown that basic categories have the highest cue validity. That is, they have many attributes common to all or most of the members of each particular category, but few attributes common with contrasting categories. Superordinate categories, whose members share fewer attributes, have lower cue validities than basic-level categories. Members of subordinate categories, although having many attributes in common, also share many of these attributes with members of different subordinate categories; therefore, subordinate categories also have lower cue validities than do basic level categories.

In summary, Rosch and her associates have developed a theory of categorization which describes the internal structure of categories (vertical and horizontal structure), explains how category members are related (family resemblance), suggests how stimuli are categorized (according to their prototypicality), explains how categorization facilitates processing information about category members (cognitive economy), and shows how categorization could provide a basis for inferences based on limited knowledge of a member's attributes (perceived world structure). The basic constructs used by Rosch are summarized in Table 11. In the following section we will use these principles to develop a model of leadership categorization.

TABLE 11
Basic Principles of Rosch's Categorization Theory

1. Cognitive Economy	Categories are organized so as to provide the most information with the least effort.
2. Perceived World Structure	Certain attributes of perceived objects are expected to occur together.
3. Vertical Dimension	Differentiates categories by degrees of inclusiveness (Superordinate, basic, subordinate).
4. Horizontal Dimension	Differentiates categories at the same vertical level of inclusiveness.
5. Prototype	Abstract representations of common attributes of category members; increase distinctiveness of categories.
6. Family Resemblance	Degree of overlap among category members at the same vertical level.
7. Cue validity	Probability of accessing a particular category given a certain attribute.

Leadership Categorization

General Model. As previously discussed, we believe Rosch's categorization principles can be appropriately applied to the area of leadership. Such an application yields a model of leadership cognitions which are hierarchically structured and vary along both vertical and horizontal dimensions. More specifically, we are proposing that leadership categorization involves three different vertical levels (superordinate, basic, and subordinate) within which different types of horizontal distinctions are made. That is, whether people are classified as leaders or nonleaders is the horizontal distinction at the superordinate level of categorization; different types of leaders (i.e., political, military, religious, business, education, sports, business, labor, finance, media, and minority) are horizontally differentiated at the basic level; and abstract types (or person types) of leaders are differentiated along the horizontal dimension at the subordinate level. Each vertical level is described in greater detail below.

The superordinate category of leader is the most inclusive level in the classification system, and therefore, it appears at the top of the vertical structure. According to the principle of family resemblance there should be few attributes common to *all* leaders. In addition, the attributes best characterizing the superordinate category, namely the attributes common to most members, should overlap very little with those of the contrasting superordinate category of nonleaders.

This assertion stems from Rosch's theory, but to us it seems to reflect aptly conclusions based on extensive research in the leadership area.

Namely, within a particular empirical study (which is analogous to a basic level category in the general model) we can find sets of traits that effectively differentiate leaders from nonleaders; however, we have not been able to find a set of traits or behaviors that clearly differentiate leaders from nonleaders across a wide range of contexts (all of the basic level categories previously mentioned) (Mann, 1959; Stogdill, 1948). This result is explainable if the superordinate leadership category is tied together by the principle of family resemblance rather than by some "critical features" which must be possessed by all leaders.

In a family resemblance model, the boundary between leaders and nonleaders may sometimes be difficult to draw. Thus, leadership like other categories that are used to classify people, may be a "fuzzy category" (Cantor & Mischel, 1979) in that there are no critical signs that differentiate *all* members from *all* nonmembers. Rosch (1978) asserts that in cases where clear-cut boundaries in stimuli do not exist, one will abstract categorizations learned and transmitted through culture rather than derived entirely from stimulus characteristics. This view implies that, as Pfeffer (1978) has argued, leadership is a social construct. However, even though leadership may be a fuzzy category, the distinction between the clearest or best leadership examples (i.e., leadership prototypes) and nonleaders may still remain relatively clear.

The basic level categories are less inclusive and reflect the different types of leaders found in the world, that is, religious versus military. The basic level categories were chosen to reflect task or contextually related differences among leaders. These differences were suggested by a content analysis of how leadership is used in the popular press. Specifically, *Time*, *Newsweek*, and *U.S. News and World Report* were content analyzed to determine how the term leadership was used. In support of this classification, Miller (1978) states that contextually determined functional characteristics are a necessary part of any identification (categorization) system. When added to the physical aspects of entities, functional characteristics help reduce vagueness, insensitivity to context, and dependence on normative conditions. Thus, by including contextual and functional information, basic categories become more clearly differentiated from contrasting categories, more vivid, and richer in detail than superordinate categories. Thus, contextual information would play a key role in distinguishing leaders from nonleaders. It would also increase perceiver ability to describe or predict leadership behavior.

The subordinate categories are the least inclusive level in the vertical structure. In our model, the subordinate level is conceptualized as an abstract representation of each basic level category. For example, the subordinate categories for the basic category of national political leader may be conservative political leader and liberal political leader. At this level of categorization we are not sure of the exact nature of categories. Moreover, due to different degrees of experience with particular basic level leaders (i.e., political leaders) or due to individual differences in cognitive capacities, different people may represent this level differently. Two alternative methods of classification are plausible: abstract representations (i.e., liberal or conservative) or exemplar representations (i.e., Kennedy type or Reagan type). An example of the alternative exemplar classification could be related to position types (i.e., presidential type or senator type). Our current research is directed at resolving some of this ambiguity.

Regardless of which classification scheme is used, based on Rosch's work we would expect members of one subordinate category to be quite similar to members of other subordinate categories under the same basic level category. Thus the detail gained by using more specific categories at the subordinate level, thereby enabling a more vivid description of typical members, would be gained at the expense of reduced category distinctiveness.

Rosch's concepts of family resemblance and cue validity which pertain to the ability to make distinctions along a horizontal dimension, can also be illustrated by our model of leadership categorization. In the illustration presented below we have focused on the superordinate and basic levels since our model is more firmly articulated for these levels. However, the principles can be extended to incorporate basic level/subordinate level relations by substituting basic for superordinate level and subordinate level for basic level in the discussion below.

Mathematical representation. The constructs of family resemblance and cue validity can easily be represented mathematically. To illustrate, let i represent the difference among a set of superordinate categories (i.e., leader versus nonleader); let j represent the basic level distinctions within each of the i superordinate categories (i.e., religious versus military); let h index the possible attributes possessed by any stimulus so represented, i.e., element a_{ij} of set A; and let a_{hij} equal 1 if the stimulus a_{ij} possesses attribute h, and 0 otherwise. Then, the degree of family resemblance (and also prototypicality) of trait h depends on the extent to which it is shared by the j members of category i. The family resemblance (FR) of trait h in category i can be defined as

$$FR_{hi} = \sum_{j=1}^{n} a_{hij}/n \qquad (1)$$

or the proportion of examples in category i possessing trait h.

This definition of family resemblance can easily be integrated with Rosch's concept of cue validity (CV_{hi}) (Rosch & Mervis, 1975), the conditional probability of being in category i given trait h. According to Bayes's rule, this conditional probability, $p(i/h)$, equals the base rate probability of i *times* the probability of h given the occurance of i *divided* by the probability of h. That is,

$$p(i/h) = p(i) \times \frac{p(h/i)}{p(h)} \tag{2}$$

However, the probability of h given i is simply FR_{hi} as defined by Equation 1. Similarly, the probability of h is merely the average family resemblance score over all i categories, $\sum_{i=1}^{m} FR_{hi}/m$. Finally, recognizing that the base rate of category i in our example equals $1/m$, cue validity can be defined as follows:

$$CV_{hi} = 1/m \; \frac{\times \; FR_{hi}}{\sum_{i=1}^{m} FR_{hi}/m} \tag{3}$$

An important aspect of Equation 3 is that the diagnosticity of trait h for category i depends on whether the family resemblance of h in category i differs from its value over the entire population, that is, whether the rightmost component of Equation 3 differs from 1 (McCauley, Stitt, & Segal, 1980). For example, decisiveness would have diagnostic value for determining leadership if leaders are more likely to be decisive than are people in general. While this conclusion may be sensible from both a perceptual and a functional point of view, applications of the same perceptual principle to other characteristics may not. Being female is less common among leaders than in the general population, thus it serves as a useful cue for making leader/nonleader distinctions from a perceptual perspective, yet there may be no functional or logical basis for excluding women from leadership positions.

Person perception. A crucial question concerning the application of these ideas to understanding person perception becomes, how do perceivers classify stimulus people into categories. Three different approaches—the classical view, the exemplar view, and the prototype view—have been taken to answer this question (Cantor & Mischel, 1979). The classical position suggests that the perceiver checks a short list of necessary and sufficient conditions for category membership to decide whether the stimulus fits into a category. The stimulus is accepted as a category member only if it possesses all the critical features. As noted earlier, this conception does not fit the fuzzy nature of person categories. A more appropriate approach is the exemplar view of categorization. According to this view, new instances (stimuli) are classified as category members on the basis of their similarity to the most salient known instance of the category. Thus, a film director might classify leading men in terms of box-office appeal by comparing them to Robert Redford. The remaining approach to categorization is the prototype view (Rosch, 1975). Rosch has proposed that categorical judgments are made on the basis of the similarity of a stimulus to a prototype, or abstration, of the category in question. This position is similar to the exemplar view in that a stimulus would be classified as a category member on the basis of the degree to which it possesses characteristics common to that category. However, it differs from the exemplar view by postulating that new stimuli are classified by comparison to an abstraction rather than a concrete example of a category.

In the prototype view, categories at the same vertical level in the hierarchical structure are considered to be essentially continuous, that is, without clear-cut boundaries. Distinctiveness of categories is achieved by conceiving of each category in terms of an abstraction of the most common attributes of category members. Clarity in judgments of category membership accrues from comparison to this prototype. That subjects can make such judgments has been demonstrated in several studies. In the object domain Rosch had found that subjects would reliably rate the extent to which an object fits their idea or image of a particular category (Rosch, 1975; Rosch & Mervis, 1975). Similarly, in the person perception field, Cantor and Mischel (1979) found that naïve judges could reliably rate the prototypicality of person descriptions which were either good, moderately good, or poor examples of extroverts.

Applied to leadership, the prototypic model implies that categorization involves the comparison of a stimulus person to a leadership prototype. If subjects are categorizing leadership in a general sense, the prototype would be of the superordinate category (i.e., an abstraction of common attributes of basic level categories). If subjects are categorizing stimuli into basic level categories, that is, business leaders, the basic level prototype would be an abstraction of attributes common to subordinate level categories of business leaders. It should be noted that such a process could easily result in a leadership rating or a general leadership impression, if subjects judged how similar the stimulus person was to the relevant leadership prototype. That is, if they use a multidimensional (multiattribute) proximity judgment to gauge the similarity of a stimulus to a prototype, they could use this same judgment to produce leadership ratings rather than a categorical judgment.

Our pilot work with leadership judgments has demonstrated that subjects can easily generate traits and behaviors which fit their prototype (ideal) of a leader or a high performing leader. They have more trouble generating characteristics of nonleaders or poor performing leaders; they generate fewer and less universal traits or behaviors. We have also found that subjects can easily rate the extent to which a given trait or behavior (such as those reflected on the LBDQ; Stogdill, 1963) fits their prototype or image of a leader. Thus, subjects seem to be capable of performing the judgments that we postulate to underly leadership perceptions.

Prototypes and implicit leadership theories. Interestingly, Cantor and Mischel (1979) hypothesize that central category attributes become the focus of attention in prototypicality judgments made on the basis of scant information. As previously mentioned, the precise structure of implicit leadership theories (ILT) is not well known, but it has been shown that under conditions of limited information (Eden & Leviatan, 1975; Rush et al., 1977) subjects can produce ratings of leadership which are virtually identical to those derived from ratings of real leaders. One explanation for this result, which is consistent with Cantor and Mischel's assertion, is that under limited information conditions subjects use their leadership prototypes to generate behavioral ratings. Furthermore, since prototypical traits or behaviors are more readily available than nonprototypical traits or behaviors, they would be judged to occur more frequently if subjects based frequency judgments on heuristics such as availability (Tversky & Kahneman, 1973). That such ratings parallel those of real leaders may simply reflect the fact that subjects encode information about real people by similar processes. That is, they use stimulus information to map the person into already existing categories. In the process much of the information about the person is assimilated with information about the category with which he has become associated.

This explanation suggests that prototypes would be central components of implicit leadership theories. In their simplest form ILT may simply be information organized around prototypes appropriate to superordinate, basic, or subordinate level leadership categories. Classification along the superordinate leader/nonleader dimension may involve judgments based on traits, behaviors, or performance information about the stimulus person. Further information specifying the task type or context would allow classification of the stimulus person into basic level categories such as political, military, or religious leaders. As we have already noted, basic level categories are richer in information and are more distinctive than are categories at other vertical levels. Thus, with limited amounts of stimulus and contextual information, one could classify stimuli into already existing categories that are fairly rich in detail, allow judgments of the likelihood of a particular behavior, and specify the functional relations of the stimuli to the perceiver. Interestingly, Calder's (1977) discussion of implicit leadership theories, though emphasizing an attributional perspective, is consistent with this model. For example, Calder notes that naïve conceptualizations of leadership are "fuzzy" and involve assigning the label of leader to people based on their behavior and its effects.

Two preliminary studies nicely illustrate the importance of leadership labels and the central role of prototypes in explaining the effects of implicit leadership theories. The first is a further analysis of results reported by Rush, Phillips, and Lord (1980). Rush et al. investigated both global leadership and LBDQ ratings using a three-factor design in which they manipulated 1) the amount of leadership behavior by showing subjects either of two 15-minute video tapes (high/low leader structure), 2) bogus performance feedback supplied to subjects prior to making ratings (good, no information, bad feedback), and 3) the length of time between viewing the videotape and making ratings (immediate ratings, 48-hour delay). They found that both stimulus behavior and performance feedback significantly affected both LBDQ and more global leadership ratings, with the effects of stimulus behavior being relatively constant over time while the effects of performance cues increased in the delayed as compared to the immediate rating condition. More importantly in *both* the immediate and delayed rating conditions almost all of the variance in subjects' LBDQ ratings could be explained by controlling for the simplified general leadership impression (a one-item measure of amount of leadership exhibited).

Rush et al. explained their findings by suggesting that subjects encoded both stimulus and contextual information using already existing categorical labels that connoted degree of leadership. According to the theory laid out in the present chapter, such a process would be based on a comparison of stimulus information to prototypes of the leader category. Further, when making LBDQ ratings subjects need not directly recall stimulus behavior. Instead, they need only recall a label (previous categorization of the leader), relying on the previously learned category prototype to "fill in" likely behaviors. In short, as Rosch (1978) maintains, categorization could provide a cognitively economical, yet fairly accurate, way of assimilating information.

To see whether such a process was capable of explaining the distortion in LBDQ ratings induced by bogus performance feedback, we had 56 undergraduate students rate the extent to which each LBDQ item characterized a good (or bad) leader. We then averaged these ratings over subjects to get one prototypicality score for each item for good leaders and another score for bad leaders. Finally, within each of the stimulus behavior and temporal delay conditions of the Rush et al. study (high structure tape-immediate rating, high structure tape-delayed rating, low structure tape-immediate rating, low structure tape-delayed rating), we correlated these prototypicality ratings with a measure of the size of the performance induced distortion for each item (item means under good performance feedback minus means under bad performance feedback). All of the resulting correlations were highly significant ($p < .001$) and were in the predicted direction. They ranged from .68 to .74 for prototypicality scores for good leaders and from −.66 to −.72 for prototypicality scores for bad leaders. Thus, LBDQ items which closely matched leader prototypes were distorted more by the bogus performance feedback. These results are consistent with the suggested assimilative role of prototypes; however, by themselves, these results do not prove that this heuristic process was actually used by subjects.

Although one should not overinterpret results based on a single study, these results have interesting potential implications for measuring leader behaviors. They imply that items of low prototypicality, items less closely related to common conceptualizations of leadership, would be less affected by contextual biases. Hence, in a purely descriptive sense, such items may be more accurate than more prototypical items. However, low prototypicality items may yield measurement scales with lower internal consistency, and they may be "forgotten" more quickly than more prototypical items.

The ability of prototypes to "explain" leadership ratings was further explored using perceptions of U.S. political leaders, that is, President Carter, Gerald Ford, and Edward Kennedy. That is, we investigated the ability of a prototype at the basic level, national political leader, to explain which of a series of traits would covary with leadership. To do this we utilized existing data from the Gallup Poll's "phrase portrait" and, in addition, obtained prototypicality ratings of these same phrases from a student sample.

The Gallup Poll was designed to assess how a national sample would describe current political leaders. It consists of a series of phrases that list 17 traits and behaviors in both positive and negative terms, a total of 34 items. Respondents were shown the phrases as pairs of opposites and were asked to choose which phrase they felt best described the political leader in question. Some examples of the phrase pairs appearing on the survey are: bright/not too bright; decisive, sure of himself/uncertain, indecisive, unsure; has strong leadership qualities/lacks strong leadership qualities. Results are given as the percentage of total respondents selecting each of the 34 items.

The Gallup Poll data yielded three kinds of information: longitudinal (change) scores, cross-sectional scores, and difference scores. Longitudinal data were available as a result of the poll being conducted four times within the time period 1977–79. Therefore, it was possible to determine change over time in President Carter's percentage rating for each item. Cross-sectional data were available as a result of obtaining the original data for some of the Gallup surveys and calculating the relationship between the item measuring leadership qualities and the remaining phrases across respondents. Difference scores were available as a result of the survey's being conducted for two different political leaders at the same time. Therefore, it was possible to determine the difference in the percentage rating for each item for each leader (i.e., Carter versus Kennedy).

Prototypicality ratings of these phrases were generated by a sample of 47 students. Specifically, for each item, subjects were asked to, "determine how well it fits your image of an ideal effective (ineffective) political leader." Each item was rated on a seven-point scale. These ratings were then averaged across subjects to provide average prototypicality ratings for each phrase. Finally, these average ratings were correlated with the longitudinal, cross-sectional, and difference scores from the Gallup Poll.

Results showed that regardless of whether one looks at longitudinal change scores, cross-sectional data, or difference scores, only those traits prototypical of national political leaders covaried with leadership ratings. That is, those items with the highest prototypicality ratings changed most when Carter's leadership rating changed, were most highly correlated with the leadership item of the Gallup Poll in the cross-sectional analysis, and exhibited the greatest discrepancy rating between national political leaders whose leadership rating differed (r's ranged from .30 to .87; Foti, Fraser, & Lord, 1980).

Results from both studies indicate that the concept of prototypicality has substantial predictive value in understanding what information is closely tied to the construct of leadership. Both behavioral information from brief exposures to videotapes of leaders and more trait related information concerning salient real leaders seems to be organized around leadership prototypes. In addition, prototypicality seems to be important for both the superordinate category of leader and at least one basic level category, national political leader.

It should be noted that, while consistent with the theory described in this chapter, neither study proves that our theory is an accurate description of the information processes used by subjects since alternative processing models could also have produced the obtained results. We should also point out that the positive results of our initial studies concerning prototypicality do not indicate that other concepts derived from Rosch's categorization theory can be appropriately applied to leadership. Clearly, judgments concerning the utility to the leadership field of constructs such as vertical and horizontal structure, family resemblance, and cue validity must await results from further research.

Implications of Leadership Categorization Theory

Although the theory we have proposed has not yet been empirically tested, we thought its heuristic value could be clearly illustrated by discussing several possible implications for real-world managers and for leadership researchers. One potential applied implication concerns the effects of our hypothesized categorical structure on the selection of leaders. Although the general model involves both contextual (situational) and person-related information, categories at the same vertical level are related by the family resemblance principle, which may cause perceivers to overemphasize the similarity between basic level leaders while minimizing situational differences in the functions they fulfill. Thus, leadership may be viewed by most people as a dispositional factor which generalizes across situations. On the other hand, within a particular context minor differences between leaders and nonleaders may be accentuated by comparing nonleaders to prototypical rather than actual leaders (see the discussion of "fuzzy categories" earlier in this chapter, under *"Leadership Categorization"*). When filling vacant leader positions, the combined effect of these two types of perceptual distortions may produce a tendency to overlook a "nonleader" from within a particular basic level category (e.g., government) who may be thoroughly familiar with that context, and instead, seek leaders from other basic level categories (military, business, or education) who lack experience with the unique functional requirements of a particular context. Thus, segmenting the environment into leader/nonleader categories, which emphasize traitlike personal qualities while underemphasizing situational factors, may lead to erroneous selection decisions. For example, high level government positions (i.e., President) may be filled by business or military leaders who are unskilled at managing the division of power between the executive and legislative branches, while congressmen possessing these needed skills are overlooked because they are perceived to lack leadership ability.

Another potential implication of this theory of categorization concerns its effects on information processing associated with managers' performance appraisals or personnel decisions (promotion, raises, termination, etc.) involving subordinates. Consider, for example, a manager evaluating the amount of leadership ability of a subordinate. Through experience, the manager has probably developed a good idea of the "type" of leader that does well in a particular situation, namely, he will have abstracted common attributes of successful managers into subordinate level leadership prototypes. Moreover, he probably will have used this perceptual schema to categorize the subordinate of interest (as well as other subordinates) on many past occasions. Thus, he will be able to rate leadership ability by relying on prior leadership perceptions as well as on memory for specific, salient events. Interestingly, if the manager uses prior leadership perceptions to cue memory (Cantor & Mischel, 1977; Phillips & Lord, 1981), he will be able to "recall" many examples of the subordinate's behavior or traits that are consistent with the appropriate prototype, some of which will accurately "describe" the subordinate in question while others will not.

In short, leader/nonleader perceptions based on subordinate level categories may provide an efficient way to process information relevant to needed judgments in a given context. Though cognitively economical, this heuristic is not necessarily optimal. Since the leader prototype would be extracted from common characteristics of managers exhibiting leadership, it may include many characteristics irrelevant to performing required managerial functions. For example, modes of dress, cultural or social class background, race, or sex may frequently be included in prototypes if they distinguish leaders (successful managers) from nonleaders (see the earlier discussion of Equation 3). The "natural" tendency is to use such information to categorize subordinates.

This discussion implies that leadership prototypes which incorporate primarily male characteristics could be a source of sex related bias in many organizations. Rosen and Jerdee (1973, 1974a, 1974b) demonstrated the existence of sex-role biases in actual organizations' situations involving selection, placement, and effectiveness of supervisory behaviors. They found that 1) the rated effectiveness of certain supervisory behaviors varied as a function of the sex of the leader, and 2) managers were biased against equally qualified women in personnel decisions involving promotion and development. Schein (1973, 1975) found that successful middle managers are perceived by male *and* female middle managers to possess characteristics, attitudes, and temperaments (i.e., leadership ability, competitiveness, self-confidence, ambitions, and responsibility) more commonly ascribed to men than women. This result is easily understood if judgments concerning successful middle managers were based, in part, on comparisons to prototypes extracted from a predominantly male population.

In addition to providing a cognitively economical means of processing information, categorization may fulfill other functions. Assuming that the content of some categories (business leaders) is widely shared, it may also provide a standard for appropriate behavior. Carver (1979) has argued that recognitory schema (prototypes) often include "response-prototypes" that provide a behavioral standard appropriate for a given context. Such standards may provide a powerful, and fairly general, model for behavior. Moreover, since such behavior would match others' prototypes, it would probably be solidified through social reinforcement. Snyder (1979) has recently argued that individuals who are high self-monitors are particularly sensitive to an image or prototype appropriate to different situations. High self-monitors are highly attentive to the behavior of other individuals and, it has been argued, that this provides high self-monitors with an extensive and easily accessible knowledge base which can then be abstracted into the appropriate situational prototype. A recent study by Snyder and Cantor (1980) has shown that high self-monitors are particularly knowledgeable and skilled at matching other people's traits to situations. Moreover, high self-monitors alter their behavior from situation to situation in order to conform to different prototypes. Thus, Snyder and Cantor have argued that these individuals should be particularly eager to enter in and pursue those situations for which there is a clearly defined prototype.

Though using prototypes as a model for behavior has obvious heuristic value, it may also lead to unnecessary conformity or it may produce some acceptable but undesirable behaviors. Articulating commonly held prototypes for familiar leadership situations/contexts (i.e., the content of basic level leadership categories) might provide a useful starting point for understanding why leaders behave as they do. Furthermore, comparing prototype based prescriptions to behavioral prescriptions derived from more sophisticated theories of leadership (i.e., the substitutes for leadership theory of Kerr & Jermier, 1978) may offer a useful approach toward identifying the types of mistakes leaders are likely to make in a given situation.

In addition to explaining leadership behavior, leadership categorization may be relevant to social influence processes in organizations. Being perceived as a leader may allow one to exert more influence (Lord, 1977) and, thereby, more easily implement one's policies or programs. Unfortunately, and ironically, when performance deteriorates so do leadership ratings, thereby undermining the ability of existing leaders to implement remedial policies. This phenomena may be particularly troublesome for political leaders whose control over the government may depend, in part, on their perceived leadership ability. For example, when a President achieves low leadership ratings, one would expect a comparable decline in his influence in Congress. One way out of this dilemma may be for low performing real-world leaders to accentuate their characteristics that are closely associated with peoples' conceptualizations of leadership, thereby counteracting the natural tendency of people to adjust their perception of all the qualities of a leader based on performance induced shifts in leadership perceptions.

We should also briefly note some of the implications of this categorization theory for social scientists. First, if social information is assimilated into important categorical systems (i.e., leadership), then perceivers (common sources of social science data) may depend heavily on these schemas when "recalling" information. Thus, behavioral dimensions or traits which are prototypical of the same categories may be difficult for respondents to separate when describing others. Hence, we might expect "halo" to be a common error which may be inseparable from accuracy in rating others (Bernardin & Pence, 1980; Borman, 1979). In addition, there would be a strong tendency for *untrained* raters to provide behavioral information that is more consistent with the dimensions of naïve theories of leadership (Calder, 1977) than with the higher order scientific theories needed to explain a leader's performance.

On a more micro level, the same process may cause an item closely tied to an important category to "hang together," giving us measurement scales with nice psychometric properties (i.e., high internal consistency). Internally consistent scales may reflect an assimilative process in which people are first categorized then subsequently "described" on the basis of the relevant prototype, as well as behaviors which naturally co-occur and are *independently* (and accurately) stored and remembered. For the most part, both processes would be fairly accurate in "describing" typical leader or nonleader behavior. However, when applied to specific individuals or behaviors, assimilation through prototype may produce particularly troublesome results. That is, once someone is categorized (on the basis of behavior, physical traits, sexual or racial attributes, or performance) both prototypical behaviors which he/she has produced and those which have not occurred will be used to describe his/her behavior (Cantor & Mischel, 1977; Phillips & Lord, 1981).

A study by Phillips and Lord (1981) illustrates the difficulty people may have in differentiating between observed and unobserved behaviors that relate to the same prototype. They showed subjects a 12-minute videotape of a group problem solving session and asked subjects to complete a specially constructed questionnaire measuring recognition for leadership behavior. The questionnaire contained 10 behaviors characteristic of leadership prototypes, 10 behaviors characteristic of nonleader behaviors, and 10 behaviors that were not characteristic of either prototype. Further, only 5 behaviors from each class were actually on the tape observed by subjects. The results showed that subjects were quite accurate in distinguishing between observed and unobserved behaviors that were prototypically ambiguous, whereas they exhibited only marginal descriptive accuracy for prototypical leadership behavior and virtually no descriptive accuracy for prototypical nonleader behavior.

Finally, it should be noted that we are not maintaining that people do not remember information that is irrelevant to categorical schema. Clearly they do, especially if such information is highly salient or unusual. What we are saying is that information relevant to widely held categories is remembered more easily and with greater frequency. As Rosch (1978) maintains, categorization provides a cognitively efficient (though not always accurate) means of processing information. Thus, where categorical structures are shared by many people and are thought to be relevant in a wide range of contexts, as they apparently are for leadership, articulating their underlying structure and role in assimilating information may be a useful approach to understanding social information processing and social behavior. We hope that this chapter has contributed this objective.

8

Leadership Activation Theory: An Opponent Process Model of Subordinate Responses to Leadership Behavior

JOHN E. SHERIDAN, JEFFREY L. KERR, and
MICHAEL A. ABELSON

Leadership research has occupied a major role in behavioral science literature for over two decades with several thousand studies having been published on leadership effectiveness (Stogdill, 1974). Yet, even in the face of this prodigious body of literature, there has been a growing discussion of the inadequacy of this research to explain the underlying leadership phenomena (Schriesheim & Kerr, 1977; Sims, 1979). John P. Campbell argued that in view of the present state of leadership research, "it would be advantageous for the field if a much greater emphasis were given simply to defining, describing, and measuring leadership phenomena. We need much more discussion and argument about what we are trying to explain, not whether a particular theory has been supported or not supported" (1977a, p. 234).

This chapter proposes a basic reformulation of the leadership construct to include the intensity of specific leadership incidents in addition to the traditional focus on the frequency of different leadership activities. It is suggested that the analysis of leadership effects from the perspective of

This research was supported in part by a fellowship from the Corporate Associates Program of the College of Business Administration, The Pennsylvania State University.

The authors gratefully acknowledge the assistance of Bruce Drake and Ray Zammuto, Wayne State University, and Donald Vredenburgh, Baruch College, for their cooperation in the development of measurement instruments used in this research, Martha Phelps, Mack Truck Company, for her effort in conducting the field study, and John Slocum, Southern Methodist University, for his helpful comments on an earlier version of this chapter.

arousal and opponent process models of motivation will add significantly to the variance explained by the conventional wisdom which explains leadership influence in terms of reinforcement or expectancy theories of motivation.

Traditional Leadership Paradigm

Many of the published leadership studies have followed a phenomenological blueprint formulated by research at Ohio State University (Stogdill, 1963), and the University of Michigan (Bowers & Seashore, 1966). This research operationalized leadership as a measure of how often the supervisor demonstrated specific leadership behaviors (i.e., schedules the work to be done and sets definite standards of performance). Previous research designs typically have asked subordinates to describe the frequency of their supervisor's activities on descriptive rating scales. For example, the Ohio State LBDQ Form XII instrument used a five-point scale ranging from "Never" to "Always." Item scores were then combined to formulate cumulative factor scores on leadership dimensions such as: Consideration (CON) and Initiating Structure (IS).

There are two important assumptions underlying this operational definition of leadership. First, the assumption is made that each scale item represents a relatively uniform level of behavior intensity on a particular leadership dimension. Each item score is, therefore, weighed equally in determining a simple algebraic summation for the composite measure on each leadership dimension. For example, it is assumed that "scheduling the work to be done" represents the same level or intensity of Initiating Structure as "setting definite standards of performance." The total Initiating Structure score is then determined simply by adding the reported frequency that the leader schedules the work plus the frequency that the leader sets clear performance standards plus the frequency of other initiating structure activities.

This additivity postulate requires a second assumption that leadership represents a composite measure of different behaviors that have a compensatory interaction within a particular dimension. For example, in determining the leader's Initiating Structure score it is assumed that "Always scheduling the work to be done" (Score = 5) can compensate for "Never setting clear performance standards" (Score = 1), since the cumulative Initiating Structure (IS = 5 + 1) is numerically equivalent to the Initiating Structure derived by "Occasionally" (Score = 3) doing both activities.

The traditional leadership paradigm thus defines leadership behavior as a composite measure of different but related activities. An examination of these activity items would suggest that the measured behaviors are not unusual activities and represent behaviors that would likely be observed on a day-to-day basis in many leader-subordinate dyads. The skewed distribution of IS and CON item scores (Schriesheim & Kerr, 1974) would indicate that subordinates perceive most of these activities occurring in a range between "frequently" to "always."

The frequency that leaders exhibit activity on different leadership dimensions represents varying leadership styles. One leader's style may be to exhibit initiating structure activities more frequently than consideration activities; whereas another leader's style may be the opposite. A large segment of leadership research has focused on the problem of determining which styles of leadership activity are most effective in different work situations. Perhaps the most cogent explanation of why the frequency of leadership behavior is posited to affect the subordinates' performance and job attitudes is found in House's Path-Goal theory of leadership effectiveness (House, 1971; House & Mitchell, 1974).

House's model explains leadership effectiveness as an extension of the expectancy theory of motivation (Evans, 1974). This model suggests that the subordinate's satisfaction and work motivation is a function of his or her expectancy that work effort will result in higher performance levels and the expectancy that higher performance will lead to desired outcomes. The frequency of the leader's Initiating Structure activities is considered to enhance and reinforce the subordinate's subjective expectancy that individual effort will result in successfully completed work assignments. The frequency of supervisor Consideration behavior is viewed as a desired outcome reinforcing the subordinate's job performance. Sims (1977) demonstrated that the leadership influence is stronger when the frequency of the reinforcement behaviors are made contingent upon subordinate performance.

The strength and need for these leadership effects on subordinate's motivation will vary depending on the structure of the work task, the subordinate's psychological and skill attributes, the work group norms, and the organization environment (House & Mitchell, 1974). Consequently, the effectiveness of different leadership styles is posited to vary between different work situations. Empirical tests of leadership influence in different work situations, however, have provided inconclusive support for the path goal model (Schreisheim & Von Glinow, 1977).

Leadership Activation Paradigm

Arousal and opponent process theories of motivation provide a different perspective for analyzing leadership effects in supervisor-subordinate dyads. These theories would view each leadership behavior incident as a specific stimulus event that occurs at a given time with a known beginning and end of the leadership incident. The intensity of each stimulus event could vary as well as the frequency or time interval between events.

Both motivation theories attempt to explain an individual's manifest response to a particular stimulus event. Arousal theory (Berlyne, 1967; Duffy, 1962) posits that the individual's motivational response can be expressed as a parabolic function of stimulus intensity. At low levels of intensity, little manifest response to the stimulus is evident since the weak stimulus event provides low hedonic disturbance. As the stimulus intensity increases the individual's motivation is activated in response to the stronger hedonic disturbance. However, at extremely high intensity levels the individual's arousal level may be accompanied by feelings of increased tension resulting from the intense stimulus events. It is suggested that at these high levels of arousal an individual may psychologically withdraw from the stressful events and the motivational response to the stimulus will begin to decline.

The opponent process theory (Landy, 1978; Solomon & Corbit, 1974) provides a useful paradigm for analyzing the individual's manifest response as a function of both the intensity of a particular stimulus event and the frequency of events. As illustrated in Figure 3, the opponent process theory posits that a particular stimulus event can create a disturbance in the individual's hedonic state in either a satisfying or dissatisfying direction. When the intensity of the external stimulus exceeds the individual's threshold of hedonic equilibrium an opponent inhibitory process is triggered within the individual. The opponent process is opposite the primary stimulus arousal and tends to dampen the individual's manifest response to the stimulus event. The opponent process is thought to continue for some time after the end of the stimulus event and serves to return the individual to hedonic equilibrium. However, a continuing opponent process may "overshoot" the hedonic neutral point immediately after the termination of the stimulus event. Consequently, the individual's emotional state may fluctuate below the neutral point immediately after the end of the stimulus arousal. Solomon and Corbit (1974) suggest that the opponent aftereffect of some extremely intense stimulus events, such as parachute jumping, results in a strong emotional state that continues for some time after the end of the stimulus event.

As illustrated in Figure 3, the individual's manifest response to a stimulus event is a summative function of the primary arousal produced by the stimulus plus the inhibiting reaction produced by the opponent process. An additional postulate of the opponent process model is that an individual's primary arousal to a particular stimulus is relatively uniform and proportional to the intensity of a specific event. Therefore, the variation in the

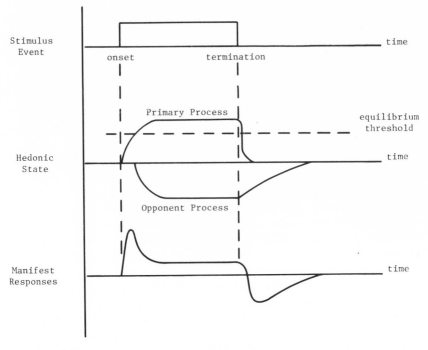

Fig. 3. Opponent process model of an individual's response to a particular stimulus event (Adapted from Solomon and Corbit, 1974)

manifest responses produced by different types of stimuli can be explained by differences in the strength of the opponent process associated with a particular external stimulus. The strength of the individual's opponent process is posited to be related to the frequency of stimulus events. The opponent process is strengthened with use and weakened with disuse of a particular stimulus. Consequently, after repeated experiences with a particular stimulus, a given event is likely to result in a weakened manifest response but one whose aftereffect may tend to linger for an extended time period after the termination of the stimulus.

Both arousal and opponent process theories were developed as within subject models to explain the dynamics of an individual's emotion response to a given stimulus event. The hypothesis of an opponent process mechanism was derived primarily from a deduction of laboratory research findings (Solomon & Corbit, 1974) although Landy (1978) has proposed widespread applications for field studies of organizational behavior. This chapter makes a heroic generalization that these models may be useful in explaining between subject variance in responses to unusually intense leadership events occurring periodically over time in a leader-subordinate dyad. It is further suggested that the manifest responses to these leadership events may be analyzed both in terms of the subordinate's job tension as well as job performance.

The supervisor's leadership behavior can be represented as a time series of stimulus events for the subordinate where the intensity of specific events and the frequency of events may vary in different dyads. If one extends the underlying opponent process phenomena to explain the subordinate's response to a time series of leadership events then the hypothesis could be made that the manifest response to intense leadership incidents will be inversely related to the frequency of the supervisor's leadership activity. When an active leader demonstrates an intensely satisfying or dissatisfying behavior, the strength of the subordinate's opponent process will dampen the hedonic disturbance and quickly return the subordinate to an equilibrium position derived from the normal leadership experiences with that supervisor. Consequently, there will be weaker manifest responses to intense leadership incidents the more active the leader is. Conversely, when an inactive leader demonstrates an intensely satisfying or dissatisfying behavior, the subordinate's weak opponent process will be less inhibiting on the level of hedonic disturbance and will be slower in returning the subordinate to an equilibrium position. Consequently, there are likely to be stronger motivational effects associated with intense leadership incidents of less active leaders.

There are various criterion variables that could be utilized to measure the subordinate's manifest response to leadership stimuli. The subordinate's job performance has often been used as an important measure of leadership effectiveness in the Path-Goal model. Arousal theory, however, would suggest that the subordinate's activation to exert high performance effort may be accompanied by a corresponding increase in perceived stress. Therefore, the criterion variables of subordinate's job performance and job tension were of particular relevance in assessing the manifest responses to intense leadership events.

Research Design

The paucity of empirical research on the functioning of an opponent process posed three important limitations on the design of this study. First, an underlying postulate of the opponent process model is the notion of an individual threshold of hedonic equilibrium. Low intensity stimuli that fall below this threshold would not trigger an opponent process and presumably would have little manifest effect. It is not known whether such a threshold exists for leadership stimuli or what relative level of intensity is needed for a leadership event to disturb the hedonic equilibrium of a particular subordinate. This study, therefore, focuses on the absolute level of stimulus intensity rather than the relative intensity in comparison with the individual's threshold level. It is assumed that all leadership events have the potential to disturb the subordinate's hedonic equilibrium and can produce a manifest motivational effect. Likewise, it is assumed that all leadership events will tend to increase the strength of the subordinate's opponent process associated with leadership stimulus. These assuptions should not prove to be strong confounding factors if the posited threshold level for leadership stimulus is low and can be considered relatively uniform across individuals.

A second design constraint results from the fact that the primary and opponent processes are posited to be dynamic and temporal in nature. The hedonic disturbance and manifest responses are thought to occur at a period of time and then disappear sometime after the stimulus event. With a strong opponent process the manifest response may fluctuate on either side of the neutral point during the decay period. Thus, a satisfying or dissatisfying event may appear to have an inverse manifest effect on subordinates immediately after the termination of the stimulus event.

With regard to the leadership stimulus, it is not known how long the subordinate's manifest response state lasts after the end of a specific leadership event, or whether the decay period is relatively uniform across individuals. Consequently, the research design views leadership influence as a time series of stimulus events rather than as an analysis of a single event. A static, cross-sectional, design is proposed to analyze the strength of any lasting manifest effects that can be associated with unusually intense leadership events that have recently occurred in the past. Thus, the intensity measures are retrospective over a previous time series of events rather than being concurrent measures of an ongoing stimulus event. The strength of the opponent process is analyzed as a relatively long run dampening effect on the subordinate's job performance and tension associated with intense leader-incidents, rather than a short run fluctuation in the manifest response immediately following the leadership incident. To the extent that the leadership stimulus produces a lasting manifest effect on subordinates, this design should provide valid results. However, the obvious shortcomings of this static design is that the manifest effects may decay quickly and may not be measurable some time after the intense leadership events have terminated.

A third limitation is that the manifest responses of the subordinate's job performance and tension may vary at extreme levels of arousal, with performance declining at higher levels of tension. In this study, the assumption was made that both the tension and performance responses would vary directly with the intensity of different leadership events. Therefore, curvilinear relationships between the intensity and criterion measures were not examined. This assumption of linear relationships appeared to be appropriate for a cross-sectional analysis of manifest responses to previous leadership events.

The usefulness of the arousal paradigm in explaining the effects of intense events was tested by the following hypotheses.

H1. The subordinate's experiences of intense leadership events will explain a significant portion of variance in job performance and job tension beyond that explained by the frequency of the supervisor's leadership activity.

The opponent process would tend to dampen the manifest response to specific leadership events. The strength of this opponent process is posited to be a function of the frequency of leadership activity occurring in a particular supervisor-subordinate dyad. Frequent leadership activity would tend to build a strong opponent process such that experiences of intense leadership events would have little manifest effects on subordinates of a highly active leader. Conversely, the intense events would have a stronger effect on subordinates if the leader demonstrated infrequent leadership activity. The strength of the opponent process dampening effect was tested by the following hypothesis.

H2. The intensity of unusually satisfying and dissatisfying leadership events recently experienced by subordinates will have a significant positive relationship with job performance and an inverse relationship with job tension. The strength of these relationships will be diminished when controlling for the frequency of the supervisor's leadership activity.

Method

Scale Development

Behavioral anchored rating scales of leadership activities (LBARS) were developed to measure the intensity of the best and worst leadership events experienced by the subordinates. The objective was to develop a LBARS instrument that could anchor the intensity levels of leadership events occurring in organizations and at the same time could be generalized to various organizational settings. Therefore, 251 MBA students, who had full-time work experience, were recruited over an 18 month period to help develop the LBARS instrument. Approximately 80 percent of participants were full-time employees taking evening MBA courses. The remaining 20 percent was comprised of full-time MBA students who had recently left their jobs to pursue graduate work. The participants had from one to twelve years' work experience in professional, supervisory, and managerial positions in various business, manufacturing, health care, education, and government organizations.

The process of developing the LBARS instrument involved the translation of specific leadership events into rating scales anchored by behavior incidents. The three phase process for scale translation was originally proposed by Smith and Kendall (1963) with subsequent modifications suggested by Campbell, Dunnette, Arvey, and Hellervik (1973) and Sheridan (1980).

Phase I. Generating Incidents of Leadership Behavior. Initially 64 students were asked to write examples of leadership behavior that they had observed during their work careers. The examples were to include critical incidents of exceptionally good and poor leadership as well as examples of typical leader behavior demonstrated by their supervisors. The students generated a list of 518 behavioral incidents with each respondent writing 4 to 10 incidents. This list was reduced to 444 incidents by eliminating those examples that were redundant.

Phase II. Sorting Behavior Incidents Into Leadership Dimensions. The objective of the second phase of scale development was to identify common dimensions of leadership activity represented in the behavior incidents. The second phase involved students participating in two different stages. In the initial stage, 29 students were given index cards containing the 444 incidents. Each student was asked to perform a Q-sort process to sort the cards into categories representing different leadership activities. The Q-sort process resulted in each student's specifying from 7 to 15 leadership categories. There was some inconsistency in the student's labelling of their Q-sort categories. However, a follow-up meeting with the students resulted in a general consensus that there were 10 distinct leadership activities demonstrated in the behavior incidents.

A short description of the 10 preliminary dimensions was written for the second stage of sorting. In this stage 70 students were asked to sort individually the 444 cards in 1 of the 10 leadership activities. A priori, the criteria were established that incidents which had at least 60 percent agreement among raters on a single dimension and no more than 20 percent agreement among raters on any other dimensions would be retained in each activity dimension. The results of this second sort indicated that some dimensions had an acceptable rater agreement on behavior incidents, but other dimensions had unacceptable agreement on scale items. The pattern of item classifications indicated a strong commonality factor among different dimensions and suggested restructuring the leadership activities from 10 to 7 dimensions. The restructured activity dimensions were labeled: 1) Task Direction, 2) Performance Feedback, 3) Performance Rewards, 4) Consideration, 5) Participation, 6) Integrity, and 7) Representation. A total of 96 behavior incidents met acceptable rater agreement criteria based on the restructured dimensions. Each dimension contained from 11 to 14 behavior incidents.

Phase III. Scaling Behavior Incidents in Each Leadership Scale. The objective of the third phase of scale development was to establish scale values for the behavioral anchors in each leadership dimension. To guard against a leniency effect in leadership intensity measures, resulting from a restricted range of scale anchors, another group of 21 students rated the level of leadership competence demonstrated by the 96 behavior incidents. The ratings were made on a five-point descriptive scale ranging from "incompetent" to "outstanding" behaviors. Five behavior incidents were found to have high variance in these competence ratings and were further eliminated from the scale construction. The researchers then selected 9 behavioral incidents for inclusion in each leadership dimension for a total of 63 incidents. Incidents were selected which represented a balanced range of leadership competence and had the highest rater agreement in being classified as a particular leadership activity.

The scale value for each behavioral anchor was established through a Thurstone scaling procedure. All possible pairs of incidents (36 pairs) in each dimension were presented to a rater who selected the incident in each pair which represented the more desirable behavior on the particular leadership activity. A ratio scale of behavioral incidents was determined by the proportion that each incident was selected by the raters in comparison with all other incidents in that dimension. A total of 67 students completed the Thurston scaling procedure. However, because of the large number of incident pairs in each scale, each rater completed the paired comparison instrument for only two leadership dimensions. Thus, scale values of behavioral anchors in each leadership dimension were based on a sample of 17 to 21 raters.

The internal reliability of each leadership scale was tested by examining the transitivity of the rater's choices among the paired incidents within each dimension. Four incidents in different dimensions were found to have an intransitive ordering of ratings. These behavioral anchors were eliminated from the final scales. The distribution of paired comparison ratings among behavioral anchors in the final scales had a significant goodness of fit (χ^2 $p < .05$) with the expected distribution assuming perfect transitivity among ratings.

The final LBARS instrument measured the intensity of experienced leadership events on seven activity dimensions.

1. Task Direction. The extent that your supervisor lets subordinates know what is expected of them on particular work assignments and provides adequate information to complete their work.

2. Participation. The extent that your supervisor encourages employee participation in decision making and is supportive of employees' ideas.

3. Consideration. The extent that your supervisor shows consideration for the personal needs and feelings of subordinates.

4. Performance Feedback. The extent that your supervisor evaluates employees' work and keeps employees informed of how well they are doing their job.

5. Integrity. The extent that your supervisor deals with employees in a forthright manner and demonstrates credibility in actions.

6. Performance Rewards. The extent that your supervisor provides recognition to employees for their accomplishments and rewards or reprimands employees based on their performance.

7. Representation. The extent that your supervisor represents the subordinates' interest with other units in the organization and acts as an effective liaison with upper management.

The scale format for the Performance Feedback dimension is illustrated in Figure 4.

Sample

The sample for the field test of the posited activation model included 66 supervisory and managerial employees working at a truck assembly plant. Each employee completed questionnaire instruments administered directly by the researchers during work hours at the plant facility. For purposes of this study, each respondent was considered to be a subordinate who reported directly to 1 of 16 different managers. The number of respondents reporting to a particular manager ranged from two to nine subordinates.

To control for possible moderating effects of different situational variables the sample was selected to represent only the production department in a single assembly plant. The respondents were not unionized and were all involved in managing production or quality control or direct supervision of workers on the assembly line.

Measures

Intensity of Leadership Events. Each respondent was asked to recall recent experiences with his supervisor over the past several months and provide three ratings on each LBARS scale: 1) a normal rating indicating the

Performance Feedback - The extent that your supervisor evaluates employees' work and keeps them informed of how well they are doing their job.

Think about your past experiences with your supervisor, recalling those incidents where he/she demonstrated performance feedback. Rate those incidents in comparison with the examples listed on this scale. Please make three ratings.

Place an H (High) rating on the scale, indicating the approximate position of the highest level of performance feedback provided by your supervisor.

Place an N (Normal) rating on the scale, indicating the approximate position of the usual level of performance feedback provided by your supervisor under normal conditions.

Place an L (Low) rating on the scale, indicating the approximate position of the lowest level of performance feedback provided by your supervisor.

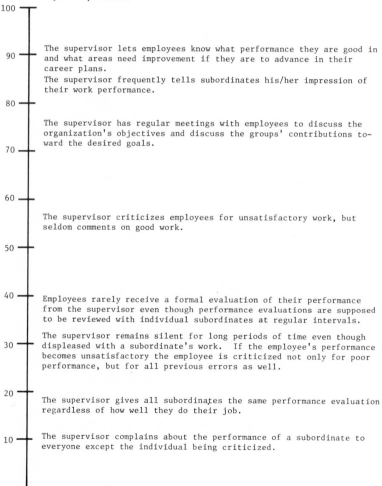

100

90 — The supervisor lets employees know what performance they are good in and what areas need improvement if they are to advance in their career plans.
The supervisor frequently tells subordinates his/her impression of their work performance.

80

70 — The supervisor has regular meetings with employees to discuss the organization's objectives and discuss the groups' contributions toward the desired goals.

60

50 — The supervisor criticizes employees for unsatisfactory work, but seldom comments on good work.

40 — Employees rarely receive a formal evaluation of their performance from the supervisor even though performance evaluations are supposed to be reviewed with individual subordinates at regular intervals.

30 — The supervisor remains silent for long periods of time even though displeased with a subordinate's work. If the employee's performance becomes unsatisfactory the employee is criticized not only for poor performance, but for all previous errors as well.

20 — The supervisor gives all subordinates the same performance evaluation regardless of how well they do their job.

10 — The supervisor complains about the performance of a subordinate to everyone except the individual being criticized.

Fig. 4. Scale format of LBARS

TABLE 12
Mean Scores for Intensity of Best and Worst Experiences on Leadership Behavior Dimensions

Leadership Dimension	Best Experience		Worst Experience		Mean
	Mean	SD	Mean	SD	Difference
Task Direction	69.3	20.1	24.4	16.1	44.9**
Participation	74.1	19.1	32.0	20.8	42.1**
Consideration	80.6	23.5	31.1	25.7	49.5**
Performance Feedback	69.9	18.4	32.2	19.8	37.7**
Integrity	70.8	22.1	34.3	19.4	36.5**
Performance Rewards	72.4	19.2	34.2	19.7	38.2**
Representation	75.6	18.8	32.1	21.1	43.5**

**$p \leq 0.1$

typical level of behavior that the supervisor usually demonstrated on the leadership activity, 2) a high rating indicating the level of the *best* incident the supervisor has demonstrated on the leadership activity, 3) a low rating indicating the level of the *worst* incident the supervisor has demonstrated on the leadership activity.

The normal rating was requested to help anchor the ratings of the "best" and "worst" experiences but "normal" scores were not utilized in the data analysis. Table 12 presents the mean and standard deviation values for reported levels of the best and worst leadership events. The results indicate a high variance in the level of experienced events but a paired "t" test indicated that the level of best experiences was significantly higher ($p < .01$) than the worst events on each leadership activity.

Frequency of Leadership Activity. Each respondent reported the frequency of his supervisor's leadership activity using the Initiating Structure and Consideration items from the Leadership Behavior Description Questionnaire (LBDQ Form XII [Stogdill, 1963]). Approximately 75 percent of the item responses ranged from "Occasionally" (40–59 percent of the time) to "Nearly Always" (80–100 percent of the time) for both Initiating Structure and Consideration items. This frequency distribution suggested that the LBDQ items represent typical leadership events that are experienced by most subordinates. The subordinate's perceptions of the supervisor's Initiating Structure and Consideration behavior was, therefore, used to measure the frequency of leadership events occurring within the particular supervisor-subordinate dyad. The internal reliability of the Initiating Structure and Consideration scales was $\alpha = .86$ and $.83$.

Job Tension. Each subordinate completed a tension instrument developed by Kahn, Wolfe, Quinn, and Snoek (1964) which measured the extent

TABLE 13
Usefulness of Leadership Variables in Explaining Job Performance and Job Tension

Predictor Sets	Performance		Job Tension	
	R^2	ΔR^2	R^2	ΔR^2
IS + CON	.14*		.22**	
Best Task Direction and Consideration Experiences	.11*		.15*	
Worst Task Direction and Consideration Experiences	.15*		.16*	
IS + CON + Best Task Direction and Consideration Experiences	.20*	.06*	.27**	.05
IS + CON + Worst Task Direction and Consideration Experiences	.23*	.09*	.26**	.04

* $p \le .05$
** $p \le .01$

that the individual perceived a stressful work environment derived from role conflict and role ambiguity. The scale reliability was $\alpha = .83$.

Job Performance. Each subordinate's current job performance evaluation was obtained after the completion of the questionnaire survey. The overall performance score represents a weighted summation of manager evaluations on seven descriptive performance scales including: Responsibility, Quality Standards, Job Knowledge, Initiative, Interpersonal Relationships, Dependability, and Potential. The performance scores could range from 0 to 250 with the participating company considering a score of 69 as representing a level of "minimum competence" and scores over 229 representing "distinguished" performance. In this sample the mean performance score was 109.7 with a standard deviation of 38.4. The internal reliability of the cumulative performance measure was $\alpha = .87$.

Results

Table 13 presents the regression analyses of the usefulness of the frequency measures (IS and CON) and intensity variables (best and worst experiences) in explaining the subordinates' job performance and job tension. The interpretation of the incremental increase in explained variance is confounded by the fact that the seven LBARS intensity measures included leadership activities that are not necessarily subsumed under IS and CON behavior. Therefore, it is not known whether the increase in explained variance is attributed to the effects of additional leadership activities or to the intensity of specific events on these activities.

The events represented by the LBARS Task Direction and Consideration dimension are most closely analagous to the IS and CON activities. Therefore, to control partially for the confounding accumulation of both intensity and activity effects, the regression analysis includes only these two LBARS dimensions. The set of IS and CON frequency scores and the sets of the best and worst Task Direction and Consideration events each explained significant portions of variance in both job performance and job tension. Moreover, the Task Direction and Consideration events accounted for a unique portion of variance in job performance since the addition of each set of best or worst intensity measures resulted in a significant increase in explained performance variance beyond that explained by the frequency measures alone. These results provided limited support for the first hypothesis. The sets of frequency and intensity variables each explained significant portions of variance in job performance and job tension. The inclusion of the intensity measures significantly increased the explained variance in job performance but not job tension.

Table 14 presents the zero and second order correlations between the intensity of the best and worst leadership events on each of the seven activity dimensions and the criterion measures. The second order partial correlation represents the correlation between the intensity of the best or worst event and the criterion variable controlling for the frequency of IS and CON activities. Since the zero and second order correlations are themselves interdependent, it is difficult to test accurately the significance of the difference between the two correlations (Stoline, 1972). Nevertheless, if a significant zero order correlation between an intensity and criterion variable is driven to near zero when controlling for the frequency measures, it is reasonable to infer that the relationship between the intensity and criterion variables was somehow affected by variation in the frequency measures either through a spurious or intervening causal relationship (Blalock, 1962; McNemar, 1969). Within the leadership activation model this suppressor effect is thought to occur as a result of an intervening opponent process associated with the frequency of the leadership stimuli.

The zero order correlations with job performance indicate that the intensity of both the best and worst experiences had significant positive relationships with job performance. That is, higher values of both the best and worst experiences were associated with higher job performance; whereas lower levels of the best and worst experiences were associated with lower job performance. Conversely, the intensity measures were inversely associated in the same manner with job tension.

The magnitude of differences between zero and second order correla-

TABLE 14

Correlations Between the Intensity of the Best and Worst Leadership Experiences with Job Performance and Job Tension

Leadership Dimension	Job Performance				Job Tension			
	Best Incidents		Worst Incidents		Best Incidents		Worst Incidents	
	r	r_2	r	r_2	r	r_2	r	r_2
Task Direction	.33**	.25*	.19*	.11	−.31**	−.19**	−.34**	−.23**
Performance Feedback	.34**	.20*	.26*	.15	−.33**	−.16	−.17	.08
Participation	.22*	.08	.17	.05	−.11	.15	−.07	.12
Consideration	.16	.00	.11	−.02	−.19	−.02	−.12	.06
Integrity	.19*	.08	.25*	.16	−.23*	−.02	−.21*	−.00
Performance Rewards	.13	−.03	.24*	.07	−.24*	−.04	−.27*	−.02
Representation	.16	−.05	−.01	−.17	−.20*	.06	−.09	.13

r_2 represents partial correlation controlling for the frequency of IS and CON behavior.

*$p \le .05$
**$p \le .01$

tions suggested two distinct patterns of results for different leadership dimensions. First, the intensity of both the best and worst experiences with Task Direction and Performance Feedback activities were significantly related with the performance and tension criterion measures. The strengths of these relationships were not greatly diminished when controlling for the frequency of IS and CON behavior. Second, the intensity of the best and worst experiences with Integrity and Performance Rewards activities were also significantly associated with the criterion measures. The strengths of these relationships, however, were diminished to near zero when controlling for the frequency of IS and CON behavior, particularly the relationships with job tension.

This second pattern of correlations thus supports the second hypothesis only with respect to the Performance Rewards and Integrity activities. The effects of intense experiences with Task Direction and Performance Feedback activities were not substantially diminished when controlling for the frequency of IS and CON behavior; while intense experiences with Participation, Consideration, and Representation activities were not strongly related to the criterion measures in any consistent pattern.

Discussion

The results of this study tend to support the usefulness of an activation phenomenon in explaining leadership influence. The subordinates' experiences of intense leadership events had significant effects on both job performance and job tension. However, any interpretation of an opponent process effect should be prefaced by noting that the opponent process is posited to be an inhibiting emotional response produced by a "slave" mechanism of the central nervous system (Solomon & Corbit, 1974). The manifest effect is not considered to be a learned or conditioned response to a particular stimulus. Solomon and Corbit, however, discuss how many of the traditional stimulus-response (S-R) explanations of behavior can be incorporated into the opponent process model.

The results suggest that different leadership activities have varying motivational effects on the subordinate. The intensity of the best and worst events on the Performance Rewards and Integrity dimensions represent unusual incidents where the supervisor did or did not provide recognition or reprimands for the subordinate in a consistent manner based on job performance, and did or did not treat the subordinate in a forthright and credible manner. Such intense interpersonal events are likely to arouse an emotional response in the subordinate and may readily disturb his hedonic equilibrium in either a staisfying or dissatisfying direction. The presence of an opponent dampening effect was particularly evident for these intense events. The significant influence of intense Performance Rewards and Integrity activities was diminished to near zero when controlling for the frequency of leadership activity in the supervisor-subordinate dyad.

Conversely, the intensity of the best and worst events on the Task Direction and Performance Feedback dimensions represent unusual incidents where the supervisor did or did not provide adequate information and guidance for the subordinate to complete his work assignments, and did or did not give feedback to the subordinate regarding his work performance. The results indicated that these intense task oriented events had significant effects on the subordinate's job performance and job tension. These effects, however, were not diminished by an opponent process associated with the frequency of the supervisor's leadership activity. It is suggested that Task Direction and Performance Feedback incidents are likely to be instrumental behaviors in either aiding or hindering the employee in the performance of his work task but would not tend to arouse a strong emotional response. Intense task oriented events are less likely to produce hedonic disturbances for subordinates. Consequently, their influence would not be strongly diminished by an opponent process effect.

The findings have important implications for leadership research. In addition to the traditional focus on learned or conditioned responses to leadership activities, the results suggest that subordinates also exhibit a slave response to intense leadership events. Active leaders are likely to evoke a strong conditioned response from subordinates, particularly to task oriented events, but will tend to have weaker emotional responses from subordinates as a result of the strong opponent process derived from the frequent leadership activity. Conversely, inactive leaders are likely to evoke a strong emotional response to their leadership behavior, particularly to intense interpersonal events, but will have a weak learned response to their leadership activity.

The subordinate's response to a time sequence of leadership stimuli can, therefore, be explained as a learned response associated with the inter-stimulus time intervals and an emotional response associated with the recent experience of an intense stimulus event (Solomon & Corbit, 1974). In this respect an important limitation of the present study was that it focused on retrospective measures of the best and worst events not knowing specifically when the events occurred, how many events occurred, or in what sequence they occurred. To better understand the motivational response to leadership stimuli there is a need for within-subject longitudinal studies which measure the occurrence of intense leadership events over time. The temporal dynamics of the subordinate's manifest response following the occurrence of intense leadership events could then be analyzed.

A second limitation of the study was that variations in individual responses to the intense leadership events were not examined. Individual differences should be measured and used to explain variation in the manifest responses demonstrated by particular subordinates, not merely treated as exogenous variables adding to the pool of residual variance (Landy, 1978). Two individual attributes appear particularly relevant in the examination of an opponent process model of leadership effects. First, the assumption of uniform hedonic thresholds needs to be more closely examined. Without valid interval scales of stimulus intensity it would be difficult to measure accurately differences between individual hedonic thresholds with respect to some absolute neutral state. However, it may be possible to infer relative ranges of hedonic equilibrium from psychological attributes such as trait anxiety (Spielberger, 1966). One might speculate that anxious individuals may have a narrow range of indifference with regard to variation in leadership behavior. Even small deviations from their leaders' normal behavior may be sufficient to create a hedonic disturbance. These individuals are likely to report a high state of tension after experiencing intense leadership events (Johnson, 1968). Conversely, individuals with low trait anxiety may perceive a wide range of indifference toward their supervisor's behavior and exhibit low manifest effects from even highly intense events.

Another important difference between individuals would be the "hedonic relevance" of the leader's behavior for the subordinate. Hedonic relevance refers to the importance of the stimulus person's behavior for the perceiver (Jones & Davis, 1965). If leadership events are important to the subordinate he or she is likely to make causal attributions about the supervisor. Subordinates who feel strongly about the interpersonal relationship with their supervisor are likely to attribute experienced leadership events as the cause of their satisfaction and behavior. These individuals may exhibit strong manifest effects associated with experiences of intense leadership events. Conversely, subordinates who perceive little importance in their leader's behavior are less likely to make such causal attributions and less likely to exhibit strong manifest responses to intense leadership events.

The hedonic relevance of leadership events can be related to the psychological traits of individual subordinates and the characteristics of specific work situations. One might speculate that subordinates with an external locus of control (Rotter, 1966) will be more likely to exhibit a stronger manifest response to intense leadership events than individuals with an internal locus of control. Likewise, there may be work situations where other organization stimuli provide "substitutes" for the supervisor's leadership (Kerr & Jermier, 1978) such that leadership events would have little hedonic relevance for subordinates in those work situations.

At this exploratory stage of research it is highly speculative to draw any conclusive managerial implications from the activation model of leadership influence. The model suggests a different line of theory development by arguing that the quality of specific leadership incidents may be as important in determining leader effectiveness as the frequency by which the leader engages in different activities. Previous leadership research has provided a generalized implication that frequent leadership activity is "good." Thus, supervisors who are "high" in Consideration and/or "high" in Initiating Structure are thought to be more effective than supervisors who are "low" in either behavior dimension. The results of the present study, however, would suggest that even inactive, "low," leaders can have a strong effect on subordinates when they demonstrate intense leadership incidents. Likewise, even the influence of active leaders can be partly attributed to the subordinate's response to intense leadership events demonstrated by the "high" leader. Thus, it is clear that what a supervisor does or does not do on a specific occasion is just as important to his or her leadership effectiveness as how often he or she demonstrates leadership activity.

9

Commentary on Part 2

Intensity of Relation, Dyadic-Group Considerations, Cognitive Categorization, and Transformational Leadership

BERNARD M. BASS

The three chapters discussed here fit nicely with the overall forward-looking theme of this book. They all represent new steps ahead in conceptualizing the phenomenon of leadership. And like most new ventures, there are problems in their execution. Nevertheless, all three efforts do a good job in pointing us in newer directions.

1. I was particularly pleased with the focus of Sheridan, Kerr, and Abelson's presentation. They call our attention to the importance of extreme rather than ordinary leader-subordinate interactions. The continuing day-to-day leader's behavior may fail to account for significant amounts of continuing supervisory-subordinate relationships. We need to attend to the dynamics of when a subordinate experiences an intense demand or when a leader experiences a highly unexpected response.

It takes only one inconsistency or fabrication by a leader to lose his or her integrity as judged by subordinates. The frequency of lying is irrelevant. A parallel argument was advanced by W. Burns (1978) that most leader-subordinate relations studied focus on a transaction (Hollander, 1978), an exchange in which the leader is instrumental or supportive in the subordinates' attainment of need satisfaction. Much more important to study than *transactional leadership*, the common form, is to study *transformational* leadership, the uncommon form, where the leader raises the subordinate's level of need (on Maslow's scale) and energizes the subordinate into accomplishments beyond the subordinate's original expectations that may transcend the subordinate's self-interests. I will say more about this later.

They may not agree but I believe Sheridan, Kerr, and Abelson have taken a first step towards developing some understanding about the transformational leader. Sheridan, Kerr, and Abelson's efforts to focus on the extremes rather than the means of leader performance are to be commended. They have completed a conscientious effort to break new ground in developing a suitable methodology to measure carefully close approximations of the theoretical constructs of consequence. Particularly interesting was their nonobvious deduction of the possible likely effect of frequency of leadership activity as performance to which subordinates would become so accustomed, that its effects would be minimal and even dampening.

Considerable care was taken to develop and validate the seven measures of intensity of leader behavior. Unfortunately, parallel measures of frequency were not used. Also instead of directly concentrating on hypotheses about the dampening effect of frequency on intensity, which was the presumed theoretical basis for the research effort, tests were run at admittedly low power for 66 subordinates of 16 managers looking at the effects of optimally combining frequency and intensity assessments.

The analyses do suggest that Sheridan, Kerr, and Abelson have ventured into a fruitful area. What I would like to see before concentrating on elegant regression analyses here is to consider more direct tests with larger samples of the initial propositions derived from opponent process theory. Presumably, if highest and lowest levels of the behaviorally anchored scales are acceptable as measures of intensity, then possibly the "normal" level can be regarded as a measure of frequency. For a given dimension, the relations between these three levels should be fully examined. Unless they are highly correlated within or between raters (which is possible), a cruder analysis more closely matching the initial theoretical position would be obtained from a cross-tabulation of job performance and tension outcomes as a function of combinations of low or high best (or worst) levels and low or high intensity. The prospects of curvilinearity of relationship between intensity and frequency are high. Curvilinear effects on outcomes are also not unreasonable to expect. For example, high frequency and high intensity may have strong effects in contrast to high frequency and low or high intensity. Optimization through multiple regression of the contributions of the measures of frequency and intensity do not, it seems to me, provide full understanding of what is happening. Partial correlation is also a fickle tool. I'd like to see more of the same kinds of data subjected to a wide variety of hypothesis tests to develop understanding of relation of frequency to intensity. Activity and opponent theory has set the stage. But I think it would now make sense to explore the combined and subtractive effects of frequency and intensity. Do they reflect qualitatively different aspects of leadership?

2. Leaders differ consistently from each other across groups but also may relate differently to different members within their group. Rather than viewing these group and dyadic considerations as "either-or," Dansereau, Alutto, Markham, and Dumas have taken a profitable next step forward which allows for analysis to include both group and dyadic relations in dealing with one set of leadership data. They have turned an Aristotelian either-or controversy into an opportunity for examination in which both dyadic and group relations can be operating simultaneously. Their analyses of differences among correlations were reasonable. However, strong inferences are made difficult to accept if we recall the erroneous law of small numbers, the large sampling fluctuations in correlation coefficients, and the problems of generating tests of sufficient power of differences between correlations. Larger samples as well as mixed effects analyses of variance may offer a more confident examination of the extent to which a leader develops differential dyadic relations with his or her differing subordinates in comparison to maintaining relations at the group level. At the same time, the mixed effects design can quantify the impact of the factors contributing to increasing or decreasing the dyadic in contrast to the group component. One can establish the proportion of variance in leader-subordinate relationships accounted for by the two models.

For example, consider where half the groups led are in a high task structure condition and half are in a low task structure situation. The subordinates of each leader are regarded as sources of replicate measurement associated with that leader. Dichotomize subordinates according to their competencies. For the dependent variable, measure the subordinates' judgments of whether they are supervised closely or loosely. The ANOVA design can then become with j leaders each with k subordinates:

A = Low or high task structure.
E_{bg} = Error (between groups).
BG = Between groups of subordinates reporting to the same leader.
C = Low or high subordinate competence.
$A \times C$ = Interaction of task structure and subordinate competence.
E_{wg} = Error (within groups).
WG = Within groups variance.
T = Total variance ($BG + WG$).
$F = \dfrac{VA}{V_{E_{bg}}}$ tests whether supervisors lead generally closely or loosely

depending on the task structure regardless of subordinate differences. $F = V_C/V_{E_{wg}}$ tests whether such supervision is associated with subordinate competence. $F = V_{A \times C}/V_{E_{wg}}$ tests whether the interaction is involved. Estimations of the proportion of variance accounted for by the components, S, C and $A \times C$ can be obtained.[1]

Analysis of covariance can be introduced to test whether, say, productivity differences among subordinates between and within groups are adjusted by A, C and $A \times C$ and what proportion of the covariance can be attributed to the three components. Additional variables affecting the differences in dyadic and group effects can be introduced by using higher order designs.

But apart from this minor methodological issue, the approach is on target. We should expect leaders to be seen differentially and to act differently to members within their group. The variables that come to mind that should make such differences include differential member competence, esteem, status, popularity, and visibility. In fact, *the very subordinate attributes that we find associated with leadership and influence in groups when attached to subordinates are likely to* affect how leaders interact with such subordinates. We should also see less dyadic effects and more uniform treatment by a leader of a given group (generating effects between but not within groups) as a function of subordinate and supervisory training, company policies, union and civil service regulations, equal task requirements, task interdependence, common fate, and leader sense of equity and fairness.

3. With reference to the Lord, Foti, and Phillips chapter, my cognitive economy and perceived world structure demands that the benefits of a new conceptualization of the leadership problem be new enough to be discriminably different from older ones and that its benefits outweigh the additional costs incurred in adding it.

This is how I see the Lord, Foti, and Phillips chapter. People sort each other into leaders and non-leaders. What for 75 years since Terman (1904) has been recognized by scholars as a continuum, is now described as a fuzzy dichotomy. (An important point to be made here is that laymen continue to dichotomize leaders and non-leaders while scholars see a continuum.) Whether one is lumped into one category or the other depends on the subsequent image remaining over time. Distortion is systematic. Perceivers fill out rating forms that say as much about themselves and their stereotypes of leaders as about the leaders they are rating (I used to say the same thing about biographers, anthropologists, and reviewers of my books). The less close in contact with the stimulus person and the more the ratings are ab-

---

1. This assumes that the total variance can be apportioned into between and within groups. The ALS model is tested by the between groups analysis and the VDL by the within groups analyses. Whether more of the variance is associated with the ALS rather than the VDL model can be tested by the ratio of the J_{BG}/J_{WG}. We must assume that the subordinates of a leader are uncorrelated or random replications and that the between groups classification, A, is independent of the within groups classifications, C.

stract the more the perceiver must rely on prototypes (stereotypes) in making general leadership ratings. Those that can be identified as about good leaders or bad leaders are more discriminating when applied to specific leaders seen as high or low in initiating structure.

What Walter Lippmann in 1922 called stereotypic thinking provides a 1980 example by the authors for what they value as another "new" formulation: the election of business and military leaders as U.S. Presidents instead of congressmen who are perceived not to be leaders. (However, of the 10 Presidents elected since 1920, 5 had been congressmen, 2 had had state legislative experience and only 3 were respectively a general, an engineer and a businessman—more recently a state governor.)

William James in 1880 talked about the world as a "blooming buzzing confusion." We deal with the world by structuring it into categories. March and Simon (1957), among others, noted that bureaucrats classify problems in order then to decide how arbitrarily to deal with them. I find the cognitive economy concept rather hoary. Saying that leadership ratings suffer from halo, generalization, and stereotyping doesn't seem to add anything that is nonobvious to the image-builders from Madison Avenue. Nevertheless, Lord, Foti, and Phillips are addressing an important and well-known pheonomenon. We are victimized by images of what leaders are supposed to be: tall, athletic, good-looking; articulate, assertive, masculine; tough, heroic, strong; honest, loyal, and brave; caring, supportive, and concerned. But I think we need to plod through this area of perceptual miasma looking for ways to map it with simple and necessary concepts that will produce new insights, not old well-known admonitions. Considerable exploitation about attribution phenomena can be applied with profit to the leader-follower relationship. The leader's behavior toward subordinates appears to be strongly determined by the reason (ability or motivation) the leader gives for the subordinate's performance—how much it is a matter of luck, situation, or within the subordinate's control. In the same way, subordinates' attributions of the reasons for the leader's behavior will strongly relate to the subordinates' satisfaction. The leader judged by subordinates as willing but incompetent seems to be more forgivable than the leader judged competent but unwilling.

Conscious perceptions may determine much of the leader's subsequent efforts. Nebeker and Mitchell (1974) found that differences in leadership behavior could be explained by the leader's expectations that a certain style of leadership would be effective in a given situation. At the same time, subordinates' descriptions of their leader's behavior may be distorted by their implicit theories about leadership particularly where they lack real information about the situation and are inclined therefore to fall back on stereotypes (Schriesheim & deNisi, 1979).

There are interesting historical implications. Consider what was expected of someone labeled as a leader in Nazi Germany. Curiously, most of the world did until modern times without the word "leadership." It didn't come into use in English until the nineteenth century when it referred to parliamentary direction and control. Could one seriously argue that leadership was not perceived, fought over, accepted or rejected because there was no label for it? Can one categorize without labeling?

Purely behavioral explanations cannot be dismissed. One can look at leadership as a perceptual phenomenon under certain conditions, or a behavioral phenomenon under others, and accurately explain what is happening in both instances. Leadership research has been heavily dependent on subordinates' reported perceptions of their leader's behavior. Yet, Gilmore, Beehr, and Richter (1979) demonstrated in a laboratory setting that, although participants failed to perceive that their leaders (instructed to be high or low in initiation and consideration) actually differed in their behavior, actual (but not perceived) high initiation coupled with high consideration by the leaders resulted in higher work quality, as expected. Least quality occurred when actual leader initiation of structure was high but leader consideration was low. It is clear we need more studies which do not depend solely on subordinate observations and descriptions.

The three contributions have directed our attention to important issues for the 80's: 1) unusual or extreme leadership acts, 2) simultaneous analysis of both dyadic and group relations with the leader, and 3) psychological implications of imaging someone as a leader or non-leader per se. All three deserve continued effort. The focus on extreme leadership acts may result in reorganizing our leadership selection and training policies as well as the performances emphasized in research. The many middle managers and bureaucrats arrested in their career development may be rescued from stagnation. Attention to both dyadic and group relations opens up a more realistic view which also is likely to impact ultimately on selection and training. The implications of being categorized as a leader or non-leader on others' expectations and reactions needs to be fully examined.

4. I would like to conclude by describing an exploration I have begun which in some sense involves all three new departures from the usual concerns in leadership research. I am trying to determine the utility of differentiating two conceptions of leadership: transactional and transformational. The distinction involves focus on the unusual, on cognitive differences and on dyadic versus group considerations.

As said earlier, we have focused on *transactional* leaders. They exchange need fulfillment for compliance. But the real movers and shakers of the world are *transformational* leaders. Such leaders raise consciousness about higher considerations. They articulate higher goals and role modeling. Aspiration levels are raised and legitimitized. Such leaders inspire confidence and a sense of purpose.

Transactional political leaders according to W. Burns (1978) are those who "approach followers with an eye to exchanging one thing for another: jobs for votes, or subsidies for campaign contributions. Such transactions comprise the bulk of the relationships among leaders and followers, especially in groups, legislatures, and parties" (p. 3). The *transforming* leader recognizes an existing need for a potential follower, but then moves forward seeking to arouse and satisfy higher needs (in terms of Maslow's need hierarchy) to engage the full person of the follower. The followers themselves may be converted into leaders.

A pilot study was recently completed to see whether the conceptualization might be useful in the world of work. Seventy senior South African male executives from a variety of organizations were asked to think of a person in their world of work who had accomplished any of the following: motivated them to do more than originally expected, raised their level of awareness about an important matter, increased level of need to a higher level (in Maslow's scale), or made them transcend their own self-interests for the good of the organization. Most respondents identified a former immediate superior as such a person. There were exceptions. Others named included a family friend, management consultants, and managers several levels higher in the hierarchy.

For many respondents, the transforming leader—always male—was seen as a benevolent father who remained friendly and treated the respondent as an equal despite the leader's greater knowledge and experience. The leader provided a model of integrity and fairness with people as well as being one who set clear and high standards of performance. He encouraged followers with advice, help, support, recognition, and openness. He gave followers a sense of confidence in his intellect, yet was a good listener. Other characteristics less frequently mentioned included: seeking others' highest good, treating others with dignity, showing respect for others and genuine interest in them. He also was seen to be firm and to reprimand when necessary, to give autonomy to followers, to encourage self-development of followers, to be participative, to be willing to teach followers, and to mix easily socially with followers. Yet he could be formal at work and be firm and reprimand if necessary. However, most respondents were inclined to see the transforming leader as informal and close. Such a leader could be counted on to stand up for his followers.

Frequent reactions of followers to the transforming leader included trust, strong liking, admiration, loyalty, and respect. These feelings in turn led followers to work "ridiculous" hours and to do more than originally expected. A fairly common reaction was the feeling that one wanted to try to satisfy the leader's expectations of the follower and to give the leader all the support asked for.

Other follower reactions included: the desire to emulate the leader, higher quality of performance, greater innovativeness, readiness to extend oneself and to develop oneself further, total commitment, belief in the organization as a consequence of belief in the leader, heightened self-confidence, and doing things not in ones' own best interest but not understanding why.

Some negative outcomes were also reported. A follower was first aroused but then "demotivated" when the leader was unable to "deliver the goods." (Was this really transformational or transactional?) Another follower's early reactions of awe and envy changed to a sense of competitiveness with the leader. One respondent mentioned overachieving in reaction against a disliked person to show that the disliked person was wrong about the respondent. In one case, respect and admiration gave way to eventual disappointment. The leader in question was charming and optimistic but tended to exaggerate and hold back the full truth.

What follows is taken from Bass and Stogdill (1981) which concludes by noting that most experimental research has focused on transactional leadership (for example, see Hollander, 1978) when the big effects on followers come from transformational leaders.

According to McCall (1977), we have been concentrating on research on the nitty-gritty, readily observable, usually short-term leader-subordinate relations. We ignore the much more important aspects of leadership to be seen in transformation leadership. We see the need for more leaders who can "initiate structure in group expectation and show us how to master and motivate institutions and individuals within a complex environment experiencing excessive internal and external stresses and changes" (Mueller, 1980, p. 19).

We should be studying such questions as: In what ways can a leader move subordinates toward the acceptance of superordinate goals? How can followers be aroused into self-transcendence? How does a leader move a group from complacency, hasty responses, inertia, or defensiveness in the face of threat to complete and adequate vigilance? (See Janis & Mann, 1977). If a group is primarily focused on its lower level safety and security needs, how does a leader move it toward concern for recognition and achievement? If a group is under stress too high for coping with the complexity of the situation, how does the leader steady and calm the group?

We can put the quantitative research spotlight on the Gandhis, Churchills, de Gaulles and Ho Chi Minhs despite the fact that their performance was exceptional. We do not have to be able to reproduce the effects in the laboratory or in simulation. Bass and Farrow (1977) showed the feasibility of using standardized survey questionnaires to study indirectly the interaction of such leaders and their immediate subordinates. Judges read the biographies of famous historical personages, then completed the Bass-Valenzi Management Styles Questionnaire *as if* they were the subordinates.

We may be avoiding study of transformational leadership because, when seen in the industrial manager, it is maybe autocratic, coercive behavior dressed up as charismatic (Culbert & McDonough, 1980).

There is some overlap between the transformational and the charismatic leader. Managers, ministers, battalion commanders, teachers, coaches, and directors can be found who fit the description of persons to whom followers form deep emotional attachment and who in turn inspire their followers to transcend their own interests for superordinate goals, for goals higher in level than previously recognized by the followers. There are even bureaucratic leaders whose competence and good connections, whose ability to mobilize and husband resources, keep their eyes on the bigger issues, take the risks required for "creative administration," give them the credit to arouse in their subordinates faith and trust in the leader.

The question is can we take what W. Burns (1978) saw primarily for transforming leadership at the mass level and apply the concept to the small group situation? Are there analogues in the world of work for the intellectual reform, revolutionary, and heroic leaders who transform societies? What are the costs of heroic leadership characterized by followers' strong belief in the leaders as persons, faith that the leader will make it possible for the group to succeed, and willingness to give the leader power to act in crises.

Mueller (1980) describes "leading-edge" leadership able to simplify problems and to jump to the (correct) crux of complex matters while the rest of the crowd is still trying to identify the problem. He sees the need for research on this "rapid reification." Second, he sees the need for leadership research on how "to integrate and relate a charismatic component with the logical and intuitive attributes which is vital to leading-edge leadership" (p. 21).

Some questions that we need to focus attention on include: What conditions promote the emergence of the transformational leader? Can we facilitate this emergence? What are consequences of moving from emphasis on social exchange which characterizes the transactional leader to leadership that mobilizes and directs members toward higher objectives. What are the costs and clear and obvious dangers as well as the benefits of transformational leadership? Can we train the average supervisor to function as a transformational leader? Can we learn how to select potential transformational leaders who probably may not show up as well on many currently available predictors as transactional leaders?

Strategies for Dealing with Different Processes in Different Contexts

IAN MORLEY

I approach leadership from the point of view of a social psychologist interested in the performance of groups. Furthermore, I follow Kelvin in taking the view that "perhaps the simplest way to regard the leader is to consider him as the individual who contributes most to the creation and maintainance of order in the group" (Kelvin, 1970, p. 223). By *order* Kelvin means a social order based on systems of power and systems of value. But power relations and value relations differ from group to group. Thus, what counts as leadership will vary from case to case. So will the qualities required of a leader. That is, the leadership skills appropriate in one context may be irrelevant or inappropriate in another. There are many different ways in which to get to this kind of conclusion (e.g., Hosking, Hunt, & Osborn, 1980). However, the point is that this kind of problem is a familiar one: How do we cope with the fact that, in some sense, different processes occur in different contexts?

Strategy No. 1

Strategy No. 1 is illustrated by the work of Dansereau and his colleagues. Essentially, the trick is to divide theories into mutually exclusive types. Then, for any dimension of performance, it becomes an empirical question: Which theory when? Dansereau, Alutto, Markham, and Dumas argue that special statistical techniques are required to answer questions of this kind. Specifically, they recommend partitioning scores into between-cell and within-cell components, as in the analysis of variance. Two kinds of correlation are computed, using the derived between-cell and within-cell scores. The pattern of correlations is then examined to see which kinds of model are ruled out.

My main criticism is that I find the opposition between average leadership style (ALS) and veritical dyad linkage (VDL) models rather forced. I am not at all sure that those who champion ALS views have to argue that all correlations derived from within-cell scores must be near zero. It is sufficient, surely, to argue that they will be *smaller* than those derived from between-cell scores.

As Dansereau, Alutto, Markham, and Dumas themselves admit, to force the opposition between ALS and VDL models (as stated) is to reify positions "that have had little credibility with those who exercise leadership." Most practitioners would agree that it is not possible to treat everyone in the same way, and they wouldn't want to do so. But their behavior must contain "some core of consistency" (Dansereau, Alutto, Markham & Dumas) if they are to "create order out of uncertainty," in Kelvin's sense (Kelvin, 1970, p. 221).

If this is true it is important to ask how "consistency" is generated: to ask what kind of order the leader is trying to create. If I were to characterize one major difference between European and American research on leadership I would say that, in Europe, researchers have paid far more attention to the analysis of the leadership task and the political context in which it is located (e.g., Batstone, Boraston, & Frenkel, 1978; Thurley & Wirdenius, 1973, 1980). European social psychology has stronger links with industrial relations research, perhaps, than social psychology in the United States (Stephenson & Brotherton, 1979; Strauss, 1979). For my own part I would say that to understand the "core of consistency" we will have to understand the threats and opportunities individuals perceive in the execution of their work. Without analysis of this kind we cannot adequately characterize the nature of leadership as a social skill (compare Morley, 1980). One contribution of the chapter by Dansereau et al. is that it invites us to consider questions of this kind.

Also, the technique of within and between analysis deserves to be used more widely in research in organizations. It is quite general and gives more information than is contained in correlations between raw scores. However, it is not the only way to pit ALS and VDL models one against the other. What is required is simply that raw score correlations be supplemented with other statistics, such as unit variances and the like. This information is not always reported but it is relatively easy to compute. My own view is that current editorial practices should be changed. Personally, I would publish fewer papers on leadership but insist that authors provide much more descriptive information about the samples and data they have obtained.

Strategy No. 2

Strategy No. 2 is illustrated by the work of Lord, Foti, & Phillips and Sheridan, Kerr, & Abelson. Broadly, it requires the identification of "basic" cognitive, conative, or affective processes which generate the behavior we observe. Researchers may then attempt to give a general account of these processes, showing how they work through in any particular case. For example, Snyder and Diesing (1977) were able to illuminate the process of crisis bargaining by articulating the processes of information interpretation/search, influence, and decision-making which were involved. Their analysis has been extended by others (e.g., Morley, 1980) and there is every reason to believe that the study of leadership would benefit from the same kind of approach (e.g., Wynne & Hunsaker, 1975).

The study of information interpretation and information search is central to both cognitive and social psychology. Furthermore, cognitive and social psychologists have begun to think about key issues in the same general kind of way. Consequently, it is possible to identify an area of "cognitive social psychology" which is breaking down some of the traditional subject boundaries and contains contributions from both sides of the "fence" (e.g., Cantor & Mischel, 1979; Eiser, 1980; Fischoff, 1976; Hamilton, 1979; Hammond, McClelland, & Mumpower, 1980; Nisbett & Ross, 1980; Rosch, 1978; Snyder, 1979; Wyer & Carlston, 1980).

Broadly, the researchers share H. A. Simon's view that people, viewed as behaving systems, are essentially simple (Simon, 1969). Apparently, we have limited capacity to process the information contained in our environment and adopt processing strategies designed to minimize cognitive strain. The strategies are *both simple and powerful* so that human expertise and human error stem (in a sense) from the same source. In particular, we err when the strategies are too simple or when a strategy (generally successful) is used in a new and inappropriate context.

Lord, Foti, and Phillips proceed from the assumption that much of the previous work can be *made relevant* to the study of leadership. I agree with them, and find much to applaud in the attempt they have made. It is only fair to say, however, that a good deal of speculation is involved since research findings rarely deal with the cognitive processes of individuals operating in an organizational context, on site (Jabes, 1978, pp. xvii–xix).

Specifically, Lord and his colleagues have adopted the theoretical perspective elaborated by Rosch in her studies of the relationship between language and thought. Originally, Rosch was interested in color names and the perception of color. She argued that certain colors became perceptually salient because our nervous systems are constructed in this way rather than that. Category labels are attached to salient colors first, and later generalized to other similar instances. In this way, color concepts are organized around "natural prototypes" or "focal colors" (Rosch, 1974).

Rosch recognized that it was unreasonable to suppose that we come equipped with natural prototypes in all domains. Accordingly, her argument became more general (Rosch, 1978). Suppose the perceived world is divided into information rich and information poor "bundles of peceptual and functional attributes." Further suppose that "basic cuts in categorization" are made when discontinuities occur. Empirically, basic categories of this kind will maximize cue validity and category resemblance (Rosch, 1978), just as we have heard. What we get is maximum information at minimum cost in terms of cognitive strain.

So far so good. But how is this relevant to the study of leadership? I take it that the category systems used by members of organizations, leaders and followers, will have the general characteristics which have been outlined. (In heretical moments I think this is more to do with the nature of taxonomies than with the nature of people.) However, what we should be moving toward is an account of the ways in which people are actually classified as being this or that type. The kind of emphasis I would like to see has been expressed very well by Hamilton (1979):

> Any given person can be classified into any number of categories, depending on the criteria that are used. . . . Obviously I do not use the same categorization scheme under all circumstances, yet . . . the person categories I employ at any given time influence what information I retain and what kinds of inferences I make about the persons I group into those categories. It therefore becomes important to understand the factors that determine what categories are likely to be employed by the perceiver, the conditions under which various alternative groupings are likely to be used, and the variables that influence the perceiver to change the basis of his social categorization scheme. (P. 59)

Actually, Lord et al. don't need Rosch's theoretical apparatus. They don't *use* it in any case. Personally, I would have used the kind of framework provided, say, by Hamilton in his work on stereotypes. This introduces the prototype concept which Lord et al. require, and produces policy implications very similar to those which Lord et al. outline (Hamilton, 1979).

Empirically, Lord et al. have conducted some very interesting experimental work, showing that ratings of leader behavior (using the LBDQ) are guided by prototypes of the leader category rather than the behavior directly observed. The person observed is categorized as a person of a certain type, and expected to behave in a certain kind of way. Cognitive strain is minimized if subjects recall the prototype and generate answers from it.

I find this argument very plausible—but I cannot resist pointing out that it can be turned round. Hamilton (1979), and others, have shown that stereotypes/prototypes can be generated as a consequence of limited processing power. Apparently, people are differentially attentive to salient or distinctive events. Furthermore, they overestimate the extent to which distinctive stimuli go together. Accordingly, categories may be selected on the basis of differential perceptions based on "illusory correlations." That is, the behavior which is observed may generate the prototype which is used.

Hamilton's work underscores the importance of salient events, the main theme of the chapter by Sheridan, Kerr, and Abelson. Once again, there is much to commend in the chapter. Once again, the most serious deficiency is the link between theory and data.

As Solomon (1980) has pointed out, the opponent process theory is "in vogue" at the moment. It is a theory about acquired motivation, designed to explain what happens when an unconditioned stimulus, reinforcer, or innate releaser is repeatedly presented to human subjects. Technically, the theory is designed to cover the phenomena of affective or hedonic contrast, affective or hedonic habituation, and the syndrome or withdrawal or abstinence which occurs after stimulus termination. In ordinary language, it is designed to explain, say, the changes in motivation shown by free-fall parachutists. Initially, they exhibit anxiety (before the jump), then terror, then relief. But as they gain experience the pattern changes to one of eagerness, then thrill, then exhilaration. To generate these kinds of effects it is assumed, first, that there are stable unconditioned reactions (a-processes) directly proportional in magnitude to the intensity of the unconditioned stimulus, reinforcer, or innate releaser. I assume that this is why Sheridan et al. measure *extremity of performance* rather than *intensity of experience*. The a-processes elicit opposing b-processes, slow to decay after the unconditioned stimulus has been withdrawn and the a-processes have stopped.

The crucial weakness is that Sheridan et al. don't test the dynamics of the opponent process per se. Rather, they end up saying that extreme behavior has more impact when leader behavior in general is relatively rare. In other words, behavior has more impact when it is distinctive. I know it's easy to be wise after the event, but to say this you don't need the opponent process theory at all. And when you jettison the theory you don't, in this case, get any mileage from the language of "opponent processes" which is used instead. The chapter isn't an "heroic generalization" of the theory: it isn't a generalization at all. Furthermore, if Landy (1978) is correct, it is a mistake to head the chapter "activation theory" since, in his view, activation theories and opponent process theories are not at all the same. Despite this, the authors seem to me to be on to something, empirically. The finding that each set of frequency and "intensity" measures accounted for unique (and sizeable) portions of variance deserves to be noted and followed up. The LBARS scales may represent an important addition to the scaling techniques we can use.

Implications

Each of the three chapters we have heard argues (in its own way) the importance of *distinctive* leadership events. I am sure it is important to maintain this emphasis in future research. For one thing I hope that the contributors will carry on with their work. But I would also like to see work on distinctiveness linked with work on values and power, perhaps along the lines suggested by Sayles (1979). Sayles made the important observation that power comes from visibility. And visibility is gained by undertaking innovation, demonstrating critical skills, and making external relationships unpredictable. In other words, power is gained when behavior is made distinctive in certain kinds of ways.

It is, however, important to note that there is more involved than just distinctiveness per se. Sayles recognized this when he wrote that: "All these structural maneuvers require more than the idea; they require forceful advocacy on the part of the leader of the group, department or faction. Since ideas will be in competition for the attention of top management . . . they have to be sold by persuasive logic and persistence" (pp. 100–101). Here, I am reminded of some of the work on minority influence by Moscovici, Nemeth and others (Moscovici & Nemeth, 1974). More generally, however, I would say that how ideas need to be sold will depend on the threats and opportunities perceived by the target. To repeat, leadership is about the creation and maintainence of social order. Essentially, it is about values and power.

A Multiplexed Response to Bass and Morley

FRED DANSEREAU, JR., JOSEPH A. ALUTTO, STEVEN E. MARKHAM, and MacDONALD DUMAS

Based on the comments of the reviewers there appears to have been at least one key issue insufficiently developed in our chapter. Our work is not intended to suggest that the VDL and ALS models must occur evrywhere at all times in all data sets. Instead, the thrust of our efforts has been to demonstrate that the question of whether an ALS, VDL, or *neither* effect occurs can be addressed empirically. Clearly, the within and between analysis (WABA) as presented in the chapter is only one technique available for testing among these alternatives. WABA does have at least one advantageous feature in that, for the purpose of empirical testing, multiple models are assumed equally plausible at the beginning of a study and data are employed to choose among these alternatives.

From this perspective, the approach identified by Bass is a step beyond the question which we addressed. In the footnote to his comments he describes Factor A as a between cell factor and Factor C as a within cell factor *before* the analysis begins thereby partially justifying use of the F-Ratio as a test for an effect. However, the purpose of our analysis is to ask a more fundamental question, namely does Factor A (for example task structure) involve a group (ALS) or dyadic (VDL) level variable or neither effect. The choice among these alternatives in WABA is based upon data and not assumptions or assertions made prior to data gathering.

Interestingly, the notion of variance seems to us to have been raised not just by Bass but also by Morley as an important potential addition to WABA. In our view this is correct. However, the way in which variance is to be incorporated into WABA may not be as simple as it appears at first glance. On the one hand, Morley suggests the use of variance in a descriptive sense. On the other hand, Bass's comments imply that variance be included in an inferential sense (i.e., ANOVA).

The solution to this substantively based statistical problem (i.e., testing for effects other than by using the F-Ratio) should have at least two characteristics. First, it should not preclude the type of analysis which Bass describes but, rather, should view his case as a very special one which applies under very particular circumstances (some of these assumptions are presented in the footnote to his comments). Second, it should not preclude the ability to specify in a descriptive sense the meaning of the ALS and VDL models as suggested by Morley. Essentially, we believe the question of how to incorporate the variance notion as suggested in both sets of comments is one worthy of future attention (see also Stogdill & Coans, 1957, and Yammarino & Dansereau, 1980).

In the same vein, there are several other issues which were raised in the comments which we also view as open questions. We agree with Morley that one condition in order to infer an ALS effect is that the within cell correlations should be "smaller" than between cell correlations. However, we are not willing to close the issue by suggesting that this is a sufficient condition. It is certainly *one* necessary condition, but it is not clear that it is the only condition which needs to be met. In a similar vein, Bass highlights a series of problems with statistical analysis in general (e.g., power, small sample sizes, etc.). We believe that most of these issues apply to the ANOVA and correlational analysis. An alternative method for addressing some of these issues may involve developing indicators of practical significance in addition to statistical significance. While this concern is reflected in our current research, here we merely note agreement on a need for decision criterion beyond that of traditional statistical significance.

Essentially, our concern in this response is not with the validity of the issues which the comments raise, but rather, with solutions to the problems which they identify. WABA is a relatively new approach and our concern, as was that of the reviewers, is that its strengths and limitations be clearly understood.

Properly Categorizing the Commentary: A Rejoinder to Bass and Morley

ROSEANNE J. FOTI, ROBERT G. LORD, and JAMES S. PHILLIPS

Although we feel that the comments made by Bass were interesting, there are four major instances where we believe his comments indicate he has misinterpreted our chapter.

One of the first points Bass makes is that the idea of stereotypes (prototypes) is not new. Bass rightfully points out that stereotypes have been in the literature for a long time. What is new, and is developed in our chapter, is explaining stereotypes from a cognitive point of view and developing a precise explanation from a social information processing perspective.

Bass goes on to say that what is needed are simple, necessary concepts that will produce new insights about leadership. He states that attribution theory can be profitably applied to the leader-follower relationship. Admittedly, categorization theory is complex, but in understanding the phenomenology of leadership perceptions, categorization theory is more, or at least as useful as attribution theory. In a recent study by Phillips and Lord (in press) investigating the importance of causal attributions in determining perceptions of leadership, categorization, not attribution theory, provided the more general explanation of subjects' leadership ratings.

In summarizing categorization theory, Bass states that whether a person is placed into one category or another depends on the subsequent image (of the target person) remaining over time. It is this third point that reflects the greatest misunderstanding of the categorization process. Whereas Bass correctly notes the impact of the category on the image someone retains over time, it is more accurate to say that the category used determines the image that remains over time.

A fourth point made by Bass is that purely behavioral explanations of leadership cannot be dismissed. He emphasizes the need for studies which do not depend on subjects' observations and perceptions. However, one implication of the categorization process we have proposed is that to the extent the contents of a particular category are widely shared, categorization may also provide a standard for appropriate behavior in a given situation. Therefore, even a behavioral measure of leadership may be affected by perceptions.

In conclusion, we would like to say a few words about the comments made by Morley. We feel they reflect an accurate summary of our chapter and raise some interesting questions. However, Morley makes the point that the work of Hamilton (1979) on stereotypes would provide a more suitable framework for the categorization process, and that the theoretical apparatus developed by Rosch (1978) is not necessary. Admittedly, the majority of the chapter deals with the prototype concept; and the positive results of our initial studies concerning prototypicality do not indicate that other concepts derived from Rosch's categorization theory can be appropriately applied to leadership. However, it is this theoretical apparatus which allows Rosch to propose such concepts as "inclusiveness" and "distinctiveness"— important in identifying the usefulness of particular categories in classifying stimuli, and the reason we have pursued this approach.

Part 3

Micro and Macro Extensions to Establishment Views

Introduction

James G. Hunt, Uma Sekaran, and
Chester A. Schriesheim

As implied by the part title, the chapters in this part focus on opposite ends of a micro (individual and group) macro (intergroup, organization, and environment) continuum. As such they are difficult to integrate but are useful in serving as a springboard which is used by Tosi in his commentary chapter to discuss an interesting reconceptualization in the study of leadership.

In considering the micro-oriented contribution by Bales and Isenberg (chapter 10) it is interesting to keep in mind a conversation between Isenberg and one of the editors. He suggested that Bales had gone "underground" from his classic group and leadership work of the 1950s (e.g., Bales, 1950) and had resurfaced at the symposium. This may be overstated a bit since one could argue that Bales's recent co-authored book, *SYMLOG: A System for the Multiple Observation of Groups* (see Bales, Cohen, & Williamson, 1979), constituted a resurfacing. If that is so, the present chapter, "SYMLOG and Leadership Theory," might be considered resurfacing within a leadership context. That is, indeed, what we had in mind when we invited the Bales and Isenberg presentation. We see it as a very interesting and innovative approach that moves beyond establishment views.

As one will note in reading the Bales et al. (1979) book, it is long and thorough. Thus, Bales and Isenberg faced substantial problems in trying to condense its content for a chapter which also treats applications to leadership. We believe they did a good job. However, where issues arise concerning methodology and the like we suggest that readers consult the book, where such questions are treated in great detail.

With respect to the essence of the chapter, SYMLOG is a theory and set of methods for research on the interplay between the dynamics of both individual perception and social interaction. The SYMLOG system is based on a three-dimensional behavior space that is the result of a considerable amount of research on interpersonal perception, social interaction, problem solving, and leadership in small groups.

SYMLOG provides a number of options for measuring the behavior of interacting group members, perceived demands, group member values, and the like. Such measures provide a means for evaluating polarization and unification tendencies within the group. Consistent with this, leadership is seen as exerting a decisive determining influence on the formation, development, or termination of a pattern of polarization-unification in the direction of behavior and/or value realization in a group. Thus, a key function of the leader is to be aware of the polarization tendencies within the group and to take actions to neutralize these. Bales and Isenberg describe this process in their chapter.

Those familiar with Bales's earlier work will recognize its roots in this approach but SYMLOG goes far beyond that earlier work. The approach allows for in-depth analysis of processes taking place in ongoing groups and their implications for the successful exertion of leadership. Its multiple methods and sophisticated conceptualizations make it quite different from other group and individually oriented micro approaches.

As the reader will note when reading the Bales and Isenberg chapter, even though multiple methods are used, there is a heavy emphasis on observation. This suggests that an alternative grouping might well have been with the Bussom, Larson, and Vicars observation chapter. Such a grouping would lead to rather different kinds of questions than might arise with the current grouping.

In sharp contrast to the micro-oriented presentation of Bales and Isenberg is the chapter by Hunt and Osborn, "Toward a Macro-Oriented Model of Leadershp: An Odyssey." There, the authors develop a leadership model with a heavy macro emphasis. It considers external environment, context (size and technology), and structure in combination with leadership. These variables are hypothesized to influence the amount of discretion available to the leader (discretionary leadership) and to interact with discretionary leadership to influence work unit outcomes. Even though the model has a heavy macro emphasis it also incorporates selected micro variables.

In addition to discussing the model, the authors describe, in some detail, its evolution from earlier work. It is quite apparent from this odyssey that "science" does not always move forward as smoothly and evenly as one might think from the way most research enterprises are described. This chapter treats the development, warts and all.

The chapter is a response to the lack of macro-oriented approaches appearing in the leadership literature. This lack has been made abundantly clear in previous symposia volumes (see Hunt & Larson, 1975, 1977, 1979) and is also emphasized by the authors. It is their contention that major advances in leadership research are not likely to be made if macro variables continue to be neglected.

One key issue that comes to mind in reading this chapter concerns discretionary leadership. The concept appears quite broad but the measure used by Hunt and Osborn is quite narrow. They point out that in this early stage of development they concentrated on trying to get a reliable and valid measure based on current work. Given the difficulty they report in being able to do even this, perhaps we are being overly optimistic to expect a broader measure of discretionary leadership, at least now. However, a broader measure would appear to be important if their model's potential is to be fully utilized.

A related question concerns the relationship between discretionary and required leadership and Stewart's demands, constraints, and choices model. As Stewart pointed out in her chapter, there appear to be some important similarities between some of these constructs, though there are differences as well.

Turning now to the commentary chapter, as we mentioned earlier, Henry Tosi uses this part's two contributions primarily as a point of departure for a novel approach of his own. While a first reaction might be that he has not fulfilled the discussant role, we feel that the innovative treatment of leadership in his model adds considerably to the content of this part.

He first points out how leadership is typically conceptualized in charismatic imagery terms but operationalized by the research establishment in terms of studying supervisors in low level jobs ("the language is mystical, the reality, mundane"). To reconcile these and other incongruencies, he argues for a paradigm shift involving changing the dependent variable to predictability, as well as considering a wide range of macro and micro dependent variables. He thus sees leadership as providing predictability in outcomes which are embedded within an ongoing organization.

Philosophically, and even to some extent operationally, he is in agreement with the thrust of Osborn and Hunt. It is quite enlightening to compare his conceptualization with theirs, and we invite the serious reader to do this.

Further, Tosi's initial arguments have something to say about the practitioner-researcher split in the leadership area which Mintzberg (chapter 13) discusses. Practitioners seem to be constantly lambasting researchers because their studies are dull and boring and do not capture the "imagery" involved in their roles (cf. D. Campbell, 1979). Tosi would seem to argue that this can be avoided, or at least minimized, by his paradigm shift. However, others such as Bass (this volume) and House (1977) argue that these are different kinds of leadership, and that charismatic or transformational leadership needs to be treated differently from the move mundane forms, at both operational and conceptual levels.

10

SYMLOG and Leadership Theory

ROBERT F. BALES and DANIEL J. ISENBERG

A recent book, *SYMLOG: A System for the Multiple Level Observation of Groups* by Bales, Cohen, and Williamson (1979) presents a new theory and set of methods for research on the interplay between the *individual* dynamics of perception and the *group* dynamics of ˌovert social interaction and communication.

SYMLOG has been developed over a long period of time in conjunction with the study of academic self-analytic groups in the setting of a college course on group psychology (Bales, 1970; Bales, Cohen, & Williamson, 1979). The guiding practical aim has been to provide the members of a laboratory self-analytic group, and their leader, the instructor, with sufficiently rich and reliable information about their own behavior and perceptions in the group to enlist and sustain their interest, to enable them to learn from their own interaction, and to monitor their progress if they wish to change. Summary data from the methods of measurement are fed back to group members for their use and evaluation. Data from past groups and experimental side studies are analyzed statistically to improve the methods and the theory.

Students in the course also regularly use the methods to study outside groups of which they are a member. Many have made case studies of their family, others make studies of roommate groups, friendship groups, cliques, teams, and work groups. Graduate students, postdoctoral fellows, and other researchers have made case studies of therapy groups, classroom groups, families, organization development teams, and small organizations. The methods are most appropriate to groups in which each member knows and interacts with each other member to some degree, although certain extensions of the approach seem appropriate to the study of intergroup relations. The methods are designed to be appropriate both for research, and for the practical guidance of leaders and consultants.

The leader of a group may not have the opportunity to make any formal or controlled measurements, but still may be able to benefit from the theory of SYMLOG. He may formalize his past experience with members of the group using the Retrospective Rating methods. But even without this preparation, he may use his observations of the behavior and communication content of members during actual interaction to provide clues for the diagnosis of the present problems of the group, and possibly effective modes of intervention. This kind of application in real time is the ultimate practical aim of the system.

The SYMLOG Space

The SYMLOG Three Dimensional Space is a theoretical construct which is conceptualized or visualized in several alternative versions. For purposes of measurement, the space may be conceptualized as a factor analytic space of three orthogonal, bi-polar factors. For purposes of mathematical reasoning about the probable dynamic effect of variables on each other, the space may be thought of as a space of vectors.

The cube model shown as Figure 5 is a *logical* diagram for the purpose of generating and displaying a formal naming system for vectors in the theoretical force field. It is not a proper geometric representation of the factor analytic space, which we suppose would be spherical. The particular rotation of the three factors is chosen in order to have a set of vector names that suggest directions in the ordinary three dimensional physical space with which everybody is familiar. We are intuitively prepared to do quite complicated calculations in our heads about the relationship of directions (and vector forces) in Euclidean space, and this is a great advantage for practical application of the theory.

The three dimensions of the SYMLOG space are represented in Figure 5 by the three lines passing through the large cube. They are imagined to intersect in the center of the cube, and each one changes in polarity at the point of intersection. From the point of intersection outward, then, each dimension may be thought of as a pair of diametrically opposed vectors. For purposes of easier visualization and remembering of names, the pairs of opposed vectors are given names that suggest directions in three dimensional physical space from a point of reference at the intersection. The vertical dimension is called the Upward-Downward dimension, or U-D. The horizontal dimension from right to left is called Positive-Negative, or P-N. The final orthogonal horizontal dimension is called Forward-Backward, or F-B.

For the purpose of deriving names for additional vectors, each dimen-

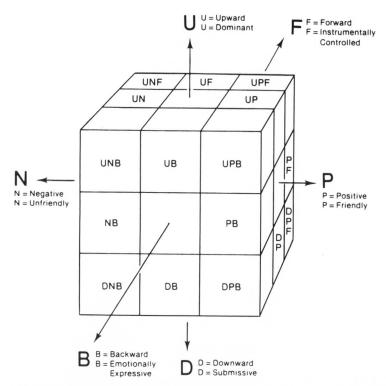

Fig. 5. The SYMLOG Three Dimensional Space, showing classes of directions, or locations, defined by logical combinations of the six named reference directions. The cube is seen from an outside point. The directions are named from a reference point at the intersection of the three dimensions, looking forward. (Reproduced by permission of the publisher from *SYMLOG: A System for the Multiple Level Observation of Groups*, by R. F. Bales, S. P. Cohen, and S. A. Williamson, copyright © 1979 by The Free Press, a Division of Macmillan Publishing Co., Inc.)

sion on the cubic diagram is imagined to be logically divided into three equal parts, one end (for example, U), the opposite end (D), and a middle part that includes the zero point where the vectors change polarity (the middle part is logically classified as neither U nor D). This division of each of the three dimensions into three equal parts results in a division of the large cube shown in Figure 5 into 27 equal smaller cubes ($3 \times 3 \times 3 = 27$). Each cube is named according to the vector that it then locates. The name UP thus designates a vector which is at an angle half way between the vectors U and P, and is at the zero point of the dimension F-B (it is neither F nor B). The cube in the center of the large cube encloses the zero point of all three dimensions and is named AVE, for Average. For practical purposes, then, there are 26 named vectors which have a definite direction.

The formal model was developed to summarize and coordinate the results of a number of different factor analytic studies. In 1950, Bales published his method for observation and classification of behavior of individuals in groups, *Interaction Process Analysis* (Bales, 1950). This method, in conjunction with various methods of rating, sociometric choice, and post-meeting questionnaires, was used in a considerable number of experimental and observational studies by Bales and his collaborators in the 1950s (see Bales, 1970). The well known distinction between "task leaders" and "social-emotional leaders" was one result of these studies, as well as the conception that "activity," "likeability," and "task-ability" should be regarded as three orthogonal factors.

In the early 1950s Couch and Carter factor analyzed observer ratings of the behavior of group members in a well designed study (Couch & Carter, 1952). They emerged with the conclusion that three orthogonal factors adequately accounted for the variance. They named the factors: Factor I, Individual Prominence; Factor II, Group Goal Facilitation; and Factor III, Group Sociability. Carter (1954) reviewed a number of previous factor analytic studies of leadership in which ratings and sociometric choices were used (Clark, 1953; Hemphill & Coons, 1957; Sakoda, 1952; and Wherry, 1950) and concluded that the results of these studies strongly supported his own results in the study with Couch.

Around 1954, Couch came to work with Bales who at this time was studying the role of value-statements in precipitating episodes of conflict or polarization in the groups he observed. Couch had a strong interest in the study of authoritarianism. Bales and Couch together searched the literature on attitudes and values, and composed a set of some 800 value statements which were then reduced to 252 for administration to a population of 552 respondents. One hundred forty-four items on which there was maximum variation across the population (signifying a relative lack of consensus for those items) were retained for factor analysis. Items on which there was low variation (or relative consensus) were dropped. The dimensions thus derived from the factor analyses tend to be *dimensions of polarization*.

The analysis revealed four orthogonal factors of agreement or disagreement with written value statements: Factor I, Acceptance of Authority; Factor II, Need-Determined Expression versus Value-Determined Restraint; Factor III, Equalitarianism; and Factor IV, Individualism.

A culminating study of the behavior of individuals in groups by Bales and Couch (Bales, 1970; Couch, 1960) included a very large number of measures (around 600) from different domains: a pre-test of agreement and disagreement with value statements derived from the study described above, a number of both standard and original personality tests, act-by-act observations of behaviors initiated and received using Interaction Process Analysis, act-by-act classification of value statements initiated by group members during interaction, using the four factors described above as the basis of categories for observation (Kassebaum, 1958), post-meeting ratings of behavior made by observers, and post-meeting ratings by group members, as well as guesses by group members as to the ratings they would receive from others.

The final interdomain factor analysis of the data was the principal base for the articulation of the SYMLOG space. Couch's study (Couch, 1960), consisting of a large number of subsidiary factor analyses in the separate domains of measures, and a final interdomain factor analysis, revealed six orthogonal factors. The first three, in order of variance accounted for, are essentially the same as those chosen for the description of the SYMLOG space:

	Couch's Factors		*SYMLOG Factors*
I—	Interpersonal Dominance vs. Submissiveness	U-D	Upward = Dominant vs. Downward = Submissive
II—	Interpersonal Affect– Positivity vs. Negativity	P-N	Positive = Friendly vs. Negative = Unfriendly
III—	Social Expressivity vs. Task Seriousness	F-B	Forward = Instrumentally Controlled vs. Backward = Emotionally Expressive

Couch interprets his last three factors as alternative modes of expression of the first three, with similar social appearance but opposite motivational roots. The first three he describes as "an '*actional*' form of expression in the overt mode of motoric actions, manifest feelings, and emotionally-toned behavior"; the last three he describes as "a '*content*' form of expression in the covert mode of the verbal meaning and symbolic content of the spoken statements" (Couch, 1960, p. 559).

Bales, working from the same set of data, adopted the first three factors as the major frame of reference, and worked out detailed conceptualizations and descriptions of all 26 vectors in what is now called the SYMLOG space, along with three 26-item sets of post-meeting questions for group members and observers designed to characterize and measure the behavior of each member on each of the vectors (Bales, 1970). Meanwhile, with his fellow teachers in the group psychology course, he continued to use and evaluate these measures with one-term, academic self-analytic groups. These measures were used with perhaps 25 or 30 groups.

The SYMLOG System of Measurement

About 1972 Bales started to work, with Cohen and Williamson, on a new observation system designed to be utilized in real time with computer assistance for fast feedback, and a cognate rating system which would take advantage of all that was then known about the space and its vectors. The post-meeting questions on behavior were converted to an adjective rating form of the kind shown in Figure 6. The items were repeatedly factor analyzed and refined, using both current data from the groups observed, and studies of outside sets of groups with varied populations. The aim was to arrive at an adjective rating form that was as simple as possible to use, and which measured the 26 vectors as exactly as possible, over as broad a population as possible. Figure 6 shows the General Behavior Descriptions form,[1] which has been described in the new book on the system of methods, called *SYMLOG* (Bales et al., 1979).

In order to obtain the summary score for the rating one person gives another on the U-D dimension, for example, the frequency scores on all of the items containing a U component in the vector name are added together, and from this sum is subtracted the sum of the frequency scores on all of the items containing a D component in the vector name. Since there are 9 items which contain a U component (see Figure 6, the first 9 items) and since each item may receive a maximum score of 2 ("often"), the highest summary score a person may receive for the U vector is 18U (9 × 2). Similarly, since there are 9 items which contain a D component (see Figure 6, the last 9 items) and the maximum score on each is 2, the highest summary score a person may receive is 18D. (The result of the subtraction is designated by a number followed by the resultant vector name, U, or D, for

---

1. Items with multiple adjectives are used in order to zero in more exactly on the desired vectors. It is desirable to describe the vectors as exactly as possible in order to be able to use the form for instruction to group members about the system, and for feedback to them, so that they may fully understand the whole space as a dynamic field, in which every vector has a polar opposite. The three-alternative rating scale of frequency (0 = "not often," 1 = "Sometimes," and 2 = "often") is chosen for speed and simplicity of use, as well as for ease of computation. A five-alternative rating scale (0 = "never," 1 = "rarely," 2 = "sometimes," 3 = "often," 4 = "always") shows very little higher reliability, if any (Bales, Cohen, & Williamson, 1979, p. 252), and makes it much harder to scale the summary scores on the three dimensions for graphic display on the Field Diagram.

		(0)	(1)	(2)
U	active, dominant, talks a lot	not often	sometimes	often
UP	extroverted, outgoing, positive	not often	sometimes	often
UPF	a purposeful democratic task leader	not often	sometimes	often
UF	an assertive business-like manager	not often	sometimes	often
UNF	authoritarian, controlling, disapproving	not often	sometimes	often
UN	domineering, tough-minded, powerful	not often	sometimes	often
UNB	provocative, egocentric, shows off	not often	sometimes	often
UB	jokes around, expressive, dramatic	not often	sometimes	often
UPB	entertaining, sociable, smiling, warm	not often	sometimes	often
P	friendly, equalitarian	not often	sometimes	often
PF	works cooperatively with others	not often	sometimes	often
F	analytical, task-oriented, problem-solving	not often	sometimes	often
NF	legalistic, has to be right	not often	sometimes	often
N	unfriendly, negativistic	not often	sometimes	often
NB	irritable, cynical, won't cooperate	not often	sometimes	often
B	shows feelings and emotions	not often	sometimes	often
PB	affectionate, likeable, fun to be with	not often	sometimes	often
DP	looks up to others, appreciative, trustful	not often	sometimes	often
DPF	gentle, willing to accept responsibility	not often	sometimes	often
DF	obedient, works submissively	not often	sometimes	often
DNF	self-punishing, works too hard	not often	sometimes	often
DN	depressed, sad, resentful, rejecting	not often	sometimes	often
DNB	alienated, quits, withdraws	not often	sometimes	often
DB	afraid to try, doubts own ability	not often	sometimes	often
DPB	quietly happy just to be with others	not often	sometimes	often
D	passive, introverted, says little	not often	sometimes	often

Fig. 6. The SYMLOG General Behavior Descriptions form (Reproduced by permission of the publisher from *The SYMLOG Case Study Kit, with Instructions for a Group Self Study*, by Robert F. Bales, copyright © 1980 by The Free Press, a Division of Macmillan Publishing Co., Inc.)

example, 5U, 3D, or 00, if the result is neither U nor D.) The summary scores for the other two dimensions are obtained by an exactly parallel process. Each of the three summary dimensional scores, U-D, P-N, and F-B, is thus based upon 18 items, 9 in each of the two opposed directions.[2]

The SYMLOG system of measurement preserves the distinction discovered by Couch between the three behavior factors and three factors of value content. Figure 7 shows a rating form for the value content of what the person says. This form is called "Value Descriptions." The items on this form are based on Bales's analysis of the results of the recording of the value statements initiated by group members in the large Bales-Couch study, presented in detail in Bales, 1970.[3]

It is important to recognize that although the same set of vector names is used for the *value content* vectors as for the *behavior* vectors, it is not assumed that one can predict the value position of a person (located from the value statements he initiates) from the behavior he or she actually shows, nor vice versa. The general implication of Couch's finding that the three verbal content factors are empirically independent of the cognate three behavior factors is that, in general, one cannot predict what an individual will do from what he or she says people should do.

SYMLOG also includes an act-by-act scoring system for observation and recording of the direction of behavior and value statements in real time. Figure 8 shows the observation form. It is typically employed by a team of four or five observers, since the amount of information required is too great for a single observer to record in real time. Each observer on his own time schedule picks out what to him or her is a "salient act" and re-

---

2. The doubly named items serve to measure two dimensions, and the triply named items serve to measure all three simultaneously. For refined research purposes the items are differentially weighted according to the amount they can be expected to contribute to a given dimensional vector, given the angle separating the item vector from the dimensional vector (see Cohen, p. 407, Bales, Cohen, & Williamson, 1979) but for practical purposes the unweighted scoring works very well, and of course, is much simpler.

Cohen's study of reliability of the form which preceded the present one, indicates correlations between split-halves of a large set of 64 raters of the same video-tape stimulus materials is .98 for the U-D dimension, .99 for the P-N dimension, and .98 for the F-B dimension. To reach a corresponding set of correlations at the .80 level will ordinarily require about 5 raters (Cohen, p. 261, Bales, Cohen, & Williamson, 1979). It is our experience that in a group of five or more, the group average Field Diagram is reliable enough that differences between it and the individual field diagrams frequently reveal important deviations in the way one individual perceives another and are not just random error.

3. This form is the result of a large amount of work in the past, although the specific items shown in Figure 7, and their direct employment in rating have not been as thoroughly tested as their counterparts in the Behavior Form, and no reliability figures are available.

		(0)	(1)	(2)
U	material success and power	not often	sometimes	often
UP	popularity and social success	not often	sometimes	often
UPF	social solidarity and progress	not often	sometimes	often
UF	efficiency, strong effective management	not often	sometimes	often
UNF	a powerful authority, law and order	not often	sometimes	often
UN	tough-minded assertiveness	not often	sometimes	often
UNB	rugged individualism, self-gratification	not often	sometimes	often
UB	having a good time, self-expression	not often	sometimes	often
UPB	making others feel happy	not often	sometimes	often
P	equalitarianism, democratic participation	not often	sometimes	often
PF	altruism, idealism, cooperation	not often	sometimes	often
F	established social beliefs and values	not often	sometimes	often
NF	value-determined restraint of desires	not often	sometimes	often
N	individual dissent, self-sufficiency	not often	sometimes	often
NB	social nonconformity	not often	sometimes	often
B	unconventional beliefs and values	not often	sometimes	often
PB	friendship, liberalism, sharing	not often	sometimes	often
DP	trust in the goodness of others	not often	sometimes	often
DPF	love, faithfulness, loyalty	not often	sometimes	often
DF	hard work, self-knowledge, subjectivity	not often	sometimes	often
DNF	suffering	not often	sometimes	often
DN	rejection of popularity	not often	sometimes	often
DNB	admission of failure, withdrawal	not often	sometimes	often
DB	noncooperation with authority	not often	sometimes	often
DPB	quiet contentment, taking it easy	not often	sometimes	often
D	giving up all selfish desires	not often	sometimes	often

Fig. 7. The SYMLOG Value Descriptions form (Reproduced by permission of the publisher from *The SYMLOG Case Study Kit with Instructions for a Group Self Study*, by Robert F. Bales, copyright © 1980 by The Free Press, a Division of Macmillan Publishing Co., Inc.)

cords it. The recording of a single act is called a "message," since it is meant to be used in feedback. As soon as a message is recorded, another "salient act" is selected, and recorded. At the end of the observation period, the records of all observers are merged to obtain a more reliable record.[4] The records are compared with each other to note peculiarities of particular observers, sorted out into small time periods, aggregated over time periods, and tabulated in a large number of ways. Computer programs are employed to perform these various mathematical and statistical operations, and to give both numerical and graphically plotted output. With simultaneous scoring and entry of data, a group can receive complex feedback on its interaction processes within five minutes of requesting such feedback.

The first three columns of the Interaction Scoring Form provide for a record of who acts toward whom and at what time. The Act/Non column (Figure 8) provides a way of distinguishing nonverbal signs of emotion (the "level Non") from intentional "Act Level" interpersonal behavior. The column called "Direction" is for the recording of the vector name of the behavior of the acting person, using the dimensions and vectors of the SYM-LOG space. The space called "Ordinary Description" is for a few uncoded key words of what was said or done, for better identification of the act on the sound record, and in particular to focus on the particular "image" contained in the verbal content, about which a value judgment is made. For example, the ordinary description of an image might be written as the key word "police." The "image" is the mental concept of the thing talked about, and about which a value judgment is made. The following column on the form is coded to show whether the value judgment is "Pro" (in favor of), or "Con" (against) the thing being talked about. The title of the next column, "Direction," means the direction or vector of the behavior or metaphoric behavior of the thing being talked about, or the value which it exemplifies. For example, a value judgment about the image "police" might be that the direction of their behavior is UNF ("authoritarian, controlling, disapprov-

4. Cohen's large study of reliability indicates that the merged scores of three to five observers are usually required to obtain satisfactory reliability on the two dimensions P-N and F-B at the ACT level, although more may be required for U-D (p. 373, Bales, Cohen, & Williamson, 1979). Polley's results with actual observer teams in the group psychology course indicate that by using the average obtained from a team of four or more, one may reasonably hope to obtain scores for the individual group members observed that will reflect their behavior with less than 20 percent of the variance due to error (Polley, Appendix T, Bales, Cohen, & Williamson, 1979). In Cohen's study correlations between two teams of nine observers each are .79 for ACT level U-D, .93 for ACT level P-N, and .88 for ACT level F-B (Cohen, in Bales, Cohen, & Williamson, 1979, p. 274). The correlations for the corresponding NON level, and the PRO and CON value content levels are somewhat lower, but range from .47 to .87 (Cohen, in Bales, Cohen, & Williamson, 1979, p. 274).

Time	Who Acts	Toward Whom	Act/ Non	Direc- tion	Ordinary Description of Behavior or Image	Pro/ Con	Direc- tion	Image Level
1:01	TOM	DAL	Act	UF	You can get it under control	Pro	UF	DAL
1:01	DAL	TOM	Act	DB	Don't have the training	Con	F	SEL
1:02	JRE	DAL	Act	PF	Maybe could apprentice	Pro	DF	DAL

Fig. 8. The SYMLOG Interaction Scoring Form (Reproduced by permission of the publisher from *The SYMLOG Case Study Kit, with Instructions for a Group Self Study*, by Robert F. Bales, coyright © 1980 by The Free Press, a Division of Macmillan Publishing Co., Inc.)

ing") or that the value direction they exemplify is UNF ("a powerful authority, law and order"). The final column, titled "Image Level," refers to the class of images to which the given image belongs, from the point of view of the speaker: Whether it is an image associated with the SELF, or with the OTHER being spoken to, or with the GROUP to which they belong, or their immediately environing SITUATION, or with the larger SOCIETY, or finally with some personal experience not accessible to the other except through his imagination, in which case the level is called FANTASY.

The Interaction Scoring system is important, even though it may not be applied in many groups for practical reasons, since it is necessary to an understanding of the more complex aspects of the theory, and is a model of the intuitive process of analyzing the interaction which one may use as a leader in the midst of actual interaction in the group.

The three coordinated measurement methods of SYMLOG, the two Rating methods, and the Scoring method for recording of observations in real time in general are convergent and reliable.[5] Together they give great

5. Although the three methods are all designed to measure the same 26 vectors in the SYMLOG space, they are utilized by different persons (individual group members, individual observers), and are intended to measure different levels of behavior and content. Hence, they are expected to reveal individual biases and the operation of psychological mechanisms of concealment, personality defenses, and distortions due to currently active processes of polar-

flexibility for applications of many kinds. One may use the rating methods to summarize one's perceptions and evaluations over any past period of time. One may use the rating forms to ask about the kind of behavior one "wishes" he might be able to show, or the kind he tries to "avoid." One may ask about the kind of values one feels he "ought" to realize, or that he tends to "reject," or feels that he actually does realize. For the clarification of group goals and group norms each member may be asked to describe the kind of behavior or values he feels a particular task or situation requires, what his own role should be, and what the role of each group member should be. One may rate other subgroups in an organization in terms of "the values they seem to be trying to realize." The conceptual images derived from all of these different kinds of rating, as well as from real-time observation, can be represented as point locations in the SYMLOG space, and from the resulting constellations additional inferences may be made.

By now it is probably quite apparent that some of the issues germane to leadership theory and research (such as the leader's behaviors, values, and perceptions of subordinates, colleagues, and superiors; the behavioral requirements of tasks; role expectations; decision-making processes; the relationship of espoused values to actual behavior, and so on) may be addressed through various uses of the SYMLOG system. It may also be clear that the SYMLOG system may be useful in the study of some leadership issues that have been difficult to approach empirically, such as the leader's position vis-à-vis the interrelationships of the subordinates (Katz, 1978). Finally, an important contribution of the SYMLOG system to the study of groups, and potentially to the study of leadership, is a theory of polarization and unification in social interaction. This will be discussed next.

---

ization and unification. Nevertheless it is important to know the general level of intercorrelations in order to extract significant information about biases. Cohen's large study found that a group of 19 trained Interaction Scorers showed the following correlations with a group of 64 naïve Raters in observations of a stimulus set of videotapes: ACT level Scoring with global Rating, on the U-D dimension, .72; on the P-N dimension, .89, on the F-B dimension, .85. The NON-verbal level Scoring was slightly less highly correlated with the Ratings. The two levels added together were higher than either alone: on the U-D dimension, .80; on the P-N dimension, .90; on the F-B dimension, .82 (Cohen, p. 276, Bales, Cohen, & Williamson, 1979). Bixby's study of nine successive meetings of a single group showed an average correlation between the ACT+NON Interaction Scores of observer teams of four, and group members short-form Ratings of each other after each meeting: on the U-D dimension, .72; on the P-N dimension, .73; and on the F-B dimension, .67 (Bales, Cohen, & Williamson, 1979, p. 344). Solomon's study (unpublished data) of the summary scores from observers' Interaction Scores over a term's interaction compared with group members' summary ratings of each other at the end of the term, averaged .64 over six separate groups, and over all three dimensions (Bales, Cohen, & Williamson, 1979, p. 464). Bixby's study showed that when Interaction Scorers also fill out Rating Forms immediately after the meeting they have scored, the correlations are high, as expected, on the average .79 (Bales, Cohen, & Williamson, 1979, p. 464).

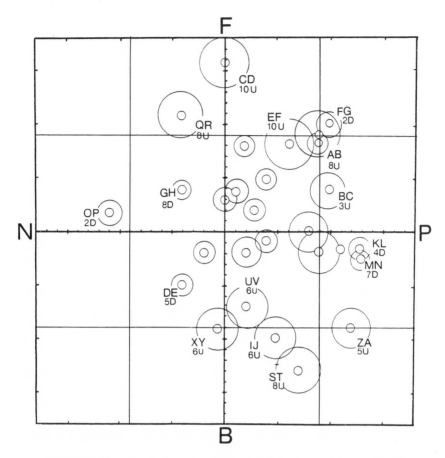

Fig. 9. Field diagram of a small organization showing location of member images as rated by member IJ

The Theory of Polarization-Unification

Figure 9 shows the behavior ratings made by one member of an actual small organization of 28 persons. The ratings are displayed graphically on a square form called the "Field Diagram" showing two of the dimensions, P-N and F-B. The Field Diagram shows the SYMLOG space viewed from the top looking downward. The "image" of each group member in the mind of the rater (in this case, IJ) is shown by a small core circle, enclosed by a larger circle, and labeled by the code name of the member and the location of the image in the U-D, Dominant-Submissive, dimension. For example, the manager of the organization, AB, is shown at a location nine units in the P direction, and nine units in the F direction. The designation just below the manager's initials is 8U, which means eight units in the U direction. The degree of dominance compared to others is shown by the size of the larger circle around the core circle. The larger the circle, the more dominant, the smaller the circle, the more submissive. (On this diagram, some of the images have been left without name labels, to reduce confusion.)

The results of the Interaction Scoring procedure can also be summarized and (after appropriate mathematical scaling) can be portrayed graphically on the standard Field Diagram. The Field Diagram makes comparison of many kinds easy (for example, the ratings of two different group members, or the average perception of the observer team members compared with the average perception of group members). But the Field Diagram is also used to prepare the data for the application of the theory of polarization-unification in order to make further inferences or predictions from the form of the constellation of images.

Figure 10 shows what is called the Polarization-Unification Template. This design is inscribed upon a transparent plastic sheet and placed on top of a Field Diagram, so that the images can be seen in relation to the inscription as in Figure 11. The inscription on the template represents the general theory of polarization-unification in abstract form, the images on the Field Diagram represent the data of a particular case; the "fitting" of the template inscription to the constellation of images according to certain rules represents the application of the general theory to the particular case.

Very briefly, the general theory holds that individuals tend to distort the location of images in their field of perception and evaluation in individually motivated ways according to various conditions (their personality defenses, wishes, fears, beliefs and values, their self-picture, presently activated emotional state, constriction of attention, etc.). These distortions are hypothesized to result in tendencies to make the total constellation of images fit within either *one* of the two large circles of the template (a unification of the cluster) or *both* circles (two unified clusters polarized in relation to each other).

The SYMLOG space is designed to be a space of the most common polarizations individuals introduce in their perception and evaluation of behavior and values. The design of the template inscription in terms of two large circles which extend to polar parts of the space along *one* dimension of vector opposition implies that under conditions that tend to distort the location of images, people tend to collapse the P-N and F-B dimensions of the space toward one dimension. Images that are similar enough to each

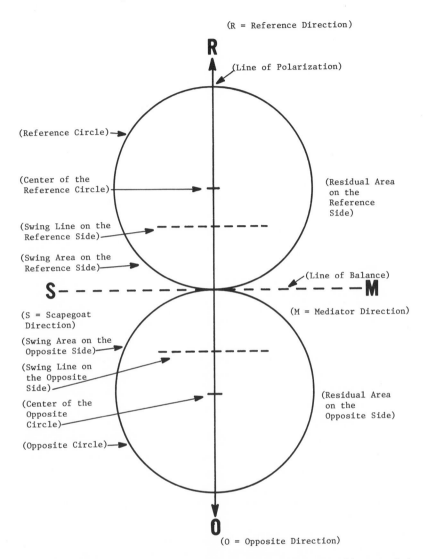

Fig. 10. SYMLOG Polarization-Unification Template (Reproduced by permission of the publisher from *SYMLOG: A System for the Multiple Level Observation of Groups,* by R. F. Bales, S. P. Cohen, and S. A. Williamson, copyright © 1979 by The Free Press, a Division of Macmillan Publishing Co., Inc.)

other (within an angle of less than 90 degrees on the plane of the Field Diagram) tend to be "assimilated" more closely into one cluster, that is, they tend to be seen and evaluated more similarly. We suppose that this tends to happen both with regard to a favored cluster (symbolized by the Reference Circle on the template), which usually contains the self-image, and a rejected opposite cluster, which contains the images of things avoided, rejected, hated, or feared (symbolized by the Opposite Circle on the template). Not all image fields show a rejected cluster. In some fields all the images that happen to be activated will fit within one cluster, in which case we say that the image field is unified.

The design of the Polarization-Unification inscription showing no overlap between the Reference Circle and the Opposite Circle implies that when a polarization is activated the two clusters of images tend to "repel" each other, that is, to appear more different from each other by a contrast effect than if the polarization were not activated. The Line of Polarization represents the average vector of all the activated images that are accepted and associated with the self-picture in the R, or Reference direction, and the average vector of the rejected images in the O, or Opposite direction. At the zero point of the Line of Polarization, between the Reference and Opposite Circles, a dashed line called the Line of Balance intersects the line of Polarization at right angles, and represents the line of locations between the two polar fields where vectors of acceptance give way to vectors of rejection. Images located along this line are theoretically expected to arouse ambivalent reactions of mixed acceptance and rejection and to be unstable in location. Two short dashed lines on either side of the Line of Balance are called "Swing Lines," and they locate an area called the "Swing Area" within which ambivalent attitudes may be significant enough to prevent definitive movement of an image toward either pole, with an "approach-avoidance" conflict toward both of the two poles. The Reference Circle, Opposite Circle, and Swing Area resemble the latitudes of acceptance, rejection, and noncommittal in Social Judgment Theory (Sherif & Hovland, 1961). Presumably many of the same principles apply, such as contrast and assimilation effects and self-anchoring of judgments.

Figure 11 shows the design of the Polarization-Unification Template inscribed upon the constellation of images shown in Figure 10. The template is fitted to the constellation by sliding and rotating the plastic template around over the Field Diagram shown as Figure 10 until the two large circles contain as much of the areas of image circles as possible.[6] The im-

---

6. The fitting procedure is not entirely formalized, and contains some elements of judgment, but it is quite carefully specified by a set of rules, which will be firmed up as the theory improves.

plication of the fit in Figure 11 is that the rater, IJ, does see the group as quite strongly polarized. A few images are left outside, or mostly outside, but the great majority of them fit within the two large polar circles of the template.

Isenberg and Ennis (1980) have shown that the constellation of images produced by a SYMLOG rating of a population of stimulus objects is essentially the same as the constellation of images produced by a multidimensional scaling (MDS) analysis of the rating of the same stimulus objects on the basis of perceived "similarity." Moreover, the first MDS dimension corresponds to the line of greatest spread on the Field Diagram, which we call the Line of Polarization. The implication is that an elongated dispersion of images on the SYMLOG Field Diagram, that is, "polarization," represents a dimension of particular salience for the perceiver, and a tendency to see images toward the extremes of the Line of Polarization as similar to other images toward the same extreme, and dissimilar to images toward the other extreme.

Isenberg (1980) has also been able to demonstrate that there are significant individual differences in tendencies to collapse the behavior description vectors toward each other, thus to cluster images with each other in the space in characteristic ways. These results have been obtained with a new personality test developed by Isenberg (1980) called the Behavioral Implications Task (BIT) which consists of asking the subject to take the description of each of the vectors in the space in turn, and rate how frequently in the experience of the subject the kind of behavior described goes together in the same person with the kind of behavior described by each of the other vectors. The image of each vector descriptor can thus be scored and placed on a Field Diagram, which can then be analyzed using the Polarization-Unification Template.

For some individuals the image of each vector is nearly in the position the descriptors were designed to measure. But for most individuals, there are characteristic and systematic distortions and simplifications in the construal of the space that can be described in a summary fashion as a tendency to polarize the space along a given line across the Field Diagram. Isenberg has shown that these individually characteristic distortions are significantly stable over time (test-retest reliability), are significantly related to the distortions that the individual introduces into his ratings of other group members with whom he interacts, and are significantly correlated with the individual's behavior as rated by other group members.

We have recently constructed a parallel test of the perception of value descriptors (the Value Implications Task, or VIT), and expect to find similar results, although the Line of Polarization at the perception-of-values level for a given individual may or may not correspond closely to that on the perception-of-behavior level. We are now in a position to test a set of hypotheses very central to the general theory of Polarization and Unification in the SYMLOG space.

First, we expect to find that the global tendency to accept or reject another person as part of one's reference subgroup is related both to the perception of the way that person *behaves*, and to the perception of the *value* position the person takes at the verbal-content level.

Second, we expect to find that the tendency to accept or reject the *behavior* of the other will be a function of the *angle of separation* between one's own Line of Polarization on the BIT, and the other's Line of Polarization on the BIT. If the angle of separation is less than 90 degrees we expect that the tendency will be to accept, and "unify" one's own image with that of the other—to perceive the two images as both within the Reference Circle of the template. If the angle of separation is more than 90 degrees we expect that the tendency will be to reject the other, and to polarize the perception of the other in relation to one's self-image.

Third, we expect to find, similarly, that the tendency to accept or reject the *value* content position of the other will be a function of the angle of separation between one's own Line of Polarization on the VIT, and the other's Line of Polarization on the VIT. As in the case of the BIT, we suppose that the critical angle between acceptance and rejection will be an angle of 90 degrees.

Fourth, we expect that the ratio of overt negative behavior compared to positive behavior addressed to the other will be correlated with an index made by adding together the two angles of separation mentioned above.

Fifth, we expect that preponderantly positive behavior between the two persons of a pair will tend to increase the perception of unification, while preponderantly negative behavior will tend to increase the perception of polarization.

Sixth, all of these effects will be amplified or diminished according to the dominance of the other member and the degree to which his value position is revealed.

These hyotheses are currently under test. They express, in operational form, the impressions we have formed through clinical observation. Most groups have a chronic pattern of polarization-unification which is quite resistant to change, but also show transient episodes which vary widely from each other in the direction of the Line of Polarization. We very frequently observe what we call "episodes" of polarization or unification, in which the focusing of attention in the group on the behavior of a particular individual or subgroup, or on an emotionally loaded content image seems to result in a prolonged build-up of interpersonal conflict, or a prolonged convergence among members in a particular direction of behavior and value content, as in a flight of fantasy or the emergence and persistence of a mood. Episodes of this kind can be detected and studied using the time plots of behavior and value content produced by the SYMLOG Interaction Scoring method.

Although we have not yet been able to bring all the resources of SYM-LOG measurement to bear upon the detection and study of these episodes it seems intuitively evident to us that they are often "set off" by specific things said and done by specific individuals and that they are often terminated by identifiable specific acts and content images. We regard these acts which seem to initiate change in the general gestalt of the interaction process as acts of leadership.

The SYMLOG theory of polarization and unification suggests that for any particular direction of the Line of Polarization in the mind of an individual, *the most strategic directions of intended leadership acts for collapsing or neutralizing the polarizing processes (if that is desired) are the directions that are exactly orthogonal to the Line of Polarization.*

The theory holds that very salient interventions of behavior or content imagery far out along the Line of Balance in a given polarization have the best prospect of neutralizing the polarization by fastening the attention of group members on a new image. If the new image elicits the positive side of the ambivalent attitudes of two polarized sub-groups, it may be called a "Mediator." If it elicits the negative side of the ambivalent attitudes of the two polarized sub-groups and so becomes the object of displaced hostility, it may be called a "Scapegoat." The *fitting of the Overlay to the constellation of images plotted on the Field Diagram locates the Mediator and Scapegoat vectors for that particular constellation,* and the general theory of the SYMLOG space provides hypotheses as to what specific kinds of behavior or value content correspond to the strategic Mediator and Scapegoat vectors.

Perhaps these hypotheses may be made more vivid by a few details from the case of the small organization represented in Figure 11. The organization is the library service of a Washington agency that performs studies for the government under contract. The security regulations are strict. Every employee is required to have a top secret clearance. The guardianship of secret information thus creates a value justification for a high degree of formal control.

IJ, our observer, who made the ratings (using the SYMLOG General Behavior Descriptions form) upon which the diagram is based, is a 23-year-old young woman, a former student of the senior author. She learned SYMLOG as a member of the undergraduate college course in group psychology. Incidentally, her position in the self-analytic course group was very similar to her self-rated position in our illustrative organization. After graduation she went to work in the Washington office as an assistant to the

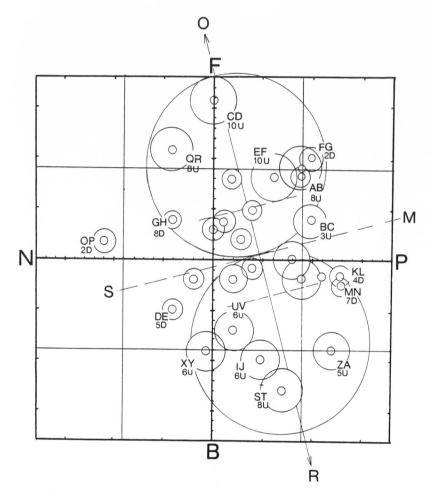

Fig. 11. Field diagram of a small organization showing location of member images as rated by member IJ (with Polarization-Unification Overlay)

manager, AB. After some time, AB asked IJ if she could give any advice that would be helpful to the organization, since many people in it seemed to be dissatisfied. Using the rating method she had learned in the group psychology course, IJ rated the behavior of all group members, including herself, made a rough diagram, and sent the data to the senior author, to see if he had any advice.

The manager of the organization, AB, is a 59-year-old woman and is shown at the location 8U, 9P, 9F, right on the UPF vector, which according to the rating system (see Figure 6) may be described in summary fashion as behavior which has the quality of "a purposeful democratic task leader." However, when the Polarization-Unification Template is fitted to the diagram, as in Figure 11, the manager AB is seen to be in IJ's Opposite Circle, along with several other dominant members, EF, CD, and QR. CD, a 53-year-old woman, is the assistant manager. She is located at the extreme task-oriented pole, in the location 10U, 00, 16F, or on the extreme UF vector, which is described qualitatively as the behavior of "an assertive businesslike manager" (see Figure 6). Near her, and to the negative side on a vector close to UNF is the member QR, a 58-year-old male, an "old-timer" at the firm who resents changes, especially when he isn't consulted, and is felt to abuse authority, as described by our informant, IJ. The UNF vector represents behavior that is "authoritarian, controlling, disapproving" (see Figure 6). The old-timer, QR, appears to embody and represent to our rater, IJ, the strict security requirements of the library, and the formal procedures which stem from them. The manager, AB, then, although herself rated as UPF, appears to be closely associated in the mind of the rater, IJ, with the (presumably rejected) cluster containing members CD and QR.

At the other extreme end of the polarization, near IJ's own image, is ST, a 30-year-old woman described by IJ as outgoing and warm, who "likes to challenge the establishment." (A later communication from IJ says that ST has recently left the organization because she couldn't feel comfortable in it.) The vector location of ST's image is 8U, 7P, 13B, or UPB, described on the Behavior Rating Form (Figure 6) as "entertaining, smiling, sociable, warm." In IJ's view, then, as portrayed by the fit of the Polarization-Unification Template on the field diagram of Figure 11, the organization appears to be polarized along an F (Instrumentally Controlled), versus PB (Positively Emotionally Expressive) line. There are indications that IJ also tends to view this as a value polarization between Conservative, verging on Authoritarian values, and those of Liberalism, verging on Radicalism. IJ identifies herself with the latter side, and is unhappy in the organization. Although the manager, AB, has asked IJ for suggestions, IJ is at least ambivalent, if not completely rejecting, in her attitudes toward AB.

According to the theory, the polarization in IJ's mind might tend to be neutralized to some extent, by the appearance of a very salient image far out on either end of the line of balance, orthogonal to the line of polarization. On the diagram (Figure 11) this line is shown as a dashed line, with S (standing for the "Scapegoat" vector) on the negative side, and M (standing for the "Mediator" vector) on the positive side. There is one image, that of member OP, near the Scapegoat vector and fairly far out. OP is a 32-year-old male systems analyst, said by IJ to be incompetent and disliked by almost all members in the organization. He is on the N vector, 2D, 11N, 2F, described on the rating form as "unfriendly, negativistic." In the eyes of IJ he seems to be in a location to be disliked by the anti authoritarian PB subgroup because his behavior is so unfriendly, and by the authoritarian subgroup because he is too rigid and incompetent to be very effective on the task. Our theory suggests that if events were to occur which made OP appear more negative and threatening—if, for example, he came to be suspected as a spy in this citadel of highly secret information, the salience of this image might well lead IJ to displace the hostility she feels for the members in the F subgroup on to OP. If enough others in the two subgroups also displaced their hostilities on OP, the two subgroups might well converge toward each other in a polarization directed at OP. If other group members see the field in ways roughly similar to the way IJ sees it, OP is in a dangerous location, apt to become a scapegoat.

On the other side of the Line of Balance, near the Mediator vector (marked M) is BC, at 3U, 10P, 4F. But she is not so very dominant, and not far out, hence not very salient. IJ describes her as "a motherly member, efficient in her work, but not overly concerned with the task." It does not appear that BC has a very strong potential as a possible mediator, in the eyes of IJ.

IJ's diagram does suggest, however, (according to the theory) that if AB herself, the manager, were able to modify her behavior toward IJ so as to become considerably more positive and less task-oriented, while retaining her salience or dominance, IJ might be able to accept her and identify with her. If AB became more identified in the mind of IJ as the leader of the PB subgroup, and less identified with the F subgroup, IJ might well be able to bring her positive feelings to the fore, and relax the polarization she feels toward the F subgroup. If AB were able to accomplish this preliminary step in modifying IJ's attitude toward her, she could then employ various means of persuasion, modeling, conditional rewards, and the like, to lead IJ in a more task-oriented, as well as more positive, direction. Concurrently, if AB were to employ the leadership rationale of SYMLOG theory, she would attempt to bring other members of the PB subgroup along with IJ. At the same time, she would try to lead members of the F subgroup in a more positive and less task-oriented direction, so that the two subgroups would tend to converge or unify in a more friendly, but still somewhat task-oriented direction of behavior. Ideally, each member would be dealt with individually be a combination of directions of behavior adjusted to the particular member's construal of the field, as represented by that individual's field diagram. Practically, of course, a manager or leader is not likely to have actual field diagrams for each individual member of the group, but the authors believe, from experience, that a workable approximation can be made by a sensitive and well-trained leader from the material provided by unobtrusive observation of the interactive behavior and value-content of member communication. In such an assessment, the rating methods and theory of SYMLOG applied by the leader alone can provide the essential means for crystallization of information acquired by participant observation to the point where inferences as to possibly effective leadership behavior can be derived.

In brief, we are hypothesizing that a better understanding of the dynamics of polarization and unification of image fields can significantly increase the success of intended acts of leadership. The dynamics of polarization-unification are powerful and often chronic, and in order to influence them in a desired way, one needs to be able to recognize them in process and to intervene at the points of their vulnerability or amenability to change. This, we believe, is true, whether one is working with a single individual (as in therapy) and so needs to take into account the dynamics of that person's perceptual-evaluative field of images, or with a group (as in leadership), and so has to take into account the *interactive* processes of polarization and unification of image fields that we call "group dynamics."

Some Implications for Leadership Theory

A working conception and definition of leadership may be derived from this view of personality and group dynamics: *to lead in a group is to exert a decisive influence on the formation, development, or termination of a dynamic interactive pattern of polarization-unification in the direction of behavior and/or value realization by whatever means.*

A great many inferences follow from this definition. A few may be stated very briefly. Leadership is measurable within an empirical action and reaction sequence taking place within specific time periods, which may be quite short. It is recognizable from the effect it produces. It is *not* recognizable from a specific predefined direction of behavior or a particular direction of values.

There may be times in a group when no leadership is taking place. It may be attempted but fail. A person who is appointed or elected to lead may not actually be able to exercise leadership. A person who does not intend to exert leadership may actually do so. A person may exercise successful leadership at one time, or with regard to particular patterns of polarization or unification, but fail at other times or with regard to other constellations.

More than one person or subgroup of persons may be attempting to exercise leadership in a particular pattern at a particular time and a successful leader may have to counteract or utilize the efforts of other aspiring leaders. There may be opposition leaders, scapegoat leaders, mediating leaders, and dominating leaders, as well as protagonist leaders. Leadership may be exercised from any direction in the space, or any value location, depending upon the dynamic constellation of the pattern of unification-polarization in the group at a particular time, thus, depending upon one's value system, leadership at a given time may be malevolent as well as benevolent.

A person may be appointed or elected as leader with the expectation that he or she will lead in a particular direction or directions of behavior and value realization, but may find that to hold leadership under changing conditions of polarization and unification, he or she must deviate from the expected directions, at times even need to controvert them.

There are various means of leadership, and a given leader may employ various means and combinations at various times, or change gradually over time. Behavior and change of behavior is one means, the expression or symbolization of values and change of value emphasis is another. A successful leader may act at one time or another as a model for emulation, as an evoker or provoker of other salient images, as a target of identification, projection, or transference, as a provoker of insight, as a therapist, teacher, trainer, shaper or modifier of behavior, or manager of rewards and punishments.

Although leadership is usually salient, it is not always so. It may be accomplished by indirect means, and may not be easily recognized. To provoke or encourage another person to become salient as a temporary or secondary leader is an indirect means. To initiate a change in the situation, task, or crisis external to the group which provokes or requires a given kind of behavior or value emphasis, or which changes the conditions of reward and punishment, is an indirect means. We may suppose that continued exercise of successful leadership in most groups and situations will require the employment of indirect as well as direct means of leadership.

It also follows from this conception and definition of leadership that, if one wishes to select, elect, appoint, or train individuals for leadership, one needs to be clear about the directions of behavior and values in the group that one wishes to have maximized in the longer run. Some kinds of leadership, though they answer the definition of leadership in the empirical sense, will be too deviant, malevolent, or ethically damaging to be acceptable even in the short run. Some kinds will be acceptable morally or ethically, but ineffective or inefficient for the directions one wishes to maximize.

Finally, it is almost certain that, even if leadership is effective in obtaining movement of the group in a desired direction, it will require dealing with transient problems, and indeed the basic complex requirements of the

group and its setting, by means of behavior and values that are deviant from the ideally desired direction to some degree at various times, and
will fail to reach the ideal of maximum movement in the desired value
direction.

An Illustrative Case: The Policy Research Department

Figure 12 is the Group Average Field Diagram of a department of a
policy research institute in international relations within an academic institution in the Boston area. The study was conducted by one of the authors (Isenberg). Through personal acquaintance with some of the members he gained access to the organization and was given permission to
conduct the study for academic purposes. Members of the organization
also wanted assurance that there would be no feedback to them. Under
these conditions they agreed to perform the rating procedure, and to give
individual interviews. Fourteen out of the 16 department members completed the ratings and interviews. One member turned in data anonymously, one failed to turn in the data, and one refused to participate.

The group average diagram shown in Figure 12 shows a mild polarization between friendly equalitarians and not-so-friendly members. However,
the more dominant members tend to be found toward the not-so-friendly
side. Member HI is the Department Head, and is found in the not-so-
friendly cluster. Indeed, HI, along with the others in his cluster, is on the side
of the polarization in the same direction from the main cluster as the Least
Preferred Co-worker LPC (Fiedler, 1972). As a matter of interest for interpretation members of the department were asked to rate on the SYMLOG
Form their "Least Preferred Co-Worker" (using Fiedler's conventional set of
instructions) as well as their concept of the "Ideal Manager (designated re-
spectively as "LPC" and "IM" in Figures 12 through 16). The Department
Head, HI, is near the opposite extreme of the polarization from the Ideal
Manager location. Several members, (JK, LM, NO, PQ) are close to the Ideal
Manager location, including RS, the female secretary of the Department
Head, who is, in addition, the most task-oriented member. Although none of
the group members is more than slightly on the emotionally expressive side,
HI is on the non-task-oriented perimeter.

It is apparent that there is something quite unusual in the behavior of
HI—although he is the appointed head of the department, one wonders if
he is the only leader. Perhaps one or more of the four associate heads of the
organization, or the secretary, RS, also function as leaders? AC is the most
dominant member shown on the diagram, and AC is in fact one of the associate heads. Two of the others are BD, located near AC, and CE, both members of the more friendly cluster. But the fourth, DF, seems to be associated

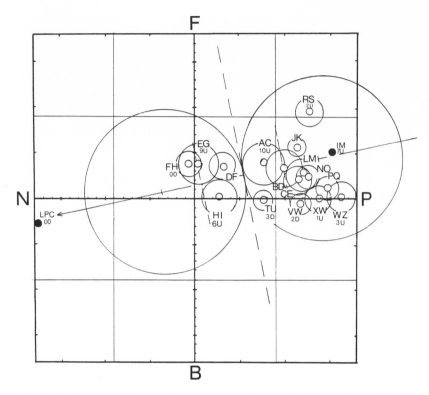

Fig. 12. Field diagram showing the average rating received by each member from all members in the policy research department (expansion multiplier = 1.51)

with the less friendly cluster, and not far from HI. Incidentally, the person who refused to participate in the ratings, and the one who failed to turn in the data, as well as the one who submitted data anonymously, are all located in the less friendly cluster. EG, the most dominant member of this cluster, is a research fellow in the department, as is FH, also in the less friendly cluster.

The interviews throw some light on the functioning of HI. Almost everyone in the department had something to say about him. Although perceptions of his behavior varied markedly in location on the diagrams of individual members, there was nevertheless consensus that he was unenthusiastic, unmotivated, did not actively lead, and was psychologically removed from the day-to-day activities of the department. Some people, particularly the research fellows, were disappointed that he did not initiate

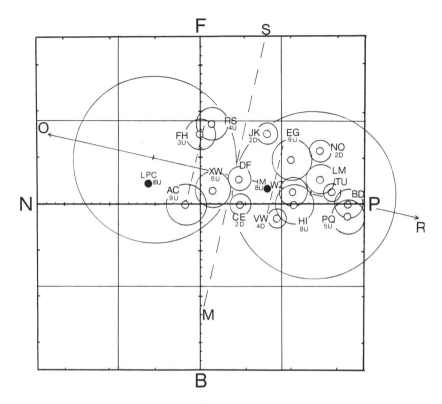

Fig. 13. Field diagram showing manager's ratings (manager = HI) of the behavior of members in the policy research department (expansion multiplier = 1.48)

research collaboration among the research fellows and instead let people pursue their research interests individually.

   Other people, particularly the associate heads, were disappointed that HI was not more active in presenting the department's resource needs to the managing committee of the research institute, in obtaining outside research funds, and in providing clearer role definitions for the associate heads. One of them mentioned that HI's laissez-faire leadership style created a power vacuum that was filled by uncertain and insecure associate heads. The associate heads and the research fellows felt that they were not clear about the roles of the associate heads of the department and this created friction and misunderstanding at times.

   Figures 13 through 16 show the individual field diagrams of four department members, HI, FH, RS, and WZ, and it is clear that each of these

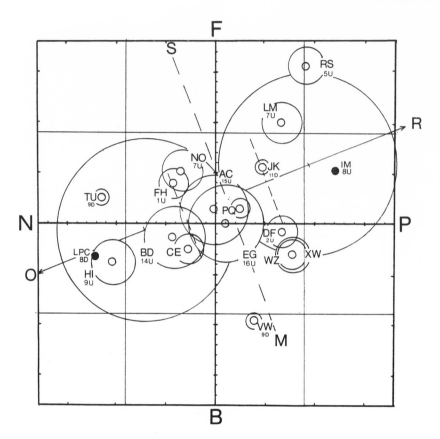

Fig. 14. Field diagram showing FH's ratings of the behavior of members in the policy research department (expansion multiplier = 1.35)

four people vary considerably in terms of their perceptions of HI. They also vary considerably in the overall structure they impose on the total field of department members, each of the four members viewing the other department members from his or her own particular viewpoint. WZ and HI are somewhat similar in the way they polarize the field, both showing NF-PB polarization, but they vary considerably as to how they view the behavior of specific members. RS, the secretary (who was rated PF) structures the field in a similar way but unifies rather than polarizes her perceptions of group members. She sees everyone as friendly, particularly HI. One wonders whether she is not showing a reaction formation, particularly given that HI, her boss, sees her as showing little or no friendliness. FH's field diagram diverges remarkably from the rest. He sees RS and HI as almost

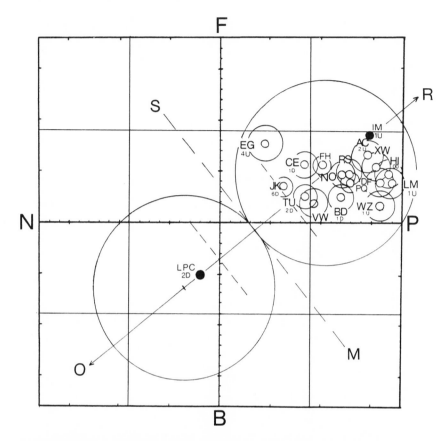

Fig. 15. Field diagram showing RS's ratings of the behavior of members in the policy research department (expansion multiplier = .922)

opposite in their behavior, and HI is quite close to the location of FH's least-preferred co-worker score.

What should the leader do? Looking at the group average field diagram the theory of polarization-unification suggests that mediation can occur if sufficiently salient images are introduced along the line of balance, orthogonal to the line of polarization. In the policy research department this could be either UPF or UPB behavior. Perhaps both are necessary to some extent, or with different organization members, but given that this is an organization with goals, responsibilities, and resources to allocate, we expect that task-oriented, friendly, and dominant behavior would be helpful in reducing the polarization, and moving the department toward its goals. Ideally, in his behavior towards FH, EG, and DF, HI would empha-

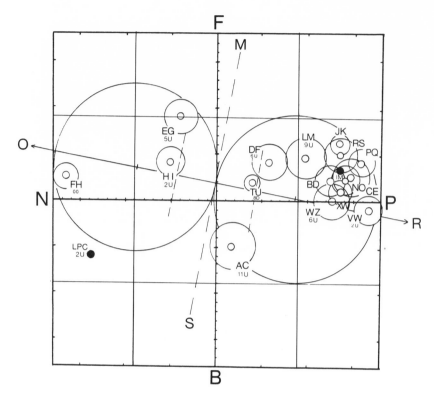

Fig. 16. Field diagram showing WZ's ratings of the behavior of members in the policy research department (expansion multiplier = .97)

size the task-oriented aspects of his behavior so as not to be overly identi-fied with the friendly subgroup. Similarly, HI should emphasize the equal-itarian and democratic aspects of his role toward the more P and PF members of the department, in order to prevent them from identifying him with the individualistic subgroup.

Some leaders have difficulty showing enough versatility in their behav-ior to meet the demands of effective leadership. HI may be in the same position and his own individual field diagram suggests that he may be in a bind. In the first place, he has a very inaccurate, or at least a diver-gent, picture of his own behavior. HI sees himself as more Dominant and Friendly than others see him, on the average, and quite close to his own conception of the ideal manager's behavior. An inaccurately positive self-image is presumably an obstacle to effective leadership. Secondly, the line of polarization suggests that HI rejects behavior in the NF quadrant and as people behave in ways that are task-oriented, HI distorts his perception of their behavior toward the negative side of the space. HI's polarization of the space apparently causes him to distort and attribute unfriendliness to instrumentally controlled behavior. For example, on the average RS was seen as clearly the most task-oriented person in the department. However, whereas the other members saw her as cooperative, friendly, equalitarian, HI saw her as very often behaving as an "assertive businesslike manager" and in an "authoritarian, controlling, and disapproving" manner. He "rarely" saw her as a "purposeful, democratic, task leader." Thus HI's dilemma is threefold. He distorts and rejects precisely the type of behavior that is necessary in the situation. The ideal managerial behavior as he conceives it would serve to increase rather than decrease the polarization. And he experiences little need to change because he sees himself as actualizing ideal managerial behavior.

Conclusion

The authors believe that the theory of SYMLOG and its coordinated methods of measurement offer significantly new suggestions and possibilities for theory and empirical research in the study of leadership. A systematic comparison of the theory advanced here with existing theories of leadership is obviously needed. On the empirical front, the methods need further perfecting, particularly the methods for measuring value content, but they are well enough developed for widespread practical use,[7] and for significant research. Research by other investigators is presently going forward on the effects of SYMLOG feedback on group performance in computer based business simulation games, on intermember relationshps in families, and in various other settings. Research on the use of the system in leadership training is a very desirable next step.

---

7. All of the forms necessary for practical application of the system are included in a compact kit, which also includes a set of instructions for a group self-study that serves as a brief introduction to the system addressed to the individual group member (Bales, 1980).

11

Toward a Macro-Oriented Model of Leadership: An Odyssey

JAMES G. HUNT and RICHARD N. OSBORN

Buried deep within an obscure, seven-year-old, final technical report lies the spirit of a macro-oriented leadership model. This chapter traces the development of the model through the conflicting thickets of theoretical integration and empirical verification. It is essentially a status report on an emerging long-range programic research effort.

The journey started in the late sixties with an analysis of leadership in mental health institutions (see Hunt, Osborn & Larson, 1973). The initial thrust was to expand and refine: 1) Fiedler's (1967) contingency approach to leadership effectiveness, and 2) the multiple administrative level leadership work suggested by Nealey and Blood (1968). Leadership was beginning to emerge from the grip of determinism toward a problematic thrust. Perhaps one leadership style was not best in all situations? Perhaps there were systematic differences between the effective leadership of supervisors and their bosses?

Our initial results in one facility were quite promising. Leadership was important and the association between leadership and various measures of performance and satisfaction was moderated by a number of group factors. Further, it appeared that the leadership of upper-level managers was important alone and in combination with the leader behavior of the first-

The investigation reported in this chapter was supported by grant DA CH 19-78-G-0010 from the United States Army Institute for the Behavioral and Social Sciences to Southern Illinois University at Carbondale (J. G. Hunt and R. N. Osborn Principal Investigators). We would like to thank Harry Martin for assistance in a number of different aspects of the investigation and Anant Balarum, John Benandi, Paul Brown, Kevin Lindsey and James Tracy for assistance in data gathering and analysis. We would also like to thank C. A. Shriesheim for critical comments.

level supervisor (Hill & Hunt, 1973; Hunt, Hill & Reaser, 1973; Hunt, Osborn & Larson, 1973). But the blush of spring was dashed by the results which emerged late in the summer of 1971. Analysis of two other mental health institutions revealed conflicting findings. We blamed the measures, questioned our statistical analyses, and searched in vain for one or a number of employee, managerial, and group factors which would produce consistency.

No one variable or series of variables held the key to consistency. Sex, age, education, and intelligence failed as did cohesiveness and group atmosphere. Analysis of individual difference variables in combination with group conditions yielded significant but low proportions of explained variance in one sample. However, results were not replicable in others.

A clinical analysis of organizational and environmental factors appeared to resolve many conflicting findings. It also appeared that the lateral leadership of middle managers was important (Duffy, 1973; Osborn & Hunt, 1974a). Further, top management attitudes toward how to treat patients was an important predictor of employee satisfaction and performance *in combination* with supervisory leadership (Hunt, Osborn, & Larson, 1975). On balance, macro factors alone and in combination with leadership seemed important.

Enter House, the Two Bureaus, and a Fraternity

Our frustrations were shared by many in the field. Although early tests of Fiedler's model showed promise, doubts about it began to enter the literature with increasing frequency (e.g., Ashour, 1973; Graen, Alvares, Orris & Martella, 1970). The notion that leadership effectiveness was contingent upon nonleader conditions was generally accepted, but an appealing theoretical explanation was illusive. While Fiedler made the mysterious LPC work, House (1971) was publishing his path-goal explanation of leadership effectiveness. We were content to seek a partial resolution between Fiedler and House in reanalysis of the mental health data and exploration of a new data base. Again the major thrust was an investigation of leadership at multiple levels in subsystems with different macro conditions.

The new data base included a number of individual, group, and leadership variables for two quite different bureaus of a state highway department. One bureau was organically structured while the other was more mechanistic. Both shared a common administrative/policy umbrella (Hunt & Liebscher, 1971, 1973). Using variables conceptually similar to those House analyzed in the early development of his approach, we did not find consistent relationships across bureaus or managerial levels. The data were consistent with clinical forecasts, but we did not explicitly measure environmental, technological, or structural conditions.

We were at a crossroads. We had decided to confine analyses to areas where there were generally well developed instruments. Exploratory analysis of organizational environments and lateral leadership appeared fruitful, and psychometrically sound instruments for measuring them now appeared to be available. It was decided to collect another round of data in a sample where units shared a common technology and structure but differed in their geographical location (see Osborn & Hunt, 1976).

It also became increasingly clear that theoretical developments in micro analysis of leadership were difficult to translate beyond the individual and small group level. The literature in organization theory was a conceptual morass of conflicting perspectives, measures, and premises. However, there appeared to be some consensus concerning the overall pattern of relationships among environmental conditions, structure, and performance. In more uncertain, dynamic settings, organizations with a more organic structure appeared to outperform their more rigidly structured counterparts (e.g., Lawrence & Lorsch, 1967). Thus, we selected a sample of rigidly structured fraternity chapters which were in different environments and which differed in size. It was proposed that the leader could alter the mismatch between environment and structure to increase the chances of unit success. Further, the leaders in larger units should be more active than heads of smaller ones.

Analysis of the fraternity data supported our a priori expectations. Thus, for example, unit size and environmental conditions (Osborn & Hunt, 1975) were found to increase substantially the explained variance in unit satisfaction and performance estimates alone and in combination with leadership. But what were the links among macro conditions, leader behavior, and leadership success?

Enter the Adaptive-Reactive Model

Data from three different types of organizations concerning over 1,000 individuals and some 200 leaders appeared to form into a pattern. Environment and organizational conditions alone and in combination with leadership appeared important. The spirit of the model in our early technical report began to assume a more substantive form in a chapter in the book covering the third leadership symposium (Hunt & Larson, 1975). There we described what we termed the Adaptive-Reactive Model (Osborn & Hunt, 1975).

While the spirit was beginning to emerge, we were not home free. There were some false starts. We first postulated a very straightforward, simple relation between macro conditions and leader behavior. Specifically, we hypothesized that leader behavior could be statistically divided into two distinct portions. One was behavior under the volition of the leader; the other was in response to macro conditions. Our weak tests using residualization and partial correlation analysis confirmed the notion that macro variables and leadership were intertwined (Hunt, Osborn, & Schuler, 1978; Osborn & Hunt, 1975, 1977). Along with this, we also investigated a number of possible linkages including cybernetics, consistency versus inconsistency of action, and socioeconomic pressures (Osborn & Hunt, 1975, 1976; Osborn, Hunt & Skaret, 1977). The silver lining was the stress on discretionary leadership—leader influence attempts beyond those prescribed by the leader's role (Hunt, Osborn, & Schuler, 1978; Osborn & Hunt, 1975, 1977).

As we were searching and testing with modest success, most of the action in leadership research revolved around individuals, their tasks, and small groups. The Fiedler and House models were generating considerable activity (e.g., Fiedler & Chemers, 1974; House & Mitchell, 1974). Graen's vertical dyad linkage (VDL) model was also eliciting some attention (e.g., Graen & Cashman, 1975). At the same time, we were being pressed to provide a psychologically based explanation of why and how macro variables impinged upon leaders, their behavior, and their success.

Shortly thereafter the tide of the literature began to turn against the popular micro models. The assault took many forms. Detailed psychometric analyses of current instruments revealed numerous flaws and inconsistencies (e.g., Schriesheim & Kerr, 1977). Popular conceptual views were deemed to be internally inconsistent, based on false premises or both (e.g., McCall & Lombardo, 1978a; Melcher, 1977; Pfeffer, 1978). Many decried the common problem of low R-squares and inconsistent results (e.g., Hunt & Larson, 1975, 1977, 1979). Some called for a "paradigm shift" while others compared the mundane scientific view of leadership with the more exciting, mysterious, and dynamic practice of leadership by "real people" (cf., Campbell, 1979). There was a "plague on both your houses" feeling by some (e.g., Miner, 1975). The ink was barely dry on an early version of our attempt to incorporate macro variables when it too was tagged methodologically unclean, psychometrically impure, and ideologically toxic. Above all it was "traditional."

Back to the Drawing Board

We again reassessed our position and began a very systematic review of the literature. A 10-year review of leadership articles in six leading journals (Hunt, Osborn, & Schriesheim, 1978) mirrored much of the more global criticisms of leadership critics. To us, however, the cardinal failure was the virtual absence of any macro information even for such global factors as the type of industry studied or the size of the organization in which the investigation was conducted. To build models and clarify relationships on previous literature alone was hopeless.

We then turned to the emerging macro literature. Our purpose was twofold. First, we were interested in writing a text in organization theory. Second, it was apparent that the normal process of reductionism, repeatability, and refutation did not appear very helpful in theory building. Thus, we began searching for theoretical integration via holism and interrelatedness. Yet it was also obvious that it was quite important to develop direct estimates of discretionary leadership based on psychologically appealing explanations. The crosscurrent between theory building and empirism led to a moratorium on data collection.

The detailed literature review reinforced our own view (Hunt, Osborn, & Larson, 1973) as well as that of others (Dansereau & Dumas, 1977; Graen & Cashman, 1975) that the distinctions among indirect, interindividual (dyadic), and group forms of influence were likely to be quite important. We began to develop a series of testable hypotheses concerning the linkages among macro factors, leader behavior (both group & individual), and leadership effectiveness. We incorporated these developments into a modification of our Reactive-Adaptive Approach which we called a "Multiple Influence Model of Leadership." An initial practitioner-oriented version of this model with no data was described in a paper written in 1976 and which appeared in print in 1980 (see Hunt & Osborn, 1980b).

Along with these theoretical intentions we were hopeful measurement improvements in the LBDQ-Form XII would help us divide leader behavior into discretionary and nondiscretionary components. Thus, we started a series of pilot tests to check the improved instruments, measure group versus individual (one-on-one) leadership, and examine some linkages between macro conditions and leadership.

The pilot tests suggested we had again started down a blind alley. First, respondents could not distinguish between group and one-on-one leadership. Leader behavior was not statistically divisible into discretionary and nondiscretionary components (see Hunt, Osborn & Martin, in press). Second, the potential number of macro-leader behavior linkages suggested by Hunt and Osborn (1980b) was too extensive. Finally, our proposed associations between macro conditions and leader action lacked an overall integrative basis.

Interviews with respondents and colleagues did seem to confirm our notion of discretionary leadership. Leaders did go beyond*role prescriptions and these efforts were recognizable. We felt that an integration of macro forces could be matched with some of the emerging theoretical explanation emanating from current micro views. Particularly important to us were reinforcement, exchange, and attribution perspectives. These are incorporated as a part of the description of the model provided below.

Description of the Multiple Influence Model

The model as it currently stands is depicted in the top panel of Figure 17. The figure summarizes the multiple classes of variables seen as affecting both leadership and work unit outcomes in organizations. In addition to leader behaviors as a determinant of outcomes, the figure shows direct and mediating influences on outcomes of leader individual differences, subordinate individual and group and task characteristics, and the broader macro features of the organization in which leaders operate.

In the model, the unit head (leader) is seen as the key link between the organization and work unit subordinates (cf. Katz & Kahn, 1978; Likert, 1961). Following our earlier discussion, the leader is seen as influencing work unit outcomes through the exercise of *required* leadership and *discretionary* leadership. Required leadership is that dictated by the leader's role and is conceptually similar to standard supervisory behaviors (Jacobs, 1971) and "headship" (Hosking, Hunt, & Osborn, 1980). Discretionary leadership involves intervention with leadership behaviors beyond those prescribed by the role.

Though both micro and macro variables are shown as influencing leader behavior and interacting with it to influence unit outcomes, our emphasis in the remainder of this chapter will be on the macro environmental and organization variables. These, along with the leader's linkage role, serve as a key feature differentiating this from most current contingency approaches. Let's now look at the role of these macro variables in the model and the reinforcement, exchange, and attributional perspectives that provide theoretical bases for their tie-in with discretionary leadership.

Macro Variables and Theoretical Bases

The macro factors vary along a broad dimension of *complexity*, which is comprised of three sources: 1) complexity associated with the *environment*

Panel A: Components of the model

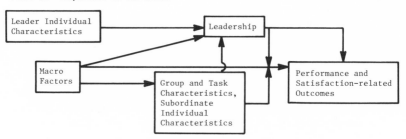

Panel B: Key macro relationships

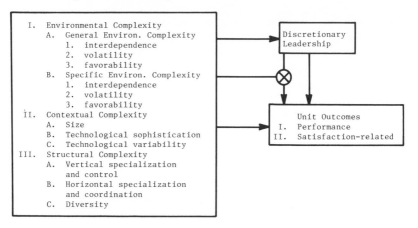

Fig. 17. Multiple influence model of leadership

and arising from interdependence, volatility, and favorability; 2) *contextual* complexity, based on size, sophistication of work unit technology, and variability of the technology between work units; and 3) *structural* complexity arising from: a) vertical specialization and control, b) horizontal specialization and coordination and, c) diversity of unit structures. The more complexity, the more opportunities and problems we see as facing the leader.

The model proposes that discretionary leadership is affected by macro factors, and that leadership and complexity interact to influence unit outcomes. Organizations are designed to accomplish objectives assuming a typical pattern of environmental, contextual, and structural conditions. However, these conditions may vary across work units. As complexity increases, these variations are assumed to increase. Leaders may fill these variations or gaps between typical and unique conditions as they relate to their subordinates and to other units by responding with discretionary actions. Why would they respond? And why would such actions increase unit outcomes? Reinforcement and exchange views can be combined to answer these two questions.

Reinforcement and exchange views center on recognition of inconsistencies in the stream of external reinforcers and the ability to make inconsistencies negotiable instruments for leadership influence. As the environment, context, and structure of a unit become more complex, there are more such streams of reinforcement and potential areas of exchange. At the same time, greater complexity from environment, context, or structure is seen as producing an imbalance among external factors. Thus, greater complexity not only increases the need for discretionary leadership but also the opportunity for such leadership. That is, alterations in complexity serve as "discriminative stimuli" indicating the extent to which discretionary leadership can be implemented.

Leader action may or may not be consistent with the stream of reinforcement entering the unit. The leader may respond with action to increases in complexity (he or she "can and does"). For instance, installation of new equipment calls for leader structuring. Conversely, the leader may not respond ("could but doesn't"). In the absence of the discriminative stimulus the leader could attempt action such as scholars have prescribed for over twenty years (Larson, Hunt, & Osborn, 1976). For instance, the leader could unilaterally increase initiating structure and considerate behavior ("can't but tries anyway"). And, of course, the leader may not act in the absence of discriminating macro stimuli ("can't and doesn't).

In the face of discriminative stimuli, the leader, as a formal linkage agent between subordinates and the organization, has a basis of exchange with subordinates (Jacobs, 1971). Leader action increasing performance is rewarding in itself and may lead to other rewards which can be dispensed through the leader. That is, complexity matched with leader discretion builds exchange credits for the leader.

A second base is from attribution views (e.g., Kelley, 1973). Leader action attributed to the superior is expected to have a more dramatic impact on subordinate affective states than action attributed to role requirements. Action attributed to the leader may be seen as direct assistance in coping with job and organizational problems. Conversely, when action is attributed to the "system" it is not seen as particularly helpful to subordinates in solving *their* particular problems. Thus action attributed to the system may be relatively non influential. For performance, the linkage is somewhat different. Following Langer (1978), leader action brings individuals out of semiunthinking modes of action and focuses their attention of information potentially salient for increasing performance. Such "awareness" helps change subordinate action toward performance improvement.

Details Concerning Components

We have briefly described the gestalt of the model together with some theoretical underpinnings. It would now be useful to examine its components from a conceptual standpoint.[1] This will set the stage for their operational treatment in the methodology section. (A summary of these components is shown in the bottom panel of Figure 17).

Environmental and Organizational Variables. We have found it useful to divide the environment into two segments—the general environment and the specific environment (Osborn, Hunt, & Jauch, 1980). The *general environment* includes environmental conditions common to all organizations operating within a particular geographical area (e.g., a state, a county, a standard metropolitan statistical area). Interdependence, volatility, and favorability are considered to be particularly important aspects of the general environment. As economic (e.g., per capita income), legal-political (e.g., per capita state expenditures), sociocultural (e.g., population density per mile), and educational (e.g., per capita educational expenditures) conditions increase, there is a tendency for more interdependence within the general environment. As the rate and direction of change of these conditions varies over time, the environment tends to become more volatile. Finally, as indicators of these conditions point to a higher degree of development or potential increase in resource availability, the more favorable we consider the general environment to be. Interdependence, volatility, and favorability are then combined to form our measure of *general environment complexity.*

The *specific environment* consists of the other organizations or units a given organization or unit works with to reach its goals (Osborn et al., 1980). Again we are interested in interdependence, volatility, and favorability. Interdependence is concerned with the relationships between a leader's unit and other units and of the other units with each other. Volatility is concerned with how stable and predictable the relationships are with and among the units. Favorability is concerned with the growth and resource availability of the units. Again, these are combined to provide a measure of *specific environment complexity.* The combined impact of both

---

1. Detailed justification for the selection of the components is treated in Hunt, Osborn, and Martin (in press), and Osborn, Hunt, and Jauch (1980).

general and specific environment complexity is obtained by combining both aspects of complexity into an overall measure.

Turning now to organizational variables, we divide them into contextual and structural. *Contextual* variables are considered to be partial determinants of an organization's or work unit's structure and outputs. Three key contextual components are size, technological sophistication, and technological variability (Osborn et al., 1980). Technological sophistication is defined in terms of the intricacy of transforming inputs such as raw materials into finished outputs. Technological variability is concerned with the range of outputs provided or the variability in duties performed by different employees (Osborn et al., 1980). Size, technological sophistication, and technological variability are combined into a measure of *contextual complexity*.

Moving from contextual to organizational *structure* variables, we are concerned with vertical specialization and control, horizontal specialization and coordination, and the diversity across a unit's dominant pattern of vertical dimensions and horizontal dimensions (Osborn et al., 1980). Vertical specialization and control is concerned with the tendency of an organization to formalize and emphasize the managerial hierarchy, techniques, and rules, policies, and procedures to control goals, technology, property, personnel, and outputs (Osborn et al., 1980). Horizontal specialization and coordination is the extent and pattern of departmentalization and use of personal and impersonal mechanisms for control (Osborn et al., 1980). Diversity in vertical and horizontal specialization is concerned wtih the variety of control and coordination mechanisms in the vertical and horizontal structures (Osborn, 1980). Vertical specialization and control, horizontal specialization and coordination, and diversity are combined to provide a measure of *structural complexity*.

Leadership. Following our earlier discussion we treat leadership in terms of vertical and lateral components. Vertical leadership is conceptualized in terms of the discretionary leader behavior discussed above. Lateral leadership is treated in terms of the leader's general orientation toward dealings with those at or near his/her own organization level. For example, to what extent do leaders think it appropriate to: a) develop specific guidelines for interunit exchanges, b) structure relations with other leaders, or c) respond to pressures from others? It has been argued by us (e.g., Hunt & Osborn, 1980b) and others (e.g., Sayles, 1964) that lateral relations of this kind are likely to be quite important—perhaps even more important than the more traditionally considered vertical leadership. Since little is known about lateral leadership, we have decided to treat it in an exploratory manner. Thus it is not shown in the figure.

Unit Outcomes. These are considered in terms of both work unit performance and several satisfaction-related variables which we have grouped together under the label *employee maintenance.* Consistent with Osborn et al. (1980), employee maintenance is a term used to describe a series of criteria centering on the attachment (or withdrawal) of employees to an organization. These criteria are considered useful in attracting and maintaining a viable work force. Examples are satisfaction, job involvement, and organizational commitment.

Conclusion

Our odyssey of initial hope, empirical disillusion, and rebirth has probably revealed most about what not to study in leadership. This wandering path, though, has now completely released the macro-oriented spirit from the technical report and transformed it into a testable model. The model reflects our contention that current leadership approaches do not predict criterion variance very well and there are not likely to be sudden, dramatic breakthroughs in the leadership area. Rather, progress will come by systematically considering a wider range of variables, primarily macro in nature and incrementally adding predictive variance.

Partial Test of the Model

Propositions Examined

The model is quite complex with a large number of variables. Thus, a complete test in a single sample is not feasible. We opted therefore for a partial test in terms of both the propositions selected for testing and the nature of the sample within which they were tested. The macro aspects of the model are emphasized here as are associations unique to our model as compared with other leadership models.

The first three propositions are based on simple, noninteractive associations among macro variables with each other and with work unit outcomes. The fourth proposition gets at the critical aspects of the model in terms of the interaction of macro variable complexity and discretionary leadership.

The noninteractive propositions are:

Proposition 1: Leaders will adjust their discretionary leadership to meet unique variations in the environment, context, and structure of their unit.

Proposition 2: Environmental and organizational variables will be associated with work unit outcomes.

Proposition 3: Discretionary leadership will be positively associated with work unit outcomes.

The interactive proposition is based on the global complexity measures for each of the macro variables and discretionary leadership.

Proposition 4: As environmental, contextual, and structural complexity increase, higher discretionary leadership will have a stronger association with unit outcomes than will lower discretionary leadership.

In addition to these propositions, our earlier discussion suggested investigating: first, the association between lateral leadership (in combination with environmental, contextual, and structural complexity) and work unit outcomes; and second, the total proportion of criterion variance for which our macro-oriented leadership model would account.

Setting and Sample

In terms of our partial test, sample selection centered on narrow variations in some conditions to provide a "strong inference test" (Platt, 1964) and more variation in those conditions which have received relatively little attention in the literature. We also determined that, to the extent possible, the sample should include "hard" performance criteria to supplement "softer" employee maintenance measures. At the same time, since questionnaires were to be a primary source of data, subjects needed to possess a high enough literacy level to provide satisfactory responses. Finally, our funding agency indicated that samples with military relevance would be desirable.

With these requirements in mind we selected U.S. Army telecommunication units. The mission of these units is to send and receive messages vital to the performance of the army's mission. The units were distributed throughout the United States, including Puerto Rico and the Panama Canal Zone. The mission of these units was similar as was the technology. Specifically, messages (e.g., orders, requests for supplies) were sent using automated equipment to the point of destination via one of five switching centers. The switching centers calculated an error rate for faulty specification of the destination and typographical errors in message headings.

Commanders were allowed to vary the structure of their units within specifications outlined by a central command. Variations centered around a generally mechanistic structure complete with a detailed manual of procedures. The units were designed by the army to minimize performance deviations (in terms of error rate) as much as possible. They were also designed to have only small deviations in technology and structure. The size variation for the units comprising our sample was also quite small (average unit size was about 15 members). Thus, context and structure had little variation. However, the geographic dispersal of the units provided for considerable variation in the general environment. Thus, the partial test of the model was based on a relatively large environmental variation and strong inference in terms of findings based on context, structure, and performance.

Procedure

The sample was restricted to message sending and receiving personnel only. No support personnel were included. The sample consisted of shift supervisors, their immediate supervisor (NCOIC), and the supervisor's immediate superior (OIC). Some units were staffed by army personnel and some by civil service employees. In still others there was a mixture. Mail questionnaires were used for most of the data but these were supplemented by clinical analysis and records, wherever possible. There were a potential 110 units available. Of these, 35 units were eliminated because they were atypical from the others in some major way or because they were so small they had no shift supervisors. Of the remainder, 49 had the three-level structure above and 26 had a two-level structure without the intermediate level of supervision.

Questionnaires were administered in the 75 units. The mail procedure utilized was developed from an earlier pilot study with a small group of telecommunication units (see Hunt et al., in press). It was designed to encourage a high return rate. Usable returns were received from 91 percent of the units. The proportion of usable returns within units varied from 81 to 91 percent. Hard performance data from 13 units were classified "top secret." Thus, the sample size was based on 55 when concerned with performance and 68 when concerned with employee maintenance. As previously indicated, a group unit of analysis was used so questionnaire data were aggregated across shift supervisors within each unit.

Measures

Data were obtained for the following variables: 1) environmental conditions (general and specific environment); 2) contextual variables (size, technological sophistication, technological variability); 3) structural variables (vertical specialization and control, horizontal specialization and coordination, and structural diversity); 4) vertical and lateral leadership; and

5) unit outcome criteria (various aspects of performance and employee maintenance).

Environment. Conditions in the general environment were drawn from census data following the work of Osborn (1976). Interdependence, volatility, and favorability across the legal-political, sociocultural, economic, and educational sectors of the general environment were assessed using one measure for each sector. As an illustration, sample items for the sociocultural sector are: interdependence (1977 population density per square mile), volatility (change in percent black 1960–70), and favorability (years of life expectancy in 1970). Items were standardized and summed across sectors. Cronbach alpha internal consistency reliabilities for these were: interdependence (.77), volatility (.63), and favorability (.72). Following theoretical and empirical arguments of Osborn (1976) the measure of general environmental complexity was obtained by multiplying by one another the standardized scores for interdependence, volatility, and favorability.

The specific environment was assessed by asking each OIC to complete a 16-item questionnaire as shown in Hunt et al. (in press). OICs were asked to specify the units important to their units' operations and then to describe them in terms of interdependence, volatility, and favorability using five-point Likert-type items. Some examples are: 1) to what extent do the actions of the units affect the operations of your unit? (interdependence); 2) what percent of the time can you predict the expectations of the units? (volatility); and 3) to what extent have the units been growing (e.g., in terms of budgets, personnel, projects) within the last three years? (favorability). Cronbach alpha reliabilities were: interdependence (.56), volatility (.86), and favorability (.61). Intercorrelations among these dimensions ranged from −.04 to .07. Specific environment complexity was calculated by standardizing the above scores and multiplying them by each other as for general environment complexity.

Context: Unit size was measured by counting the number of direct full-time operators and supervisors in the unit as indicated by organizational rosters. Following Kimberly (1976) a log transformation was used to adjust for skewness and for the diminishing impact on criteria typically reported as size increases.

Technological sophistication was measured by asking each shift supervisor and his/her superior to complete a four-item, between-unit modification of Van de Ven's (1975) work-flow scale. The items are concerned with variations in work flow from independent, through sequential and reciprocal, to a team work-flow case. Reliability coefficients were not calculated because the scales are Guttman type. A lower score was interpreted as indicating less sophistication. Following Van de Ven, shift supervisor scores were averaged, combined with their superior's score, and divided by two to provide a composite index.

Technological variability was measured by a modification of a three-item specialization scale developed by Ford (1976). A sample item is: What percent of the employees in your work unit perform the same job? Cronbach alpha was .65. The higher the score the less the degree of variability. Scores were combined in the same manner as for technological sophistication. Standard scores for the three contextual variables were calculated and multiplied by each other to provide a measure of contextual complexity.

Structure. Vertical specialization and control was measured by formalization and decentralization (as decisions are delegated more people are involved in decision-making, hence there is more specialization). The 9-item formalization measure was adapted from Van de Ven (1975). An example item is: What percentage of nonsupervisory employees are given written operating instructions? The 12-item decentralization measure was adapted from Ford (1976) and Melcher (1976). An example item is: Approximately what percentage of the budget for a typical unit is directly under the boss' control: In units such as these with similar missions and numbers of organizational levels, one way of measuring horizontal specialization and coordination is by means of within-unit work flow. Such a measure was used here. It was a 4-item Guttman-type scale. Its items are similar to those above for between-unit work flow but concentrate within units.

Again, with the similarity of mission and hierarchical levels of the units in mind, structural diversity was measured by a standardization scale modified from Van de Ven (1975). The scale taps the extent to which rules and procedures govern the work to be done. The more of these, the less the diversity is considered to be. Where relevant, Cronbach alphas averaged about .65 for the above measures. Shift supervisor and superior data were aggregated as for technology. Standard scores for vertical and horizontal specialization and diversity were multiplied by each other to form the structural complexity index.

Leadership. The heart of the Multiple Influence Model is the measure of discretionary leadership. It evolved through four pilot studies which are described in detail in Hunt et al. (in press). The dimensions used in the present study were based on the work of Schriesheim (1978) and Jermier and Berkes (1979). These, in turn, were based on modifications of the earlier LBDQ-Form XII dimensions of consideration and initiating structure (Stogdill, 1963) and consist of: 1) support, 2) role clarification, 3) work assignments, and 4) rules and procedures. All scales consist of five items and were completed by shift supervisors to describe their superiors. An example item follows for each dimension: 1) support—my boss helps make working on my job more pleasant, 2) role clarification—my boss gives vague explanations of what is expected of me, 3) work assignments—my boss puts me on specific jobs, and 4) rules and procedures—my boss tells me how to go about doing my job.

While we believe discretionary leadership to be considerably broader in scope than the relatively narrow range of behaviors covered in these four dimensions, these were used initially because of their previous conceptual and empirical base. Schriesheim (1978) provides considerable justification for the dimensions. Our strategy was to utilize these as a base for determining convergent-discriminant validity. If we were successful in that, we could expand the dimensions in future work. Our convergent-discriminant validity tests used questionnaire measures of the discretionary leadership construct. One set was based on the reinforcement approach discussed earlier. The other set was based on attribution. These measures evolved through the previously mentioned four pilot studies. The difficulty of obtaining convergent-discriminant validity necessitated the large number of pilot studies.

In the reinforcement approach, four response alternatives were used for each of the items in Schriesheim's (1978) four dimensions. Each was given a weighting justified on a priori grounds: "can and does" = 4 (stimulus present and appropriate response); "can't and doesn't = −1 (stimulus absent); "could but doesn't" = −2 (stimulus present but opportunities are lost); and "can't but tries anyway" = −3 (stimulus absent but inappropriate response).[2] Sum scores were then calculated for each of the four dimensions. Items which did not pass an item analysis test were deleted, leaving a total of 14 rather than the original 20 items for the four dimensions.

The attribution approach was operationalized in the present study by asking shift supervisors to allocate 100 points between their superior and outside forces in terms of control over leader behavior. This was done for each of the four dimensions of support, role clarification, work assignment, and rules and procedures. The point values attributed to the leader were then correlated with the sum scores for each of the four dimensions based on the reinforcement approach.[3]

On the basis of data from the fourth pilot test and the present study, it was concluded that there was considerable support for convergent and discriminant validity for two of the four dimensions—support and rules and

---

2. Alternative weighting schemes, e.g. "can and does" = +1, all other outcomes = −1 as well as other possibilities were found to correlate in the vicinity of .9 with this one.

3. This approach was used in the fourth pilot study as well as the present investigation. We should note that a number of other variations were used in the earlier pilot studies. As previously indicated, we were not able to obtain convergent-discriminant validity with them. (See Hunt, Osborn, and Martin, in press, for details.)

procedures. In the pilot, the convergence test showed r's of .57 for support and .45 for rules and procedures between the reinforcement and attribution measures. For discrimination, these correlations were, with one exception, larger than those with the other dimensions. The method test showed an r of .35 between support and rules and procedures for the reinforcement approach and .50 between these dimensions for the attribution approach. Spearman-Brown internal consistency reliabilities were .84 and .85 for support and rules and procedures for the multiple-item reinforcement approach. The kurtosis values clustered around 1.0.

Corresponding data for the present study were as follows: convergence, r's of .60 for support and .50 for rules and procedures, reinforcement and attribution, respectively. Discrimination, these correlations were considerably larger than those with the other dimensions. Method, r between support and rules and procedures equaled .40 for reinforcement and .16 for attribution. Spearman-Brown reliabilities were .80 for support and .76 for rules and procedures, reinforcement. Again, kurtosis values were in the 1.0 range.

Lateral leadership was measured by a 30-item scale given to OICs. They were asked how typical managers in their position should behave in dealings with others at or near their own organizational level. It was based on the work of Osborn (1971), Duffy (1973), Osborn and Hunt (1974b), and Osborn, Hunt, and Skaret (1977). A sample item is concerned with the extent to which he (the leader) should maintain tight control over his unit's resources. A confirmatory factor analysis (N = 67) of the 30 items provides support for four dimensions developed a priori and from analyses in previous studies. Three of these were: pressure for action, network development, and adaptation to pressure. Respective Cronbach alpha reliabilities were .79, .72, and .66. The fourth dimension had an unacceptably low reliability coefficient, so was dropped.

Criteria. Performance measures consisted of: 1) machine error (percentage of mistakes in message headings sent for a one-month period), and 2) machine down time (number of hours per month a machine was inoperable). These data were provided by the army. Consistency in performance over time was considered an important criterion so that it was not used as a reliability indicator. However, 15 units had two machines. Here, the correlation between error rates was above 0.9. For down time, older machines had lower performance. Thus, down time on the newest equipment was used. Machine age could not be partialled from the analysis because of security considerations. Figures for both measures were averaged over the most recent six-month period preceding the study. Because of skewness and other considerations these scores were adjusted using a log transformation. To tap consistency in performance over time we used variability over the above six month period for error rate and down time. This was measured in terms of the standard deviation of each. All of these measures were provided by army records and were automatically adjusted for variations in unit size.

Measures of job satisfaction, job involvement, intent to leave, system rewards, and system and unit goal congruence were used as employee maintenance indicators. All were obtained from shift supervisor questionnaires and aggregated across shift supervisors within a unit. The Job Descriptive Index (Smith, Kendall, & Hulin, 1969) (JDI) was used to measure satisfaction with work, supervision, co-workers, pay, and promotion. In this study, data were summed across dimensions to provide one kind of overall satisfaction measures. Cronbach's alpha for this measure was 0.91.

A conceptually and empirically different measure of overall job satisfaction used was the Kunin (1955) single-item, Job in General Measure.

Job Involvement tapped the involvement of an individual with his or her job. It was measured by the six-item Lodahl and Kejner (1965) scale. A sample item is: "I live, eat and breathe my job." Cronbach's alpha was 0.64.

An intent to leave measure was used to indicate the likelihood of leaving army (seven-items) or civil service (five-items) employment. The items utilized were adapted from Patton (1970) by T. N. Martin (personal communication, July 1977). A sample item is: "Do you plan to reenlist or continue your commission?" Cronbach's alpha was .78. This kind of measure has been shown to correlate significantly with later turnover (see Hunt et al., in press).

System rewards was a three-item criterion developed from feedback by army officials from the earlier army pilot data. It was designed to tap equity of rewards. A sample item is: "Rewards here are given to those who deserve them." Cronbach's alpha was .79.

System and unit goal congruence measures were the final employee maintenance criteria and, like system rewards, were developed by the authors. Five items were devoted to each. A sample item for system congruence is the extent to which a respondent agrees with the army's goals. Respective Cronbach alphas were .83 and .75.

Data Analysis

The first three propositions are concerned with main effects. To minimize the likelihood of chance findings given the large number of relationships to be examined, canonical correlations using Wilke's Lambda (Cooley & Lohnes, 1962) were used to test for significance among a group of predictors and criteria. Then zero-order correlations were used to isolate specific contributors to the overall relationship.

The fourth proposition calls for interactive tests. The interactions were tested using moderated regression (Cohen & Cohen, 1975; McNeil, Kelly & McNeill, 1975). Here, a "full" model containing the interactive term was tested against a "restricted" model without the interactive term. An F-test of the full versus restricted model R-square was then used to determine the unique variance contributed by the interactive term. The two supplementary research questions were tested using moderated regression with more complex models than those for the fourth proposition.

Results

The first proposition was concerned with the association between macro variables and leadership. The second proposition examined the relationship between macro variables and work unit outcomes. The third proposition investigated the discretionary leadership-outcome relationship. Results for these noninteractive propositions[4] show:

1. Partial support for the first proposition. Structure components were significantly associated with discretionary leadership (Canonical R = .49, df = 16, Lambda = .65, p = .028). Environment and context components were nonsignificant.

2. Partial support for the second proposition. Specific environment components were significantly associated with performance (Canonical R = .55, df = 16, Lambda = .66, p = .037). Structure components were significantly associated with employee maintenance (Canonical R's = .66 and .57, df = 28 and 18, Lambda = .32 and .57, p = .001 and 0.49).

3. Substantial support for the third proposition. Discretionary leadershp dimensions were significantly associated with performance (Canonical R = .51, df = 16, Lambda = .58, p = .044) and employee maintenance (Canonical R's = .66 and .52, df = 28 and 18, Lambda = .32 and .57, p = .001 and .034).

The fourth proposition was the critical interactive one based on macro complexity measures and discretionary leadership. Results are summarized in Table 15.

In terms of performance, the table shows the most consistent pattern to be for contextual complexity. Specifically, there are significant interactions for both discretionary leadership dimensions for down time and variability in down time. In all four cases of significance the interactions are

---

4. Details of these and the supplementary zero-order correlations are reported in Hunt, Osborn, and Martin (in press).

Complexity Interactions (ΔR^2) of Macro Variables with Discretionary Rules and Procedures and Support

	Environmental Complexity with				Contextual Complexity with				Structural Complexity with			
	Rules & Procedures		Support		Rules & Procedures		Support		Rules & Procedures		Support	
Criteria	R^2_f	ΔR^2	R^2_f	ΔR^2	R^2_f	ΔR^2	R^2_f	ΔR^2	R^2_f	ΔR^2	R^2_f	ΔR^2
Performance												
Log Error Rate	.09	.03	.06	.00	.06	.00	.07	.01	.08	.01	.06	.00
Log Down Time	.09	.01	.14	.07*	.16	.08a**	.08	.01a	.08	.00	.12	.05*
Log Variability Error Rate	.17	.02	.08	.00	.15	.00	.09	.01	.16	.02	.08	.00
Log Variability Down Time	.03	.01	.16	.08**	.07	.05a*	.13	.05a*	.02	.00	.17	.09*
Employee Maintenance												
JDI Total	.38	.11aa**	.37	.10aa**	.27	.00	.28	101	.33	.06*	.34	.06a*
Job in General Satisfaction	.16	.01a	.18	.04aa*	.15	.00	.14	.00	.23	.08a**	.24	.10a**
Job Involvement	.02	.00	.04	.01	.03	.00	.03	.00	.03	.01	.03	.00a
Intent to Leave	.20	.06aa*	.23	.02	.18	.05*	.23	.01	.14	.00a	.30	.09aa**
System Rewards	.11	.02	.08	.00	.10	.01	.09	.02	.10	.01a	.10	.03a
Unit Goal Congruence	.28	.05aa*	.37	.00	.27	.03	.39	.01	.26	.03a	.39	.02
System Goal Congruence	.25	.09a**	.25	.03a	.19	.03	.22	.00	.17	.01	.23	.01

N = 51 for performance (varies from 61 to 68 for employee maintenance).

Note. a's indicate where components of the macro complexity measures were significant at the .05 level or better (one a = one significant component; two a's = two or more significant components). Decision rules for testing for significant interactions for the two criterion sets (performance and employee maintenance) for each of the complexity measures and: 1) inspect the pattern of significant interactions for the two complexity measures; 2) if there is a consistent pattern, say, 4 of 8 for performance, trace the interactions for the components of each of the complexity measures; 3) repeat for employee maintenance; 4) if only the global interactions are significant, stop; 5) if only the second-level interactions are significant, stop; 6) if both the global and second-level interactions are significant, check the third level component interactions, where applicable as for environment.

*$p \le .05$ (1-tail)
**$p \le .01$ (1-tail)

attributable to components of complexity—size for rules and procedures and technological sophistication for support.

In terms of employee maintenance, Table 15 shows a more complex pattern of relations. First, environmental complexity interacts with rules and procedures for all the criteria but job involvement and system rewards. Second, contextual complexity does not form a clear pattern. Third, structural complexity interacts with both leadership dimensions across several criteria. The table also indicates that for environmental complexity, the significant interactions can be attributed to either the general or specific environment complexity measure or to a still more specific component within one of these two dimensions. The situation is similar for contextual complexity. On balance, there is considerable support for this interactive proposition.

Results for the investigation of lateral leadership are based on an examination of possible macro complexity interactions with the three lateral dimensions discussed earlier (see Table 16). Concerning performance, the table shows the most consistent pattern of results to be with environmental and structural complexity. System rewards, unit goal congruence, and system goal congruence are the employee maintenance criteria with the most consistent pattern of significance. This is especially true for contextual complexity where all three lateral dimensions are involved. Environmental complexity is also important, especially for adaptation to pressure.

Earlier we indicated that our final question of interest in this study was concerned with how much criterion variance might be accounted for by this macro leadership model. To investigate this, we formulated specific regression models for each criterion where there was a pattern of significant findings. These global models were formulated for all performance measures and all employee maintenance criteria except job involvement, which had few significant relationships.[5]

---

5. To minimize including too many predictors, the following decision rules were applied in formulating the models: (1) only significant findings with an incremental R-square magnitude of 5 percent or greater were considered; (2) main effects of complexity variables were included in each equation for employee maintenance criteria, but only where significant for performance because of the smaller sample size for the latter; (3) only if a dimension of leadership was a significant predictor or component of a significant interaction term was it included; and (4) no more than four interactions were considered in any final model. To isolate the relative importance of interaction effects, all main effects were first included and then interactions were added on the basis of the incremental addition to explained variance. As an example, the model for error rate consisted of environmental complexity + structural complexity + the three lateral dimensions + the interaction of lateral pressure for action and network development with environmental complexity and lateral adaptation to pressure with structural complexity.

TABLE 16
Significant Macro Interactions (ΔR^2) for Lateral Leadership

| Criteria (CR)[a] | Environmental Complexity (E) Lateral Dimension | | | | | | Contextual Complexity (C) Lateral Dimension | | | | | | Structural Complexity (St) Lateral Dimension | | | | | |
| | Pressure for Action | | Network Dev. | | Adaptation to Pressure | | Pressure for Action | | Network Dev. | | Adaptation to Pressure | | Pressure for Action | | Network Dev. | | Adaptation to Pressure | |
	R_f^2	ΔR^2	R_f^2	ΔR^2	R_f^2	ΔR^2	R_f^2	ΔR^2	R_f^2	ΔR^2	R_f^2	ΔR^2	R_f^2	ΔR^2	R_f^2	ΔR^2	R_f^2	ΔR^2
Performance																		
Log Error Rate	.18	.14**	.28	.20**	.23	.00	.07	.03	.09	.02	.23	.01	.11	.07*	.10	.03	.29	.07*
Log Down Time	.07	.02	.05	.00	.05	.01	.05	.00	.05	.00	.05	.01	.06	.02	.05	.00	.10	.05*
Log Variability Error Rate	.15	.08*	.29	.19**	.28	.00	.10	.02	.10	.00	.31	.04	.11	.04	.12	.02	.30	.03
Log Variability Down Time	.07	.04	.07	.00	.06	.01	.07	.05*	.07	.00	.05	.00	.07	.04	.08	.01	.07	.02
Employee Maintenance																		
JDI Total	.23	.01	.22	.01	.27	.04*	.25	.03	.21	.00	.24	.01	.22	.01	.21	.00	.23	.01
System Rewards	.11	.04	.08	.00	.14	.06*	.36	.29**	.09	.01	.22	.15**	.17	.11**	.07	.01	.07	.01
Unit Goal Congruence	.27	.05*	.24	.01	.30	.07*	.53	.30**	.37	.14**	.36	.14**	.22	.00	.25	.02	.26	.02
System Goal Congruence	.28	.12**	.17	.01	.40	.23**	.49	.33**	.32	.16**	.52	.35**	.29	.13**	.16	.00	.19	.01

Note. N = 50 for performance and 61 for employee maintenance. Interactions compare: Cr = E + C + St + appropriate lateral dimension + (appropriate complexity dimension × appropriate lateral dimension) against E + C + St + appropriate lateral dimension.

* $p < .05$ (2-tail)

** $p < .01$ (2-tail)

[a] To simplify the table, only those criteria are listed with interactions significant at the .05 level or better (2-tail).

Space precludes tabulation of specific results here; they are shown in Hunt et al. (in press). The R-squares for performance ranged from .23 to .49. Adjusted for shrinkage (Cohen & Cohen, 1975) the range was from .07 to .39 with the largest R-square for the primary criterion (error rate) used by the army to evaluate the units. For employee maintenance the R-squares ranged from .31 to .88 (adjusted for shrinkage from .22 to .85). There was about an equal balance between main and interaction effects in the models for these criteria. The criterion variance accounted for suggested to us that macro-oriented leadership models such as this one possess the potential of accounting for relatively substantial proportions of criterion variance. Thus, such models appear to be potentially useful for both theoretical and practical reasons.

Discussion

This study partially examined a heavily macro-oriented leadership model. The model was partially tested in army telecommunication units. These units operated in a highly variable general environment with little variation in specific environment, context, and structural variables. Performance was also designed by the army to be as strongly machine controlled as possible. We thus considered the investigation to combine traditional hypothesis testing with strong inference for a number of the variables. The design works against successful tests of the model. Statistically significant results found under these circumstances hold promise of being replicable in future samples with more variability.

We found partial support for our propositions. In terms of the first three noninteractive propositions, environment had less influence than predicted, while structure had more. Structure was associated not only with performance and employee maintenance but with discretionary leadership. Discretionary leadership, in turn, had the expected positive associations with performance and maintenance criteria.

There was considerable support for the predicted interactive relationships between the macro variables and discretionary leadership. In predicting criteria, a number of significant interactive relationships with lateral leadership were also revealed. Interestingly, the patterns were different for the two kinds of leadership, emphasizing the inclusion of lateral leadership in the model.

While macro complexity was an important interactive variable, the fact that individual components were important in many cases suggests that this is an especially important area for future study. The question has important conceptual and empirical ramifications for the model. As now conceptualized complexity serves as a convenient "umbrella" construct to pull together a large number of separate predictors and to help tie our work more solidly into the organization theory literature. We would expect replication of complexity results in future studies. However, we would expect significant components to differ from sample to sample.

In terms of criterion variance, the macro variables in the Multiple Influence Model appear encouraging. The R-square values for both the performance and employee maintenance criteria were large enough to be of both practical and theoretical significance. They are larger than those typically reported in current contingency models. While one can argue that they *should* be larger, given the number and range of variables included in our model, micro leadership models have implicitly been formulated as if such macro variables were not necessary. As we argued earlier, it is our contention that systematic inclusion of macro variables will add substantial portions of variance in leadership models. We believe that this is a more viable strategy than looking for the magical pot of gold at the end of the leadership rainbow (see Hosking, Hunt, & Osborn, 1980).

Implications

Some of the practical implications of this model are discussed in Hunt and Osborn (1980a, 1980b) and Hunt et al. (in press). These focus especially on its use in organizational design but cover leader placement and training as well.

The implications we wish to focus on in the remainder of this chapter are concerned with the model's role in programmatic research. It is our contention that not only does the leadership field need to include macro variables if it is to advance but carefully designed programatic efforts are also necessary. With the exception of Fiedler, Graen, and Bass and their associates (e.g., Bass & Valenzie, 1974; Fielder & Chemers, 1974; Graen & Cashman, 1975), there is relatively little such research now being conducted.

As previously indicated, our initial investigations underlying the current model set out to extend the range of contingency variables applicable to then-developing approaches. Over time this evolved into a program of research which systematically investigated organizations with common and similar properties. Thus, large, multiunit organizations (e.g., the highway department, the business fraternity, the army telecommunication units) were focused upon. In these kinds of organizations, while there are sometimes dramatic technological changes, there has more often been a tendency to rely on much the same equipment and processes for several years.

Organizations such as these also frequently attempt to establish a common or similar structure which can be used for numerous units. The army units are prototypical of this with their similar mission, technology, structure, and varying environment. Based on work in these kinds of organizations, our model postulates that unique opportunities and threats (as exemplified by complexity), in combination with leadership, help predict substantial portions of criterion variance. That is, discretionary leadership is postulated to be particularly important where the existing bureaucratic structures and processes are inadequate.

Consistent with this, two types of studies are proposed to continue this examination of large, bureaucratic organizations. The first concentrates on wider variations in structure and begins to investigate the issue of causality which has become a central issue of many current leadership researchers (e.g., Graen & Cashman, 1975; Greene, 1975). Here sample units share a similar mission and technology, but with different environmental settings and structures. Structures more suited to the mission, technology, and environment would be expected to call for less discretionary leadership. While this is a commonsense notion, the type of structure(s) needed for different combinations of mission, technology, and environment is still an open question. The extent to which a manager high in discretionary leadership could help close the gap between structure and setting better to reach mission objectives is a particularly important question to be investigated.

The causality issue, while important generally, is especially crucial in a complex model such as this. The knowledge is needed for a better theoretical and scientific understanding of the model and to implement its full organization design and other applications-oriented implications.

To summarize, this type of study would investigate structural parameters alone and in combination with leadership and focus on causality in large organizations which operate nationally.

A second type of study challenges an important but often implicit assumption underlying many organization and leadership investigations. Specifically, many organizations must be structured for crisis conditions even though crises occur infrequently. Performance during the crisis may be the ultimate criterion of success as in military or quasi-military units. The Multiple Influence Model suggests that discretionary leadership should be particularly important in such crisis units.

To continue the program of research so that results can be compared with those in similar organizations that do not face crises, the sample units should be part of a large organization and should share a similar mission, context, and structure. The model suggests that discretionary leadership is important where there are variations in setting. By comparison with parallel studies, the importance of the crisis versus noncrisis conditions could be more carefully estimated.

In terms of the first type of study, a longitudinal sample of United Way of America agencies is now in the process of being obtained. This sample meets the varying environment, varying structure, but constant technology parameters outlined above. In terms of the second type of study, military units undergoing simulated battle conditions and returning to readiness are one example. Fire departments are another. Work is now underway with a colleague at the University of Aston in Birmingham, England, to study a major metropolitan British fire fighting service. The model will be tested with the firemen in the stations contrasted with their behavior on the fireground.

Both of these are multiyear studies designed to build carefully on previous work and to serve as a bridge to additional future investigations of the model.

12

Commentary on Part 3

Toward a Paradigm Shift in the Study of Leadership
HENRY J. TOSI, JR.

The two chapters in this part are too diverse to try to integrate. They do, indeed, represent micro and macro ends of a continuum based on extensions to establishment views. Given this, then rather than attempt an impossible integration or even to write a critique, my preference is to comment briefly on the approaches and then move into a proposed paradigm shift which I see as portended by the Hunt-Osborn contribution.

The first chapter, by Bales and Isenberg, proposes a new metric, of sorts. SYMLOG is a method for mapping relationships among individuals in a three-dimensional space. The location of persons and the distances from other persons in a group are plotted along three vectors: 1) an upward-downward dimension, 2) a positive-negative dimension, and 3) a forward-backward dimension.

Bales and Isenberg propose that this mapping process has some utility for leadership theory and research. First, they argue that these dimensions have some commonality with those frequently used in leadership research, Initiation of Structure and Consideration. Secondly, they suggest that the mapping process can identify the degree of polarization between individuals or subgroups within the unit of analysis.

The usefulness of SYMLOG remains to be demonstrated. Certainly the method has face validity as an assessment of group cohesiveness, an oft used dependent variable in leadership study. Perhaps a relationship may be found between leadership styles and the several general group conditions that Bales and Isenberg propose. Additionally, SYMLOG patterns may be related in some way to group output or productivity. There is little question that SYMLOG will find some use in the future study of leadership.

The "Odyssey" chapter by Hunt and Osborn struck a more resonant chord. The theme on which the authors' analysis is based is consistent with my belief that leadership can only be understood within the organizational context in which it occurs (Tosi, 1979). This contextual tone is not an obvious part of current leadership work. I am less impressed with the results in the Hunt-Osborn contribution and much more interested in the journey which led the authors to introduce organization factors into their analysis. They are quite correct in noting that there is little research which includes "macro" variables, yet they fail to point out that there is little theory to guide this research. Their chapter is more important in that it portends a shift in the direction of leadership research—a shift in the direction of a broader range theory.

To move in such a direction is no mean task. There is need for a theoretical model, the skeleton of which I will outline in the remainder of this chapter. But, more importantly, it is necessary to bring about a change in the conceptual set of those who write and think about leadership from the establishment view. I describe below what I believe to be the basis for the current conceptual stereotype which permeates leadership study. The argument I advance is that there is a nonisomorphic relationship between the imagery of leadership and the manner in which it is studied. Then, I suggest a minor, but what I believe to be an important, shift in the paradigm for leadership research.

From Charisma to Leadership

There is a remarkable inconsistency in the logic which links the concept of leadership to its translation to research. The general definition of leadership is drawn from charismatic imagery, the measurement of leadership is undertaken with technique designed to study managers or military officers, and the stereotype which often dominates selection of leaders is rather Hollywood-like.

The Charismatic Imagery of Leadership

Consider, first, the images from which the definition of leadership is drawn. It is charismatic, without doubt. Ask any group, without prompting, to imagine a specific person engaging in a leadership act. A fairly consistent set of images emerge: Hitler rallying the German population; Vince Lombardi extracting extreme physical and mental effort from football players; Martin Luther King at the head of a group marching to Selma, Alabama; Churchill demanding blood, sweat, and tears; and so on. (Women are rarely mentioned when I have asked groups to imagine leaders). Such an image of leadership naturally leads to a definition which has wide acceptance in the "establishment" of leadership theory and research; leadership is the ability of one person to influence another to act in a way desired by the first.

The Measurement of Leadership

Consider, now, how current approaches to studying leadership relate to the imagery, or concept, above. There is a nonisomorphic relationship between the concept of leadership (as I have speculated above) and the character of the tools used in its research. First, the development of most instruments to study leader behavior begins with a focus on the characteristics or the behavior of effective military officers, managers, or basketball players. It takes a great stretch of the imagination to accept a premise that 1) charisma, the base of the definition of leadership, is so generally distributed throughout the population that it will be found in those who hold such positions and, 2) that the emotionally charged situations in which the charismatic person generally exerts leadership is present in many, if any, of the settings in which the research is executed.

Second, the charismatic image of leadership and the operational version of leadership do not share similar outcomes. The "establishment" construction of the leadership paradigm typically considers effectiveness and satisfaction as dependent variables (the effects of successful leadership). While it is true that many charismatic leaders were effective in the sense that they and their followers conquered in wars, won in games, or changed society, it is also the case that many were unsuccessful. In the end, Napoleon was exiled and Hitler was defeated. Yet these two men must be regarded as effective leaders.

Neither is it likely that the charismatic leaders were concerned with satisfaction in the same way that satisfaction is viewed in the "establishment" model. Charismatic leaders ask their followers to sacrifice, to work, to hurt. Commitment to a belief, a cause, is a far more accurate dependent variable as it should be drawn from leadership imagery, not satisfaction and effectiveness. This is not meant to minimize the organizational and human importance of satisfaction and effectiveness. Rather, it may be useful to point out that the translation of leadership imagery, both in behavior and outcomes, to current theory and practice is inconsistent.

The Selection Stereotype

The final twist in the path that begins with the leadership imagery is the selection stereotype that is used in choosing managers. There seems to be a rather steady and extended empirical literature which demonstrates the following: When a person is asked to choose which of several individuals is most likely to perform well, to be trusted, to receive higher pay, unless the decision maker has some evidence upon which to base the choice, the most attractive and tallest male will be chosen. Such evidence about the effects of appearance suggests the rather simple conclusion that height, attractiveness, and being male are attributes generally associated with influence, or leadership.

The logic that leads to this point is, indeed, convoluted. The charismatic image begins with an assortment of men diverse in height, age, attractiveness, and ethnic background and ends with Hollywood-like leading men.

Leadership Begins Where Managing Ends

The irony that permeates the current established leadership paradigm is that it is charisma in which the field is interested yet it is ordinary managers, quite often in very low level jobs, who are studied. The language of leadership is mystical, the reality mundane. Our imagery of leadership is a mental cinema in which heroic figures watch a battle from atop a nob as Napoleon, prowl the sideline of a football field like Vince Lombardi, or march down a highway toward Selma, Alabama, as did Martin Luther King. The images are of leaders in action, pleading, cajoling, and demanding that their constituents follow.

There is another side to this image which is less visible and less attractive. This other side has not found exposure in the establishment literature, theory, or research. With few exceptions, behind the popular charismatic image, the leader acted as a manager. A good deal of time was spent acquiring resources, making decisions, assigning responsibilities, and so forth. These managerial practices may account for as much of the individual's success as do the personal qualities, which are the base of charisma. If this is so, then any theoretical construction of leadership influence which does not include such managerial elements is likely to be far too inadequate.

Katz and Kahn (1978) propose a definition of leadership that seems theoretically sound and consistent with the view that effectiveness has both charismatic, or influential, antecedents as well as managerial antecedents. They "consider the essence of organizational leadership to be the influential increment over and above mechanical compliance with a routine directive of an organization." This concept of leadership makes rather explicit the point that a great deal of effective organizational behavior may occur which is attributable to causes other than leadership.

The utility of an incremental concept of leadership is quite clear. If leadership is interpersonal in character, generally charismatic, and construed solely as an influence process, there is little possibility that it can be taught or trained. This is a disappointing state. However, if performance of individuals and groups can be affected by "managing" behavior and if that behavior is composed of planning, designing organizations, controlling, budgeting, and so on, then a more positive case exists. People can learn how to do these "managerial" things easier then they can learn how to "exert influence." To put it in other words, a person can learn to manage but may be unable to learn to lead. If this is true, it is important to ask, "How much performance is attributable to managing and how much is attributable to leadership?"

Toward a Paradigm Shift

It follows from the arguments presented to this point that there is a need for a paradigm shift in leadership theory and research. Such a shift should lead to a set of constructs which mirror reality in a less blurry way than the current constructions of leadership theory. The argument for a paradigm shift, briefly stated, is: The leadership establishment considers organization effectiveness, in a general sense, to be the appropriate dependent variable for theory and research. The role of other practices and forces which might lead to effectiveness are not significant elements in current leadership theory and research.

Certainly one would be disadvantaged to hold a position that the current status of leadership theory and research, founded on such premises as I have outlined above, is alive and well. Neither does it seem warranted to believe that any substantive gains can be expected by psychometric improvement of instruments or minor shifts in the focus of analysis, that is, individuals, units, dyads, and the like. Rather, the focus and the imagery of leadership must be changed. I propose two rather basic changes and further argue that such a shift is worth some investigation and consideration. These are: 1) Change the dependent variable in leadership theory and research, and 2) broaden the scope of the independent variables.

Change in the Dependent Variable

With the exception of psychometric development of instruments, theory and research in the leadership literature examines how leadership behavior, characteristics, or traits relates to effectiveness and/or satisfaction. Satisfaction is an affective, individual response. Effectiveness is generally some form of productivity or performance indicator, objective or subjective. Of course, such a set of dependent variables ostensibly makes sense.

The research and theory to date are most concerned with demonstrating the force of interpersonal influence on both the individual's and the organization's performance as well as human affective responses to that influence.

There are two basic problems with this form of dependent variable. First, there is no strong conceptual or theoretical structure for "organizational effectiveness." At best, effectiveness is theoretically construed as an aggregation of productivity, individual satisfaction, group cohesiveness, and social responsibility, each having perhaps a different weight.

Secondly, and pragmatically, effectiveness has an amorphous meaning. There is disagreement among managers about what it is. A researcher, trying to define effectiveness as a dependent variable for research purposes, may find little convergence among managerial perceptions about effectiveness. This leads, naturally, to 1) research which uses broad subjective judgments of effectiveness that are obvious products of varying conceptions and perceptions of effectiveness or 2) to research in which effectiveness is narrowly construed, say in terms of productivity.

Here is the difficulty. If the broad construction of effectiveness is used, it is likely that there is too large a variance in the perceptions on which it is based to be useful for research purposes. If the more narrow construction, productivity, is used it is likely that many other factors (independent variables, as it were) would have at least as great an effect on it as leadership. Surveys of the leadership literature, with regularity, conclude that effectiveness is not consistently related in any fashion to leader behavior.

But the findings on individual satisfaction do not seem to provide such divergent results. In general, there seems to be a fairly consistent and positive relationship between satisfaction and "considerate" leadership styles. Perhaps the reason that there are divergent results for the effectiveness research and convergent results in satisfaction research is that there is a far greater agreement as to what satisfaction is rather than what effectiveness is.

To get around some of these problems, I propose that some strong consideration be given to a theoretical reconstruction which shifts the focus to a different dependent variable, *predictability*. This is based on the following logic. It is a reasonable position to take that organizations may be viewed as patterns of predictable behavior which occur over some relatively long period of time. Yet, it is not equally plausible to argue that these behavior patterns are necessarily the most optimal, or effective, from an organizational point of view. Even the most rational of organization theorists would accept the proposition that there are often structural and managerial elements present which lead to suboptimal behavior and performance. To put it in reinforcement theory terms, the structure of organization contingencies is often such that the behavior patterns which do emerge are not the most effective.

If this is true, it then seems promising to seek to understand what causes a particular structure of behavior patterns rather than to study organization effectiveness. The reason for this is obvious. If one understands the structure of the contingencies which reinforce behavior patterns then it is a more simple matter to rearrange these contingencies to reinforce preferred behavior patterns.

The difficulty with such a proposed shift in the dependent variable is, I believe, one of transforming the concept of predictability into a useful operational measure. Conceptually, predictability means the amount of stable variance in a behavior over time. Some, certainly not all, of the behaviors which must be assessed in terms of frequency and of level of effort are: 1) task activities, 2) nonwork behavior, 3) absenteeism frequencies, and 4) affective states, and so forth.

Of course, the issue of aggregation of these behaviors must also be resolved as well as the question of whether individuals or groups may be the most appropriate unit of analysis. This is no simple matter. A theoretical structure to provide guidance as to how the specific content of these behaviors vary by the type of work, by type of organization, and by organizational level is necessary. There is also the need to formulate useful measurement strategies. This surely poses a challenge for the "leadership establishment."

Broaden the Scope of the Independent Variables

Most leadership theory and the vast majority of research considers, primarily, the relationships between leader behavior and some dependent variable. There have been some few attempts to broaden the set of independent, or causal, variables in leadership research and theory but they have only trickled into the literature. Fiedler's (1967) contingency theory, the House-Evans path-goal model (House, 1971; Evans, 1968) and the Vroom-Yetton approach (1973) are the most prominent of these models.

We know two things about leadership for certain, and these should be a more integral part of leadership theory and research. First, many factors other than leadership (defined as influence) affect or cause 1) how well a person performs, 2) the level of personal commitment, and 3) the amount of work satisfaction. Secondly, we know that these causal factors will be different as a function of, at least, the type of work and organization level.

Therefore, to understand the effects of leadership it is necessary to know what portion of the predictability (variance) in behavior patterns is accounted for by interpersonal influence and what portion is accounted for by other factors. Yet it is specifically these *other* factors which are rarely integrated into leadership theory and research is systematic fashion. These factors are, at least, the following: 1) Formalization (Fo), 2) Technology (Te), 3) Socialization (So), 4) Selection (Se), 5) Reward Systems (RS), 6) Work Relationships (WR), and 7) Leadership (Le).

Formalization is both how much and how restrictive are rules, procedures, and policies. Organizations develop formalistic tendencies early in their existence and it is unquestionable that these affect behavior patterns.

Technology may affect behavior in two ways. First, it may be a determinant of the upper and the lower limit of performance. A person can rarely produce more than the capacity of the machine with which he or she works. Secondly, technology may affect interpersonal relationships between a person with peers, supervisors, and subordinates. When a work process is automated, for instance, it reduces the need for personal supervision, substituting machine control for human control.

Socialization is the learning process by which the institution (a society or an organization) inculcates its members with values, beliefs, and norms. One's early experiences affect how individuals learn how to adapt, or cope with organizations. Of particular importance is the nature of organizational commitment and responses to authority which emerge from socialization. Organizational socialization, the learning of norms after one joins an organization, also effects commitment.

Socialization is important because of its effect on the individual's motivational structure. To the extent that values, beliefs, and norms have a systematic effect on behavior patterns, it is necessary that the socialization element be an integral part of leadership theory and must be considered in research.

Selection processes may, if systematic, restrict the range of behavioral and attitudinal variance in an organization. Selection procedures which systematically include or exclude a particular class of individuals will have obvious effects on behavior patterns. For example, a firm may systematically choose persons with very high ability and not those with moderate or low skills. Another effect of selection may be due to the regular choice or exclusion of persons with a particular attitude set, or point of view.

Reward systems may affect behavior patterns. Pay, promotion, and/or recognition systematically given or withheld will be a determinant of behavior patterns. Understanding the bases for allocation of reward and sanctions is fundamental to understanding predictability of behavior.

Work relationships among peers and with subordinates are often reflected in both productivity and compliance norms. The nature of these relationships and the strength of group pressures for compliance can be strong forces in shaping behavior.

Finally, *leadership*, as interpersonal influence of a higher level organiza-

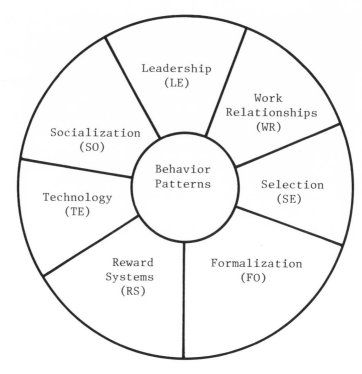

Fig. 18. Factors which determine organizational behavior patterns

tional official, affects behavior patterns. This occurs to the extent that a person complies with such influence attempts.

Figure 18 illustrates these several factors and their relationship to the dependent variable, predictability of behavior. These several factors account for different amounts of the variance in behavior patterns. It is also likely that some portion of the variance in predictability may never be accounted for, though this notion is not illustrated here. Three questions immediately emerge: 1) How much variance in behavior patterns is accounted for by each factor? By all these factors combined? 2) Do these factors have a simple additive or interactive effects on behavior patterns? 3) Are there circumstances (and what are they) in which different patterns of these factors would result in the similar level of predictability? To deal with these questions requires two things, a model and a measurement approach.

First, the model must more fully explicate the structure of the causal factors under different circumstances. For example, these factors should account for different portions of the variance in different types of organizations and at different organization levels.

Consider the most simple organization taxonomy, organic and mechanistic forms of organization. It is by definition that formalization is more predominate in the mechanistic than in the organic organization. Thus, it is reasonable to conclude that formalization should be a more influential dimension in the mechanistic organization.

One could easily draw hypotheses about how other factors would vary in influence on behavior patterns between organic and mechanistic organizations. The organization models proposed by Burns and Stalker (1961) and elaborated later by Tosi and Carroll (1976) provide some theoretical guidance for the formulation of such propositions.

There is also a consistent theme in the management literature which posits that managerial work differs by organizational level. Mann (1965), for instance, suggests that the importance of administrative, human, and technical skills would be different at lower, middle, and top levels of an organization. Katz and Kahn (1978) describe managerial role differences by level. Mahoney, Jerdee, and Carroll (1965) found that top managers spend more time planning and less time controlling than lower level managers. The evidence is quite clear, that is, there are important organizational level differences in what managers do.

Integrating concepts about both organizational type differences and organizational level differences seems a rather logical extension for leadership theory. The effects of such differences are suggested in Figure 19. Figure 19 illustrates how the different factors might account for predictable behavior patterns in the mechanistic and in the organic organizations at different organization levels. For example, at lower organizational levels, formalization and technology would be a more significant source of influence in a mechanistic organization while professional socialization, leadership, and work group relationships may be more influential in the organic organization.

At mid-levels of the mechanistic organization, formalization has less infuence than it does at lower levels. Organization socialization has a more significant effect than at lower levels. This would be the case particularly where certain attitudes and values are prerequisite for promotion to that level. At mid-levels of the organic organization, socialization and leadership may account for the largest portion of variance in behavior patterns. Formalization, technology, and the reward system may be of much less effect.

At the top levels the mechanistic and organic organization may be most similar in terms of the structure of the causal factors. Formalization,

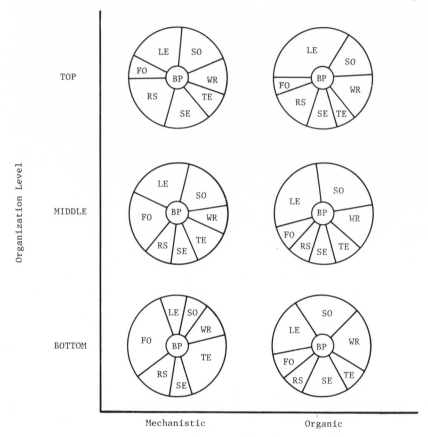

Organization Level

TOP

MIDDLE

BOTTOM

Mechanistic   Organic

Type of Organization

Fig. 19. Hypothetical relationship between factors which cause behavior patterns, by type of organization and by organization level

selection, and technology are likely to have very minimal effect on the behavior patterns of senior managers. Other elements, such as socialization, leadership, and work relationships are likely to account for larger portions of the variance.

Second, the measurement implication of such a model is that techniques must be used which assess each of these factors simultaneously. It is not enough merely to assess any one of the dimensions, that is, leadership, or formalization, or selection. One would expect to find very different correlations between any factor and the dependent variable, behavioral predictability, in different research settings. It is how they are combined which must be studied.

Summary

The paradigm shift suggested in here is on one hand in a direction *away* from establishment views, but on the other hand clearly *toward* a theoretical structure more congruent with the objective case. It has two readily apparent benefits.

First, it directs attention toward a more complete set of dimensions which affect performance. More importantly, it postulates that the effects of each of these may be different, one accounting for larger amounts of variance in the dependent variable than others. Such a model will point out the importance of leadership, relative to other factors, as a cause of performance patterns.

Second, such a model provides a base for clarifying the difference between a conception of "leading" and of "managing." In this model, *leading* is an influence process. *Managing* may be seen as the act of making choices about the form and structure of those factors which fall within the boundaries of managerial discretion. For example, decisions can be made about selection criteria, the particular technology which might be used in work, and the specifics of the reward structure. Less managerial discretion may exist with respect to work relationships and socialization experiences. A distinction between controllable and uncontrollable factors facilitates improving organization performance.

Such a change in the conceptualization of leadership seems long overdue. The leadership problem is an important one, it will not go away. Current theory and the research which derives from it are too simplistic and have not been particularly rewarding. A new and a different view must find its way into the open. There are some beginnings, such as the chapter by Hunt and Osborn and a recent article by Kerr and Jermier (1978). Such ideas need more exposure and much more theoretical development.

Part 4

Overview, Epilogs, and Conclusion

Introduction
James G. Hunt, Uma Sekaran, and
Chester A. Schriesheim

The four chapter in this last part, again, provide a diverse treatment of leadership and management phenomena. Mintzberg's invited overview chapter ("If You're Not Serving Bill and Barbara, Then You're Not Serving Leadership") deals with several provocative issues, including the practitioner-academic dichotomy. The next two chapters ("Beyond Establishment Leadership Views: An Epilog," and "Leadership Research and the European Connection: An Epilog") are epilogs written by the editors and Hosking and Hunt, to review recent research trends and develoments in the United States and Europe, respectively. Finally, the last chapter ("Conclusion: The Leadership-Management Controversy Revisited") is by the editors, and it highlights several issues which permeate both this book and the field at large.

Mintzberg's chapter is an attempt both to deal with and be provocative about several areas of conflict in the field. And, although Mintzberg disclaims some of his more extreme stances as rhetorical devices, readers may suspect the sincerity of his disavowal. In any event, however, this chapter is stimulating and clearly congruent with the overviewer role. It also reiterates and brings into focus issues raised in previous symposia volumes (Hunt and Larson, 1975, 1977, 1979) as well as a recent exchange in *Contemporary Psychology* between David Campbell (1979) and Hunt (in press).

The chapter begins by introducing Bill and Barbara (two "intelligent practitioners"), and by briefly summarizing the "essence" of each noncommentary chapter in this book. These summaries are then used to critique the contributions with respect to Bill and Barbara's likely perspective, and several insightful questions are raised about each. In general, the chapters do not fare well, although Mintzberg suggests that three might be viewed as at least somewhat worthwhile by Bill and Barbara. Mintzberg then presents

Bill and Barbara's actual commentaries, and notes that his anticipation of their reactions proved to be overly optimistic.

Mintzberg spends considerable time defending his "Bill and Barbara test," and contends that the use of jargon and the lack of relevance-testing is largely accountable for present dissatisfaction with leadership as a field. He argues that leadership research must have a practitioner constituency, and then explores the methodological implications of this perspective.

Mintzberg argues that we need to depart from traditional structured methodologies, and move to unstructured methods which can yield more informal, intuitive knowledge. He advocates abandoning constructs prior to data collection, abandoning instruments, and, more generally, abandoning nonorganizational measures. He also suggests the elimination of the independent-dependent variable distinction and, perhaps, even the development of "precise" conceptual definitions. He concludes by suggesting some avenues worth exploring from his research on managerial roles and behavior and, again, defends his "Bill and Barbara test" as necessary for the field.

As one might suspect, Mintzberg's presentation at the symposium generated substantial audience discussion, and perhaps highlights should be mentioned to alert readers to some key issues which were raised. In general, much of the discussion was centered around more provocative portions of his presentation, with the audience attacking what they viewed as extreme positions, or with the audience expressing sympathy for Mintzberg's views.

One theme which ran throughout the discussion concerned possible strategies for generating knowledge on leadership and managerial processes. It was suggested that one might synthesize the more anthropological approaches, for example, by integrating biographies which have been written about leaders and historical figures. This would yield richness, while at the same time provide some indication concerning the generality of conclusions. Interestingly, Bass and Farrow (1977) have already made a start in this direction.

The appropriate approach to take to developing research in this field occupied considerable discussion. It was debated whether the field needs to stop developing theory, and just begin observing what managers do, how they do it, and so forth. Mintzberg felt strongly about the necessity for this, while some members of the audience violently disagreed. One possible compromise suggested was that in the early stages of research, investigators "wallow around" in the field, grounding their theories in observations before they became solidified. An issue raised here was whether constructs and variables should be used in research at all (Mintzberg's initial position was to deny the need for these), or whether they should be formulated after research has sharpened up relevant issues. (This became Mintzberg's final position—that constructs and variables should be constructed from observations, not from data forced into preconceived categories.)

Mintzberg suggested some interesting ideas about theory testing, including that the process is basically one of intervention, and therefore cannot be replicated. He also outlined four different ways to test a theory, an approach which seems interesting and innovative. Briefly, these methods are 1) the traditional manner, 2) to employ an innovative methodology and see if the same results are obtained, 3) to employ Kaplan's (1964) idea of examining the "beauty" or aesthetic quality of a theory, and 4) to ask practitioners whether a theory provides an improved approach to their problems and concerns. According to Mintzberg, method 4 is the ultimate test; a number of the audience strongly disagreed with this general conclusion.

The issue of single, universal, versus multiple theories in the field was raised and discussed briefly. It seemed to be the general consensus that multiple theories are needed, and that no one theory will ever be useful in the leadership and management area. (This issue is echoed in the European epilog and conclusion chapters of this part, and we touched on it briefly in the introductory chapter.) It was also noted that we deal with complex systems and that our methods for dealing with such systems are currently underdeveloped. This, therefore, was seen as representing one possible avenue for future exploration and development.

Mintzberg spent some time, and several members of the audience seemed to agree, emphasizing the point that in the social sciences (as opposed to a field like physics), precision in research may not be what we want. It was contended that as precision in the social sciences increases, generalizability decreases. If true, this suggests that to develop a field of rich generalizations, we may have to be less "rigorous," at least in the traditional sense.

Considerable discussion centered around Mintzberg's "Bill and Barbara test," and the debate was heated and emotional at times. Some members of the audience emphasized that employing practitioners as ultimate evaluators of research raises the danger of reinforcing existing prejudices and "conventional wisdoms," which may be highly dysfunctional to both practitioners and academics alike. Mintzberg countered with his argument that if they are not applied, theory and research are of little worth. In conclusion, the audience and Mintzberg raised several important points not covered in his formal presentation (chapter 13), and readers might want to consider these while reading his chapter.

The U.S. epilog which follows Mintzberg's contribution is intended to chart the current state of the field, as well as to showcase recent ongoing research and possible new directions for future inquiry. While both con-

ceptual integration and critical commentary are avoided, over sixty studies
are categorized and summarized in eight major areas (research related to
Mintzberg's managerial roles, instrument development and testing, perception and attribution, participation and other leader behaviors, leadership within a broader context, process studies, extensions to current approaches, and training and development work). Some linkages are provided
to chapters in the current and previous volumes, and conclusions briefly
drawn about differences in trends between current research, as exemplified
in the studies discussed, and previous research on leadership and managerial phenomena.

The U.S. epilog is followed by a European epilog by Hosking and
Hunt, which summarizes presentations and discussions at a recent informal European workshop on leadership and managerial behavior. Emphasis
is placed on highlighting the European perspective, and on contrasting
it with the U.S. point of view. This chapter notes considerable diversity in
approach, research methods, and topical areas covered, and suggests a number of exciting issues which might be usefully explored in an American context. Thus, in addition to highlighting for Europeans interesting work of
their colleagues, this chapter may stimulate interest among U.S. researchers
on a number of fronts. While this chapter is not lengthy, it contains a richness
of ideas and, hence, warrants careful reading and contemplation.

The concluding chapter by the editors attempts to treat selected issues
raised by Mintzberg and others, through the use of a metaphor involving ice-cream production and consumption. Although not a reply to
Mintzberg or other commentators on the field, it deals with issues pertinent
to Mintzberg's contribution and may be read as a companion piece. Essentially, differences in ontological and epistomological viewpoints are treated
metaphorically, and the desirability and need for diverse approaches to
leadership are advanced. Linkages to the European epilog are also briefly
considered.

This last chapter represents an attempt, at least in part, to bring the
infighting among persons interested in leadership and managerial phenomena to a halt, and to direct our energies in what we see as more useful
avenues of inquiry. Although readers may or may not agree with the editors' perspective, we thought this a useful contribution with which to end
the volume. The last part of the chapter deals with the "fun" of scientific
inquiry, and suggests that diversity may be required to generate the commitment necessary to advance the field. We found the diversity of this volume stimulating to us, and we hope that readers will derive as much insight
and enjoyment from its contents as we had in assembling it.

13

If You're Not Serving Bill and Barbara, Then You're Not Serving Leadership

HENRY MINTZBERG

This past Monday I had dinner with Bill and Barbara. Bill is an old, close friend. I wrote *The Nature of Managerial Work* (Mintzberg, 1973); Bill, by editing it, virtually rewrote it, and taught me a great deal about writing. Recently, he was promoted over his boss's boss to the position of Director of Distribution (head of marketing) of the National Film Board of Canada, with about 300 people in his charge. Bill drew Barbara out of the department in the Maritimes to head up his largest subunit, Canadian distribution, with a staff of 200. Thus, Bill and Barbara are now managers—leaders of one sort. Both are young and very bright, and both are concerned with trying to understand and better cope with their new responsibilities. When Barbara came across a paper of mine about the hemispheres of the brain and the management of organizations, and she expressed interest to Bill, he proposed the dinner—to talk about their concerns.

In preparing this overview, a few days later, one question dominated my thinking. Which of these eight contributions, or any others in the research literature, should I give to Bill and Barbara? Think about that. If the question makes you uneasy, then perhaps something is wrong with the research. If any of these presentations is potentially relevant to Bill and Barbara, then, without trying to trivialize it, I should be able to capture its essence in a sentence or two, at least to entice them to read it. Let me try.

Were Sheridan, Kerr, and Abelson ("Leadership Activation Theory:

My thanks to Bill Litwack and Barbara Janes for their contributions—both real and metaphoric—to this overview and to Sam Jelinek, Blair Sheppard, and Jim Waters for their comments.

An Opponent Process Model of Subordinate Responses to Leadership Behavior") asked to pull one brief passage out of their chapter, my guess is that it would come from the last paragraph, probably the following, "The quality of specific leadership incidents may be as important in determining leader effectiveness as the frequency by which the leader engages in different activities." Would that grab Bill and Barbara? Is there something new or startling in this comment, some clue to leader effectiveness? It would come as no surprise to Bill and Barbara that how they do things is at least as important as how often they do them. But their real concern is to get inside those hows. What is "quality"; what kind of quality works, and when? In the concluding "discussion" section, the authors comment that their "findings have important implications for leadership research." But do they have important implications for leadership?

Trying to pull the essence out of the Dansereau, Alutto, Markham, and Dumas chapter ("Multiplexed Supervision and Leadership: An Application of Within and Between Analysis") leads me, if they will excuse my paraphrasing, to the conclusion that sometimes leaders must treat their employees the same and sometimes differently. So? I am sure Bill and Barbara would agree. They might even say this is of some concern to them, though hardly a burning issue. But discovering the problem is not the point—dealing with it is. Again, does this chapter make a contribution to leadership, or to leadership research? Is it a reorientation for misguided managers, or misguided colleagues? And does anyone believe that the "Average Leadership Style model" or/and the "Vertical Dyad Linkage model," at least as characterized by Dansereau et al., would be of any interest at all to Bill and Barbara, even if these were labeled comprehensibly?

Bill and Barbara might say that the Lord, Foti, and Phillips chapter ("A Theory of Leadership Categorization") as well as that by Bales and Isenberg ("SYMLOG and Leadership Theory") are not really about leadership, but about categorization in one case and group process in the other. Leadership seems to be an afterthought in both. The potential may be there, but the ideas are not sufficiently developed. In one case, Bill and Barbara would want to see the categories before being able to make an assessment of relevance; in the other they might ask that a broader perspective be taken of leadership (and of group process). Had they heard Isenberg say in response to a question, "This is not a good example—it's a real-life example" (as opposed to one from a carefully controlled laboratory), perhaps they would have thought, "Maybe that's the problem."

Bill and Barbara would probably react in a more positive way as they began to read the Hunt and Osborn chapter ("Toward a Macro-Oriented Model of Leadership: An Odyssey"), happier with a broader, more comprehensive approach. Until, I suspect, they come to the notion of "discretion." If they spoke in our terms, my guess is that they would' say: "Hey, wait, discretion is not a variable, as you describe it, and certainly not a *dependent* one. We succeed by *creating* discretion. To help us, you have to probe into this notion deeply, to find out where we can find it. Not in general. In our jobs, on Tuesday, at 8:45. 'Macro variables' will aid in the search for 'the magical pot at the end of the rainbow' no more than micro variables; you'll need a telescope, and a shovel, not variables and questionnaires."

When Bill and Barbara come to Bussom, Larson, and Vicars's presentation ("Unstructured Non Participant Observation and the Study of Leaders' Interpersonal Contacts"), I think they would say, "Ah, now we're getting closer." But in reading on, they might add: "But not yet. There's a wealth of data here—real data, not quantified abstraction—but it has yet to be mined, for our purposes. (That will take an impressive shovel.) If the researchers can really go further in their conclusions, then the chapter will serve our needs. (Aren't all managers police chiefs of a sort?)" In other words, for Bill and Barbara, it is not the methodology that counts, not even the data, but the ability of the researchers to deal with data creatively. Especially the anecdotes—the "quality" in addition to the frequency.

That leaves two chapters. Bill and Barbara would certainly appreciate the way Rosemary Stewart ("The Relevance of Some Studies of Managerial Work and Behavior to Leadership Research") writes—no jargon, accessible to leaders. And I think they would like her trichotomy, would find it useful to think about their jobs in terms of demands, constraints, and choices. Indeed, we spent Mondey evening over dinner talking about such issues, though we did not use those labels. My guess is that Bill and Barbara would, as in the case earlier with discretion, say to her: "Couldn't you play some more at the margin of these three concepts? How can constraints be removed, choices created, and demands, if not avoided, at least partially circumvented and used to enhance choices? What is the link between these three notions and leader effectiveness? For example, are weak managers the ones who perceive no choices? Should we promote only managers who believe they have wide latitude for choice, avoiding the ones who always complain about demands and constraints?

And then Bill and Barbara would come to the Lombardo and McCall presentation ("Leaders on Line: Observations from a Simulation of Managerial Work"). "Finally," they would say, "Henry doesn't know what he's talking about when he criticizes the laboratory approach. This presentation shows that a clear head (one free of overly specified methodology) and a creative mind can function within any rich data base, even a simulated one." Reading through the chapter, they might comment on the following points:

"The problem certainly is the appropriate unit of analysis—we spent Monday evening talking about problems. And leadership (in the narrow way used in a number of other chapters) does fold into problem solving."

"You bet being caught in the middle—for us between the organic structure (now they're learning our jargon) of filmmaking and the bureaucratic structure of government administration—is chaotic."

They would be nodding point after point (e.g., that "there are no simple dependent variables," to "stop thinking group"). At least, until they came to the argument near the end that "leadership can make a difference." There they would laugh, believing that Lombardo and McCall's need to make such a point only shows what a dismal state the research literature is in. You see, Bill and Barbara have worked under different commissioners (the Film Board's name for its chief executive). They might even say: "If you didn't have to waste energy arguing that it made a difference, maybe you could spend more time finding 'how, why, and when' instead of having to admit you 'do not know.'" Were Bill and Barbara in as poetic a mood as Lombardo and McCall, they might conclude that here, at last, was a song with a score as well as lyrics.

In summary then, I think Bill and Barbara would find two of the presentations of interest and a third potentially so, depending on how the data were used. That is somewhere between 25 and 38 percent of the chapters, a far better average, I am willing to bet, than most of the "establishment" research literature would receive if submitted to our "Bill and Barbara test."

In fact, after I had written all this I became curious as to what would happen if I actually carried out the test. Accordingly, because I recalled that somewhere in the literature we are told that managers are busy and don't like to read, I gave Bill and Barbara the short versions of the eight contributions—exactly the same ones that were given out to the symposium participants. (These averaged about five pages; Barbara, after reading them, asked for the full copies of five of the presentations—those of Lord et al., Bales and Isenberg, Bussom et al., Stewart, and Lombardo and McCall. Bill, in typical managerial fashion, and because of *our* deadlines, read them on a plane to China, and so could not ask for the full versions.) I told Bill and Barbara nothing at all when I gave them the chapters, except that I would like some "pithy" comments on each—and more general ones if they so wished—vis-à-vis the concerns they had expressed Monday evening. Barbara, in fact, expected something quite germane to those concerns.

In her opinion, she did not get it. Indeed, my anticipation of her reactions was rather optimistic. For his part, Bill reported that he was positively angered by this material. Their reactions are shown in the accompanying extract.

Bill and Barbara's Comments
Bill   Barbara
Overall

Many presentations go to incredible and convoluted lengths and explanations, only to finish by stating the obvious. Complex and overinflated jargon is often used to camouflage emaciated ideas. Many seem more interested in studying the subtleties of a particular research approach— or even worse, studying other studies—than they are in contributing to a real understanding of leadership itself.

Leadership is an important subject and one that interests me a lot, but if these contributions are an indication of the current state of leadership research, then the gulf between academia and the real world is even greater than I feared. What bothered me most, as I read the presentations, was the gnawing suspicion that all the research was being carried out as an end in itself. Hence relevance was really a side issue. Perhaps I am too much of a pragmatist, but I persist in thinking that research, even in academic circles, should mean something.

Stewart

The study seems to be taking an approach which is more pragmatic than most of the others and therefore it should be more useful. But while the propositions for future research touch on valid areas, it is still frustrating that the major result is simply to indicate additional research that needs to be done.

More interesting and readable than most of the other presentations, but considering the competition, that is not exactly a rave review. I cannot say that I really learned anything new from it, apart from some terminology. The five propositions for leadership research, however, sounded more relevant than the work described in the other presentations.

Bussom et al.

The presentation spends most of its length defining the problem and explaining the approach taken—and it is quite practical and reasonable in this. But then it is very unclear about the analysis undertaken with the data, and ultimately says absolutely

A very promising beginning, but the presentation ended up going nowhere. Such an awful lot of work to establish that "there is a great amount of dissimilarity and complexity in how leaders carry out their interpersonal contacts." Eureka! The observa-

nothing about what it all might mean. [The complete chapter by Bussom et al., which Bill did not get a chance to read, does discuss the meaning of the analysis in considerably more detail.]

tional method is certainly valid, but is it being put to good use here?

Lombardo and McCall

This presentation is clearer and simpler than the others. It is more concrete and practical, and seems more closely to describe what actually happens in real life. But it still doesn't say much about leadership. The presentation succeeds more in clarifying what the considerations are rather than in coming to real conclusions. On the other hand, much can be said for not trying to offer artificial conclusions. The presentation does suggest specific and reasonable directions for future study. Finally, a presentation that includes the observation "effectiveness is a function of who defines it" is light-years more helpful and realistic than the other contributions which give the impression that the issues being dealt with can be neatly defined and analyzed.

At least this one is written in readable English. However, I did not find it particularly interesting or significant. Can one really learn much about the nuances of leadership behavior in a simulated situation? I doubt it; too many intangibles are absent. In the final analysis I think Lombardo and McCall are more interested in leadership research than in leadership.

Dansereau et al.

At least this presentation is understandable. But if it is of interest at all, it is to those studying leadership and not to leaders themselves. Whatever insight it contains relates to research approaches and not to the actual exercise of leadership. The insights gained as a result of what

A moderately interesting introduction followed by a boring discussion of research methods. What does all this have to say about leadership?

the presentation calls a "derivation" seem banal and self-evident, for example, that "it is possible for a superior to treat subordinates equally on one dimension and unequally on a second dimension." If this sort of thing passes for an acceptable and meaningful result in academia, then clearly the performance demands for academic research are less exciting than those for leaders in real life.

Lord et al.

Instead of studying what leadership is this presentation studies the structures of various theories of leadership. This is beyond navel-gazing—it is solipsism. Moreover, studying other studies is a perilous business that should not be undertaken lightly. If the quality of the presentations you gave me is any indication of the quality of the presentations being studied by this presentation (is that clear?), then it should not be undertaken at all. The whole thing is like a Russian matrioska doll—doubtful studies enveloping doubtful studies enveloping studies that were banal, superficial, and uninteresting in the first place. To make matters worse, much of the presentation is written in a style that can only be described as excruciating.

Much too theoretical to be relevant to me and written in very contorted prose. How can I take seriously a presentation that contains sentences like, "Though cognitively economical, this heuristic is not necessarily optimal"? The mathematical formulae left me dumbfounded.

Sheridan et al.

This presentation describes an "arousal and opponent process theory of motivation" that views

Another awful title; (sounds like something written by Pavlov). The ensuing presentation is not

each "leadership behavior incident" as if it were neatly definable and separable. It thus betrays an ignorance of the variety and complexity of day-to-day managerial work. The study attempts to link the frequency of leadership incidents and their intensity in simplistic ways. I think such an attempt is doomed by definition because it is trying to measure things which are intrinsically nonquantifiable—at least on neat scales. It is like an art critic saying that if the ceiling of the Sistine Chapel were one foot higher and the index fingers of God and Adam one inch further apart, the impact would be 2 percent less. Such an approach is devoid of imagination and misses the point in a truly monumental way. The study forgets that "leadership" is a social and communications phenomenon that happens between human beings and not a set of rules for some managerial chess game. Moreover, most of the conclusions, even if by some accident they turned out to be accurate, are staggeringly banal and obvious—for example, "different leadership activities have varying motivational effects on the subordinate." The mind boggles. It also vastly oversimplifies the subtleties of job performance and "credible" treatment of subordinates. The appendix showing the questionnaire is quite interesting—but the article itself leaves the impression that it could have been much better. Only the appendix was written in clear English, but I did not really understand what it was supposed to prove. The conclusion, as stated, seemed incredibly banal. Did I miss something?

pression that the concrete questions contained in the questionnaire have been transformed into mush.

Bales and Isenberg

This presentation spends most of its length describing the general theory, model, or approach that was used—and tells very little about what the actual results were when the theory was applied to leadership. It culminates with a working definition of leadership that is vague and not particularly helpful. When you cut through the jargon the definition amounts to the following: "To lead is to exert a decisive determining influence . . . by whatever means." It hardly seems worth the effort.

A mildly interesting foray into the much plowed field of group dynamics. Readable, but I doubt that it holds any surprises for a reasonably alert manager. The problem with "how to" guides to interpersonal skills is that good leaders do not need them (that's how they got to be leaders!) and bad ones cannot really be taught to use them.

Hunt and Osborn

As research, it may be exemplary. As something that is relevant and meaningful to managers, it is of limited interest. To say "managers are seen as those who stand between and link subordinates with their organization" is not only wrong, it is offensive. It implies that these subordinates are somehow not already part of the organization but need to be linked to it. It is the sort of facile and meaningless jargon which leads in the following sentence to the "discovery" that managers interact with their subordinates! Two plus two also equals four. I still have no idea who the contribution was written for. The conclusions

Obviously aimed at academics, not at managers. Even the title put me off. Could scarcely wade my way through the jargon. After a first reading, from which I gleaned very little, I considered rereading, then decided it was not worth the effort.

seem slim, obvious, and not particularly useful in understanding
what leadership is and how managers manifest it. In sum, the
presentation was too interested
in its research model and not interested enough in showing how
the model and the supposed results stemming from it related to
the work of managers.

I should emphasize that I wrote my comments on the material before I ever
saw Bill and Barbara's (and made no changes subsequently), while they
wrote their comments without ever seeing mine or being given any clue
about them. Let me reiterate that these are two well-educated, bright, articulate people who can handle concepts. If you cannot get through to Bill and
Barbara, then I firmly believe you have no chance of getting through to any
important segment of the leadership community out there.

The Question of Constituency

When I first wrote all this, I asked myself if I was belittling a lot of hard
work. Is the Bill and Barbara test a fair one? Shouldn't researchers be given a
chance to sort things out before having to be judged relevant? Is there not a
place for pure, as opposed to applied, research on leadership? And then I
said, "Damn it, no." Leadershp researchers have had almost a century to sort
things out. (In his *Handbook of Leadership*, Stogdill, 1974, traces research on
leadership traits back to 1904.) The absence of such a test is what has left the
field in such a mess. I believe in pure research—that having to come up with
a "how to" conclusion can spoil a useful line of thinking. But I have also
discovered that intelligent practitioners are as interested as researchers in
the results of pure research—and by that I mean descriptive insights devoid
of prescription. So long as the results have some relevance to their own
concerns. And are expressed in clear English. I have never come across a
good insight in organizational behavior or management that could not be so
expressed. Jargon is too often a smokescreen that clouds the emptiness of
the findings. The Bill and Barbara test is designed to blow it away.

Let me emphasize that I am not promoting a public relations campaign,
not making a call to include some kind of executive summary at the front of
every research report. I am talking about how the research is conceived

in the first place and how the results are then developed—who they are designed to serve. And I fully recognize all the dangers of fooling some practitioners with slick writing that has no substance. But those are not the practitioners I have in mind for this test. I am talking about intelligent practitioners, ones who can handle concepts and see through shallowness. There are plenty of them out there. If you like, imagine the test will be restricted to Ph.Ds. in organizational behavior who have become full-time line managers.

My point is that if leadership researchers can talk only to each other, then they ultimately serve nobody. They form a closed system which ingests resources and offers nothing in return. If the field of leadership is to function effectively, then it must have a constituency. Without that it lacks a "belay," to use McCall's nice term. Interestingly, the authors of the two chapters I believe most directly relevant to leaders have clear belays. Rosemary Stewart has spent her career training practicing managers: she has to have something to tell them or they will simply go away. Likewise Lombardo and McCall work at the Center for Creative Leadership, where they are constantly in touch with practicing managers. The rest of us, myself included, can hide in the university if we so choose; these people cannot.

As implied, I believe that constitutency is first of all leaders themselves—and in our society that means mostly (or at least conveniently) managers. Managers want to know how to select other managers, how to train them, above all how they themselves can lead more effectively. But it is not only advice they need, perhaps not even primarily advice, at least from us as researchers. They need insight—startling insight, ideas that will change their perceptions. With such insight, they—or the staff people and consultants close to them—will know what to change. How many of the presentations in this book, or in the research journals over the past ten years, properly translated, provide that kind of insight? How many would you give to the managers you know—say to your dean, to help him serve you more effectively? Better still, how many would you take to heart if *you* became dean?

A second constituency—less easily pinned down—is society itself, increasingly concerned about the quality of its leadership. America, with its Carters and Reagans, previously its Fords and Nixons, is facing a crisis of immense proportions in its political leadership. Is that not an issue that leadership researchers should address? Do you? Can you? Do consideration and initiating structure or the Vertical Dyad Linkage model help us to understand what were Carter's problems? (I must add an afterthought here. The morning following the U.S. presidential election, a radio commentator suggested that Jimmy Carter's problem was that "he was not really in contact with his constituents"—the South, new immigrants, the poor, and so forth.

The implication, that leadership is the capacity to connect to a relevant constituency, has its own intriguing implication: that leadership researchers have themselves exhibited no leadership.)

In short, without a constituency, I believe leadership research can go nowhere. And for the most part, the research has no constituency.

The State of the Leadership Literature

This volume is entitled "Beyond Establishment Views". Those who have occupied the overviewer position before me have decried the state of leadership research, as have many others. So much so that this has become the establishment view. So let me say that I think the literature on leadership is in great shape. But not the "establishment" research literature, by which I mean the material that fills the refereed journals.

When I first looked at that literature, in the mid-1960s, I was frankly appalled: traits pursued fruitlessly for decades, consideration and initiating structure being rediscovered in the research year after year, risky shifts that were eventually discredited, and so on. And what has changed since the 1960s? Every theory that has since come into vogue—and I shall not name them for fear of losing all my friends—has for me fallen with a dull thud. None that I can think of has ever touched a central nerve of leadership— approached its essence. Even the old ones endure. I find in these chapters, intended to move beyond establishment views, that consideration and initiating structure are not dead—they come up repeatedly. Sometimes I think I must be awfully dense: I just do not get the point, and never have.

Even the titles of the theories—new no less than old—reveal the nature of their content—plodding and detached. Since the beginning, there seems to have been a steady convergence on the peripheral at best, and all too often on the trivial and the irrelevant.

Early in their program, our doctoral students read Kaplan's *The Conduct of Inquiry*. In looking at it again recently, I was struck by the author's inclusion, under "Validation of Theories," of the criterion of their "esthetic qualities": "A scientist sometimes needs the courage, not only of his convictions, but also of his esthetic sensibilities" (1964, p. 319). Picking up on this, I suspect that if a theory is not beautiful, then the odds are good that it is not very useful. Which theory of leadership is beautiful? Consideration and initiating structure? The Vertical Dyad Linkage model? About which leadership theory can we say, as did Watson about the double helix, "the structure was too pretty not to be true" (1968, p. 134). When I read most of the literature, I want to say, "The structure is so ugly it has to be false." What Kaplan wrote in 1946 seems to apply to the leadership literature of 1980: "The esthetic norm . . . has little bearing on behavioral science in its present state, which may be characterized—without undue offense to anyone, I trust [!]— as one of almost unrelieved ugliness" (p. 319).

The literature that is in great shape is another literature. It is the literature of biographies, the more articulate practitioner literature, and the literature of a fifth column of academic types, but outside the establishment— from people such as Weick, Sayles, Kotter, McCall. (I would have included Rosemary Stewart, but she described herself at this symposium as an outsider in this gathering of leadership researchers. I too was going to say that. But why? Rosemary Stewart has spent her career studying leaders; I am a professor of management policy whose best known work is a study of leaders, and even now our research on strategy formation is all wrapped up with trying to understand the influence of leadership, among other factors, on that process [Mintzberg & Waters, 1980]. Neither I nor Rosemary Stewart am an outsider to the study of leadership. I and apparently she as well simply feel compelled to disassociate ourselves from what leadership research has become in so much of the literature.)[1]

In other words, I believe we know a good deal more about leadership than we realize (and I want to return to that word "know"). But the knowledge is in other places, and it is being generated by people doing other things—people outside the mainstream of academic research. Let me take one example. Consider a special issue entitled "Leadership" of the *Executive* magazine, put out by the Cornell business and public administration school. I am going to give it to Bill and Barbara, asking them to look especially at the article by Thomas Peters (1980), of the McKinsey consulting firm, because I think it touches one of those central nerves. Peters makes the simple point—based on "the experience of a score of companies that have executed major shifts of direction with notable skill and efficiency" (p. 12), that effective leadership is related to "brute persistence" or obsession. "Repeatedly and conspicuously, the chief executive officers of these companies exhibited a common pattern of behavior: namely, obsessive at-

1. My study of five managers reported in *The Nature of Managerial Work* was actually my dissertation in a doctoral program in management policy. I believed that without an understanding of managerial work, we had no hope of understanding any issue related to management policy. I wrote the book for policy people and, much to my surprise, it was the organization behavior people who adopted it. Leadership, in the narrow sense—relationships between the leader and the led—was the "least convincing" of the roles I discussed, in the opinion of Karl Weick (1974, p. 117) and myself as well. In his review of the book, Weick wondered how much was to be gained by "invoking the concept of leadership" (p. 117) at all, as opposed to attaching it to the other roles.

tention to a myriad of small ways of shifting the organization's attention to the desired new theme" (p. 12). Supporting this, Peters found the attributes of "consistency in support of the theme, usually over a period of years," the focussing of the theme on "building or enhancing just one or two basic organizational skills" such as customer service or cost reduction, "conscious use of symbolic behavior," "strong encouragement of experimentation," "an extraordinary amount of time in the field" often bypassing formal authority, and so on (p. 12). When I told Barbara, after she had given me her comments on the presentations, that I would give her this magazine, and described this article briefly, she said, "Now *that* sounds interesting!"

Why should this be the case? Why should the interesting material be in the practitioner literature, or in a very different kind of research literature? To go beyond establishment views, I should do more than comment on the state of the literature—I should make tangible suggestions as to how it can be improved. The previous overviewers have, I believe, been rather mild in their prescriptions. I wish to go farther out on a limb, saying things that may seem a little outrageous. That way I can better make my points. And so the reader is warned that from here on everything is meant to be overstatement (including this).

Some Overstated Prescriptions

I believe that the root of the problem in what I have been calling the mainstream research literature on leadership is methodological. In *Zen and the Art of Motorcycle Maintenance*, Pirsig (1974) makes the intriguing point that we cannot define "quality" (and presumably cannot measure it), but we "know" it when we see it. I am struck by the same thing about leadership. We are unable to define it, we fail at measuring it, but we sure seem to know it when we see it. And why not? Is good leadership not one kind of quality. And therein seems to lie the difference between one kind of literature and the other—the fact that there appears to be two kinds of knowing. There are those things we know formally, or analytically—by definitions and measures. And there are those things we know informally, intuitively—deep in our brains, although we do not know why. An expert has been defined as someone with no elementary knowledge. An amusing point, because it appears to contain a grain of truth. That truth seems to be that the expert is all too often someone who blocks out the second kind of knowing. He or she "knows" analytically, but not intuitively. The expert has certain sophisticated knowledge—which may or may not be relevant—but he or she lacks certain basic elementary knowledge. And leaderhsip seems to require a good deal of elementary knowledge. That is probably why everybody seems to understand it except the experts, at least formally. Thus we have the Lombardo and McCall comment that leaders know far better than researchers what leadership is all about, but the researchers don't know how to ask them and the leaders don't know how to tell the researchers.

Let me illustrate. It has become fashionable among researchers (not practitioners) to argue that leadership does not matter. A well-known colleague of ours, who has been saying these things, visited us at McGill recently and I asked him why it is that those who make this claim always seem to fight so hard when deans are being changed. Our colleague smiled, slightly embarassed, admitting that he had in fact been deeply involved in such a process recently. When asked why, he answered, "Just in case!" A cute answer, for a cute hypothesis. But pure bull! In his practical mind, he doesn't believe it any more than I do. We both "know" very well that leadership matters, that while some situations are unmanageable, in the vast majority of cases leadership can make an enormous difference. Both he and I have seen what has happened to different business schools under different deans.

And if we "know" leadership makes a difference, then I think we "know" a good deal more, for example that effective leaders probably do exhibit certain traits or styles under certain conditions. But we do not know them in the establishment literature, for there we are forbidden to discuss what cannot be defined or measured precisely. Another thing we know is how fundamentally intuitive the job of leading is, and how lacking in inherent structure. Indeed, here we know formally as well as informally: we know about the brevity, variety, and fragmentation of the job, its oral characteristics and its emphasis on soft data, the absence of patterning in the work, the dynamic and unprogrammed nature of its decision making. If the job is so unstructured, then how can research with so much structure capture it? If the job is so intuitive, then how can research that precludes the use of intuition—by keeping the researchers so far removed from its rich reality—help us to understand it?

Pirsig writes: "The subject for analysis, the patient on the table, was no longer Quality, but analysis itself. Quality was healthy and in good shape. Analysis, however, seemed to have something wrong with it that prevented it from seeing the obvious" (1974, p. 213). Likewise our patient is not leadership but leadership research, specifically methodology. Until it is changed to help generate other kinds of knowledge—knowledge less obsessed with definition and measurement—I do not believe it will serve leadership. What we need are research methods that are unconventional—not unconventional for the world at large but for the world of experts—methods that do not get in the way. Methodology has been the problem in leadership research because of the nature of *this particular* phenomenon. We need to study leadership *simply*, *directly*, and *imaginatively*—that is all. In this regard, let me take another look at the three chapters that I believe are or might be of use to Bill and Barbara.

Rosemary Stewart asks us to look at leader behavior. I ask you to look at her behavior, as a researcher, over time. What struck me about her contribution—knowing her previous work—is how she has loosened up on methodology (and the diary was hardly a highly rigorous method to begin with). She has become far more eclectic, not only using a wider variety of methods, but also reverting to almost no method at all for some of her data. More interesting is the absence of numbers in her chapter. In general, her only numbers are those that identify the year of each reference. Even her tables are all words. As Rosemary Stewart herself commented at this symposium: "I have tried to measure various things. Most of them I've given up." Similarly, the Lombardo and McCall contribution is one of words, based on the simplest of methods (at least once the simulation was built!). They just observed what their managers did, and drew some conclusions— simply, directly, and with imagination. And Bussom et al., interestingly, argue the case for *un*structured observation (although as they note, theirs was structured, but not highly so—they just observed and recorded). They certainly present numbers, but these are believable numbers, close to what managers actually do.

An expert has also been defined as someone who avoids all the many pitfalls on his or her way to the grand fallacy. I think the grand fallacy in leadership research has been rigor—artificial rigor, detached rigor, rigor not for insight, but for its own sake. That kind of rigor has interfered with the researchers' capacity to understand what goes on. All those statistical tests, questionnaire designs, and the like contain the pitfalls. We sometimes forget that "significance" is not a word owned by the statisticians. It matters more that the conclusions be significant than the results. Does one kind of significance in fact interfere with the other?

With this in mind, let me present some methodological challenges, reiterating first that I am purposely overstating and second that I mean these comments to apply *only to leadership research*, not to research in management or even in organizational behavior in general. My challenges are not meant to promote a "one best way"; rather they are designed to avoid what I believe to be the "one worst way" to do research on leadership.

First, get rid of constructs, at least before collecting the data. Stop trying to fit the world into your abstract categories, especially ones so far removed from how leaders actually behave. I do not know what initiating structure has to do with answering the telephone at 9:43; I have never been able to identify any clear degree of discretion in a single managerial decision; I have no idea what intensity of behavior means as a general construct, or amount of control, or even participation. Isolating some abstract construct and then measuring it in some detached way serves no one. (What construct, no matter how half-baked, cannot be measured on a seven-point scale?) We do not need to measure constructs, we need to enrich them—to give them some real meaning, through deep probes into leadership activity. What does participation really mean and what forms can it take? How do leaders exercise control? How does discretion manifest itself in the complex job of being a leader? Discretion itself is an enormously complicated issue. My MBA students recently described the heads of a school board they are studying as having the capacity "to prepare themselves for doom." Is that discretion? In other words, do your research *in order* to create richer, more relevant constructs, and when you have them, do more research to enrich them still further. And then, one day, when intelligent practitioners believe you really have something insightful—and you yourselves truly find it beautiful— then go out and test. But don't hold your breath waiting.

Second, get rid of instruments. Following from the first point, throw away your questionnaires and set foot in places where real leaders and rich behaviors can be found. Watch them, talk to them, talk to the people around them. Study what is really going on out there, as I believe Stewart, Bussom et al., and Lombardo and McCall (in one sense) tried to do. Don't let instruments get in the way of your intuition. Some years ago we did a paper describing how 25 strategic decisions were made in organizations. Then came the first request for our "instrument" and they have been coming regularly ever since. On receiving that first request I had to laugh to myself: all I had was a typed list of 21 banal questions. Research is not instruments. It is detective work. Bussom et al. found out that my instrument in *The Nature of Managerial Work* was a clipboard, a pen (preferably a pencil, with a good eraser), and a watch. What matters is being there, with your eyes wide open, and then what you do with what you see. The point is, keep yourself open. There is a rich complicated reality out there. Let it surprise you. If it doesn't, then you haven't learned anything.

Third, get rid of measurement, or, at least, if you insist on it, measure in organizational terms. In other words, if you have to count, count real things. Not your own inventions, brought to an artificial life on seven-point scales. There are indeed a great many interesting things to count out there. (We are studying strategies in an airline by counting aircraft bought, new routes opened up, and the like.) But I am not sure that counting is what we need to get at the essence of leadership. I counted a great deal in *The Nature of Managerial Work*, and I think that helped me understand what managers do. But not what makes a manager successful. That will require more intensive probes into the ways individual managers work—*how* they perform their different tasks, not *what* tasks they perform.

What is so sacred about measurement anyway? I think it was Charlie Brown's friend, Peppermint Patty, who said that "Nothing spoils arithmetic faster than a lot of numbers." Does the same thing apply to leadership research? The organizational behavior literature tells us quite clearly that organizational goals are often displaced by attempts to quantify them. I wonder if researchers in OB ever considered applying that finding to themselves. Is it not possible that the ultimate goal of research—insight—is being displaced in fields such as leadership by an overemphasis on quantification? For example, it could be that the more organization itself is able to measure performance or effectiveness in certain managerial jobs, the less leadership counts in those jobs. If true, that could have damaging consequences on studies, such as the one by Hunt and Osborn, which use samples of leaders selected on the basis of the presence of objective measures of effectiveness. To repeat what I said earlier, maybe what matters in leadership is beyond measurement. Maybe highly structured research will not allow us to understand people who function intuitively yet perhaps succeed by acting in counterintuitive fashion (yet still intuitively), as Lombardo and McCall suggest. What is wrong with words anyway? To my mind, words are what distinguish the establishment research literature from both the practitioner and the fifth-column research literature, the more closed-ended studies from the open-ended probes, the literature that serves itself from the literature that serves leaders.

Fourth, get rid of variables, and especially the notion of dependence and independence. The logical consequence of getting rid of constructs, instruments, and measurement is getting rid of variables. That way we can stop pretending that the world is divided into dependent and independent variables. Since von Bertalanffy, it has been clear that the world is a system in which everything impacts on everything else. Again, let us study the world as it comes.

Fifth, perhaps get rid of definitions. We often tie ourselves up in knots trying to define things that are easily "known" in other ways. Kaplan (1964) makes the intriguing point that a definition is not contained in that one sentence so labeled; it must be inferred from the entire text. (How often have we read a piece in which the definition-in-use—that is, the definition that can be inferred from the entire text—directly contradicts the reconstructed definition—the formal one.) Indeed, the object of leadership research is to define leadership! That is what all those years of research have been all about. What sense does it make to sit back in the abstract and throw out a one sentence definition at the outset, or debate different ones?

To summarize, *get rid of methodology that gets in the way.* This is not a plea for fuzzy thinking or fishing at random, not a suggestion to go knock at the door of some organization and say: "Hi. Are there any leaders here because I'd like to study leadership." A sense of focus is necessary in research, as is some orderly way to collect data. But as I have stated elsewhere (Mintzberg, 1979), I firmly believe that the best methodologies to study organizational and managerial phenomena are usually the simplest, most direct ones, the ones that give full vent to the researcher's imagination. And I believe that is what has characterized all the best research on leadership too, research from outside the establishment.

Some Leadership Concerns

One final note, on this issue of focus—the content of research rather than the method of doing it. When I published *The Nature of Managerial Work,* I hoped that subsequent research would probe deeply into some of the manager's roles or activities, to try to get at *how* managers worked— essentially the issue of style and its relationship to effectiveness. I also hoped that what I saw as the most important issue in the book would be taken up and investigated. That is the problem of superficiality, that managers, in whose decisions the future of our society is entrusted, are forced by the very nature of their work to make these decisions quickly and superficially. Instead I see a number of replications emerging. That is good for the ego. But I have always felt that *The Nature of Managerial Work* exposes perhaps 1 percent of that proverbial iceberg. Would it not be more useful to go after chunks of the other 99? There is so much to investigate. Above all, we need to understand the whole integrated phenomenon of leadership— leader by leader or, as Lombardo and McCall suggest, issue by issue. And that will mean studying managers a few at a time, intensively, looking at their activities as well as their styles as well as their effectiveness as well as their situations. And style is more, much more, than how managers deal with subordinates; it is how quickly they make their decisions, what kinds of data they prefer, which contacts they favor, how often they tour their facilities and how they do so, and a thousand other things, informational and decisional as well as interpersonal.

In the context of such research, we need to address the real concerns of managers and organizations. For example, we need to find out:

What discretion means in the context of managing an organization, and how it is found or created.

What the leader's role is in the formation of an organizational culture or ideology; in the words of Selznick (1957), how a leader infuses his organization with purpose; what charisma means, what it has to do with the vision of the leader.

What the word "planning" means in the context of the work of managing an organization; how a manager's vision of the future gets translated into concrete action, formally and informally.

How managers balance the conflicting needs for change and continuity in their organizations.

Why turnover is so high in some important managerial jobs (such as police chiefs who, Bussom et al. tell us, average 13 months' tenure).

What inhibits the emergence of strong leaders in certain situations (the U.S. presidency?; General Motors?); or more to the point, what conditions nurture "great" leaders.

As for the problem of superficiality, I have done somewhat of a flip on this one. I used to think that managers had to learn to be superficial in order to succeed, to become, if you like, effective in their superficiality (for example, by being able to judge the people making proposals if they could not understand the proposals themselves). Now I am beginning to think that superficiality may be at the root of many of the problems of our large organizations. Could the growing crises of leadership, behavior, and performance of large organizations—public as well as private, capitalistic not much less than communistic—be related to superficiality, to the problems leaders of giant organizations have in knowing what is going on, in keeping in touch? Are such leaders being increasingly forced to know in the expert's way—through detached information systems and the like? (In other words, do these leaders face the same problems mainstream researchers do in trying to undrstand their data? Is there a bureaucratic mode that is prevailing in—and destroying—research and practice alike?) Increasingly, our organizations seem to survive and grow for political reasons. They sustain themselves through power relationships rather than effective service to their clientele (a point reflected in the most recent literature of organization theory, e.g., Pfeffer & Salancik, 1978). Are many of our large organizations too political, too detached, above all too large to serve us? Is this a problem of leadership? I certainly believe so. Is it one that leadership researchers should care about? I certainly hope so.

Back to Bill and Barbara

Let me come back to the Bill and Barbara test in conclusion, because I am perfectly serious about it. Announce that any request for research funding or any submission to a journal will have to undergo screening by an intelligent practitioner. A member of that constituency will have to find it relevant before it is approved. Then watch what happens. That is my challenge to you—if you really want to change things, instead of just decrying them. If you cannot serve leaders, then how can you hope to serve leadership?

14

Beyond Establishment Leadership Views: An Epilog

UMA SEKARAN, JAMES G. HUNT, and CHESTER A. SCHRIESHEIM

In the epilog to the previous symposium volume, some 60 studies, at various stages of development (from conception to recent publication), were highlighted (see Hunt & Larson, 1979). This stream of studies was envisioned as helping move leadership research to a new stage of development. It is in this spirit and hope that this epilog was prepared. The studies here help balance this volume, by providing a more complete picture of the state of the field and its probable future direction.

To do this, we report information on more than 60 studies currently in various stages of development—from a conceptualized theory, to research proposals, to papers in press. These are occasionally supplemented with recently published works where they help round out the picture. The materials were obtained through: 1) summaries provided in response to a blanket request by the editors to researchers working in the leadership or managerial behavior areas, 2) paper presentations obtained from proceedings or presented at recent professional meetings, 3) unsolicited papers sent by authors, and 4) responses to personal requests from the editors to researchers working in specific areas. Based on past experience, it seems that the sample of studies obtained is fairly representative of current research in the leadership area, including managerial work and behavior studies as well.

Below, we try to capture the essence of these studies and, where appropriate, link these to the 1979 epilog and try to project future trends. As before, we group all material together by main themes, even though some studies may have one or more subsidiary themes contained within them. Again, depending on the details in our possession, and the stage of development of the work, more emphasis is placed on some studies than others.

Neither a tight theoretical integration, nor a comprehensive, critical review is attempted in this summary.

We have classified studies into eight categories: 1) work of the Center for Creative Leadership and follow-ups to Mintzberg, 2) instrument development testing, 3) perception and attribution, 4) participation and other leader behaviors, 5) leadership within a broader setting, 6) process studies, 7) extensions to currently emphasized approaches, and 8) training and development.

Work of the Center for Creative Leadership, Follow-ups to Mintzberg and Other Managerial Role Studies

The 1979 epilog briefly reviewed, among other things, the work of McCall and his associates at the Center for Creative Leadership, and some replications and extensions of Mintzberg's managerial role work. Also offered was a brief preview of the potential contributions of simulations to the study of leadership in dynamic, complex organizations. Let's update this review.

Center for Creative Leadership Work

The Lombardo and McCall chapter in this volume, and the commentator and overviewer reactions, provide ample testimony to the interest and enthusiasm with which the Looking Glass simulation has been received by scholars. An interesting feature of the ongoing work of McCall and his associates is their efforts to validate the simulation as a viable research method which offers findings applicable to the corporate world. In this connection, McCall and Segrist (1980) report that they have just completed a study relating individual performance, as measured in the Looking Glass simulation, to individual performance as measured by the corporation from which the sample was drawn. They find significant relationships between various measures in the simulation and several corporate measures of performance.

These findings augur well for the validity of the simulation. Lombardo and Stein (1980) are also studying job analysis techniques to analyze the job requirements in the simulated organization. The results thus far indicate that job ratings and clusters for the simulated positions are analogous to corporate norms on the instrument they employed. Lombardo and Stein feel that the content validity of managerial simulations can thus be empirically assessed. Based on their experience with Looking Glass, McCall and Lombardo have written an article describing how simulation can be used for management research (McCall & Lombardo, in press). As we pointed out earlier in this volume, that article is a useful supplement to their present chapter in giving a "feel" for research uses of simulation.

We may, with a reasonable degree of certainty, expect that in the next decade simulation will gain increasing popularity and acceptance as a research method, especially when its external validity is more fully established. We may thus expect to hear further from the Center for Creative Leadership on the Looking Glass simulation.

Other research endeavors by the center include a research review by McCall on the leadership of scientists and engineers, an area that has not been stuided very much. An article by McCall, scheduled to appear in Connolly (in press), will discuss: 1) characteristics of scientists and engineers, and effective supervision among professional groups; 2) leadership at the interface between professional units and large organizations; and 3) the implications of promotion into management for scientists and engineers. Other recent work focusing on R and D scientists is by Dailey (1980) and Hoffman and Pearse (1980); both studies concentrate on project leaders. The center has also been actively involved in follow-ups to Mintzberg's (1973) study of managerial work. We cover that below, along with the work of other investigators.

Follow-ups to Mintzberg's Work

Most of the ongoing follow-ups of Mintzberg's original studies basically relate to establishing the author's 10 managerial roles and developing instruments to tap them, or to further examining the question of whether managers engage in the planning function.

Argue (1979) used Mintzberg's 10 roles in a diary study of nine school principals. He reports a number of work pattern similarities between his sample of principals and Mintzberg's chief executives. McCall and Segrist (1980) published their first technical report on the development of an instrument to measure Mintzberg's managerial roles (i.e., the beginnings of this effort were reported in the 1979 epilog). Further refinement of their instrument was undertaken, and it is now being used to explore the relationship between each managerial role and various managerial levels and functions. Previously, the effects of hierarchy and functional area on the extent of required managerial roles was studied by Alexander (1979). Using a sample of 225 managers, he found that both level in the hierarchy and functional area have a strong effect on the assumption of managerial work roles.

Managerial roles have also been studied in the public sector. Lau, Broedling, Walters, Newman, and Harvey (1979), using a multimethod approach and U.S. Navy Civilian Executives (initial phases of the study were reported in the previous symposium volume), concluded that organization structure (centralization, decision-making demands, etc.) has an impact on how the roles are exercised. These researchers noted that an executive selection, development, and appraisal system can be designed around a common core of skills, knowledge, and abilities required by executives.

A different approach to executive development through the identification of managerial job requirements has been proposed by Lau, Pavett, and Park (1980). While their study of 210 managers and executives in the public sector and 220 in the private sector did not identify all 10 managerial roles proposed by Mintzberg, the authors found that managers in both sectors performed similar jobs. Based on this, they suggest that executive development programs can be designed based on similar job requirements. This study is interesting to compare with two earlier ones using Mintzberg's roles as a starting point (Gingras, Zeghal, & Alain, 1977; Morse & Wagner, 1978) as those studies emphasized the importance of contingencies in managerial behavior research.

Along with this examination of Mintzberg's 10 managerial roles, research has also addressed the question of whether managers plan. Interest in this topic is understandable in the context of Mintzberg's findings that managers hardly ever plan. To reconcile this discrepancy, Snyder and Glueck (1980) supplemented structured observations of school and hospital chief executives with interviews. As the chief executives explained what they were doing and why, it became clear that they extensively engaged in planning activities and functions.

In a study of community mental health institutions (organized anarchies) and branch banks (rational organizations), Kaplan (1979) concluded that organizational setting is an important variable in explaining managerial action. While community mental health systems had a greater portion of their work planned than the branch banks, they did not show greater adherence to the plans. The organized anarchies monitored less, counseled employees more, and legitimated organizational norms more. They also interacted more with public representatives and with members of larger organizations. These differences among nonindustrial organizations suggest that setting variables be taken into account while studying managerial activities and roles.

Some interesting propositions regarding the nonplanning profile of managers are offered by Kurke and Aldrich (1979), who replicated Mintzberg's study using CEOs from a public hospital, a school system, a high-technology plant, and a bank. Deliberating on how organizations can tolerate "nonplanning" managers, these researchers suggest that relevant external pressures are not organization-wide, but instead selectively impinge on specific subunits and that as long as these subunits respond effectively to their environments, CEOs do little damage. An alternative proposition was also put forth based on the "population ecology model." That is, organizations survive or fail by their relative standing vis-à-vis other organizations. As long as most managers behave in the same way, no organization is at a disadvantage. Also, when environmental niches are forgiving (there is more than one way to achieve profits and legitimacy), managers have a cushion between their behavior and reality.

A study which linked roles based on Mintzberg's work to organizational success was conducted by Harrison (1980). Four pairs of chief executives heading "successful" and "unsuccessful" firms across four different industries were sampled. Role data were obtained using expanded diaries covering five working days. Among the most important conclusions were that the successful manager engages in more leader activity (motivation and staffing), monitors more, and receives more unsolicited information from subordinates than the unsuccessful manager. Also, leader and monitor role performance were found to be tightly linked and central to organizational success.

Finally, an update on the Vicars, Larson, Bussom (1979) observational study proposal (reported in the previous volume) is in order. Apart from their current chapter, the researchers have completed nationwide data collection on police chiefs and school superintendents, and are now attempting to move beyond Mintzberg's classification scheme in analyzing their data. Their data base should prove useful in both the leadership and managerial work areas.

Summarizing the above literature, by-and-large, Mintzberg's ten managerial roles have not been unequivocally established empirically. Vicars et al., the McCall group, as well as a number of other studies mentioned above have found difficulty in operationalizing the 10 roles. There is also some question about Mintzberg's coding scheme, as it does not allow for recording a rich variety of events, and it may obscure some of the managerial functions that are performed by executives. Given the popularity and general acceptance of Mintzberg's studies, the viability of the roles and the coding system need to be established further, before more investigators take off on the Mintzberg model.

Related Studies of the Managerial Role

Morris (1980) contemplates an observational study of 16 Chicago public school principals for 12 days. The purpose is to study the discretionary decision-making activities undertaken by the principals, how they perceive the limits of their power, and what aspects of their discretionary life are most related to job success or failure. This aspect of studying discretionary decision-making could parallel the concept of discretionary leadership, and may mesh with Stewart's work as well.

A study examining managerial decision-making, coordination, communications, and technical competency of U.S. Civil Service engineer and scientist managerial personnel was conducted by Ellison, Abe, Fox, and Guest (1980). These dimensions were examined in conjunction with biographical inventories and sketches, among other things, in order to determine how well they could be predicted.

Conclusion

The variety of methods of data collection used in these studies is impressive. It reinforces the argument for multimethods of data collection in single studies. Of course, it takes enormous amounts of time and effort to coordinate different methods and establish data reliability and validity. But, the use of multiple methods appears to offer considerable potential in the study of leadership, and managerial behavior.

Instrument Development and Testing

Some instrument development work was reported above as a by-product of managerial behavior studies. Here, the emphasis is more directly on such work, and is heavily focused on Stogdill's (1963) LBDQ-Form XII.

The first study, by Markham (1980a), is related to the within and between analysis contribution by Dansereau, Alluto, Markham, and Dumas (chapter 6). It is concerned with analyzing Form XII to reflect different units of analysis. Markham's goal is thus similar to that reported in the work of Hunt and Osborn (this volume) and Schriesheim (1976). Neither of these earlier studies was successful in making a unit of analysis differentiation.

Kavich (1980) and his associates are in the process of conducting tests among a wide range of educational institutions, to determine the potential usefulness of Form XII in that setting. Similarly, Ramirez, Ramirez, and Richek (1980) are using Form XII with business and education administration students (who are potential leaders). They have been involved with conducting higher order factor analyses and other psychometric examinations of the instrument.

While the consideration and initiating structure dimensions of Form XII have been widely used, there are relatively few studies which have employed all 12 dimensions. The work above, in addition to whatever other usefulness it may have, is of interest because it uses all of the dimensions. In this sense it is reminiscent of a study by Hawley (1969), who reports factor analysis results for the complete instrument.

The final work considered here-is by Alvares, Silverman, and Dalessio (1980). It reports on a scale to measure subordinate liking or positive affect toward a superior (the Favorable Affect Scale). Early psychometric properties are reported to be encouraging, and the potential moderating effects of the scale on relationships between leader behavior and various criteria will be tested in field settings.

Perception and Attribution

Some of the studies reported here deal solely with perceptions, some solely with attributions, and some with both. The 1979 epilog dealt with studies relating to power, influence, and attribution. We have broken away from that grouping, since very few of the current studies are directly related to power or influence. We will consider the studies dealing solely with perceptions first, and the attributional studies second.

Perception

The studies on perceptions—at various stages of development—focus on a number of concerns: 1) individual need states of subordinates and their perceptions of leader behavior, 2) perceptions of leadership climate, 3) effects of leader behavior on subordinate perceptions of job characteristics, 4) contrasts between superior and subordinate perceptions of leadership, 5) subordinate perceptions of the "transforming" leader, 6) the impact of organizational structure on perceptions of leader behavior, and 7) the effects of attributional factors on perceptions. Let's look at some details.

A hospital field study conducted by Niebuhr, Bedeian, and Armenakis (1980) found that subordinates' need states influenced their perceptions of leader behavior. Individuals with high needs of achievement, power, and independence perceived their leaders as less active, particularly with regard to instrumental supervisory behavior. Interpreting this and the other results from their study, the authors conclude that dyadic leader-follower relationships should be investigated and that pattern variables should also be taken into account. Striking a similar note, in a study of 46 naval health research center supervisors, Jones, Butler, and Dutton (1980) argue that perceptions of required activities are more strongly related to the need strength of the supervisors than to division goals, allocated authority, or work climate (which were also generally unrelated to self-described leadership patterns). Thus, a supervisor's choice of behavior toward subordinates may be tied more closely to the supervisor's needs and characteristics than the requirements of the job or task goals.

A series of U.S. Army studies investigated perceptions through leadership climate surveys administered to troops and leaders in a brigade twice, seven to eight months apart (Sterling, 1980; Sterling & Carnes, 1980a, 1980b). Key results focus on causal relations concerning leadership and the combination of current and later punishments and rewards. These results were interpreted by the researchers as indicating the importance of leaders' modeling effective versus ineffective behaviors for future leaders and the proper use of rewards and punishments for shaping future personnel readiness.

Jones and Butler (1980) postulated a model of superior-subordinate communication where communication initiated by the leader leads to increased structure and reduced ambiguity for subordinates, while communication initiated by subordinates is in response to role ambiguity. A path analysis of responses by 184 military and civilian employees of five outpatient health care facilities revealed that role ambiguity and subordinate-initialed communication were negatively related, and superior and subordinate-initiated communication were positively associated. Based on these results, it was suggested that subordinate-initiated communication might be considered as a response to communication demands perceived as imposed by the leader, group decision-making structure, and the subordinate's own propensities, rather than an attempt to obtain clarity.

A recent study (whose initial efforts were cited in the 1979 epilog) investigated the effects of leader behavior on subordinate perceptions of job characteristics (Griffin, 1980). The study involved first interviewing 29 supervisors in a large manufacturing plant (to determine their task-related supervisory behaviors), and then obtaining questionnaire responses from two subordinates (of each supervisor concerning the perception of task characteristics). The results supported the hypothesis that supervisory behavior which is intended to promote task variety, identity, autonomy, and feedback may be related to subordinate perceptions of the same attributes in their tasks. A large-scale field experiment is now in progress, where Griffin is testing and validating these pilot study findings.

A number of other studies are in progress in the field of perception. One such is by Alvares, Silverman and Dalessio (1980), on the degree of similarity between perceptions of ideal and actual leader, the leader's understanding of subordinates, and subordinate understanding of the leader as predictors of subordinate satisfaction and performance. The authors' investigation also shows that supervisors perceive their behavior as more multidimensional than do subordinates, and they are now trying to use Graen's (e.g., Graen & Cashman, 1975) vertical dyad linkage approach to investigate these issues further.

Bass's recent work on transformational leadership, reported as a part of chapter 9, is also perceptual in nature. Transformational leaders (who raise consciousness about higher considerations) elicit a number of positive perceptions from subordinates, as well as negative perceptions when they are unable to "deliver." This work, and part of Tosi's discussion in chapter 12, are related to House's (1977) recently developed charismatic theory of leadership.

In still another perceptual study, the relationship between organizational structure—defined as stable networks of interaction—and the formation of perceptions is explored by Feather (1980). Feather believes that the network concept of structure may offer a better link between the formation of perceptions and structure than other conceptions of structure. He proposes to show that subordinate perceptions of leader behavior vary systematically according to the subordinate's position of centrality in the network.

Attribution

Turning now to attribution, we focus on a study which looks at the effects of attributional factors on leadership perceptions. Phillips and Lord (1980a) manipulated leader salience and plausible explanations for group performance either to augment or discount attributions to leaders. Both factors affected leadership and LBDQ ratings, even though all subjects saw exactly the same leader behavior. The researchers highlight the importance of attributional and categorization processes in understanding leadership perceptions (and thus supplement their chapter in this volume).

In another stream of attributional studies, researchers at the University of Washington are continuing work reported in the 1979 epilog. Some of these studies concentrate on how attributions of good leadership are made and how superiors' attributions influence their responses to subordinates' performance. Mitchell and Wood (1980) showed in a study of nursing supervisors that a) information about consensus, consistency, and distinctiveness helped supervisors in making attributions, b) internal attributions led to punitive responses by supervisors, and c) supervisors used more internal attributions and punitive responses when performance consequences were serious as compared to not serious. A second study by Knowlton and Mitchell (1980) dealt with attributions made by supervisors concerning both good and poor performers. This study showed that a supervisor faced with a high performing subordinate will be more rewarding if the supervisor believes the performance is due to effort rather than ability. However, a poor performer was more likely to be severely punished for low effort than for low ability. A third study by Mitchell and Kalb (1980) dealt with the effects of outcome knowledge on attributions. The results showed that simple knowledge of outcomes (whether good or bad) lead to the supervisor's saying that poor performing subordinates should have known better, and therefore are more responsible and at fault. Lastly, a study by Ilgen, Mitchell, and Fredrickson (in press) manipulated the degree of supervisor dependence on poor performers. In the high interdependence condition, the supervisor was less blaming and punishing than in the low interdependence condition. A review of earlier work of these researchers will be forthcoming in volume 3 of the Staw and Cummings series on *Research in Organizational Behavior*.

A study of leadership attribution from administrative scenarios highlights our possible need to change societal stereotypes of leaders as consistent persons. Staw and Ross (1980) designed an experiment wherein 95 practicing managers, 48 undergraduate business students, and 79 undergraduates in a psychology course were asked to study one of eight descriptions of an administrator's behavior. By manipulating several factors, it was found that the administrator was highly rated when he followed a consistent course of action, allocated minimum resources, and was ultimately successful. The effect of consistency on ratings was strongest among practicing managers, and weakest among psychology students. This attribution of consistency for desirable leadership may be detrimental in a society that needs change and experimentation.

Finally, a 2×2 repeated measures experimental design is being used to assess the main and interaction effects of objective performance information and attributions about employee performance on leader verbal behavior. Data are now being gathered on this by Gioia and Sims (1980). The same researchers are also using a videotape of manager-subordinate interaction under three different behavior styles—positive, punitive, and goal setting—to determine how descriptions of observed leader behaviors are affected by attributions of observers' impressions of salient leader behavior. A somewhat similar design to test the effects of "modeling" on leadership training is also reported later in this epilog.

Implicit leadership theories. A special case of attribution has been said to be implicit in leadership theories (Hunt & Larson, 1979). In the 1979 epilog, the editors reviewed the work of Lord and his colleagues at the University of Akron. Their most recent work has focused on perceptual processes involved in leadership and links to social information processing and leadership measurement. A lab study of problem solving groups by Lord, Phillips, and Rush (1980) showed that rater characteristics were significantly related to leadership and social power ratings, and accounted for about a third of their variance. Phillips and Lord (1981) also show that people have trouble separating observed leadership behaviors from unseen behaviors, if the behaviors are highly related to leadership—i.e., if they are prototypical of either leaders or nonleaders. However, descriptive items unrelated to leadership were recalled with much more accuracy. This, according to the authors, suggests that subjects integrate information around a leadership construct, and once so integrated, they have difficulty recalling the original information. Exploring the effects of a temporal delay on LBDQ ratings of videotaped leaders, Rush, Phillips, and Lord (1980) found that a 48-hour delay did not reduce the effect of stimulus factors. However, all the variance associated with behavioral or performance information could be explained by a simple one-item rating of "leadership exhibited." The authors conclude that people heuristically reorganize information about leaders into simpler, more easily remembered forms. This is consistent with the cognitive economy principle presented in the Lord, Foti, and Phillips chapter.

In a laboratory study of 246 college juniors and seniors, Jermier (1980), investigated the importance of two aspects of implicit leadership theories—sexual and physical attractiveness. They were examined in the presence of information about general (organizational) and specific (recent leader-subordinate interactions) contexts. It was found that raters did not ignore descriptive information about the formal leader or the situation in favor of cultural stereotypes when making inferences about leadership. The implications of this study, while not challenging the existence of implicit leadership theories, raises some basic questions about the way raters use implicit theories.

Looking at the growing interest in the area of perception and attribution, we may expect these studies to multiply in the near future. Implicit theories of leadership and the controversy around them suggest that we need to explore social information processing as it relates to leadership processes.

Participation and Other Leader Behaviors

Both participation and other leader behaviors are treated here. Participation is more heavily emphasized in the first four studies and other leader behaviors are concentrated on in the final study. The differing treatments of participation are interesting to compare with the way it is treated in the European research discussed in the next chapter.

Halal and Brown (1980) were interested in practices and attitudes concerning different types of participation (e.g., in communication and consultation, compensation and personnel actions, work processes and the job) in U.S. firms. The authors found a large gap between interest in participation and actual practice as reported by respondents, and concluded that considerable potential exists for improving performance and satisfaction by developing selected aspects of participation. Kay (1980) looks at participation within the context of McGregor's theory X and theory Y in a sample of business, government, and educational organizations. The author argues that McGregor's original description of theory Y has become exemplified by the wishful notion that people, if treated responsibly, will develop altruistic drives to help the employer rather than the view that individuals have intensive selfish drives for esteem and fulfillment. Kay's research, which looks at variations of participation and task characteristics, is designed to investigate the argument that if these latter drives can be properly channeled, they can be productive.

Klauss and Bass (1980) consider participation and other leader behaviors within the context of communication styles. In a sample of 71 subordinates describing 28 "focal" superiors, the researchers found that satisfactory communication behavior was strongly related to participative, consultative, and delegative types of behavior, and less strongly related to directive or negotiative behaviors. The focal superiors, on the other hand, saw much less linkage between leadership and communication behavior. They did report, however, that if they were negotiative they were much less likely to communicate with attention, care, and trustworthiness.

Derakhshan (1980) looks at the relationship between span of supervision and the extent to which participative-directive leadership is used in a sample of fast-food outlets. The author reports preliminary results indicating significant associations between span of supervision and various aspects of participative-directive leader behaviors, and concludes that a benevolent autocracy might be the most appropriate overall style of behavior. He also shows no significant relationship between the supervisor's concept of ideal leader behavior and his/her behavior as perceived by subordinates. In this, his results are not dissimiliar to those of Klaus and Bass and are in line with previous findings (e.g., Hunt, Osborn, & Larson, 1973).

Shifting from participation to the familiar consideration and initiating structure, Korabik (1980) examined the relation of these behaviors to sex role-orientation. The author found sex role orientation to be a better predictor of these behaviors than sex per se. As predicted, those with strong male sex role orientations emphasized more initiating structure and those with female orientations were higher on consideration.

Leadership Within a Broader Setting

Turning now to a broader context, an issue which seems likely to gather momentum as a topic of research interest in leadership concerns substitutes for leadership. While the leader is considered a significant component of the stimulus world for subordinates, Naylor, Pritchard, and Ilgen (1980) make the point that leader behavior must be understood from this frame of reference.

Exploring the issue of whether leaders are needed for organizational outcomes, Howell and Dorfman (1980b) found in a study of 220 hospital workers that organizational formalization emerged as a strong substitute in the instrumental leader behavior-organizational commitment relationship. With a different sample of hospital managers and engineers, the same results emerged. Similarly, Hunger and Akin (1980), in their exploratory study of student project groups, found that neither a designated nor an emergent leader was necessary for group performance.

In a broader but related perspective, Sheridan, Vredenburgh, and Abelson (1980) argue for a research model which would include a comprehensive set of micro and macro variables in leadership research. By doing so, the authors believe that it may be possible to develop a taxonomy of contextual factors describing sociotechnical variables that can either substitute for, or neutralize, the leader's influence in any given work situation.

In still another context, that of dangerous and extremely dangerous environments, Jermier (1980) identified space-time concepts in the study of interpersonal influence styles. Using data on urban police officers, Jermier contends that contingency theories of organization may be strengthened by explicitly recognizing space-time concepts.

Studying leadership in voluntary organizations and the controversy over social action in Protestant Churches, Wood (1981) contends that voluntary organizations do not necessarily lead to oligarchies, and that, as a corollary, leaders cannot legitimately act counter to the majority will. Two interesting questions raised by Wood are: why do members oppose policies that derive from the core values of the organization, and what is the role of legitimacy in inducing members to support unpopular policies?

Finally, in what may be the most comprehensive model of all, Bryson (1980) is in the process of developing a model of leadership emergence, stabilization, and change in organizational and interorganizational networks. The study focuses on the political economy of leadership. In the context of organizations being viewed as bargaining and influence systems, leadership is conceptualized as "produced" and "consumed" and is seen as crucial to the structuring and maintenance of political "markets."

All of these models are consistent with the macro-oriented spirit reflected in the Hunt and Osborn chapter in this volume.

Process Studies

Here we take a broad perspective and consider work on leadership succession, in addition to studies of leadership as an ongoing dynamic process. Zahn and Wolf (in press) define the leadership process as behaviors and messages exchanged by supervisors and subordinates in task and relationship domains. These behaviors are arranged in a cycle of recurring patterns of transactions. A Markov model is used to simulate behavior of different superior-subordinate relationships, illustrating such effects as risk-taking defensiveness, and the impact of close supervision. Implications of the model and applications to selection and training are discussed.

Zierden (1980) discusses an interesting process model oriented toward practitioners. This model concentrates on leadership requirements in terms of addressing a set of questions in the minds of followers. These are: Where am I going? How can I get there? Who will I be when I arrive there? Can I feel good about myself in the process? The author discusses the implications of these questions in terms of successful ongoing leadership.

A quite different approach is discussed by Bello and Mackenzie (1979). That approach explains how leaders identify, reduce, and prevent task process uncertainty in *ad hoc* emergent groups. Four major processes are involved: 1) selecting structures, 2) implementing structures, 3) correcting errors, and 4) revising structures. Experimental tests with five-person laboratory groups were conducted, and the researchers conclude that the approach has considerable support.

Still another process approach to leadership called the "Response to Power Model" (RPM) is described in a progress report by Sweney (1979). The report summarizes results of a long-term programmatic research effort. The RPM is an interactional one which predicts actions and reactions of superiors and subordinates in their differing organizational roles. It makes no assumptions of permanent styles but instead argues that the roles may be altered to fit the circumstances of the interactions so that changes in counterparts or situations will militate changes in roles. Transactions of power and obligation define the role interactions most likely to occur. These differ in terms of authoritarian, equalitarian, and permissive role preferences on the part of supervisors and rebel, critic, and ingratiator role preferences on the part of subordinates. Relevant instrument development work is discussed as well as evidence concerning the model itself.

Turning now to succession, we focus on a series of four studies by Taylor. The first of these has been prepared in manuscript form (Taylor, 1980), while others are in preparation. In these, Taylor is concerned with acceptance of a new first-level supervisor as a function of different variables, including: subordinate liking and frustration with the predecessor and the successor, congruence of behavior between predecessor and successor, and fate of the predecessor and successor origin. These studies are consistent with work such as that of Rosen (1970) and Gordon and Rosen (1979), which work argues that consideration of newly placed supervisors adds a vitally needed dimension to leadership research.

Extensions to Currently Emphasized Approaches

Here, as in the 1979 epilog, we briefly examine updates and extensions of well-known leadership models. We cover the models of Vroom and Yetton (1973), Fiedler (Fiedler & Chemers, 1974), and Graen (Graen & Cashman, 1975).

Vroom and Yetton

The 1979 epilog detailed three studies refining problem sets for measuring differences in leadership style in the Vroom-Yetton (1973) model. Two studies by Jago and Vroom (1980) add to this by dealing with sex differences in leadership styles. The researchers used a multifactorial experiment, with various groups of male and female managers and students. They conclude that females tend to be significantly more participative in their leadership style than males. The authors feel that these differences are a function of widely shared role expectations, as supported by the fact that females who were perceived to have an autocratic style were judged more negatively on both males and females than were males who were perceived to be autocratic.

Fiedler

Strube and Garcia (1980) examined the validity of Fiedler's contingency model, using data from 127 validity tests of the model and from the 33 studies used in its original development. Employing a meta-analytic technique (e.g., Rosenthal, 1978, 1979) to test significance in combined samples, they concluded that the model was extremely robust in predicting group performance.

Also, a study testing Fiedler's model with male and female leaders at the U.S. Military Academy was conducted by Rice, Bender, and Vitters

(1980). In a laboratory investigation of 72 four-person *ad hoc* groups, the researchers found significant relationships between LPC scores and objective measures of task performance. The researchers conclude that difficulty in interpreting whether their results support the model indicates a need to develop direct measures of situational factors. They also conclude that the LPC scale is an important measure of leadership for both males and females, and that criticisms calling for a halt to LPC research are not valid (their plea is not to throw the baby out with the bath water).

Graen

The studies reported here are not investigations per se of Graen's vertical dyad linkage (VDL) model. Rather, they owe their origin to the dyadic versus group notion embodied in the model (complementing the Dansereau, Alluto, Markham, and Dumas work in chapter 6). Consistent with chapter 6, Bruning and Skaret (1980) compared dyadic leader behavior differentiated for each group member with average behavior directed at the group. Both methods of leadership made unique contributions to variance in attitudes about the leader. Again, as in chapter 6, these authors argued for theoretical integration of group and individual analyses. Nachman, Dansereau, and Naughton (1980) have applied the within and between analysis approach of chapter 6 to an examination of the negotiating latitude scale, a key indicator in VDL-oriented research (see Graen & Cashman, 1975). The authors suggested that other measures may be examined using within and between analysis, to infer whether they reflect group or dyadic phenomena.

Training and Development

A special feature of the current epilog is the inclusion of current ideas and experiences in training and developing leaders, managers, and professionals. The techniques range from daily developmental processes to field research with U.S. Air Force systems using nominal group techniques and O.D. efforts.

Cohen and Bradford (1980) propose that excellence is achieved through the creation of superordinate goals and a constant developmental emphasis with individuals and groups. According to them, few managers understand the interpersonal dimensions of developmental efforts, or approaches to implementation on a daily basis. Their book in progress, entitled *Managing for Excellence*, is oriented toward managers interested in outstanding rather than good performance.

From a different perspective, Goodman (1981) argues that anecdotal evidence in his research points very strongly to the role of managers in influencing the professional growth of subordinates. The relationship seems to be stronger in less developed organizations (such as theaters) than in more developed organizations (such as research and development). The nature of professional development in systems such as theaters where the supervisor can perform all subordinate tasks is one of building technical skills. In systems such as R & D units, where the supervisor can only provide general direction, learning is more managerial in nature.

In-basket exercises and simulations have been developed by Gill (1979), to assess management potential and to train managers. These simulations and exercises have been found by Gill to be a better way of assessing and developing than traditional psychometric tests. Normative data are being currently gathered, and an in-basket exercise for a simulated small business enterprise is also being pilot tested (Gill, 1980).

Manz and Sims (1980) propose leadership training with behavioral models for leader behavioral change and subordinate satisfaction. The authors used three interventions to reveal positive reward behavior, punitive behavior, and goal setting behavior. They conclude that modeling interventions led to changes in leader behavior and subsequently to subordinate satisfaction. They advocate, in agreement with Latham and Saari (1979), an overall program of modeling training.

Tolle (1980) has developed a nondeterministic approach to executive-level development. Integrating the models of Chris Argyris and Carl Rogers, the author has developed a client-centered maangement development program. Basically, it is an organizational effectiveness workshop which has six phases: 1) intrapersonal knowledge building and interpersonal experiential use of this knowledge, 2) working in autonomous learning groups, 3) team building, 4) working on pre-workshop questionnaire feedback data, 5) designing follow-up programs, and 6) reviewing the effects of the workshop. This intensive, introspective learning is expected to enhance ability to experience organizational life as an ongoing learning and growing process.

As a consultant to U.S. Air Force acquisition units, Fox (1980) is involved in three areas of training field research. They involve 1) use of Nominal Group Technique with various problem-solving groups, 2) O.D. efforts involving role-playing, modeling, and feedback, and 3) planning and implementing a survey feedback intervention program.

In a U.S. Army battalion setting, R. L. Miller (1980) examined the effectiveness of a program of structured interviews (COMTRAIN) in facilitation command transition at the company level. Comparisons between 45 experimental and control commanders showed the utility of the COM-

TRAIN. There was no overall increase in performance, but, for external locus of control commanders without experience, improvement occurred in performance ratings. Evaluations by COMTRAIN users were also positive as to its benefit.

Finally, an ongoing training program to upgrade the leadership and managerial competencies of naval officers and enlisted personnel has been developed by McBer and Company (e.g., Winter, 1979). The program is labeled Leadership and Management Education and Training (LMET). Its cornerstone is 16 competencies grouped into five clusters for training purposes. These competencies are broad skills or personal qualities which have demonstrated a relationship to superior leadership performance, and which can be increased through educational and training procedures.

These programs illustrate the range of training and development activities currently in use in the armed forces, private, and public sectors.

Conclusions

Two trends apparent in the 1979 epilog were the emphasis on measuring what leaders do and attribution and perception. These trends are even more noticeable in this epilog, as exemplified in the first three sections. There is also an emphasis on process studies, and extensions to currently emphasized approaches—both areas which received attention in the 1979 epilog.

A key difference between the two epilogs, however, is in the more recent emphasis upon the wider settings. We are encouraged by this emphasis, which was largely absent in the 1979 epilog, as well as from earlier symposia volumes. We are hopeful that the work cited in this epilog, along with that earlier in the volume (e.g., Lombardo & McCall; Hunt & Osborn), is indicative of a trend that will receive more emphasis in the future.

While there is a heavier emphasis on the wider setting in this epilog, there is also less emphasis on some topics which previously received considerable treatment—operant or reinforcement approaches, emergent leadership, and consideration of behavioral criterion variables. Whether this relative lack of emphasis is real or apparent cannot be said with certainty, since our sampling is imprecise, a reflection of materials gathered by imperfect means. Given the way the field in general seems to be moving, however, we feel that operant and behavioral work is likely to again be emphasized in epilogs which follow this one. That is an empirical prediction, however, and only two years from now shall we know if its accuracy.

15

Leadership Research and the European Connection: An Epilog

DIAN-MARIE HOSKING and JAMES G. HUNT

What if we held a leadership research conference and nobody came? This was a key concern of ours based on the arguments of some that European scholars are not interested enough in leadership as a research area to participate in a conference. We need not have worried. More than 30 participants from England and continental Europe responded to an announcement, distributed in early 1980, for an informal, scholarly "Workshop in Leadership and Managerial Behavior." The conference was held at the University of Aston Management Centre while Hunt was spending a semester on sabbatical leave there. This chapter is designed to capture the flavor of the conference and to compare and contrast that flavor with leadership research (establishment and otherwise) in the United States.[1]

The conference was designed to be extremely informal, so as to help promote a discussion forum for those interested in the scholarly study of leadership and managerial behavior. Hence, the emphasis on "workshop" in the title. Like the contents of this book it was also intended to cast a

The partial conference support of the United States Office of Naval Research, London Branch, and the British Social Science Research Council is gratefully acknowledged. We also wish to acknowledge the support of the University of Aston Management Centre and particularly the help of Ronald Amey, Katherine Carmody, Peter Clark, Peta Small, and Barbara Richards.

1. A more detailed summary of the individual contributions is included in reports by Hunt and Hosking (1981), Hosking, Hunt, and Child (1980) or may be obtained from the individual contributors referenced as appropriate. In addition to these referenced contributors we also wish to acknowledge the assistance of the following individuals who served as discussion leaders and summarizers: David Butcher, John Chapman, Peter Clark, Charles Cox, Ray Loveridge, John McWilliams, and Diana Pheysey.

broad net. Hence the emphasis on *both* leadership and managerial behavior. The conference lasted two and one-half days and had 22 contributions spread across eight topic areas together with four integration-discussion sessions and a concluding overview-discussion session. The presentations varied from formal papers to extended outlines of ongoing or proposed research. Most of the contributors came from England but also present were those from Holland, Poland, and Sweden as well as two representatives from the United States. In addition, work being done in other countries such as West Germany, Yugoslavia, and Switzerland was covered as a part of the presentations.

Given the informal, workshop nature of the conference, much of its flavor came from the extensive interactions which took place in the discussion periods. We have written the chapter with that in mind. Thus, we concentrate on the broad concerns emanating from these integrative discussions rather than on detailed summaries of the presentations. Ideas coming from the presentations are interspersed as an integral part of these integrative discussions. With this as a background let's look at the content by starting with our overall impressions. We then turn to a more detailed picture.

Some Overall Impressions

We were struck by the very diverse approaches to the study of leadership adopted by European leadership scholars. Perhaps this is a major reason why there is no clearly defined and obvious caucus of persons who recogize themselves as leadership researchers, as in the United States. Instead we find sociologists, psychologists, management theorists, and practitioners engaged in both "pure" and "action" research in many relatively autonomous but overlapping areas of interest. For example, there are those who pursue the study of small groups and the cognitive processes assumed to underlie social interactions; at the same time others are studying the distribution of control in organizations, degree of member participation in decision-making, and the effects of new forms of work organization and organization design. Yet another set of interests focuses on what appointed officials do, who they interact with, how they spend their time, how they maintain the flow of production, and how they build and shape organizations. This contrasts with much more specific analyses and training to develop the basic skills believed to underlie interactions which may be described as involving "leadership."

Issues, Aims, and Interests

Views on Leaders and Leadership

A pervasive but usually implicit theme concerned the meaning of the terms "leaders" and "leadership." It was very apparent that people used them to mean totally different things but on the whole—or so it seemed to us—did not see this as a problem. Indeed we saw little evidence of any desire to develop a common language. Perhaps the general view could be more positively described: moves towards agreed and collective definitions and perspectives seemed to be restricted as inappropriate and unconstructive. This position clearly contrasts with the views of at least some U.S. critics who claim that leadership research should have a "unified and generally accepted paradigm" (McCall, 1977, p. 376).

Approaches favored by a number of European scholars included treatment of leadership activities as a subset of managerial tasks, or use of the terms leadership and management interchangeably. The presentations of Stewart (1980), Rubenowitz (1980), and Wlodarczyk (1980) are representative of this. Such viewpoints do not necessarily preclude the possibility that leadership may be exercised by persons other than those formally appointed to managerial positions. Such possibilities were typically left unconsidered, however. The relative lack of interest in informal leaders (i.e., those not sanctioned by the organization) and the possible leadership roles of those such as trade union officials mirrors the situation in the United States. It seems particularly surprising that such possibilities are largely ignored by those who conduct their studies in countries where management authority is probably more problematic than in the United States. This appears particularly true of Britain.

The size and vagueness of the vocabulary of leadership led some to view it as a "ragbag" in need of conceptual clarification. In this sense some saw the diversity of approaches to leadership as having dysfunctional consequences causing major obstructions to future developments in understanding. Such persons felt it was essential to distinguish clearly different aspects of leadership and between such related terms as leadership and management.

Among those most strongly supporting this view were Hosking (1980), Heller (1980), and Dachler (1980). Others were of the opinion that the term "leader" should be dispensed with altogether—a proposal powerfully argued by Miner (1975) in an earlier symposium volume. Various partial substitutes were offered, many of which focused on particular tasks or functions to be performed. These included generating commitment and creating energy and purpose (Pettigrew, 1980), handling disturbances and "steering" performance (Thurley & Wirdenius, 1980), and problem owner-ship roles having the basic objective of achieving a "fit" between the prefer-ences of different interest groups (Madron, 1980).

Those such as Margerison (1980) placed the question of definitions firmly in the context of objectives; depending on the purpose of one's re-search, certain definitions were felt to be more appropriate and others less so. We felt that this was an attitude which many shared but which few made explicit. It became particularly apparent in discussions of an expressed desire for research to become more client-oriented and more problem-oriented (e.g., Heller, 1980; Kakabadse, 1980; Margerison, 1980). For ex-ample, in discussing new forms of work organization, questions were raised regarding the implications of these changes for the meaning of terms such as "leader," "leadership," and "participation." In many respects the flavor here was not unlike that conveyed in Mintzberg's overview chapter.

Perhaps it is not surprising that discussions of this sort led to consid-eration of leadership as a political process. A number of participants felt that this aspect of leadership has been relatively neglected, particularly by those who seek conceptual and methodological rigor. We may note that while valuable analyses have been made of both political leadership (e.g., Neustadt, 1960) and the political aspects of leadership in social, commer-cial, and industrial organizations (e.g., Sayles, 1964), such approaches are relatively rare. Furthermore, at least where establishment U.S. leadership research is concerned, there seems to be little evidence of much interest in these perspectives.

To summarize, European scholars evidence little agreement in their treatment of an area which may be broadly represented as dealing with leadership. If we try to use such terms as "second degree constructs" (Cal-der, 1977, p. 181), they are certainly found wanting. We can only agree with Katz and Kahn that "the concept of leadership has an ambiguous status" (Katz & Kahn, 1978, p. 526). However, in contrast to the United States, there seems little evidence of much effort toward convergence.

Managerial and Leader Behaviors

There was a strong move toward increasing the range of behaviors typically considered as being performed by managers and leaders. How-ever, underlying this high degree of consensus was considerable disagree-ment about why and how this should be achieved. For example, Stewart (1980) argued that attempts to break out from the traditional emphasis on task and socio-emotional dimensions are to be applauded. At the same time, as in her present chapter, she indicated that many such efforts tend to reflect on overly structured "classical management" view of relevant behaviors. As she noted, research on what managers do has seriously questioned the validity of such a perspective. Thus it was argued that future attempts to measure leader and managerial behaviors should include items indicated by this broader body of data (see, e.g., Mintzberg, 1973; Stewart, 1976).

A number of those whose fundamental interests are in leadership effectiveness and training felt that progress would be facilitated by greater attention to underlying specific behavioral processes (Alban-Metcalfe, 1980; Randell, 1980; Wright & Taylor, 1980). They take a "skills approach." Thus they argue that while we need to go beyond traditional task and socio-emotional categories of behavior, this should be in the direction of identifying the basic building blocks of interactions. These include analysis of words, gestures, and tones of voice used to gather information, influence behavior, and handle emotion. One of the distinctive features of this approach is a call for increased precision in the definition and measurement of leader behaviors. While those U.S. scholars such as Argyris (1979) have recently become concerned about this, Randell and his colleagues have been involved with ongoing research in the area for some time (see, e.g., Randell, in press).

Given the diversity of people's approaches and interests in leadership, we were not surprised that many felt the need to research new factors and dimensions of behavior to supplement the conventional and well-known ones. Political and ideological categories seemed in demand and were emphasized by those such as Hosking (1980), Morley (1980), and Pettigrew (1980). Our problem was to determine when people were talking about leaders' *tasks*, for example, managing political processes, legitimizing and justifying actions, as treated by Pettigrew, and when they were referring to *behaviors*. This problem largely stems from the conventional lack of precision of behavioral descriptions mentioned earlier.

Concern was also expressed over the criteria employed for selecting certain behavioral items and rejecting others. For example, T. Watson (1980) showed that use of conventional criteria can result in a researcher's discarding items that respondents say are most important. In his view, traditional item-analysis criteria should be supplemented with others to pick up concerns like importance. This argument also has some conceptual implications. For example, it may be that we should devote more attention to measuring not just the "content" of a leader's or manager's behavior, but also its importance as perceived by the "receiver." This may lie in its distinctiveness (i.e., the behavior is seldom employed), its criticalness (it is often employed but seen as essential), or its timing. The relative neglect of timing and "phase changes" in behavior were seen to be major deficiencies in the literature. The thrust of the Sheridan et al. contribution in this volume is certainly consistent with this general argument.

Questions were also raised regarding the degree to which leaders' and managers' behavioral repertoires are constrained. This issue was developed by Wlodarczyk (1980), who asked a radical and fundamental question: to what extent are leaders'/managers' behaviors specific to particular settings? While contingency theorists have argued for many years that different behaviors will be employed in different situations (see, e.g., Fiedler & Chemers, 1974), they have typically assumed that a given set of behavioral dimensions will be generally appropriate. In other words they have assumed that the variation will be of the *level*—more or less of the same—rather than something completely different as Wlodarczyk argues.

To summarize, many felt that existing attempts to measure managerial and leader behaviors are inadequate. Less consensus was revealed in ideas of how to improve matters. Some called for the measurement of precisely defined specific behavior processes; some felt the need to consider a wider range of behaviors than has typically been studied; others felt the need to examine additional features of behavior other than the *frequency* with which particular acts are performed. The view that different behavioral universes might be applicable in different situations was also expressed. Clearly, many of these views are compatible.

The Characteristics of Leaders' and Managers' Domains

We were impressed with the wide variety of organizational settings dealt with in the studies reported. These included hospitals, schools, banks, public theatres, social services, insurance, printing and publishing, manufacturing, and the construction industry. Within such settings, analysis was usually focused at the level of the leader-subordinate dyad (e.g., Alban-Metcalfe, 1980; Randell, 1980; Wright & Taylor, 1980), or relations between the leader (or manager) and their work unit: a department, a plant, or a project (e.g., Hunt & Osborn, 1980c; Kakabadse, 1980; Quince & Lansley, 1980). These practices are very similar to those reported in the U.S. literature in that "psychological groups" (as distinct from "aggregates" and "classes," see Gibb, 1969) were relatively ignored as entities for which leaders and managers are responsible. Hosking (1980) and Morley (1980) focused on this concern.

It was argued that there is a strong managerial bias in much U.S. leadership research and that a similar bias seems to pervade European studies. A number of participants commented on this bias and argued that it was obstructive. For example, it tends to lead to biased views about goals, leadership tasks, and interactions. This was not seen as a problem for those primarily interested in *managerial* effectiveness. It is interesting to contrast this view with that expressed in Mintzberg's overview where researchers are taken to task for a lack of management relevance.

Much less similarity is evidenced between European and U.S. treatments of the wider context within which leaders and managers operate. In the U.S. literature, critics have often bemoaned the "failure to extend situational factors beyond the immediate work group" (McCall, 1977, p. 378). And of course, Hunt and Larson in previous symposia volumes (1975, 1977, 1979) have lamented this lack so often as to sound like a broken record. If the research reported at the workshop provides a representative picture of the scope of variables typically considered by Europeans, the above-mentioned criticism does not apply. For example, there are those who examine setting (e.g., environmental, cultural, technological, structural) characteristics as they affect opportunities to display leadership (Quince & Lansley, 1980) and the behaviors employed (Terry, 1980; Wlodarczyk, 1980).

Others study their influence on supervisory functions with particular emphasis on participation (e.g., Forsblad, 1980; Heller, 1980; Rubenowitz, 1980; Thurley & Wirdenius, 1980) and on the consequences of leaders' behaviors (e.g., Geersing, 1980; Heller, 1980; Rubenowitz, 1980). Of especial interest is the cross-national flavor of some of the European research where managerial samples across a number of differing countries and cultures are utilized. The workshop presentations of Heller (1980) and Rubenowitz (1980) are representative of this as is the cross-cultural work of Hofstede (1980, in press) not directly represented at the workshop.

While varying roles of setting factors are examined they have usually been treated as independent variables. Two researchers, Mangham (1980) and Pettigrew (1980), have cast them in a dependent role by viewing leaders as creators of organizations and manipulators of culture. This contrasts, for example, with recent U.S. work on "constraints"—setting actors which limit discretion and leader activity (e.g., Salancik, Calder, Rowland, Leblebici, & Conway, 1975). We found this work very interesting and expect to see greater concern with the ways in which leaders and managers manipulate their setting. We hope interested parties will then tackle questions, such as those raised by Hunt and Osborn (1980c and the chapter in this volume) at the workshop and an earlier chapter, of the relative *degree* to which leaders act on, and are acted upon by their environment.

Perspectives and Methodologies

As we have already seen, considerable diversity was apparent in the ways in which contributors conceptualized their area of concern. That diversity was sufficiently great as to render it likely that people would have very different ideas about appropriate and useful methodologies. This was indeed the case. Both laboratory and field studies were reported (the latter forming the majority). Simulations and field experiments seemed to find little favor, as in the United States. The "law of the instrument," discussed by Heller (1980), whereby available methods determine lines of research, seemed much less dominant than in the United States. Indeed, a significant proportion of the research reported did not use standardized instruments. Furthermore, many researchers made use of a *variety* of investigative techniques rather than, for example, just questionnaires or rating scales. Some of the work of Heller and his colleagues summarized at the workshop (Heller, 1980) and reported in more detail elsewhere (Drenth, Koopman, Rus, Odar, Heller, & Brown, 1979; Heller, Drenth, Koopman, & Rus, 1977) is particularly interesting in this regard.

Even so, there were clear and strongly held preferences for so-called psychometric or impressionistic approaches. Only a few appeared to see strengths and weaknesses in each and consequently be prepared to cross what seemed to be firmly drawn "battle lines." Indeed, these battle lines were not unlike the researcher-practitioner split emphasized so strongly in Mintzberg's chapter.

The methods employed by particular researchers obviously reflected the preferences mentioned above. They also seem to be related to the chosen conceptual orientation or perspective. For example, both Mangham (1980) and Pettigrew (1980) were interested in changes, in the evolution of organizations, and leaders' roles in managing transitions. Clearly some form of processual analysis is best suited to this perspective and this is what the researchers chose. Interestingly, their particular solution differed from the method with which we are familiar in U.S. studies. Instead of relying on standardized questionnaires and collecting "waves" of comparable data at different points in time, they relied on records, interviews, and informal observations which they analyzed in terms of "social dramas" (Turner, 1969). Dramaturgical analysis does not figure in U.S. studies of leadership, and as we know, longitudinal studies seem rare in both continents.

In the opinion of Osborn (1980), who overviewed the workshop, the considerable range of perspectives and methodologies probably reflects the involvement of very diverse groups all having different interests in leadership. As Osborn noted, governments, unions, and managements all have a very real interest in leadership and participation in organizations. Owners, shareholders, executives, and the like have an interest in the consequences of leadership. Furthermore, some of these groups may bias research activity in the direction of their own partisan interests with little regard for its possible theoretical contribution. That is, the study of leadership may become "politicized," in Osborn's terms. Osborn felt that these interest groups appeared to be much more influential in directing the course of research than is true in the United States—where academics seem to exercise more exclusive "rights of ownership." Perhaps it is for these reasons that "leadership" does not constitute a distinct or discipline-based area of study in the European literature. According to Osborn, it is seen as a construct in Europe but as a distinct area of study, albeit a too narrow, psychologically dominated one in the United States.

As we noted earlier, many appeared to find this European diversity both necessary and fruitful. The main argument against it seems to be that it makes it very difficult to communicate ideas and understandings when there is little in the way of a common language. Contributors spoke of "disturbance handling," "steering functions," "problem owners" (appointed officials), "leaders," "heads," "managers," "supervisors," participation and "power distance." Perspectives included use of role theory, leadership as a decision-making activity, discussions of leadership tasks, social skills, functions, and objectives. A small minority felt that multidisciplinary research had considerable potential but in the absence of a shared language and philosophy of science, little synergy was likely to result. Osborn proffered an alternative to the present situation where leadership is treated as a politicized catch-all term as in Europe and as a too-narrow psychologically oriented discipline as in the United States. This was to root the subject within the discipline of organizational analysis and to develop a perspective whereby any act which is strategic, which is part of a patterning or sequencing of activities, would be defined as leadership.

This patterning might be achieved through developing and focusing attention on particular goals and paths to those goals and by reinforcing behaviors which contribute to their achievement. Such a perspective assumes that leadership does not constitute a set of distinct actions separable from other, different activities (e.g., managerial behavior). A specific action derives its status as an act of leadership by virtue of its being part of this pattern which cuts across areas of activity.

From this perspective Osborn argued that those who are unwilling to pattern activities, focus attention, and reinforce selectively would not be seen as practicing leadership. Given this, it would be possible to arrive at some global estimate of an individual's leadership by assessing how much patterning is in existence over and above some "typical" level. Such analysis could be done at individual subsystems, organization, and/or institutional levels of analysis.

Osborn suggested that such a perspective, while admittedly imprecise, might help those active in the area to communicate more effectively. He suggested that this approach might bring us closer to that found in economics—one which cuts across interest groups and units of analysis and which might more readily encourage leadership researchers to build upon each others' work.

The Consequences of Leadership and Leadership Training

Of the many issues and interests discussed at the workshop we single out one more for attention. This was a general concern for leadership research to have some practical pay-off. There were some (e.g., Margerison, 1980) who argued this perhaps as strongly as Mintzberg's earlier chapter. And of course it comes as no surprise that participants differed in their views on how this might best be achieved or even its desirability. Some concentrated on the possible benefits that training of individual managers might provide. For example, those mentioned earlier who adopted a skills approach argued that trainees must receive instruction in the basic components of behavior. They questioned the value of training which deals with fairly abstract and poorly defined behavioral categories such as "supportive"—trying to change the degree to which an individual displays these behaviors. If it is accepted that it requires a great deal of skill to enact appropriately particular behaviors—even when they are clearly defined and their purpose is understood—it is clear that such an approach is extremely deficient. Such a view obviously challenges most traditional approaches to leadership training (e.g., Blake & Mouton, 1964; Fiedler, Chemers, & Mahar, 1976).

The value of individual training received a more fundamental challenge from Terry (1980) whose research led him to conclude that much of managerial behavior is powerfully influenced by the culture within which it is located. Cultural factors were also seen to influence organizational outcomes. Thus he argued that organizational dysfunctions will probably require interventions at that level, rather than individual training and development.

Organizational characteristics have long been known to affect the likely long-term consequences of training (e.g., Fleishman, 1953). They have also been seen as open to manipulation such that, for example, organizational performance might be improved by redesigning rules and procedures centralizing decision-making, and so on. Leadership researchers interested primarily in performance outcomes have recognized this as an alternative to individual training but, in the United States, at least, have tended to deal with relatively micro, situational characteristics such as the nature of the work group and its principal task. Some participants argued for increased attention to this approach and extending it to include more macro-organizational dimensions.

As was noted by Pfeffer (1978) those who seek to train leaders or modify their situations so as to improve their effectiveness assume (often implicitly) that leadership has a significant effect on performance. As pointed out earlier in this book, a number of American researchers have recently been questioning the validity of this assumption (see, e.g., Pfeffer and Salancik, 1978; Vaill, 1978). This issue was addressed during the workshop in the context of changing forms of work organization. Forsblad (1980), Heller (1980), and Rubenowitz (1980) were among those scholars who considered the possibility that leadership roles might have diminished significance in more participative, "vertically loaded" production systems. Interestingly, there was little evidence that this was the case.

To conclude, we felt there was a widespread concern for research to have some "practical pay-off" for organizations. This was reflected in attempts to improve the training and development of individuals, and to understand the roles of organizational characteristics.

Conclusion

Not long ago Fiedler and Chemers remarked that the "overwhelming part of leadership research has been conducted in the United States" (Fiedler & Chemers, 1974, p. 2). The output of the United States is certainly considerable. However, if the evidence of the European workshop is anything to go by, significant contributions are certainly being made elsewhere. It is just that they are more difficult to recognize because the terms "leader" or "leadership" are seldom used.

We were struck by a number of substantial differences between European and U.S. approaches. First, in the former there seems very little interest in developing models or theories of leadership: studies tend to be more "broad brush" and descriptive or action-oriented. Second, when theoretical propositions are tested, they are typically concerned with the distribution of control and decision-making authority within organizations, little or no reference being made to "leadership." Third, perhaps for the reasons already given, there is relatively little concern with getting down to definitional problems: by not studying leaders and leadership it is possible to focus on members of organizations (usually appointed officials). Fourth, little effort was expended in testing or refining the models of leadership so well known in the U.S. literature (Fiedler, 1967; House, 1971; and the like). Fifth, and again presumably as a function of the reasons already mentioned, little attention seemed to be devoted to detailed issues which rear their heads in the developmental evolution of models. For example, models may focus on leader-group interactions or leader-individual interactions; the validity of these various approaches has received much debate in recent years (see, e.g., Hosking & Schriesheim, 1980). European researchers seem relatively untroubled by such problems.

Other differences between the approaches of European and U.S. scholars include: emphasis on the development and use of standardized instruments (greater in the United States), consideration of a wider scope of variables (especially organizational characteristics) by Europeans, little European interest in developing an integrated approach.

While similarities were also evident, they are fewer in number. First, researchers in both continents seem relatively uninterested in leadership in group settings (defined in terms of shared norms and goals, perceptions of "we" versus "they," and the like. It is probably for this reason that characteristics of groups (status congruence, homogeneity, etc.), emergent leadership, group development, and other such variables receive relatively little interest in the leadership literature. Second, certain methodologies are still employed relatively infrequently, for example, longitudinal and processual analysis, experimental field studies, and simulation. Third, research has usually been focused at the level of behavior rather than going to underlying cognitive processes.

As was noted by Evans (1979), North American journals and texts have increasingly protested about the narrowness of much research on leadership in organizations. This is certainly not a problem with European research in the area. However, as we have seen, diversity has drawbacks as well as advantages. In particular, it renders progress on a "united front" most unlikely. But this is only a problem for those who seek a corporate philosophy rather than a loose federation.

16

Conclusion: The Leadership-Management Controversy Revisited

CHESTER A. SCHRIESHEIM, JAMES G. HUNT, and UMA SEKARAN

In assembling the contents of this volume, through both invited and competitively selected chapters, we have tried to illustrate and highlight some of the conflicting points of view and approaches available to persons interested in studying leadership phenomena. In large part, the diverse background and approaches of this volume's contributors account for some of the unevenness and lack of integration in the individual contributions and the book as a whole. We have chosen to edit minimally the chapters of our contributors (and, undoubtedly, to allow ourselves to be taken to task by one or more book reviewers for this), rather than ruin their individual qualities by homogenizing them (as in a blender) into one continuous stream of material which has no discernible taste and, perhaps, an unappetizing color. What we have here, then, is a collection of different types of ice cream, varying in texture, ingredients, consistency, hardness, and flavor. We have applied to this potpourri a topping (and, we hope, some cherries), which we hope enhances its flavor and does not prohibit savoring the flavor of each. That topping is our integrative material (introductory and concluding chapters, part introductions, etc.), and we have tried to provide just enough of it to make the entire dish pleasing to the connoisseur. It is for the reader to judge by his or her own taste buds whether we have been successful or not but, nonetheless, we feel very positive about our creation, although we will undoubtedly alter the recipe in the future.

Before concluding this volume, we would like to highlight briefly some issues which permeate the book and, in fact, the field at large. Although we can only touch on these issues here, we nonetheless wish to raise them for open debate among researchers interested in leadership and management (for recent treatments of some of these issues, see Behling, 1980; Boehm,

1980; Morgan and Smircich, 1980). The two most recent symposia volumes (Hunt & Larson, 1977, 1979) have also dealt with some of these from a different perspective than here.

The Leadership-Management Controversy

One of the most respected scholars in managerial research, Henry Mintzberg, has expressed in this volume a strong desire not to be labeled as a "leadership researcher," due to serious misgivings about the usefulness of leadership research as a means of advancing either knowledge or practice. And, by comments made by numerous others (including previous symposium overviewers), he is not alone in either his misgivings or his disavowal of leadership as a field.

This reaction to the leadership area seems instructive, and it highlights what we might label the "leadership-management controversy." Although there are undoubtedly many origins of this controversy, two seem particularly apparent and are considered at some length below. In addition, we treat a third major topic, the "fun" of scientific inquiry, since this lies at the very heart of all our professional enterprise.

The Constituency Issue

One of the distinguishing differences between "leadership" researchers and "managerial" researchers appears to be that of underlying purpose—who research is to serve (the constituency of research). Most researchers in the management realm seem to have a strong value orientation toward serving practicing managers, while leadership researchers seem to be more oriented toward serving scholars in the academic community. Thus, we see Mintzberg's strong statements (and, perhaps, feel his strong emotions) that research which makes a contribution to leadership research but not leadership practice is of limited or no redeeming value.

Continuing our earlier gastronomical metaphor, arguments over the constituency of research seem, in many ways, like those over which flavor of ice cream is best. Some people like chocolate, some like vanilla, and some like both or neither. It seems foolish to argue about a topic as trivial (to some people) as ice cream preferences but, undoubtedly, some people do. So, too, do we argue about an important topic (constituency) but, again, there is no objective referent which can be employed to resolve the dispute. The constituency issue involves one of values and cannot be confirmed or proven right or wrong.

Although one might argue that ours is an applied field and therefore *should* serve an applied clientele, there is no inherent reason why we *must*. Indeed, our purposes might be better served if we operate like the typical ice cream manufacturer—by not assuming that one flavor is best or that the consuming public can be convinced that one is best, but, instead, by trying to meet multiple tastes by producing a diversified product line which is specialized to appeal to different market segments.

Do we need diversity if we are to serve adequately our different consumer clienteles? In other words, do our market segments have different needs or desires which cannot be met by a single offering? Mintzberg's comments seem to suggest so. For example, he notes that practitioners need creative approaches which get through to them by providing startling insights (based on intuitive knowledge) and which produce changes in their perceptions about desirable activities and behaviors (i.e., research with strong action implications). Academic scholars, on the other hand, seem to have adopted a natural science model of inquiry (Morgan & Smircich, 1980), and seem more interested in systematic analytical knowledge, designed to yield a cumulative knowledge base which may or may not have immediate action implications (Behling, 1980). This suggests that the needs of practitioners and scholars may be different, and it also has numerous implications for how research is conducted (these are discussed later). Although one might argue that we should be serving the practitioner (or academic) community, or that we should convince practitioners (or academics) to change their orientation, this, again, involves value issues which seem unlikely to be resolved. Thus, a more fruitful way to proceed might be to recognize these value differences and, instead of trying to mold our markets to our products, try to serve these different markets as best we can. In other words, as we suggested earlier in this volume, a pluralistic approach to leadership and management research may be desirable—not just a tolerance for a multiplicity of flavors in our collective product line, but an active production of the same.

An ice cream manufacturer's perspective. Carrying our ice cream metaphor even further, how might we proceed if we adopted an ice cream manufacturer's perspective? That is, allowing that there may be different market segments in our environment with different needs or tastes, how might we deal with them?

For a start it would seem that we would not assume knowledge about our customers but, instead, might undertake a market analysis to determine how many subsegments exist (and who constitute each), what sorts of products they desire, and how we might deliver our products to them. To this end, we would examine such things as flavor preferences (e.g., chocolate, vanilla, etc.), and the uses to which ice cream are put (e.g., as a basic food staple, as a family "treat," as dessert for guests, etc.). This might result in a highly complicated marketing program, but it might also be more likely to result in increased success in serving our consuming publics.

Although we have not undertaken a systematic market analysis, some ideas immediately come to mind and can be used to illustrate the implications of our metaphor. A more in-depth analysis is needed, however, before actually applying a diversity-based approach to leadership and management research.

Flavor preferences. Recognition of differences in flavor preferences leads to some fundamental differences in ingredients and, perhaps, in production processes underlying our various outputs (more is said concerning needed production processes later). For example, if restaurant customers (practitioners) prefer creative, novel, and startling products, we may produce a line of ice creams for them which has high fat content (is rich), incorporates surprises (raisins, nuts, bits of pralines, etc.), and is unstandardized (the menu varies form week to week). On the other hand, if our home market (academics) prefers products of more uniform consistency (with few surprises) which are available in standardized form throughout the year, we may want to produce a line of basic flavors (chocolate, vanilla, etc.) to suit their preferences. Although we may want to consider trying to market creative ice creams to the home market, and standard products to the restaurants, we are unlikely to succeed if each market perceives its needs or preferences as being incongruent with these products. Thus, although we may try to expand our sales by various promotional strategies (e.g., packaging, advertising, etc.), we may expect to be unsuccessful, at least in the long run, if such preference incompatabilities exist.

In sum, if we recognize that practitioners and academics may have varying preferences for different research outputs, diversity becomes imperative. Collectively, we cannot produce only one kind of output, although some of us may choose to specialize to reduce complexity, gain economies of scale, or to fit our own visions of the type of product we wish to produce.

Use preferences. Accepting that different market segments may have different tastes, we might also consider the different uses of our product outputs. This, in turn, might lead us to not only differentiate more finely among our market segments (e.g., distinguish between fast-food outlets and ice cream parlors), but also lead us to expand our product line.

If our fast-food customers prefer simple products for high-volume sales and minimal inventory, we might market a product line of only basic flavors. On the other hand, if our ice cream parlor segment caters to a broad range of consumers, we might endeavor to supply them with basic flavors, as well as more exotic delights (such as praline and almond coffee nut fudge) for multiple uses (plain, sundaes, and banana splits, etc.). We might also seek to provide complements to our ice cream line, by adding such things as toppings, cones, nuts, and so on.

The implications of use differences for leadership and management research seem enormous and, therefore warrant a brief excursion from our metaphor to highlight further some possibilities. In the academic community, different types of research may be needed, for example, to develop theories as compared with testing existing frameworks. One could distinguish, for example, between hypothesis-generating and hypothesis-testing types of inquiry. Similarly, within practitioner circles, one could envision differences in research aimed at prescriptions for top-level versus supervisory management, new versus established managers, initial training versus skill maintenance, and so on. In the training domain, for example, one might wish to concentrate on conducting research which is congruent with, or has a focus on self-diagnosis, attitude change, and learning principles. Accessories offered could include such things as training manuals, action guides, and self-programmed texts, in addition to startling and insightful theoretical treatments (our ice cream).

In sum, adoption of a diversity-oriented approach suggests that we not only accept that different market segments have different output preferences, but that we also need to consider end uses and necessary accouterments for spurring use of our output.

Additional considerations and summary. Obviously, we could develop our ice cream metaphor even further (although, perhaps, we have carried it too far already) to include issues such as packaging (e.g., fancy versus plain containers), promotion (e.g., giving away sample "tastes"), place (e.g., regular supermarkets, discount houses, etc.), or price (e.g., market skimming versus penetration strategies).

We have concentrated on a limited set of "product" issues, however, to illustrate some implications of taking our metaphor seriously, and of adopting a widely defined user-oriented perspective (which is sometimes called the "marketing approach"). In sum, we believe that viewing our research endeavor in metaphorical terms leads to numerous insights, not the least of which involves recognition of differences among consumers in terms of tastes, uses, and the like. Such a perspective on the constituency issue seems, at least to us, a more useful approach than collectively attempting to be a manufacturer who produces only one product and then forcefully tries to sell that one product to an undifferentiated public.

The Research Strategy Issue

Although the constituency issue discussed above is important, another issue which seems to differentiate "managerial researchers" from "leadership researchers" is apparent in Mintzberg's comments, and was mentioned earlier by Stewart (chapter 2). This concerns the research strategy issue—how knowledge is discovered and systematized.

Sources of the research strategy issue. The research strategy issue obviously relates to our earlier discussion concerning differences needed in production processes to meet the needs of different constituents. It also arises as a result of differences in beliefs about the phenomena we investigate. Differences in perceptions of underlying phenomena (ontology) lead to differences in beliefs about needed inquiry modes (epistomology), and this seems to be the source of arguments over research strategies (Morgan & Smircich, 1980).

Thus, we see Mintzberg's view that leadership and management phenomena are so unstructured as to preclude study by more structured means. Intuitive knowledge (as compared with analytical knowledge) is therefore needed, and only less structured means can be used to obtain such knowledge and the startling insight associated with intuitive knowing.

Adopting a marketing perspective. Adopting a marketing (diversity-based) approach, it again seems unfruitful to argue that research should be structured to yield analytic knowledge or that research should be structured so as to produce intuitive knowledge. This epistomological argument derives from two different world views (ontology) and, hence, seems incapable of objective resolution. If some people believe that ice cream has bumps (e.g., nuts, berries, etc.), while others see it as homogeneous, can we change these beliefs and, perhaps more importantly, should we try? Our earlier discussion of constituency suggests that trying to change these beliefs may be dysfunctional, since our constituency may best be served by producers holding different viewpoints and developing and offering different products to the consuming public. Similarly, if beliefs about ice cream composition are the result of differential socialization, upbringing, and experience (e.g., households where only one type of ice cream was purchased and consumed by the parents), how likely is it that even showing people "objective evidence" (bumpy or homogeneous types of ice cream) will change their views? They might deny that such products could be ice cream, because their backgrounds have proven otherwise.

Although we are more inclined toward lumpy and bumpy ice cream, we do not wish to argue our point of view here (this is discussed later). Others have equally strong desires for a more homogeneous product, as well as some compelling reasons for arguing their tastes (cf. Behling, 1980). Again, what seems most useful is to recognize that different products may be needed, that these may require different production processes, and that we need to develop processes compatible with our product line.

Thus, for example, if we are intent on serving restaurant (practitioner) customers we may have to produce ice creams which are rich, contain surprises, and vary from week to week. Such a group of products may have to be produced either by hand or by very sophisticated machinery (designed for short production runs, not to clog with ingredients of varying consistency, etc.). On the other hand, if we serve the home market (academics), and if they want basic flavors with a uniform consistency, these products may be more amenable to using either less sophisticated or more automated production equipment. In either case, we would want to analyze output economics and marketing implications of various production strategies before implementing them, but still we might expect some fundamental production differences which are related to the very nature of our products.

In sum, if we accept the need for a collectively diverse product line, we may also have to accept that different means may have to be used to produce them. Diverse research strategies therefore seem both necessary and desirable if we are to serve adequately our consumer market segments.

Some Concluding Thoughts

Before concluding this volume, we would like to deal with two issues which are interrelated, and which we believe warrant some discussion: our perspective, and the "fun" of scientific inquiry.

Our Perspective

Morgan and Smircich (1980) suggest that researchers should explicitly communicate their basic assumption about ontology and epistomology, so that readers can keep underlying biases in mind. In this respect, our orientation should be obvious. Our arguments for diversity are rooted in taste buds which rejoice in sampling a smorgasbord of ice creams—ranging from the simple yet sublime to more exotic and exciting concoctions. As noted in the introduction to this volume, and by our selection of contributions for this book, we believe that leadership is an aspect of the managerial job, and that broadening our collective menu can only lead to a more healthy and stimulating diet for the field. We also believe that diverse research strategies are equally viable, and that both structured and unstructured methods can and should be used to complement each other.

This advocacy of diverse methods comes not only from recognition of the need for different products, but also from realizing the inherent impurities in both structured and unstructured approaches. These shortcomings require the use of both research modes in our field, if we are to ensure that our knowledge is not to be method-dependent or method-bound. Furthermore, since our knowledge of the spectrum of leadership and managerial phenomena is very limited and fragmentary, diverse research methods may also be useful in first generating knowledge and then testing it. Although some have argued that this distinction is undesirable (e.g., Mitroff & Pondy, 1978), we, nonetheless, feel it may be useful in resolving epistomological disputes and in advancing the field.

We would also like to point out that if we look back at our European epilog (chapter 15), we see there indication of considerable tolerance of and, in fact, respect for diversity. We feel that this is healthy, and hope to encourage such developments both here and abroad. In fact, as this book goes to press, we are tentatively planning on holding the next symposium in Europe, and striving for balance of North American contributions and contributions from the rest of the world. We feel that diversity is a necessity, and that the European model may be helpful in broadening our perspective. In sum, we cherish diversity and see it as needed for our collective endeavor.

The "Fun" of Scientific Inquiry

Having explicitly stated our value preferences above, we would now like to conclude this volume with a brief discussion of a topic of interest to us all—"fun". We mentioned earlier that one criterion which might be applied to our productive enterprise is our own individual vision of the type of product we wish to produce. What we are trying to highlight here is that choice exists on both sides of the producer-consumer exchange, and that each of us may select our products to fit our beliefs, needs, and self-images. Do we have such a right? We would argue that we do and, furthermore, that we must exercise that right if our collective enterprise is to prosper.

Our profession is a demanding one in many ways: we pay heavily for our jobs in terms of many years in school, long apprenticeships, poor remuneration, unremitting pressure ("productivity-or-perish"), long hours, limited promotional opportunities (a three-tier hierarchy), and little recognition from the public-at-large. Given these costs of production, and the fact that most of us have chosen to be ice cream manufacturers for freedom to produce products congruent with our own self-images (using methods of our own choice), we would argue that we should be allowed to engage in free market competition, to enact our visions as best we can.

Furthermore, we believe that only through such a process will our production system succeed. Besides serving diverse public needs, only if we are allowed to pursue our own conceptions of academic enterprise will our commitment to advancing knowledge be enhanced. Surely, at the root of any professional value system is what some have termed "commitment to calling"—a fundamental belief in the worth of the profession and a lifelong desire to serve in it (Kerr, Von Glinow, & Schriesheim, 1977)—and this may dissipate if we do not exercise freedom of choice.

However, if we enhance commitment by allowing researchers to have "fun," to do research congruent with their desires, might not more and better products result? Mitroff (1980) tells us that "the history of science shows repeatedly that science has been advanced by persons who passionately believed in their pet hypotheses" (p. 514). Where is our passion? Might not freedom of choice lead to passion development? Might it not also lead to the diversity needed to explore the domain of leadership and management phenomena?

In sum, our values and beliefs suggest that research should be fun if we are to advance the field, and that we should therefore encourage diversity if we are to achieve that end. We want to be able to enjoy our enterprise and, at the same time, to serve constituencies of our own choosing, with products compatible with their needs and ours.

References
Name Index
Subject Index

References

Alban-Metcalfe, B. *Leadership—who does what to whom, and how?* Unpublished manuscript, University of Bradford Management Centre, West Yorkshire, England, 1980.

Alexander, L. D. *The effect which level in the hierarchy and functional area have on the extent to which Mintzberg's roles are required by managerial jobs.* Paper presented at the Western Academy of Management meeting, Portland, OR, April 1979.

Alutto, J., & Acito, F. Decisional participation and sources of job satisfaction: A study of manufacturing personnel. *Academy of Management Journal*, 1974, *17*, 160–67.

Alutto, J., & Belacco, J. A typology for participation in organizational decision making. *Administrative Science Quarterly*, 1972, *17*, 117–25.

Alvares, K. M., Silverman, W. H. & Dalessio, A. *Scale development: Affective component in leadership.* Working paper, Department of Psychology, Bowling Green State University, Bowling Green, OH., 1980.

Argue, A. R. What do principals do? *The B.C. Teacher*, November–December 1978, 68–70.

Argyris, C. How normal science methodology makes leadership research less additive and less applicable. In J. G. Hunt & L. L. Larson (Eds.), *Crosscurrents in leadership*. Carbondale: Southern Illinois University Press, 1979.

Ashby, W. R. *An introduction to cybernetics*. London: Chapman & Hall, 1956.

Ashour, A. S. The contingency model of leadership effectiveness: An evaluation. *Organizational Behavior and Human Performance*, 1973, *9*, 339–55(a).

Bales, R. F. *Personality and interpersonal behavior*. New York: Holt, Rinehart, and Winston, 1970.

Bales, R. F. *Interaction process analysis: A method for the study of small groups*. Cambridge, MA: Addison-Wesley, 1950. (Reprinted in paperback by the University of Chicago Press, Chicago, 1976).

Bales, R. F. *The SYMLOG case study kit, with instructions for a group self study*. New York: Macmillan, Free Press, 1980.

Bales, R. F., Cohen, S. P., & Williamson, S. A. *SYMLOG: A system for the multiple level observation of groups.* New York: Macmillan, Free Press, 1979.

Bales, R. F., & Slater, P. E. Role differentiation in small decision-making groups. In T. Parsons, & R. F. Bales, *Family, socialization, and interaction processes.* Glencoe, IL: Free Press, 1955.

Bass, B. M. *Transformational leadership.* Working paper, School of Management, State University of New York at Binghamton, Binghamton, NY, 1980.

Bass, B. M., & Farrow, D. L. Quantitative analyses of biographies of political figures. *Journal of Psychology,* 1977, *97,* 281–96.

Bass, B. M., & Stogdill, R. S. *Revised handbook of leadership.* New York: Macmillan, Free Press, 1981.

Bass, B. M., & Valenzie, E. R. Contingent aspects of effective management styles. In J. G. Hunt and L. L. Larson (Eds.), *Contingency approaches to leadership.* Carbondale: Southern Illinois University Press, 1974.

Batstone, E., Boraston, I., & Frenkel, S. *Shop stewards in action: The organization of workplace conflict and accommodation.* Oxford, England: Basil Blackwell, 1979.

Behling, O. The case for the natural science model for research in organizational behavior and organization theory. *Academy of Management Review,* 1980, *5,* 483–90.

Bell, G. The influence of technological components of work upon management control. *Academy of Management Journal,* 1965, *8,* 127–32.

Bello, J. A., & Mackenzie, K. D. *Leadership as an uncertainty control process.* Unpublished manuscript, School of Business, University of Kansas, July 1979.

Bennis, W. G. Leadership: A beleagured species? *Organizational Dynamics,* 1976, *5* (1), 3–16.

Bennis, W. G., & Shepard, H. A. A theory of group development. *Human Relations,* 1956, *9,* 415–37.

Berlyne, D. E. Arousal and reinforcement. In D. Levine (Ed.), *Nebraska Symposium on Motivation* (Vol. 15). Lincoln: University of Nebraska Press, 1967.

Bernardin, H. J., & Pence, E. C. Effects of rater training: Creating new response sets and decreasing accuracy. *Journal of Applied Psychology,* 1980, *65,* 60–66.

Bixby, T. D. *Action and speech content: Perception in small group interaction.* Unpublished honors thesis, Department of Psychology and Social Relations, Harvard University, 1978.

Blake, R. R., & Mouton, J. S., *The managerial grid.* Houston: Gulf, 1964.

Blalock, H. M. Four variable causal models and partial correlation. *American Journal of Sociology,* 1962, *68,* 182–94.

Boehm, V. R. Research in the "real world"—A conceptual model. *Personnel Psychology,* 1980, *33,* 495–503.

Borman, W. C. Format and training effects on rating accuracy and rater errors. *Journal of Applied Psychology,* 1979, *64,* 410–21.

Bowers, D. G., & Seashore, S. E. Predicting organizational effectiveness with a four-factor theory of leadership. *Administrative Science Quarterly,* September 1966, *11,* 238–63.

Brown, R., & Turner, J. Interpersonal and intergroup behavior. In J. C. Turner and H. Giles (Eds.), *Intergroup behavior.* Oxford, England: Basil Blackwell, in press.

Bruning, N. S., & Skaret, D. J. *Leadership: A test of two models.* Paper presented at the American Institute of Decision Sciences meeting, Las Vegas, NV, November 1980.

Bryson, J. M. *A model of leadership emergence, stabilization and change in organizational and interorganizational networks.* Work in Progress, Hubert H. Humphrey Institute of Public Affairs, University of Minnesota, Minneapolis, MN, 1980.

Burns, T. The directions of activity and communication in a departmental executive group: A quantitative study in a British engineering factory with a self-recording technique. *Human Relations*, 1954, *7*, 73–97.

Burns, T. Management in action. *Operational Research Quarterly*, 1957, *8*(2), 45–60.

Burns, T., & Stalker, G. *The management of innovation.* London: Tavistock, 1961.

Burns, W. *Leadership.* New York: McGraw-Hill, 1978.

Bussom, R. S. *Cybernetic modeling in health: An application to head nurse behavior.* Unpublished doctoral dissertation, Ohio State University, 1973.

Bussom, R. S., Larson, L. L., Vicars, W. M., & Ness, J. J. *Non-participant observation as a research approach: Problems and issues.* Paper presented at the annual meeting of the Academy of Criminal Justice Sciences, Oklahoma City, March 1980.

Calder, B. J. An attribution theory of leadership. In B. M. Staw & G. R. Salancik (Eds.), *New directions in organizational behavior.* Chicago: St. Clair Press, 1977.

Campbell, D. The cutting edge is dull. *Contemporary Psychology*, 1979, *24*, 248–49.

Campbell, D. T., & Fiske, D. W. Convergent and discriminant validation by the multitrait-multimethod matrix. *Psychological Bulletin*, 1959, *56*, 81–105.

Campbell, J. P. The cutting edge of leadership: An overview. In J. G. Hunt & L. L. Larson (Eds.), *Leadership: The cutting edge.* Carbondale: Southern Illinois University Press, 1977. (a)

Campbell, J. P. On the nature of organizational effectiveness. In P. Goodman, J. Pennings, & Associates (Eds.), *New perspectives on organizational effectiveness.* San Francisco: Jossey-Bass, 1977. (b)

Campbell, J. P., Dunnette, M. D., Arvey, R. D., & Hellervik, L. V. The development and evaluation of behaviorally based rating scales. *Journal of Applied Psychology*, 1973, *57*, 15–22.

Campbell, J. P., Dunnette, M. D., Lawler, E. E., III, & Weick, K. E., Jr. *Managerial behavior, performance, and effectiveness.* New York: McGraw-Hill, 1970.

Cantor, N., & Mischel, W. Traits as prototypes: Effects on recognition memory. *Journal of Personality and Social Psychology*, 1977, *35*, 38–48.

Cantor, N., & Mischel, W. Prototypes in person perception. In L. Berkowitz (Ed.), *Advances in experimental social psychology* (Vol. 12). New York: Academic Press, 1979.

Carlson, S. *Executive behavior: A study of the work load and the working methods of managing directors.* Stockholm: Strombergs, 1951.

Carter, L. F. Recording and evaluating the performance of individuals as members of small groups. *Personnel Psychology*, 1954, *7*, 477–84.

Carter, L. F., Haythorn, W., Shriver, B., & Lanzetta, J. The behavior of leaders and other group members. *Journal of Abnormal and Social Psychology*, 1951, *46*, 589–95.

Cartwright, D. S., & Zander, A. (Eds.). *Group dynamics: Research and theory* (3rd ed.). New York: Harper & Row, 1968.

Carver, C. S. A cybernetic model of self-attention processes. *Journal of Personality and Social Psychology*, 1979, *37*, 1251–81.

Clark, R. A. Analyzing the group structures of combat rifle squads. *American Psychologist*, 1953, *8*, 333.

Cohen, A. R., & Bradford, D. *Managing for excellence*. Working Paper, Whittemore School of Business and Economics, University of New Hampshire, Durham, 1980.

Cohen, J., & Cohen, P. *Applied multiple regression/correlation analysis for the behavioral sciences*. Hillsdale, NJ: Lawrence Erlbaum Associates, 1975.

Cohen, M. D., & March, J. G. *Leadership and ambiguity*. New York: McGraw-Hill, 1974.

Cooley, W. W., & Lohnes, P. R. *Multivariate procedures for the behavioral sciences*. New York: Wiley, 1962.

Couch, A. A. *Psychological determinants of interpersonal behavior*. Unpublished doctoral dissertation, Harvard University, 1960.

Couch, A. S., & Carter, L. F. *A factorial study of the rated behavior of group members*. Paper presented at the Eastern Psychological Association meeting, Boston, March 1952.

Culbert, S. A., & McDonough, G. G. *The invisible war*. New York: Wiley, 1980.

Cummings, L. L. Assessing the Graen/Cashman Model and comparing it with other approaches. In J. G. Hunt and L. L. Larson (Eds.), *Leadership frontiers*. Kent, OH: Comparative Administration Research Institute, Kent State University, 1975.

Dachler, P. *A social systems perspective of leadership*. Unpublished manuscript, Hochschule St. Gallen, Guisarstrasse 11, 9010 St. Gallen, Switzerland, 1980.

Dailey, R. C. *Project leader's locus of control and task certainty as antecedents of members' satisfaction with leadership and R & D team performance*. Working Paper, Graduate School of Business Administration, Tulane University, New Orleans, LA, 1980.

Dansereau, F., Cashman, J., & Graen, G. Instrumentality theory and equity theory as complementary approaches in predicting the relationship of leadership and turnover among managers. *Organizational Behavior and Human Performance*, 1973, *10*, 184–200.

Dansereau, F., & Dumas, M. S. Pratfalls and pitfalls in drawing inferences about leader behavior in organizations. In J. G. Hunt and L. L. Larson (Eds.), *Leadership: The cutting edge*. Carbondale: Southern Illinois University Press, 1977.

Dansereau, F., Graen, G., & Haga, W. J. A vertical dyad linkage approach to leadership within formal organizations: A longitudinal investigation of the role-making process. *Organizational Behavior and Human Performance*, 1975, *13*, 46–78.

Derakhshan, F. *Leadership directiveness and span of supervision: A study of fast-food restaurants*. Work in progress, Indiana University, Kokomo, IN, 1980.

Drenth, P. J. D., Koopman, P. L., Rus, V., Odar, M., Heller, F. A., & Brown, A. Participative decision making: A comparative study. *Industrial Relations*, 1979, *18*, 295–309.

Dubin, R. Supervision and productivity: Empirical findings and theoretical considerations. In R. Dubin, G. Homans, F. Mann, & D. Miller (Eds.), *Leadership and productivity*. San Francisco: Chandler, 1965.

Dubin, R. Metaphors of leadership: An overview. In J. G. Hunt & L. L. Larson (Eds.), *Crosscurrents in leadership*. Carbondale: Southern Illinois University Press, 1979.

Duffy, E. *Activation and behavior*. New York: Wiley, 1962.

Duffy, P. J. *Lateral interaction orientation: An expanded view of leadership*. Unpublished doctoral dissertation, Southern Illinois University, Carbondale, 1973.

Dumas, M. *An empirical approach to the study of leadership in organizations*. Unpublished doctoral dissertation, State University of New York at Buffalo, 1977.

Duncan, R. B. Characteristics of organizational environments and perceived environmental uncertainty. *Administrative Science Quarterly*, 1972, *17*, 313–27.

Dunnette, M. D. Fads, fashions and folderol in psychology. *American Psychologist*, 1966, *21*, 343–52.

Eden, D., & Leviatan, U. Implicit leadership theory as a determinant of the factor structure underlying supervisory behavior scales. *Journal of Applied Psychology*, 1975, *60*, 736–41.

Eiser, J. R. *Cognitive social psychology: A guidebook to theory and research*. London: McGraw-Hill, 1980.

Ellison, R. L., Abe, C., Fox, D. C., & Guest, C. W. *The development and evaluation of managerial selection/promotion procedures*. Technical Report, Department of the Army, Construction Engineering Research Laboratory, Champaign, Illinois, July 1980.

Evans, M. G. *The effects of supervisory behavior in worker perceptions of their path goal relationships*. Unpublished doctoral dissertation, Yale University, New Haven, CT, 1968.

Evans, M. G. Extensions of a path-goal theory of motivation. *Journal of Applied Psychology*, 1974, *59*, 172–78.

Evans, M. G. Leadership. in S. Kerr (Ed.), *Organizational behavior*. Columbus, OH: Grid Publishing, 1979.

Feather, J. *Organizational structure and the formation of perceptions*. Working paper, Department of Sociology, State University of New York at Buffalo, 1980.

Feilders, J. F. *Action and reaction: The job of an urban school superintendent*. Unpublished doctoral dissertation, Stanford University, 1978.

Fiedler, F. E. Engineer the job to fit the manager. *Harvard Business Review*, 1965, *43*(5), 115–22.

Fiedler, F. E. *A theory of leadership effectiveness*. New York: McGraw-Hill, 1967.

Fiedler, F. E. Personality, motivational systems, and behavior of high and low LPC persons. *Human Relations*, 1972, *25*, 391–412.

Fiedler, F. E., & Chemers, M. M. *Leadership and effective management*. Glenview, IL: Scott, Foresman, 1974.

Fiedler, F. E., Chemers, M. M., & Mahar, L. *Improving leadership effectiveness: The Leader Match concept*. New York: Wiley, 1976.

Fischhoff, B. Attribution theory and judgement under uncertainty. In J. H. Harvey,

W. J. Ickes, & R. F. Kidd (Eds.), *New directions in attribution research.* Hillsdale, NJ: Lawrence Erlbaum Associates, 1976.

Fiske, S. T., & Cox, M. G. Person concepts: The effects of target familiarity and descriptive purpose on the process of describing others. *Journal of Personality,* 1979, *47,* 136–61.

Fleishman, E. A. Leadership climate, human relations training and supervisory training. *Personnel Psychology,* 1953, *6,* 205–22.

Ford, J. D. *The interaction of size, technology, and environment on intended dimensions of structure.* Paper presented at the 36th Annual Academy of Management Conference, Kansas City, August 1976.

Forsblad, P. *Changes in Swedish industry and their implications for leadership.* Unpublished manuscript, The Economic Research Institute at the Stockholm School of Economics (IFL), Stockholm, Sweden, 1980.

Foti, R. J., Fraser, S. L., & Lord, R. G. *Leaders, prototypes, and labels: What does the word "leader" imply?* Unpublished manuscript, Department of Psychology, University of Akron, 1980.

Fox, W. M. *Use of the nominal group technique with various problem-solving groups with the NGT procedure modified to accommodate pre-meeting and meeting-time anonymous inputs.* Work in progress, University of Florida, Gainesville, 1980.

Geersing, J. *Leadership and participation: Implications for action research.* Unpublished manuscript, Subfaculteit Psychologie, State University of Groningen, Groningen, The Netherlands, 1980.

Gibb, C. Leadership. In G. Lindzey and E. Aronson (Eds.), *The handbook of social psychology* (2nd ed., Vol. 4). Reading, MA: Addison-Wesley, 1969.

Gill, R. W. T. The in-tray (in-basket) exercise as a measure of management potential. *Journal of Occupational Psychology,* 1979, *52,* 185–97.

Gill, R. W. T. *A trainability approach to assessing management potential using the in-basket technique.* Work in progress, State University of New York at Binghamton, 1980. (a)

Gill, R. W. T. *What is the content in "content validity?"* Paper presented at the 88th annual meeting of the American Psychological Association, Division 14, Montreal, Quebec, September 1980. (b)

Gilmore, D. C., Beehr, T. A., & Richter, D. J. Effects of leader behaviors on subordinate performance and satisfaction: A laboratory experiment with student employees. *Journal of Applied Psychology,* 1979, *64,* 166–72.

Gingras, A., Zeghal, M., & Alain, M. *A study of managers' work in public organizations.* Unpublished summary, Ecole nationale d'administration publique, Sainte-Foy, Quebec, Canada, 1977.

Gioia, D., & Sims, A. P. *The influence of performance and performance attributions on leader verbal behavior.* Working paper, College of Business Administration, Pennsylvania State University, University Park, PA, 1980.

Goodman, R. A. *Temporary systems: Professional development, manpower utilization, task effectiveness and innovation.* New York: Praeger, 1981.

Gordon, G. E., & Rosen, N. *Critical factors in leadership succession.* Unpublished manuscript, New York State School of Industrial and Labor Relations, Cornell University, 1979.

Graen, G. Role-making processes within complex organizations. In M. D. Dunnette (Ed.), *Handbook of Industrial and organizational psychology*. Chicago: Rand McNally, 1976.

Graen, G., Alvares, K., Orris, J. B., & Martella, J. A. Contingency model of leadership effectiveness: Antecedent and evidential results. *Psychological Bulletin*, 1970, *74*, 285–96.

Graen, G., & Cashman, J. F. A role-making model of leadership in formal organizations: A developmental approach. In J. G. Hunt and L. L. Larson (Eds.), *Leadership frontiers*. Kent, OH: Comparative Administration Research Institute, Kent State University, 1975.

Graen, G., Dasereau, F., Minami, T., & Cashman, J. Leadership behaviors as cues to performance evaluation. *Academy of Management Journal*, 1973, *16*, 611–23.

Graen, G., & Schiemann, W. Leader-member agreement: A vertical dyad linkage approach. *Journal of Applied Psychology*. 1978, *63*, 206–12.

Greene, C. N. Limitations of cross-lagged correlational designs and an alternative approach. In J. G. Hunt and L. L. Larson (Eds.), *Leadership frontiers*. Kent, OH: Comparative Administration Research Institute, Kent State University, 1975, 121–26.

Griffin, R. W. *The effects of leader behaviors on subordinate perceptions of job characteristics*. Paper presented at the American Institute for Decision Sciences meeting, Las Vegas, NV, November 1980.

Guilford, J. *Fundamental statistics in psychology and education*. New York: McGraw Hill, 1965.

Halal, W. E., & Brown, B. *Participative management: Myth and reality*. Working paper, Department of Management Science, School of Government and Business Administration, George Washington University. Washington, DC, 1980.

Hamilton, D. L. A cognitive-attributional analysis of stereotyping. In L. Berkowitz (Ed.), *Advances in experimental social psychology* (Vol. 12). New York: Academic Press, 1979.

Hammond, K. R., McClelland, G. H., & Mumpower, J. *Human judgment and decision making*. New York: Praeger, 1980.

Harrison, A. M. *The operational definition of managerial roles*. Unpublished doctoral thesis, University of Cape Town, Cape Town, South Africa, 1980.

Hawley, D. E. *A study of the relationship between the leader behavior and attitudes of elementary school principals*. Unpublished M.Ed. Thesis, University of Saskatchewan, 1969.

Hays, W. L. *Statistics*. New York: Holt, Rinehart, and Winston, 1963.

Head, L. K. *Summary of leadership/managerial behavior work*. Working paper, Department of Educational Psychology and Foundations, University of Northern Iowa, Cedar Falls, IA, 1980.

Heller, F. A. *A multinational study of managerial competence*. Unpublished manuscript, Centre for Decision-Making Studies, Tavistock Institute for Human Relations, London, England, 1980.

Heller, F. A., Drenth, P. J. D., Koopman, P. L., & Rus, V. A longitudinal study in participative decision-making. *Human Relations*, 1977, *30*, 567–87.

Heller, F. A., & Wilpert, B. *Competence and power in managerial decision making.* New York, London: Wiley, 1981.

Hemphill, J. K. *Dimensions of executive positions.* Research Monograph No. 98. Columbus: Bureau of Business Research, Ohio State University, 1960.

Hemphill, J., & Coons A. E. Development of the Leader Behavior Description Questionnaire. In R. M. Stogdill and A. E. Coons (Eds.), *Leader behavior: Its description and measurement.* Columbus: Bureau of Business Research, Ohio State University, 1957.

Hill, J. W., & Hunt, J. G. Managerial level, leadership, and employee need satisfaction. In E. A. Fleishman and J. G. Hunt (Ed.), *Current developments in the study of leadership,* Carbondale: Southern Illinois University Press, 1973.

Hodgson, R. C., Levinson, D. J., & Zaleznik, A. *The executive role constellation: An analysis of personality and role relations in management.* Boston: Division of Research, Harvard Business School, 1965.

Hoffman, L. R., & Pearse, R. W. *Behavior of leaders in project groups.* Work in progress, Rutgers University, Newark, NJ, 1980.

Hofstede, G. *Culture's consequences: International differences in work-related values.* Beverly Hills, CA: Sage Publications, in press.

Hofstede, G. Motivation, leadership, and organization: Do American theories apply abroad? *Organizational Dynamics,* 1980, *9*(1), 42–63.

Hollander, E. P. *Leadership dynamics: A practical guide to effective relationships.* New York: Macmillan, Free Press, 1978.

Hosking, D. M. *A critical evaluation of Fiedler's predictor measures of leadership effectiveness.* Unpublished doctoral thesis, University of Warwick, England, 1978.

Hosking, D. M. *The social psychology of leadership—Mark I.* Unpublished manuscript, University of Aston Management Centre, Birmingham, England, 1980.

Hosking, D. M., Hunt, J. G., & Child, J. *Summary report: European Workshop in Leadership and Managerial Behavior.* Unpublished document, University of Aston Management Centre, Birmingham, England, 1980.

Hosking, D. M., Hunt, J. G., & Osborn, R. N. *Leadership: Not one rainbow, not one pot of gold.* Working paper, University of Aston Management Centre, Birmingham, England, 1980.

Hosking, D. M., & Schriesheim, C. A. *Issues and non-issues in leader-group interactions.* Unpublished manuscript, Department of Organizational Behavior, University of Southern California, Los Angeles, 1980.

House, R. J. A path-goal theory of leader effectiveness. *Administrative Science Quarterly,* 1971, *16*, 321–38. Reprinted in E. A. Fleishman and J. G. Hunt (Eds.), *Current developments in the study of leadership.* Carbondale: Southern Illinois University Press, 1973.

House, R. J. A 1976 theory of charismatic leadership. In J. G. Hunt and L. L. Larson (Eds.), *Leadership: The cutting edge.* Carbondale: Southern Illinois University Press, 1977.

House, R. J., & MacKenzie, K. D. *Paradigm development in the social sciences: A proposed research strategy.* Unpublished manuscript, Faculty of Management Studies, University of Toronto, 1976.

House, R. J., & Mitchell, T. R. Path-goal theory of leadership. *Journal of contemporary business*, 1974, *3*(4), 81–97.

Howell, J. P., & Dorfman, P. W. *Substitutes for leadership: An empirical study.* Paper presented at the American Psychological Association Annual Convention, – Industrial/Organizational Psychology Division, Montreal, Quebec, Canada, September 1980. (a)

Howell, J. P., & Dorfman, P. W. *Substitutes for leadership: Test of a construct.* Working paper, Department of Management, New Mexico State University, Las Cruces, NM, 1980. (b)

Howland, D. Cybernetics and general systms. *General systems yearbook*, 1963, *8*, 227–32.

Howland, D., Pierce, L. M., & Gardner, M. *The nurse-monitor in a patient-care system.* Final Technical Report, February 1970, Ohio State University, Grant No. NU00095, U.S. Public Health Service.

Hunger, J. D., & Akin, G. *Dimensions of productive work groups: Is a leader necessary?* Working Paper, McIntire School of Commerce, University of Virginia, October 1, 1980.

Hunt, J. G. Curiouser and curiouser: An incestuous academician strikes back. *Contemporary Psychology*, in press.

Hunt, J. G., Hill, J. W., & Reaser, J. Leadership behavior correlates at two managerial levels in a mental institution. *Journal of Applied Social Psychology*, 1973, *3*(2), 174–85.

Hunt, J. G., & Hosking, D. *Summary Report: European Workshop in Leadership and Managerial behavior.* O.N.R.L. Conference Report, London, England, U.S. Department of the Navy, Office of Naval Research, 1981.

Hunt, J. G., & Larson, L. L. *Leadership frontiers.* Kent, OH: Comparative Administration Research Institute, Kent State University, 1975.

Hunt, J. G., & Larson, L. L. (Eds.). *Leadership: The cutting edge*, Carbondale: Southern Illinois University Press, 1977.

Hunt, J. G., & Larson, L. L. (Eds.), *Crosscurrents in leadership.* Carbondale: Southern Illinois University Press, 1979.

Hunt, J. G., & Liebscher, V. K. C. *Leadership behavior effects at multiple management levels in a highway department.* Paper presented at TIMS, College on Organization, Washington, DC, March 1971.

Hunt, J. G. & Liebscher, V. K. C. Leadership preference, leadership behavior, and employee satisfaction. *Organizational Behavior and Human Performance*, 1973, *9*, 59–77.

Hunt, J. G., & Osborn, R. N. *Beyond contingency approaches to leadership.* Working paper, University of Aston Management Centre, Birmingham, England, 1980. (a)

Hunt, J. G., & Osborn, R. N. *Summary of a multiple influence model of leadership.* Unpublished manuscript, University of Aston Management Centre, Birmingham, England, 1980. (b)

Hunt, J. G., & Osborn, R. N. A multiple influence approach to leadership for managers. In J. S. Stinson and P. Hersey (Eds.), *Perspectives in leader effectiveness*, Athens, OH: Center for Leadership Studies, Ohio University (1980). (c)

Hunt, J. G., Osborn, R. N., & Larson, L. L. *Leadership effectiveness in mental institutions*, National Institute of Mental Health, Final Technical Report, Department of Administrative Sciences, Southern Illinois University at Carbondale, 1973.

Hunt, J. G., Osborn, R. N., & Larson, L. L. Upper level technical orientation and first-level leadership within a non-contingency and contingency framework. *Academy of Management Journal*, 1975, *18*, 476–88.

Hunt, J. G., Osborn, R. N., & Martin, H. J. *A multiple influence model of leadership*. Alexandria, VA: Army Research Institute for the Behavioral and Social Sciences, in press.

Hunt, J. G., Osborn, R. N., & Schriesheim, C. A. Some neglected aspects of leadership research. In C. N. Greene and P. H. Birnbaum (Eds.), *Proceedings of the 21st Annual Midwest Academy of Management Conference*. Bloomington/Indianapolis, IN: Graduate School of Business, Indiana University, 1978.

Hunt, J. G., Osborn, R. N., & Schuler, R. S. Relations of discretionary and non-discretionary leadership to performance and satisfaction in a complex organization. *Human Relations*, 1978, *31*, 507–23.

Ilgen, D. R., Mitchell, T. R., & Frederickson, J. W. Poor performers: Supervisor and subordinate responses. *Organizational Behavior and Human Performance*, in press.

Industrial Democracy in Europe (IDE)–International Research Group, *European industrial relations*, London: Oxford University Press 1980. (a)

Industrial Democracy in Europe (IDE)–International Research Group, *Industrial democracy in Europe*, London: Oxford University Press 1980. (b)

Isenberg, D. J. *Individual differences in social-knowledge structures*. Unpublished manuscript, Department of Social Relations, Harvard University, 1980. (A shorter version was presented at the American Psychological Association Annual Convention, Montreal, Quebec, Canada, September 1980.)

Isenberg, D. J., & Ennis, J. *A Comparison of imposed and derived dimensions of group structure*. Unpublished manuscript, Department of Social Relations, Harvard University, 1980.

Jabes, J. *Individual processes in organizational behavior*. Arlington Heights, IL: AHM Publishing Corporation, 1978.

Jacobs, R., Kafry, D., & Zedeck, S. Expectations of behaviorally anchored rating scales. *Personnel Psychology*, 1980, *33*, 595–640.

Jacobs, T. O. *Leadership and exchange in formal organizations*. Alexandria, VA: Human Resources Research Organization, 1971.

Jago, A. G., & Vroom, V. H. *Sex differences in the incidence and evaluation of participative leader behavior*. Working paper, Department of Management, University of Houston, Houston, Texas, 1980.

Janis, I. L. *Victims of groupthink*. Boston: Houghton Mifflin, 1972.

Janis, I. L., & Mann, L. *Decision making: A psychological analysis of conflict, choice, and committment*, New York: Macmillan, Free Press, 1977.

Jermier, J. M. *Ecological hazards and organizational behavior: A study of dangerous and extremely dangerous urban environments*. Working paper, Department of Management, Graduate School of Business, University of Florida, Gainesville, 1980.

Jermier, J. M., & Berkes, J. L. Leader behavior in a police command bureaucracy:

A closer look at the quasi-military model. *Administrative Science Quarterly*, 1979, *24*, 1–23.

Jermier, J. M., & Young, J. W. *Influence of cultural stereotypes, organizational type, and immediate behavioral episodes on leadership inferences.* Working Paper, Department of Management, Graduate School of Business, University of Florida, Gainesville, 1980.

Johnson, D. T. Trait anxiety, state anxiety, and estimation of elapsed time, *Journal of Consulting and Clinical Psychology*, 1968, *32*, 654–58.

Jones, A. P., & Butler, M. C. *Influences of perceived superior-subordinate communication patterns on subordinate performance.* Working Paper, Naval Health Research Center, San Diego, 1980.

Jones, A. P., Butler, M. C., & Dutton, L. *Correlates of self-described leader behavior among navy supervisors.* Paper presented at the Western Psychological Association meeting, Honolulu, Hawaii, May 1980.

Jones, E. E., & Davis, K. E. From acts to dispositions: The attribution process in person perception. In L. Berkowitz (Ed.), *Advances in experimental social psychology* (Vol. 2). New York: Academic Press, 1965.

Kahn, R. C., Wolfe, D. M., Quinn, R. P., & Snoek, J. D. *Organizational stress.* New York: Wiley, 1964.

Kakabadse, A. *Designing social service organizations.* Unpublished manuscript, Management & Organizational Development Research Centre, Cranfield School of Management, Cranfield, Bedford, England, 1980.

Kaplan, A. *The conduct of inquiry: Methodology for behavioral sciences*, San Francisco: Chandler, 1964.

Kaplan, A. L. *Managerial activities in an organized anarchy and a rational organization: Community mental health centers contrasted to branch banks.* Unpublished doctoral dissertation, Stanford University, 1979.

Karmel, B. Leadership: A challenge to traditional research methods and assumptions. *Academy of Management Review*, 1978, *3*, 475–82.

Kassebaum, G. G. *Value orientations and interpersonal behavior: An experimental study.* Unpublished doctoral dissertation, Harvard University, 1958.

Katz, D., & Kahn, R. *The social psychology of organizations*, New York: Wiley, 1966.

Katz, D., & Kahn, R. *The social psychology of organizations* (2nd edition). New York: Wiley, 1978.

Katz, R. Towards a theory of the leadership process. In B. King, S. Streufert, & F. Fiedler (Eds.), *Managerial control and organizational democracy.* Washington, DC: Winston/Wiley, 1978.

Kavich, L. Analysis of the LBDQ–Form XII in educational institutions. Work in progress, Educational Psychology Department, University of Northern Iowa, Cedar Falls, Iowa, 1980.

Kay, L. I. *Theory Y and participative management are not synonyms!* Paper presented at the Academy of Management annual meeting, Detroit, MI, August 10–13, 1980.

Kelley, H. H. The process of causal attribution. *American Psychologist*, 1973, *28*, 107–28.

Kelvin, P. *The bases of social behavior.* London: Holt, Rinehart, & Winston, 1970.

Kerr, S., & Jermier, J. M. Substitutes for leadership: Their meaning and measurement. *Organizational Behavior and Human Performance*, 1978, *22*, 375–403.

Kerr, S., Von Glinow, M. A., & Schriesheim, J. F. Issues in the study of "professionals" in organizations: The case of scientists and engineers. *Organizational Behavior and Human Performance*, 1977, *18*, 329–45.

Kimberly, J. R. Organizational size and the structuralist perspective: A review, critique and proposal. *Administrative Science Quarterly*, 1976, *21*, 571–97.

King, C. D., & Van de Vall, M. *Models of industrial democracy*. The Hague, Paris, New York: Mouton, 1978.

Kirscht, J. P., Lodahl, T. M., & Haire, M. Some factors in the selection of leaders by members of small groups. *Journal of Abnormal and Social Psychology*, 1959, *58*, 406–8.

Klauss, R., & Bass B. *Communication and leader behavior*. Paper presented at the Academy of Management annual meeting, Detroit, MI, August 10–13, 1980.

Knickerbocker, I. Leadership: A conception and some implications. *Journal of Social Issues*, 1948, *4*, 23–40.

Knowlton, W. A., Jr., & Mitchell, T. R. Effects of causal attributions on a supervisor's evaluation of subordinate performance. *Journal of Applied Psychology*. 1980, *65*, 459–66.

Korabik, K. *Sex role orientation and leadership style*. Paper presented at the Institute for Women and Psychology, Canadian Psychological Association, Calgary, Alberta, June 1980.

Korman, A. K. Contingency approaches to leadership: An overview. In J. G. Hunt and L. L. Larson (Eds.) *Contingency approaches to leadership*. Carbondale: Southern Illinois University Press, 1974.

Kotter, J. P., & Lawrence, P. *Mayors in action: Five studies in urban governance*. New York: Wiley, 1974.

Kunin, T. Development of a new measure of job satisfaction, *Personnel Psychology*, 1955, *8*, 65–77.

Kurke, L. B., & Aldrich, H. E. *Mintzberg was right! A replication and extension of The nature of managerial work*. Paper presented at the Academy of Management annual meeting, Atlanta, GA, August 1979.

Lammers, C. L., & Hickson, D. (Eds.). *Organizations alike and unlike*. London: Routledge and Kegan Paul, 1979.

Landy, F. J: An opponent process theory of job satisfaction. *Journal of Applied Psychology*, 1978, *63*, 533–47.

Langer, E. Rethinking the role of thought in social interaction. In J. H. Harvey, W. Ickes, & R. Kielel (Eds.), *New directions in attribution research*, New York: Lawrence Erlbaum Associates, 1978.

Larson, L. L., Bussom, R. S., & Vicars, W. M. *The nature of a school superintendent's work*. Unpublished manuscript, Department of Administrative Sciences, Southern Illinois University at Carbondale, 1978.

Larson, L. L., Hunt, J. G., & Osborn. R. N. The great hi-hi leader behavior myth: A lesson from Occam's Razor. *Academy of Management Journal*, 1976, *19*(4), 628–41.

Latham, G. P., & Saari, L. M. Appliction of social-learning theory to training supervisors through behavioral modeling. *Journal of Applied Psychology*, 1979, *64*, 239–46.

Lau, A. W., Broedling, L. A., Walters, S. K., Newman, A. R., & Harvey, P. M. *The nature of the navy civilian executive job: Behavior and development.* Technical Report, Navy Personnel Research and Development Center, San Diego, CA, 1979.

Lau, A. W., Pavett, C. M., & Park, A. *The nature of managerial work: A comparison of public and private sector managers.* Paper presented at the Academy of Management annual meeting, Detroit, MI, 1980.

Lau, A. W., Newman, A. R., & Broedling, L. A. The nature of managerial work in the public lector. *Public Administration Review*, 1980, *40*, 513–20.

Lawrence, P. R., & Lorsch, J. W. *Organization and environment: Managing differentiation and integration.* Homewood, IL: Irwin, 1967.

Levinson, D. L. *The seasons of a man's life.* New York: Knopf, 1978.

Lewin, K. *Field theory in social science.* D. Cartwright (Ed.). New York: Harper & Row, 1951.

Lieberson, S., & O'Connor, J. F. Leadership and organizational performance: A study of large corporations. *American Sociological Review*, 1972, *37*, 117–30.

Likert, R. *New Patterns of Management.* New York: McGraw-Hill, 1961.

Lincoln, J. R., & Zeitz, G. *Organizational properties from aggregate data: Separating individual and structural effects.* Paper presented at the 74th annual meeting, American Sociological Association, Boston, August 1979.

Lodahl, T. M., & Kejner, M. The definition and measurement of job involvement. *Journal of Applied Psychology*, 1965, *49*, 24–33.

Lombardo, M. W., Jr., & Stein, T. *Job analysis in Looking Glass.* Work in progress, Center for Creative Leadership, Greensboro, NC, 1980.

Lord, R. G. Functional leadership behavior: Measurement and relation to social power and leadership perceptions. *Administrative Science Quarterly*, 1977, *22*, 114–33.

Lord, R. G., Binning, J. F., Rush, M. C., & Thomas, J. C. The effect of performance cues and leader behavior on questionnaire ratings of leadership behavior. *Organizational Behavior and Human Performance*, 1978, *21*, 27–39.

Lord, R. G., Phillips, J. S., & Rush, M. C. Effects of sex and personality on perceptions of emergent leadership, influence, and social power. *Journal of Applied Psychology*, 1980. *65*, 176–82.

Luthans, F. Leadership: A proposal for a social learning theory base and observational and functional analysis techniques to measure leader behavior. In J. G. Hunt & L. L. Larson (Eds.), *Crosscurrents in leadership.* Carbondale: Southern Illinois University Press, 1979.

Machin, J. L. J. A Contingency Methodology for Management Control. *Journal of Management Studies*, 1979, *16*, 1–29.

Madron, R. *Leading an open democracy.* Unpublished manuscript, Manchester Business School, University of Manchester, Manchester, England, 1980.

Mahoney, T. A., Jerdee, T. H., & Carroll, S. J. The job(s) of management. *Industrial Relations*, 1965, *4*, 97–110.

Mangham, I. *Interaction in theatrical enterprises: Some features of communication and authority.* Unpublished manuscript, School of Management, University of Bath, Bath, England, 1980.

Mann, F. C. Toward an understanding of the leadership role in formal organizations. In R. Dubin, G. C. Homans, F. C. Mann, & D. C. Miller (Eds.), *Leadershp and Productivity.* New York: Chandler Publishing, 1965.

Mann, I. L., & Janis, L. *Decision-making.* New York: Macmillan, Free Press, 1977.

Mann, R. D. A review of the relationship between personality and performance in small groups. *Psychological Bulletin,* 1959, *56,* 241–70.

Manz, C. C., & Sims, H. P. *A social learning perspective: Behavioral change and subordinate satisfaction from leadership training with behavioral models.* Paper presented at the Academy of Management annual meeting, Detroit, MI, 1980.

March, J. G., & Simon, H. A. *Organizations.* New York: Wiley, 1957.

Margerison, C. *Practical research in management and organization.* Unpublished manuscript, Cranfield School of Management, Cranfield, Bedford, England, 1980.

Markham, S. *Leadership and motivation: An empirical examination of exchange and its outcomes.* Unpublished doctoral dissertation, State University of New York at Buffalo, 1978.

Markham, S. *Factor analysis of LBDQ—Form XII: A WABA approach.* Work in progress, Department of Management, Virginia Polytechnic Institute, Blacksburg, VA, 1980. (a)

Markham, S. *The independence of the supervision and leadership networks.* Work in progress, Department of Management, Virginia Polytechnic Institute, Blacksburg, VA, 1980. (b)

Markham, S. *Pay and performance: A within-unit analysis.* Work in progress, Department of Management, Virginia Polytechnic Institute, Blacksburg, VA, 1980. (c)

Markham, S., Dansereau, F., & Alutto, J. Fundamental problems in leadership research. *Proceedings of the 22nd Annual Conference of the Midwest Academy of Management.* E. L. Miller (Ed.). Ann Arbor, MI: Division of Research, Graduate School of Business Administration, University of Michigan, 1979.

Marshall, J., & Stewart, R. Managers' job perceptions: Part 2. Opportunities for, and attitudes to, choice. *Journal of Management Studies,* in press.

Maurice, M., Sorge, A., & Warner, M. Societal differences in organizing manufacturing units: A comparison of France, West Germany, and Great Britain, *Organization Studies,* 1980, *1,* 59–86.

McCall, M. W., Jr. Leaders and leadership: Of substance & shadow. In J. Hackman, E. Lawler, and L. Porter (Eds.), *Perspectives on behavior in organizations.* New York: McGraw-Hill, 1977.

McCall, M. W., Jr. Research on scientists and engineers. In T. Connolly (Ed.), *Scientists, engineers and organizations.* Monterey, CA: Brooks/Cole, in press.

McCall, M. W., Jr., & Lombardo, M. M. (Eds.). *Leadership: Where else can we go?* Durham, NC: Duke University Press, 1978. (a)

McCall, M. W., Jr., & Lombardo, M. M. *Looking Glass, Inc.: An organizational simulation.* Technical Report No. 12, Operational Manual, Vol. 1. Greensboro, NC: Center for Creative Leadership, 1978. (b)

McCall, M. W., Jr., & Lombardo, M. M. *Looking Glass, Inc.: The first three years.* Technical Report No. 13, Greensboro, NC: Center for Creative Leadership, 1979.

McCall, M. W., Jr., & Lombardo, M. M. Using simulation for leadership and management research: Through the looking glass. *Management Science*, in press.

McCall, M. W., Jr., Lombardo, M. M., & Rice, S. S. *Looking Glass, Inc.: Norm tables*. Greensboro, NC: Center for Creative Leadership, 1979.

McCall, M. W., Jr., Morrison, A. M., & Hannan, R. L. *Studies of managerial work: Results and methods*. Technical Report No. 9. Greensboro, NC: Center for Creative Leadership, May 1978.

McCall, M. W., Jr., & Segrist, C. A. *In pursuit of the managers job: Building on Mintzberg*. Technical Report No. 14. Greensboro, NC: Center for Creative Leadership, March 1980.

McCauley, C., Stitt, C. L., & Segal, M. Stereotyping: From prejudice to prediction. *Psychological Bulletin*, 1980, *87*, 195–208.

McNeil, K. A., Kelly, F., & McNeil, J. *Testing research hypotheses using multiple linear regression*, Carbondale: Southern Illinois University Press, 1975.

McNemar, Q. *Psychological statistics*. New York: Wiley, 1955.

Melcher, A. J. *Structure and process of organizations: A systems approach*. Englewood Cliffs, NJ: Prentice Hall, 1976.

Melcher, A. J. Leadership models and research approaches. In J. G. Hunt and L. L. Larson (Eds.), *Leadership: The cutting edge*, Carbondale: Southern Illinois University Press, 1977, 94–108.

Meyer, M. W. Leadership and organizational structure. In M. W. Meyer and Associates (Eds.), *Environments and organizations*. San Francisco: Jossey-Bass, 1978.

Miller, G. A. Practical and Lexical knowledge. In E. Rosch & B. B. Lloyd (Eds.), *Cognition and categorization*. Hillsdale, NJ: Lawrence Erlbaum Associates, 1978.

Miller, R. L. *The effects of leader transition on unit performance: An evaluation of the Comtrain Transition Guide*. Unpublished manuscript, Army Research Institute, APO New York, 1980.

Miner, J. B. The uncertain future of the leadership concept: An overview. In J. G. Hunt and L. L. Larson (Eds.), *Leadershp frontiers*, Kent, OH: Comparative Administration Research Institute, Kent State University, 1975, 197–208.

Mintzberg, H. *The nature of managerial work*. New York: Harper & Row, 1973.

Mintzberg, H. Patterns in strategy formation. *Management Science*, 1978, *24*, 934–48.

Mintzberg, H. An emerging strategy of "Direct" research. *Administrative Science Quarterly*. 1979, 582–89.

Mintzberg, H., & Waters, J. A. *Tracking strategy in an entrepreneurial firm*. Unpublished manuscript, Faculty of Management Studies, McGill University, Montreal, Canada, 1980.

Mitchell, T. R. The construct validity of three dimensions of leadership research. *Journal of Social Psychology*, 1970, *80*, 89–94.

Mitchell, T. R. *Attributional model of leadership*. Working paper, Graduate School of Business Administration, University of Washington, Seattle, 1980.

Mitchell, T. R., & Kalb, L. S. *Effects of outcome knowledge on supervisors' judgements*. Paper presented at the American Psychological Association annual convention, Montreal, Quebec, Canada, September 1980.

Mitchell, T. R., Larson, J. R., & Green, S. G. Leader behavior, situational modera-tors, and group performance: An attributional analysis. *Organizational Behavior and Human Performance*, 1977, *18*, 254–68.

Mitchell, T. R., & Wood, R. E. Supervisors' responses to subordinate poor perfor-mance: A test of an attributional model. *Organizational Behavior and Human Per-formance* 1980, *25*, 123–38.

Mitroff, I. I. Reality as a scientific strategy: Revising our concepts of science. *Acad-emy of Management Review*, 1980, *5*, 513–15.

Mitroff, I. I., & Pondy, L. R. Afterthoughts on the leadership conference. In M. W. McCall & M. M. Lombardo (Eds.), *Leadership: Where else can we go?* Durham, NC: Duke University Press, 1978.

Morgan, G., & Smircich, L. The case for qualitative research. *Academy of Manage-ment Review*, 1980, *5*, 491–500.

Morley, I. E. *The social psychology of leadership—Mark II*. Unpublished manuscript, Department of Psychology, University of Warwick, Coventry, England, 1980.

Morley, I. E. Negotiation and bargaining. In M. Argyle (Ed.), *Handbook of social skills* (Vol. 2). London: Methuen, 1981, in press.

Morris, V. C. *The urban principal: A comparative inquiry into discretionary decision-mak-ing in a large educational organization*. Working paper, College of Education, Uni-versity of Illinois at Chicago Circle, 1980.

Morrison, C. T., & Randell, G. A. Problems in developing behaviourally anchored rating scales. *Journal of Occupational Psychology*, in press.

Morse, J. J., & Wagner, F. R. Measuring the process of managerial effectiveness, *Academy of Management Journal*, 1978, *21*, 23–25.

Moscovici, S., & Nemeth, C. Social influence II: Minority influence. In C. Nemeth (Ed.), *Social psychology: Classic and contemporary integrations*. Chicago: Rand McNally, 1974.

Moses, J. L. Lack of application of leadership findings to real world problems. In J. G. Hunt & L. L. Larson (Eds.), *Crosscurrents in leadership*. Carbondale: South-ern Illinois University Press, 1979.

Mueller, R. K. Leading-edge leadership. *Human Systems Management*, 1980, *1*(1), 17–27.

Mulder, M. *The Daily Power Game*. Leiden, The Netherlands: M. Nijhoff, 1977.

Nachman, S., Dansereau, F., Jr., & Naughton, T. J. *Beyond the traditional vertical dyad linkage model of leadership: A within and between analysis of negotiating latitude*. Pa-per presented at the Academy of Management annual meetings, Detroit, MI, August 1980.

Naylor, J. C., Pritchard, R. D., & Ilgen, D. R. *A theory of behavior in organizations*. New York: Academic Press, 1980.

Nealey, S. M., & Blood, M. R. Leadership performances of nursing supervisors at two organizational levels. *Journal of Applied Psychology*, 1968, *53*, 414–22.

Nebeker, D. M., & Mitchell, T. R. Leader behavior: An expectancy theory ap-proach. *Organizational Behavior and Human Performance*, 1974, *11*, 355–67.

Neustadt, R. *Presidential power: The politics of leadership*. New York: Wiley, 1960.

Niebuhr, R. E., Bedeian, A. G., & Armenakis, A. A. Individual need states and their influence on perceptions of leader behavior. *Social Behavior and Personality*, 1980, *8*, 17–25.

Nisbett, R., & Ross, L. *Human inference: Strategies and shortcomings of social judgment.* Englewood Cliffs, NJ: Prentice-Hall, 1980.

Osborn, R. N. *Organizational effectiveness: A model and a test.* Unpublished doctoral dissertation, Kent State University, 1971.

Osborn, R. N. The search for environmental complexity. *Human Relations*, 1976, *29*, 179–91.

Osborn, R. N. *Overview: European workshop in leadership and managerial behavior.* Unpublished manuscript, Department of Administrative Sciences, Southern Illinois University at Carbondale, 1980.

Osborn, R. N., & Hunt, J. G. An empirical investigation of lateral and vertical leadership at two organization levels. *Journal of Business Research*, 1974, *2*, 209–221. (a)

Osborn, R. N., & Hunt, J. G. Environment and organizational effectiveness. *Administrative Science Quarterly*, 1974, *19*, 231–46. (b)

Osborn, R. N., & Hunt, J. G. An adaptive-reactive theory of leadership: The role of macro variables in leadership research. In J. G. Hunt and L. L. Larson (Eds.), *Leadership frontiers*, Kent, OH: Comparative Administration Research Institute, Kent State University, 1975.

Osborn, R. H., & Hunt, J. G. Design implications for mechanistically structured systems in complex environments: Alternatives in contextual variables. In R. H. Kilmann, L. R. Pondy, and D. P. Slevin (Eds.), *The management of organizational design: Research methodology* (Vol. 2). New York: American Elsevier, 1976.

Osborn, R. N., & Hunt, J. G. *Environment and leadership: Discretionary and nondiscretionary leader behavior and organizational outcomes.* Unpublished manuscript, Department of Administrative Sciences, Southern Illinois University at Carbondale, 1977.

Osborn, R. N., Hunt, J. G., & Jauch, L. R. *Organization theory: An integrated approach.* New York: Wiley, 1980.

Osborn, R. N., Hunt, J. G., & Skaret, D. J. Managerial influence in a complex configuration with two unit heads. *Human Relations*, 1977, *30*, 1025–38.

Patterson, W. N. *A day in the life of Berkeley superintendent Dick Foster: An event analysis.* Paper presented at the American Educational Research Association annual meeting, Washington, DC, 1975.

Patton, J. A. *Relation of job attitudes to later turnover.* Unpublished manuscript, I.B.M. Canada, Don Mills, Ontario, 1970.

Peters, T. J. A style for all seasons. *Executive*, Graduate School of Business and Public Administration, Cornell University, Summer, 1980.

Pettigrew, A. *Symbolic and political aspects of leadership.* Unpublished manuscript, Centre for Industrial & Business Studies, University of Warwick, Coventry, England, 1980.

Pfeffer, J. The ambiguity of leadership. In M. W. McCall, Jr., & M. M. Lombardo (Eds.), *Leadership: Where else can we go?* Durham, N.C.: Duke University Press, 1978.

Pfeffer, J., & Salancik, G. R. *The external control of organizations*. New York: Harper & Row, 1978.

Phillips, J. S., & Lord, R. G. Causal attributions and perceptions of leadership. *Organizational Behavior and Human Performance*, in press.

Phillips, J. S., & Lord, R. G. *Leadership prototypes: Effects on memory for leader behavior*. Unpublished manuscript, Department of Psychology, University of Akron, Akron, OH, 1981.

Pirsig, R. M. *Zen and the art of motorcycle maintenance*. New York: Bantam, 1974.

Pitner, N. J. *Descriptive study of the everyday activities of suburban school superintendents: The management of information*. Unpublished doctoral dissertation, Ohio State University, 1978.

Platt, J. R. Strong inference. *Science*, 1964, *146*, 347–53.

Popper, K. *The poverty of historicism*. London: Routledge and Kegan Paul, 1961.

Quince, T., & Lansley, P. *Leadership and managerial orientation in construction management*. Unpublished manuscript, Ashridge Management College, Berkhampsted, Hertfordshire, England, 1980.

Ramirez, E., Ramirez, M., & Richek, H. G. *Research on leadership behaviors and locus of control*. Work in progress, University of Oklahoma, Norman, 1980.

Randell, G. A. *The chasm between theory and practice in leadership*. Unpublished manuscript, University of Bradford Management Centre, West Yorkshire, England, 1980.

Randell, G. A. Management education and training. In W. T. Singleton (Ed.), *Management skills*, Baltimore: University Park Press, in press.

Reed, S. K. Pattern recognition and categorization. *Cognitive Psychology*, 1972, *3*, 382–407.

Rice, R. W., Bender, L. R., & Vitters, A. G. *Validity tests of the Contingency Model for female and male leaders*. Working paper, Psychology Department, State University of New York at Buffalo, 1980.

Richardson, F. L. W., Jr., & White, K. *Executive action—Stimulating others to greater performance* (Document No. 8426). Washington, DC: American Documentation Institute, Photoduplication Service, Library of Congress, October, 1964.

Roethlisberger, F. J., & Dickson, W. J. *Management and the worker*. Cambridge, MA: Harvard University Press, 1939.

Rosch, E. Linguistic relativity. In A. Silverstein (Ed.), *Human communication: Theoretical explorations*. Hillsdale, NJ: Lawrence Erlbaum Associates, 1974.

Rosch, E. Cognitive representations of semantic categories. *Journal of Experimental Psychology: General*, 1975, *104*, 192–233.

Rosch, E. Principles of categorization. In E. Rosch & B. B. Lloyd (Eds.), *Cognition and categorization*. Hillsdale, NJ: Lawrence Erlbaum Associates, 1978.

Rosch, E., & Mervis, C. Family resemblances: Studies in the internal structure of categories. *Cognitive Psychology*, 1975, *7*, 573–605.

Rosch, E., Mervis, C., Gray, W., Johnson, D., & Boyes-Braem, P. Basic objects in natural categories. *Cognitive Psychology*, 1976, *8*, 382–439.

Rosen, B., & Jerdee, T. H. The influence of sex role stereotypes on evaluations of male and female supervisory behavior. *Journal of Applied Psychology*, 1973, *57*, 44–48.

Rosen, B., & Jerdee, T. H. Effects of applicant's sex and difficulty of job on evaluations of candidates for managerial positions. *Journal of Applied Psychology*, 1974, *59*, 511–12. (a)

Rosen, B., & Jerdee, T. H. Influence of sex-role stereotypes on personnel decisions. *Journal of Applied Psychology*, 1974, *59*, 9–14. (b)

Rosen, N. A. Open systems theory in an organizational sub-system: A field experiment. *Organizational Behavior and Human Performance*, 1970, *5*, 245–65.

Rosenthal, R. Combining results of independent studies. *Psychological Bulletin*, 1978, *85*, 185–93.

Rosenthal, R. The "file-drawer" problem and tolerance for null results. *Psychological Bulletin*, 1979, *86*, 638–41.

Rotter, J. Generalized expectancies for internal control of reinforcement. *Psychological Monographs*, 1966, *80* (No. 609).

Rubenowitz S. *The impact of management-style on participation and co-determination.* Unpublished manuscript, Department of Psychology, Goteborg University, Goteborg, Sweden, 1980.

Rush, M. C., Phillips, J. S., & Lord, R. G. *The effects of memory demands on leader behavior descriptions and perceptions of leadership.* Unpublished manuscript, Department of Psychology, University of Akron, Akron, OH, 1980.

Rush, M. C., Phillips, J. S., & Lord, R. G. The effects of a temporal delay in ratings on leader behavior descriptions: A laboratory investigation. *Journal of Applied Psychology*, in press.

Rush, M. C., Thomas, J. C., & Lord, R. G. Implicit leadership theory: A potential threat to the internal validity of leader behavior questionnaires. *Organizational Behavior and Human Performance*, 1977, *20*, 93–100.

Sakoda, J. M. Factor analysis of OSS situational tests. *Journal of Abnormal and Social Psychology*, 1952, *47*, 843–52.

Salancik, G. R., Calder, B. J., Rowland, K. M., Leblebici, H., & Conway, M. Leadership as an outcome of social structure and process: A multidimensional analysis. In J. G. Hunt & L. L. Larson (Eds.), *Leadership frontiers*. Kent, OH: Comparative Administration Research Institute, Kent State University, 1975.

Salancik, G. R., & Pfeffer, J. Who gets power—and how they hold on to it: A strategic-contingency model of power. *Organizational Dynamics*, 1977, *5*(3), 3–21.

Sayles, L. R. *Managerial behavior: Administration in complex organizations*. New York: McGraw-Hill, 1964.

Sayles, L. R. *Leadership: What effective managers really do . . . and how they do it.* New York: McGraw-Hill, 1979.

Schein, V. E. The relationship between sex-role stereotypes and requisite management characteristics. *Journal of Applied Psychology*, 1973, *57*, 95–100.

Schein, V. E. The relationship between sex role stereotypes and requisite management characteristics among female managers. *Journal of Applied Psychology*, 1975, *60*, 340–44.

Schneider, B. *Different levels of an analysis in data aggregation: Problems, pitfalls, and a potential solution for survey research.* Paper presented at the Symposium on Data Aggregation in Organizational Research, American Psychological Association Annual Convention, Toronto, Ontario, Canada, September 1978.

Schriesheim, C. A. *A preliminary report on new individually-worded initiating structure and consideration subscales.* Unpublished manuscript, Department of Administrative Sciences, Kent State University, Kent, Ohio, 1976.

Schriesheim, C. A. *Development, validation and application of new leadership behavior and expectancy research instruments.* Unpublished doctoral dissertation, Faculty of Management Sciences, Ohio State University, 1978.

Schriesheim, C. A. The similarity of individual directed and group directed leader behavior descriptions. *Academy of Management Journal,* 1979, *20,* 345–55.

Schriesheim, C. A., & DeNisi, A. S. Task dimensions as moderators of the effects of instrumental leader behavior: A path-goal approach. In R. C. Huseman (Ed.), *Proceedings of the 39th Annual Academy of Management Meeting.* Athens, GA: University of Georgia, 1979. Pp. 103–6.

Schriesheim, C. A., & Kerr, S. Psychometric properties of the Ohio State leadership scales. *Psychological Bulletin,* 1974, *81,* 756–65.

Schriesheim, C. A., & Kerr, S. Theories and measures of leadership: A critical appraisal of current and future directions. In J. G. Hunt and L. L. Larson (Eds.), *Leadership: The cutting edge,* Carbondale: Southern Illinois University Press, 1977.

Schriesheim, C. A., and von Glinow, M. A. The path-goal theory of leadership: A theoretical and empirical analysis. *Academy of Management Journal,* 1977, *20,* 398–405.

Scott, M., & Eklund, S. J. *Ecological methods in the study of administrative behavior.* Paper presented at U.C.E.A. and Indiana University School of Education Seminar on Methodological Issues in Administrative Inquiry, Bloomington, Indiana, November 1978.

Secord, P., & Backman, C. *Social psychology.* New York: McGraw Hill, 1974.

Senger, J. The co-manager concept. *California Management Review,* Spring 1971, *13,* 71–83.

Sheridan, J. E. *Measures of job performance in nursing homes.* Final technical report on Grant No. 5R01 NU00612-02 from the Division of Nursing, Health Resources Administration, DHEW, 1980.

Sheridan, J. E., Vredenburgh, D., & Ableson, M. A. *Contextual model of managerial roles in hospital units.* Working paper, Pennsylvania State University Park, 1980.

Sherif, M., & Hovland, C. I. *Social judgement: Contrast and assimilation effects in communication and attitude change.* New Haven: Yale University Press, 1961.

Simon, H. A. *The sciences of the artificial.* Cambridge, MA: M.I.T. Press, 1969.

Simonton, D. K. Was Napolean a military genius? Score: Carlyle 1, Tolstoy 1. *Psychological Reports,* 1979, *44,* 21–22.

Sims, H. P. The leader as a manager of reinforcement contingencies: An empirical example and a model. In J. G. Hunt and L. L. Larson (Eds.), *Leadership: The cutting edge,* Carbondale: Southern Illinois University Press, 1977.

Sims, H. P. Limitations and extensions to questionnaires in leadership research. In J. G. Hunt and L. L. Larson (Eds.), *Crosscurrents in leadership.* Carbondale: Southern Illinois University Press, 1979.

Sims, H. P., & Szilagyi, A. D. Leader reward behavior and subordinate satisfaction and performance. *Organizational Behavior and Human Performance*, 1975, *14*, 426–38.

Smith, P. C., & Kendall, L. M. Retranslation of expectations: An approach to the construction of unambiguous anchors for rating scales. *Journal of Applied Psychology*, 1963, *47*, 149–55.

Smith, P. C., Kendall, L., & Hulin, C. L. *The measurement of satisfaction in work and retirement: A strategy for the study of attitudes*. Chicago: Rand McNally, 1969.

Snyder, C. H., & Diesing, P. *Conflict among nations: Bargaining, decision making, and system structure in international crisis*. Princeton, NJ: Princeton University Press, 1977.

Snyder, M. Self-monitoring processes. In L. Berkowitz (Ed.), *Advances in experimental social psychology* (Vol. 12), 85–128. New York: Academic Press, 1979.

Snyder, M., & Cantor, N. Thinking about ourselves and others: Self-monitoring and social knowledge. *Journal of Personality and Social Psychology*, 1980, *39*, 222–34.

Snyder, N., & Glueck, W. F. How managers plan—The analysis of managers' activities. *Long Range Planning*, 1980, *13*, 70–76.

Solomon, R. L. The opponent-process theory of acquired motivation: The costs of pleasure and the benefits of pain. *American Psychologist*, 1980, *35*, 691–712.

Solomon, R. L., & Corbit, J. D. An opponent process theory of motivation: Temporal dynamics of effect. *Psychological Review*, 1974, *81*, 119–45.

Spielberger, C. D. *Anxiety and behavior*. New York: Academic Press, 1966.

Staw, B. M., & Ross, J. Commitment in an experimenting society: A study of the attribution of leadership from administrative scenarios. *Journal of Applied Psychology*, 1980, *65*, 249–60.

Steers, R. M. *Organizational effectiveness: A behavioral view*. Santa Monica, CA: Goodyear, 1977.

Stephenson, G. M., & Brotherton, C. J. (Eds.). *Industrial relations: A social psychological approach*. Chichester, England: Wiley, 1979.

Sterling, B. *Company leadership climate and objective measures of company effectiveness*. Paper presented at the American Psychological Association Annual Convention, Montreal, Quebec, Canada, September 1980.

Sterling, B., & Carnes, D. *The relationship between perceptions of company leadership climate and measures of unit effectiveness*. Technical Report, ARI Field Unit, USAREVR, 1980. (a)

Sterling, B., & Carnes, D. *The relationship between perceptions of leadership and measures of personnel readiness over time: Across lagged analysis*. Technical Report, ARI Field Unit, USAREVR, August 1980. (b)

Stewart, R. *Managers and their jobs*. London: Macmillan, 1967.

Stewart, R. *Contrasts in management: A study of the different types of managers' jobs: Their demands and choices*. London: McGraw-Hill, 1976.

Stewart, R. The manager's contacts: Demand or choice? *Journal of European Industrial Training*, 1979, *3*, 2–5.

Stewart, R. *The relevance of research into managerial behavior for leadership studies*. Unpublished manuscript, Oxford Centre for Management Studies, Kennington, Oxford, England, 1980.

Stewart, R., Smith, P., Blake, J., & Wingate, P. *The district administrator in the National Health Service.* London: King Edward's Hospital Fund for London, 1980. (Distributed by Pitman.)

Stogdill, R. M. Personal factors associated with leadership: A survey of the literature. *Journal of Psychology,* 1948, *25,* 35–71.

Stogdill, R. M. *Manual for the Leader Behavior Description Questionnaire–Form XII.* Columbus: Bureau of Business Research, Ohio State University, 1963.

Stogdill, R. M., *Handbook of leadership: A survey of theory and research.* New York: Macmillan, Free Press, 1974.

Stogdill, R. M., & Coons, A. E. *Leader behavior: Its description and measurement.* Columbus: Bureau of Business Research, Ohio State University, 1957.

Stoline, M. R. *Examples of hypothesis tests concerning correlated correlation coefficients.* Mathematics Report No. 21, Kalamazoo, MI: Western Michigan University, January 1972.

Strauss, G. Can social psychology contribute to industrial relations? In G. M. Stephenson & C. J. Brotherton (Eds.), *Industrial relations: A social psychological approach.* Chichester, England: Wiley, 1979.

Strube, M. J., & Garcia, J. E. *A meta-analytic investigation of Fiedler's contingency model of leadership effectiveness.* Paper presented at the American Psychological Association Annual Convention, Montreal, Quebec, Canada, September 1980.

Sweney, A. B. *Leadership: The management of power and obligation.* (Prepublication edition.) Wichita: Test Systems, Inc., 1979.

Taylor, G. A. *An investigation into acceptance levels of new supervisors associated with subordinate frustration, and subordinate job satisfaction with comparative work units.* Working paper, Western Illinois University, Macomb, Illinois, 1980.

Taylor, S. E., Fiske, S. T., Etcoff, N. L., & Ruderman, A. J. Categorical and contextual basis of person memory and stereotyping. *Journal of Personality and Social Psychology,* 1978, *36,* 778–93.

Terman, L. M. A preliminary study of the psychology and pedagogy of leadership. *Pedagogical Seminary,* 1904, *11,* 413–51.

Terry, P. *English culture and management behavior.* Unpublished manuscript, Cummins Engines Co., Ltd., New Malden, Surrey, England, 1980.

Thurley, K., & Wirdenius, H. *Supervision: A reappraisal.* London: Heinemann, 1973.

Thurley, K. & Wirdenius, H. *Leadership: A production systems perspective.* Unpublished manuscript, London School of Economics, London, England, 1980.

Tolle, E. F. *Client-centered management development.* Unpublished manuscript, IBM Corporation, Lexington, KY, 1980.

Tornow, W., & Pinto, P. The development of managerial taxonomy: A system for describing, classifying and evaluating executive positions. *Journal of Applied Psychology,* 1976, *61,* 410–18.

Tosi, H. L. The need for theoretical development in organizational behavior. *Exchange: The organizational behavior teaching journal,* 1979, *4*(3), 5–7.

Tosi, H. L., & Carroll, S. J. *Management: Contingency, structure and process.* Chicago: St. Clair Press, 1976.

Turner, V. A. *In the ritual process: Structure and anti-structure.* London: Routledge and Kegan Paul, 1969.

Tversky, A., & Kahneman, D. Availability: A heuristic for judging frequency and probability. *Cognitive Psychology*, 1973, *5*, 207–32.

Vaill, P. B. Towards a behavioral description of high-performing systems. In M. W. McCall, Jr., & M. M. Lombardo (Eds.), *Leadership: Where else can we go?* Durham, NC: Duke University Press, 1978.

Van de Ven, A. H. *Organization assessment measurement manual.* Philadelphia: Wharton School, University of Pennsylvania, 1975.

Vecchio, R. A dyadic interpretation of the Contingency Model of leadership effectiveness. *Academy of Management Journal*, 1979, *22*, 590–600.

Vicars, W. M., Larson, L. L., & Bussom, R. S. The nature of a police executive's work. Unpublished manuscript, Department of Administrative Sciences, Southern Illinois University at Carbondale, 1979.

Vroom V., & Yetton, P. *Leadership decision-making.* Pittsburgh: University of Pittsburgh, 1973.

Wall, T. D., & Lischeron, J. A. *Worker participation.* London, New York: McGraw Hill, 1977.

Watson, J. E. *The double helix.* New York: Mentor, 1968.

Watson, T. *Inconvenient findings: Loose ends or pointers?* Unpublished manuscript, Centre for Industrial and Business Studies, University of Warwick, Coventry, England, 1980.

Weick, K. E. Review Essay: The nature of managerial work. *Administrative Science Quarterly*, 1974, *19*, 111–18.

Weick, K. E. The spines of leaders. In M. W. McCall, Jr., & M. M. Lombardo (Eds.), *Leadership: Where else can we go?* Durham, NC: Duke University Press, 1978.

Weick, K. E. *Loosely coupled systems: Relaxed meaning and thick interpretation.* Working paper, Graduate School of Business and Public Administration, Cornell University, 1980.

Wherry, R. J. *Factor analysis of officer qualification form QCL-2B.* Columbus: Ohio State University Research Foundation, 1950.

Winter, D. G. *An introduction to LMET theory and research.* Task planning document EG-29B, McBer and Company, Boston, August 1979.

Wlodarczyk, C. *Some doubts on the leadership studies concept.* Unpublished manuscript, Organization and Management Section, Institute of Occupational Medicine, Lodz, Poland, 1980.

Wood, J. R. *Leadership in voluntary organizations: The controversy over social action in Protestant churches.* New Brunswick, NJ: Rutgers University Press, 1981.

Wright, P., & Taylor, D. *The interpersonal skills of leadership: A conceptual framework.* Unpublished manuscript, University of Bradford Management Centre, Bradford, West Yorkshire, England, 1980.

Wyer, R. S., & Carlston, D. E. Social cognition, ingerence, and attribution. Hillsdale: NJ: Lawrence Erlbaum Associates, 1980.

Wynne, B. E., & Hunsaker, P. L. A human information-processing approach to the process of leadership. In J. G. Hunt & L. L. Larson (Eds.), *Leadership frontiers.* Kent, OH: Comparative Administration Research Institute, Kent State University, 1975.

Yammario, F., & Dansereau, F. *Interpretations and misinterpretations of the F-ratio.* Working Paper No. 457, State University of New York at Buffalo, 1980.

Yukl, G. A., & Nemeroff, W. F. Identification and measurement of specific categories of leadership behavior: A progress report. In J. G. Hunt & L. L. Larson (Eds.), *Crosscurrents in leadership.* Carbondale: Southern Illinois Press, 1979.

Zahn, G. L., & Wolf, G. Leadership and the art of cycle maintenance: A simulation model of superior-subordinate interaction. *Organizational Behavior and Human Performance,* in press.

Zierden, W. E. Leading through the follower's point of view. *Organizational Dynamics,* 1980, *8*(4), 27–46.

Name Index

Subject Index